An International History of
BRITISH POWER
1957–1970

An International History of
BRITISH POWER
1957–1970

Michael J. Turner

\<teneo\>
// press

YOUNGSTOWN, NEW YORK

ISBN: 978-1-934844-20-5

Requests for permission should be directed to:
permissions@teneopress.com, or mailed to:
Teneo Press
PO Box 349
Youngstown, New York 14174

For
Pump, Gruber, Jillbo, and Popdude
with lots of love

TABLE OF CONTENTS

ACKNOWLEDGMENTS

I am grateful to Paul Richardson, Toni Tan, Nicole Ford, and everyone at Teneo Press who had a hand in the publication of this book. I would also like to thank current and former students in Britain and in the United States. I wrote this book in response to their interest in and questions about Britain's international role during a period when imperial power, economic success, and global reach became increasingly difficult to sustain—though, as I argue below, this does not necessarily mean that Britain ceased to be 'great'. Most of all, I want to thank family and friends who have been kind enough to ask about my work and—even more—to listen long-sufferingly to me whenever I told them about it!

An International History of
BRITISH POWER
1957–1970

Introduction

Substantial savings will be made in the demands of defence on the nation's manpower and financial resources. More of our forces will be based in Britain. We plan no major change in the size of our contribution to NATO. The savings will be chiefly obtained from a significant reduction in our military presence outside Europe, and from some changes in its deployment.

—'Supplementary Statement on Defence Policy', July 1967[1]

Our commitment is not to police the world. We have made it clear that we do not believe that to be the role of this country, but we have pledged this Government against any war…in which Britain would go it alone. This is the basis of our policy. Equally, it is our policy that we cannot police the world on the basis of far-flung military stations.

—Harold Wilson, prime minister,
in the House of Commons, July 27, 1967[2]

I imagine historians will best remember my six years at the ministry of defence for the liquidation of Britain's military role outside

Europe, an anachronism which was essentially a legacy from our
nineteenth-century empire...When I left office, for the first time
in its history, Britain was spending more on education than on
defence.

—Denis Healey, secretary of state for defence 1964–1970,
in his autobiography (published in 1989)[3]

These remarks reflect the motives and concerns behind the effort to scale
down Britain's international responsibilities during the 1960s. An irresistible combination of political pressures, economic and financial imperatives, strategic reassessments, military limitations, diplomatic priorities,
and general trends in interstate relationships meant that the British had to
adjust their methods and goals in order to uphold their interests and retain
influence in a rapidly changing world. This, indeed, had been a primary
task of successive British governments (both Labour and Conservative)
since the end of the Second World War. Many historians discuss Britain's
postwar international position in terms of 'decline'. Britain 'retreated',
was 'eclipsed' and 'overruled', and experienced an inexorable 'descent
from power'. It cannot be denied that Britain suffered reverses and disappointments on the world stage and that these appeared to multiply during
the second half of the twentieth century. The extent of the decline, however, is easily exaggerated. Using failure and weakness as leitmotifs—as
a framework within which to assess Britain's global role in the decades
after 1945—is simplistic, inappropriate, and misleading.

Britain *did* decline relative to the other great powers in the world,
particularly in economic performance and military strength, which are
usually regarded as the foundations for status and influence, but this does
not mean that Britain *ceased* to be a great power. In fact, Britain remained
a great power and was treated as such by the other great powers. The
British used what resources they had to good effect. As options were lost
and opportunities decreased, Britain nevertheless retained the ability to
influence events abroad, and its power rested on more than the condition
of the economy and the size and capability of the British armed forces.
It rested also on tradition and history, on the experience and expertise
of leaders and policymakers, on Britain's long record of involvement in

many parts of the world, on continuing links with those regions, and on past achievements and present relationships. It rested on the ability to coerce, persuade, or satisfy others—friends as well as foes—and on Britain's success in convincing allies and enemies alike that its opinions and wishes really mattered. The British manoeuvred themselves into a place of prestige and importance after 1945 and were normally treated with a respect that the true level of their economic and military effectiveness no longer merited. Despite relative decline, Britain strove to limit the compromises, withdrawals, and concessions that had to be made. Decline was painful, and it was denied, hidden, and glossed over. It was not rapid or dramatic. It was resisted and delayed. There was no choice but to accept it, yet the crucial point is not that it happened but that it was well managed.

This book offers a detailed examination of Britain's role and influence in a difficult period. At the end of the Second World War, many contemporaries supposed that world affairs would be reorganised and urgent problems addressed under the supervision of the 'Big Three' victors in that war, including Britain. The 'Big Three' approach soon broke down. The postwar international order had more or less taken shape by the mid-1950s, but much was still unsettled; in these circumstances, Britain could make the most of its opportunities even while recognising that it was not the equal of the United States of America or the Union of Soviet Socialist Republics. British priorities changed and different ways to exercise influence had to be found in view of pressing needs, both at home and abroad, but the continuing desire was to shore up Britain's position in those parts of the world that were relevant to its security, wealth, strategy, and reputation. This book elucidates the motives behind the vital decisions of the age. It discusses the far-reaching consequences of those decisions and places British policymaking in its proper contexts. It offers an appreciation of the international environment within which policymakers had to operate. In order to understand why British leaders considered some options to be more attractive than others at key moments, it is necessary to consider the activities of the other great powers and to treat British policy as one component of an evolving international order. It is also important not to overstate or misrepresent the nature of Britain's decline.

The post-1945 international order featured new institutions and new patterns of coalition and rivalry. These structures and relationships became integral to the Cold War as the liberal democratic West led by Washington and London confronted the communist Soviet Union and its allies and satellites. The Cold War began in Europe and divided that continent. It quickly spread to other regions and competition in Europe spilled over into conflicts across Asia, Africa, the Middle East, and Latin America.

Yet there had been hopes that the end of the war would open the way for international cooperation and the blessings of peace and prosperity. The United Nations (UN) was established in 1945. The UN Charter emphasised joint endeavours, international law, security, economic development, social progress, human rights, and world peace. Plans had already been made to rebuild international trade and finance. Representatives from more than forty nations had attended a conference in the United States, at Bretton Woods, New Hampshire, and agreements were signed in 1944 to cover monetary regulation. The International Monetary Fund (IMF) and the International Bank for Reconstruction and Development became operational in 1945. Each member of the Bretton Woods system undertook to maintain the exchange rate of its currency within a fixed limit, linked to the value of gold and the U.S. dollar. The IMF was responsible for bridging temporary imbalances of payments. The idea was to promote stability in order for national economies to advance and international economic relationships to improve.

The British played a leading part in these initiatives. Britain became one of five permanent members of the UN Security Council, for example, and Britain's prominence and influence accorded with the aspirations of its leaders. They assumed that Britain would remain a great power with a global reach. The wartime leader Winston Churchill, who served as prime minister from 1940 to 1945 and again from 1951 to 1955, spoke of the 'three circles' of power: the 'English-speaking alliance' between Britain and the United States, the British empire-Commonwealth, and the emerging 'United Europe'. Churchill, and those who thought like him, regarded Britain as specially favoured, for it belonged to each 'circle' and was the only link between them. In such a position, how could Britain not remain great?

There were challenges to this comforting scenario, however, as when the U.S. Congress placed restrictions on the exchange of nuclear technology and information with the McMahon Act of 1946. During the war, the British had assisted in the development of the atomic bomb; now they were angered by the American decision to end this close collaboration. Still, Britain focused on its own weapons programme and had the atomic bomb by 1952 and the hydrogen bomb by 1957. The security of Britain and of Western Europe had been enhanced, meanwhile, by a series of agreements that culminated with the formation of the North Atlantic Treaty Organization (NATO) in 1949. Its original members were Britain, the United States, France, Belgium, the Netherlands, Luxembourg, Canada, Portugal, Italy, Norway, Denmark, and Iceland. Greece and Turkey joined in 1952. The establishment of NATO was largely a British success, for it was a principal British foreign policy aim to bind the Americans into collective security arrangements. NATO was both a consequence of and a support for the 'special relationship' between Britain and the United States.

Anglo-American relations were complicated by anticolonial sentiment in the United States and by the American wish to capture markets and weaken Britain as an economic competitor, all of which affected Britain's dealings with the empire and Commonwealth. A process of decolonisation gathered momentum in the postwar period, mainly because of the pressure for self-rule that had arisen in some colonies and because of the expectation in London that amicable settlements would ensure the survival of beneficial links (especially economic and strategic) after the granting of independence. The sensible course, it was decided, would be to avoid the trouble, expense, and bloodshed that might result if Britain tried to cling to colonies and refused to engage in talks with their nationalist leaders-in-waiting. India, which had long been Britain's most valuable overseas possession, became independent in 1947. Though several former colonies did not join the Commonwealth, most did. The Commonwealth grew and was greatly altered. An intergovernmental association of free and equal states, it had formerly consisted of the old self-governing white Dominions—Canada, Australia, New Zealand, and South Africa—but now, as new nations joined, Britain had to attend to their needs and desires. In time British leadership was questioned within the Commonwealth, and in Britain doubts arose about the usefulness of the Commonwealth and the remaining colonies. Could they really prop up British power in the world? Moreover, in 1951, Australia and New Zealand signed a security treaty with the United States—the ANZUS Pact—from which Britain was excluded. Two important members of the Commonwealth, it appeared, no longer had confidence in Britain's will and ability to protect them and to police the Far East and Pacific. British leaders made light of this, expressing gratitude to America for extending its commitments and pointing out that the issue of British adhesion to the ANZUS Pact would not arise unless the pact was opened to others. Yet the British, still operating a global defence system, did regard their nonmembership of the pact as an anomaly.

Conversely, Britain still had a strong military presence in the Far East, and the Middle East, and a network of bases, colonies, client regimes, and allies, trading concerns, and spheres of influence that traversed the entire globe. British power in its political, military and diplomatic manifestations was backed up by commercial and financial activities, and the sterling area was particularly important in this respect. The British pound had been the most important international currency and the City of London by far the world's most important financial centre. In the early twentieth century, about 60 percent of global trade was financed, invoiced, and settled in sterling, and the largest proportion of official reserves, apart from gold, was held in sterling. Many countries outside the empire-Commonwealth, as well as most of its members, fixed the value of their local currencies in relation to sterling. This led to the emergence of a sterling bloc. At the beginning of the Second World War, sterling bloc countries within the empire-Commonwealth decided to protect the external value of the pound by forming a single exchange control area. These countries also held sizeable sterling balances in London for the purpose of conducting overseas trade. After 1945 the sterling area was the largest currency bloc in the world. It provided its members with full freedom of payments, stable exchange rates, and access to the financial services of the City of London. The British government was able to use the pooled reserves of the entire area to support sterling when it was under pressure, which it more frequently was after the war as Britain's economic performance gave cause for concern, as international trade was transformed, and as the U.S. dollar rose to become the world's strongest currency.

In Europe, Britain's political, military, and economic activities were also changing. The postwar occupation of Germany by British, American, French, and Soviet forces, and the similar four-power division of Berlin, could not be ended quickly because there was no definitive or comprehensive peace treaty after the Second World War. The Soviets, who did not want to give up the territorial and other gains that the war had delivered to them, insisted that a new Germany should be created, one that was neutral and demilitarised. In London, Washington, and Paris, there was suspicion of Soviet designs and a determination not to lose the power-potential of Germany. This quarrel resulted in the establishment of two German states in 1949: the British, American, and French occupation zones in the west became the Federal Republic of Germany (FRG) and the Soviet zone in the east became the communist German Democratic Republic (GDR). The first chancellor of the FRG was Konrad Adenauer. By the mid-1950s, he had allayed fears (especially in France) about German recovery, regained sovereignty for the federal government in Bonn, and merged the FRG into economic and security structures in Western Europe. The FRG was one of 'The Six'—the FRG, France, Belgium, the Netherlands, Luxembourg, and Italy. These countries adopted proposals for European integration and gave the idea of a new Europe institutional form by setting up the European Coal and Steel Community (ECSC) in 1952. The British stayed out of the ECSC and opposed most of the other integrationist schemes of the time because they disliked supranational bodies. They preferred limited agreements between national governments and refused to involve themselves in any plan that entailed loss of sovereignty. Britain was willing to increase its security role in Europe, and did so, enlarging the British military presence on the continent as part of a bargain that expanded and reinforced NATO in 1954–1955, when the FRG was admitted to the alliance. This bargain was promoted by the British foreign secretary, Anthony Eden. But the type of economic and political integration favoured by 'The Six' did not appeal to the British, who still had global interests, who believed that more formal and binding links with Europe were not advisable or necessary, and whose trade was mainly extra-European.

To Moscow, economic progress and integration in Western Europe and the strengthening of NATO were developments that had to be countered. After 1945 the Soviets refused to withdraw from the territories they had invaded in Eastern Europe during the war. Moscow saw these territories as a security buffer and set up satellite communist regimes there. None of the countries in this eastern bloc was permitted to pursue an independent foreign policy or to rely on the West for economic support. Comecon, the Council for Mutual Economic Assistance, was formed in 1949. The original members were the USSR, Bulgaria, Czechoslovakia, Hungary, Poland, and Rumania. Comecon directed the economic affairs of member states according to Soviet interests and facilitated trade within the bloc. In 1955 Moscow created an alliance for mutual defence, the Warsaw Pact, consisting of the USSR, Albania, Bulgaria, Czechoslovakia, the GDR, Hungary, Poland, and Rumania. An attempted revolt in Hungary in 1956, with demands for political reform, free elections, and withdrawal from the Warsaw Pact, was suppressed by Soviet troops.

For all the tension in Europe, the situation was even more alarming in the Far East. After a bitter civil war, China had fallen to the communists under Mao Tse-tung in 1949. Nationalist Chinese forces had been pushed off the mainland to the island of Taiwan under their leader, Chiang Kai-shek, who remained an ally of the United States. Mao planned to invade Taiwan, while defending it was crucial to the broadening U.S. effort to contain communism in Asia. Political chaos in Korea led to a war there, which was internationalised in 1950 when the United States gained a mandate at the UN for military action against communist insurgents, who were backed by Mao and by the Soviets. Britain and the Commonwealth contributed to the UN force. The division of Korea into two states was confirmed after a ceasefire in 1953. North Korea was governed by an authoritarian communist regime and South Korea signed military and economic agreements with the United States. The region remained unstable. War broke out in Vietnam, part of the French colony of Indochina, as the French prepared to withdraw. A peace agreement was concluded in Geneva in 1954—another diplomatic success for Eden—but the agreement was soon broken. Instead of being united as an independent country after elections, Vietnam remained partitioned. North Vietnam was ruled by communists. Washington supported the separate state of South Vietnam as a barrier to the further spread of communism. Containment was boosted by the formation of the South East Asia Treaty Organization (SEATO) in 1954. The members of SEATO were the United States, Britain, France, Australia, New Zealand, Pakistan, Thailand, and the Philippines. Britain had for some time been calling for the establishment of a security system in the region. The idea was that alliances would better enable Britain to protect its interests and sustain its influence around the world.

This was also one of the motives behind Britain's pursuit of collective defence agreements in the Middle East. The Americans were not willing to participate on Britain's terms, however, and other avenues had to be explored. When Iraq and Turkey signed a security treaty in 1955, the Baghdad Pact, the British quickly joined the pact, as did Iran and Pakistan (the Baghdad Pact later became CENTO, the Central Treaty Organization). Britain's role in the Middle East was by this time under threat from Arab nationalists, and especially the government of Egypt; the British needed the Baghdad Pact as a means of maintaining status and authority in the region. But there was no placating Egypt. After a coup in 1952, the Egyptian monarchy had been abolished and army generals took control. Gamal Abdel Nasser became Egypt's prime minister in 1954 and its president in 1956. His agenda was assertively nationalistic and anti-British.

In the early 1950s, the biggest concentration of British forces outside Europe was in the Suez base complex. The Egyptians wanted the British to leave, however, and this was arranged under the Suez base agreement of 1954. The British moved their regional headquarters from Suez to Cyprus. In London it was thought that the advent of nuclear weapons had removed the need for large military bases and that withdrawal from Suez might help to persuade Egypt to take part in regional security arrangements. Nasser, who had negotiated the Suez base agreement and liked to pose as the man who had freed Egypt from British domination, flatly refused to accept any defence plans that involved Britain or other western powers. He condemned the Baghdad Pact and urged other Arab states not to join it. He visited Moscow, purchased arms from the eastern bloc, and formally recognised Mao's regime in China. The Americans agreed with Britain that Nasser had gone beyond the pale, but there was a disagreement about what should be done. British patience ran out in 1956 when Nasser nationalised the Suez Canal Company, an Anglo-French concern that administered the world's most important international waterway. Eden, now Britain's prime minister, attempted to find a peaceful solution, but Nasser's intransigence (in which he was encouraged by the Soviet Union) led the British and the French to opt for military intervention in league with Israel. The leaders of Israel wanted to strike at Egypt in pursuit of security goals that they deemed not to have been achieved during the war that had accompanied the creation of the state of Israel in 1948–1949. The intervention in Egypt, justified by the British as the only way to safeguard the Suez Canal and ensure that it remained open for all its users, was condemned around the world. Under pressure from the Americans, Eden decided to stop the military operation. He had been warned by the U.S. president, Dwight Eisenhower, and by the U.S. secretary of state, John Foster Dulles, that America could not approve of a resort to arms—especially not in a year when Eisenhower was seeking reelection on a peace platform—but Eden had apparently assumed that the U.S. government would not actively oppose the military operation once it was in progress. This had also been the view of such senior ministers as Harold Macmillan, chancellor of the exchequer in the Eden Cabinet.

The Suez crisis was a blow to Britain. It seemed to indicate that the capacity for independent action was limited, that Britain was becoming reliant on U.S. goodwill, and that it was losing influence even in parts of the world that had traditionally been under British control.

Within Britain there were expressions of doubt about the global role, the future of the empire, the use of force abroad, and the worth to Britain of many of its overseas commitments. Suez certainly undermined Britain's confidence, but not for long. There was no rush to decolonise or to abandon responsibilities and surrender interests. The Middle East and Far East were still considered to be strategically and economically vital to Britain; Britain was still a global as opposed to merely a European power. The Americans concurred, and although the 'special relationship' was damaged by the Suez crisis, cooperation and consultation were soon restored.

This book explores the main determinants of British foreign policy from the aftermath of Suez through to the beginning of the 1970s. Britain's international role changed tremendously during this period; indeed, it probably changed more between 1957 and 1970 than in any other thirteen-year period in British history. This book explains what happened. While acknowledging that Britain lost influence and declined as a great power relative to other great powers, however, this book draws attention to British triumphs as well as failures, to signs of strength as well as examples of retreat, in order to provide a balanced picture. Despite the changes to Britain's international role, many of which were regretted at elite and popular levels, Britain did not become a nonentity in world affairs.

The arrangement of the book is partly thematic and partly chronological. This mixed approach brings out the main topics for analysis while providing detailed insights that serve to illustrate general points. Among the book's leading concerns are the shifts in the Cold War and the increase in tension (both in intensity and in geographical spread) between the Americans and the Soviets and between the western powers and the communist camp; the course of the 'special relationship' between Britain and the United States; Britain's wish and ability to take independent action when necessary; and efforts to maximise Britain's influence and preserve British interests in the 'three circles' identified by Churchill and others after the Second World War.

These major concerns are explored with reference to specific events and issues:

- the improvement in Anglo-American relations after Suez and the waning of the 'special relationship' during the mid-1960s;
- defence reforms, nuclear deterrence, the need to pay for nuclear and conventional forces, the fate of British weapons programmes, increasing military coordination with the Americans, the appeal of disarmament, and the eventual withdrawal from East of Suez;
- Britain's involvement in and relations with the UN, NATO, and other bodies;
- the development of the western alliance and the problems therein associated with nuclear weapons and multilateralism, forward defence, joint strategy, and political cohesion;
- international crises over Berlin, Cuba, the German question, Vietnam, the Middle East, and Czechoslovakia;
- the end of empire, British decolonisation, Britain's relationship with the Commonwealth and the complications created by apartheid and Britain's arms sales to South Africa, overseas aid, immigration policy, the turn to Europe, wars in Congo and Nigeria, and disputes concerning Gibraltar, Kashmir, and Rhodesia;
- instability in South East Asia and the Pacific, China's assertive policy and the Sino-Soviet split, the confrontation between Indonesia and Malaysia, and controversial British attempts to arrange a settlement in Vietnam;
- friction in the Middle East produced by Arab nationalism, internal regional politics, the 'Eisenhower Doctrine', continuing British military and political involvement (notably in Jordan, Kuwait, Aden, and the Persian Gulf), and British policy during and after the Arab-Israeli War of 1967;
- relations with Moscow, the nature of Soviet foreign policy, and the extension of the Cold War into new areas (especially Africa);
- breakthroughs such as the Test Ban Treaty of 1963, international summitry, the superpower thaw, and European détente;

- the impact of French and West German overtures to the eastern bloc and the consequences of economic, social, and political change in the bloc;
- Cold War politics, propaganda, intelligence, and espionage; technological, ideological, and cultural competition; and the contributions of science and research and development;
- the new Europe, the Paris-Bonn axis and quickening European integration, the formation of the European Economic Community and why Britain made two unsuccessful applications to join it; and
- the underperformance of the British economy and the gap between resources and commitments, concerns about sterling and the balance of payments, and recurring economic and financial problems.

This is a long list, which reflects the fact that much was going on in this relatively short but very busy period. How Britain coped, and the extent to which British goals were accomplished, will become clear in what follows. A basic question suggests itself, one that will be taken up at the end of the book: How did Britain's international role at the beginning of the 1970s compare to its role in the late 1950s?

CHAPTER 1

FOREIGN POLICY, DEFENCE, AND BRITAIN'S WORLD ROLE

Anthony Eden's successor as prime minister, Harold Macmillan, led the government from January 1957 to October 1963. Macmillan was not without experience in the field of diplomacy and international relations. During the Second World War, he served as British minister in North Africa, the Mediterranean, and Italy, and he was initially Eden's replacement as foreign secretary when Eden became prime minister, although he had only held this post between April and December 1955 before being appointed chancellor of the exchequer. The Macmillan government faced many difficulties. Some of Britain's most important connections—with the United States, the empire, and Europe—had to be rearranged; defence policy was in need of a thorough review; and adjustments had to be made in order to marry together resources, goals, and opportunities. As challenges arose to threaten Britain's role and position as a global power, boldness, imagination, flexibility, and perseverance were required on the part of British leaders if the problems of the time were to be fruitfully addressed.

In the aftermath of Suez, Macmillan focused on restoring relations with the United States. He told Eisenhower that if the 'special relationship' between Britain and America fell apart, their shared principles would be defeated. He agreed with Churchill's 'three circles' idea and hoped to show the Americans that partnership with Britain meant partnership with a great power, with the Commonwealth, and with the real leaders of Europe. Macmillan also saw Britain as the mediator between East and West. He believed that the British still had a major role to play in global affairs, even if their military and economic resources were not what they had been in former times. Macmillan later recalled that restoring relations with the United States was 'the most urgent, and at the same time the most delicate, task which confronted me'. He and his colleagues were 'not at all in the mood...to put ourselves in a humiliating posture', but there was a need for 'a new strategy', which entailed reorganisation, retrenchment, and a careful analysis of domestic and international contexts.[1]

If Britain was to remain America's partner it would be in a junior capacity, but it was natural for the prime minister to talk up Britain's strength and potential. Anglo-American relations did improve. Now that the U.S. elections were over, Eisenhower admitted that the situation in the Middle East might necessitate intervention. According to the 'Eisenhower Doctrine', announced in January 1957, regimes in the Middle East could expect American assistance when threatened by communists. In April 1957 King Hussein of Jordan appealed for help as the pro-Nasser faction in his country stepped up its destabilisation campaign. The coup in Iraq in July 1958, which brought down the pro-British regime of Nuri el-Said, deepened the sense of crisis in the region. American troops were sent to Beirut to protect the government of Lebanon, and the instability in Jordan prompted British military intervention there, with U.S. approval. The 'Eisenhower Doctrine' was meant to curb disorder in the region and keep the Soviets out. It was controversial in the United States and elsewhere it also had a mixed reception. Leaders in the Middle East were divided, Moscow and Peking were hostile, London and Paris were favourable. The government of India warned Eisenhower that military action was not the answer, to which he replied that his only aim was to promote peace and prosperity. The Americans became more active in the Middle East. Eisenhower realised that Britain had been right about Nasser and pan-Arab radicalism. At the same time, the Americans were determined that their involvement would be selective. They were sure that the British would try to trick them into a heavier commitment and that this would be used by London to compensate for the damage done to British interests by Suez, to protect Britain's oil supply, and to pressurise Nasser. Macmillan hoped that the situation in Jordan would lead to greater Anglo-American cooperation, but he knew that Washington was reluctant, and he probably exaggerated the dangers in the region in order to gain leverage. It is also possible that the British covertly aggravated the crisis in Jordan so as to justify an expansion of Britain's military role in the Middle East.[2]

The coup in Iraq in 1958 was a serious blow to Britain. It reinforced London's fears about Arab nationalism and made Britain's bases in Muscat and Aden more vulnerable. Indeed, Arab demands for a British withdrawal increased. London was also worried about Soviet ambitions, although in some ways this helped because states in the Persian Gulf still regarded Britain as their protector (America, as the friend of Israel, was not an option for them). The need for a show of force partly explains the intervention in Jordan. Remaining in the Middle East was a strategic necessity for Britain, which had ongoing interests and commitments East of Suez and could only project influence across the globe by protecting allies and clients and maintaining a chain of bases. Commitments were kept up despite pressure from the Labour opposition in Parliament and advice from military chiefs, strategists, and others that the world role had to be scaled down. Britain's overseas obligations in the early 1960s would not be significantly fewer than they had been in 1957.[3]

Macmillan reported on the Middle East to the House of Commons on July 17, 1958. He spoke of the revolution in Iraq and disturbances in Jordan, about the movement of Syrian forces towards the Jordanian border, and about the intelligence concerning a plot against King Hussein, who had requested British assistance. British troops had been sent to help the Jordanians maintain their independence and integrity. Macmillan argued that friendly Arab states needed support and that dictatorship had to be prevented from spreading across the region. Labour MPs objected that the legality of Britain's action was debatable, that British interests would be damaged in the long run, and that even in the short term it was not clear that Jordan could be stabilised. Some speakers wanted the government to refer problems to the UN Security Council before taking military action, not afterwards, and Macmillan and his fellow ministers were subjected to a barrage of questions on specific aspects of the operation in Jordan. Members of Parliament expressed concern about the likely Soviet response to British and U.S. intervention in the Middle East.[4]

The Times argued that Britain's prestige, relationships in the Middle East, and need for oil made the sending of troops to Jordan 'justifiable'. *The Times* backed the government's view that inaction would have been worse than action and that Arab leaders could not be allowed to think that Britain was no longer strong or reliable. Like the U.S. involvement in Lebanon, Britain's intervention in Jordan was necessary and appropriate. The main difficulty lay ahead: when their mission was over, American and British forces would have to withdraw in a way that did not expose the governments of Lebanon and Jordan to their enemies. The *Economist* was unimpressed by the American operation in Lebanon, claiming that the popular cry there was for U.S. troops to leave. In Jordan, meanwhile, it was not clear what the British presence could achieve. King Hussein had declared that Jordanian intervention in Iraq might become necessary, but he realised that this would test the loyalty of his army, and above all he needed the army to put down domestic disorder. British troops had been sent to Jordan not to put pressure on the new leaders of Iraq, the *Economist* assumed, but to protect Hussein's government. By bringing them in, however, Hussein had offended other Arab countries. Instability was worrisome for him and if it spread it would endanger the wider interests of Britain and the West.[5]

The emergencies in Lebanon and Jordan were dealt with and U.S. and British troops were withdrawn within four months. A resolution was passed at the UN to promote stability in both countries. Moscow complained about the American and British intervention and there were also protests from Israel, which had not been consulted (and may have been hoping to take advantage of the turmoil to seize more territory). For Britain, the successful action in Jordan and cooperation with the United States gave cause for self-congratulation. Macmillan hoped that Washington would pay more attention to London's advice about the Middle East in future. Some commentators warned that the Americans were out to replace Britain as the dominant power in the region, but others interpreted the 'Eisenhower Doctrine' as a confession of error and a recognition that America needed to work with, not against, Britain. In December 1958 the British government reaffirmed its commitment to joint action as and when necessary. It considered that Britain's position in the Middle East was threatened primarily by Arab nationalism. The USSR and communism were secondary threats, although on December 17, 1958, the chiefs of staff recommended that London and Washington should arrange for military action to prevent any country in the Middle East from coming under Soviet control. Considerable tension still existed between the British and Americans, however, and Britain's military chiefs and strategists continued to think the Americans clumsy and ill-informed with regard to the Middle East. Those Lebanese leaders who had called for U.S. help were soon removed from power. In British eyes the U.S. intervention in Lebanon was mismanaged, in contrast with the smaller, more discreet and mobile British operations in Jordan and elsewhere in this period.[6]

Nevertheless, Anglo-American relations were generally improving. In March 1957 Macmillan and British foreign secretary Selwyn Lloyd met Eisenhower and Dulles for talks in Bermuda. The discussions, Eisenhower recorded, were marked by 'frankness and confidence'. Later in 1957, Queen Elizabeth II and Prince Philip went on an official visit to the United States, and Macmillan and Eisenhower signed a 'Declaration of Common Purpose'. These were the outward signs of a restoration of Anglo-American friendship. The British government would not apologise for Suez, Macmillan said, but it no longer mattered.[7]

Other circumstances were less satisfactory. The British could not ignore the growing gap between their commitments and the available resources. A time of reassessment was necessary. Britain's hydrogen bomb was tested in 1957, but the programme was expensive, as was the system of national service. A review of April 1957 resulted in reforms named after the defence minister, Duncan Sandys. The idea was to cut costs by relying on an independent nuclear deterrent and smaller, better-equipped conventional forces. Though Britain would still be able to claim great-power status, with hydrogen bombs, new aircraft, and Blue Streak missiles, there was no option but to make savings. Before the Second World War, defence spending had taken only 3 percent of the national wealth and the armed forces numbered less than 300,000. By 1957 defence spending stood at 8 percent of the national wealth and Britain maintained armed forces of 700,000. The French were spending 6 percent of their national wealth on defence and the Federal Republic of Germany only 4 percent, at a time when Britain was facing stiff economic competition, especially from Western Europe. Sandys proposed that conscription should cease by 1960. The army would be cut to 165,000 by 1962, the armed forces as a whole would fall to 400,000, and defence spending was to be held at 7 percent of the national wealth.[8]

The Times was sceptical. The plan to develop missiles and warheads appeared to make sense in that America's willingness to come to Britain's aid might decline with the proliferation of intercontinental ballistic missiles (ICBMs), but Sandys had also stressed the need for collective defence, and it was plain that Britain could not protect itself without allies. Sandys had suggested that his measures would save money, yet he was apparently ready to spend heavily on missiles. According to *The Times*, policy 'has been determined mainly by the desire to get rid of national service and...by mistaken notions about national prestige'. There was a 'lack of balance between our nuclear and conventional preparations'. The *Observer* agreed. Deterrence had to be a primary goal, but would the focus on nuclear forces represent the best use of resources? Britain's deterrent 'constitutes only a marginal contribution to an American programme which is already nearing saturation point'. The *Observer* insisted that the most urgent need was to enlarge the army. It was too small to meet its growing NATO obligations, and too small to perform essential tasks outside Europe, even if these were going to be reduced. Without improvements it would never reach the required levels of strength and efficiency.[9]

Following a heated Commons debate on April 16 and 17, 1957, the government's defence plan was approved, with Sandys telling MPs that it had been well received by the British public and 'abroad, after some initial doubts, it has in the main been received with understanding and a good deal of respect'. Sandys explained that 'we cannot go on devoting such a large part of our resources—and, in particular, of manpower—to defence', and that because 'adequate protection against all-out nuclear attack is impossible', Britain had to concentrate 'not upon preparations to wage war so much as upon trying to prevent that catastrophe from ever happening'. Sandys linked together deterrence, disarmament, civil defence, and other aspects of national security, but his critics were unimpressed. Opposition MPs denied that the government could achieve what it claimed it wanted to do. Labour spokesman George Brown regretted the focus on deterrence and contended that the government would have done better to postpone Britain's nuclear testing and press for an international agreement on arms limitation.[10]

Labour's misgivings did not alter defence policy. There had been various recommendations while Eden was prime minister and Macmillan and Sandys were determined to press ahead, believing that more attention had to be given to the condition of the economy, but the reorganisation of defence policy was not easy. The process was hindered by quarrels, delays, and compromises. Some measures were pushed through despite strong objections from the service chiefs. This is not to suggest that their advice was simply ignored; on many points it was Sandys who had to give way. There was a lot of misrepresentation surrounding the changes. In part, the government justified them by exaggerating British power, by emphasising the independent deterrent and arguing that more adaptable conventional forces would enhance Britain's ability to act alone when necessary. This was because Macmillan and Sandys wished to heighten perceptions of British power both at home and abroad. However drastic they seemed when first announced, though, the Sandys proposals were not radical in practice. The Churchill and Eden governments of 1951 to

1957 had repeatedly discussed Britain's defence needs and capabilities and the basic assumption remained the same throughout this period: Britain would remain a world power. Sandys sought to retain this status while cutting costs, but savings on the conventional side were smaller than predicted. The focus on the nuclear deterrent entailed greater dependence on the United States and the continuation of high defence spending exacerbated Britain's economic difficulties.[11]

The Eisenhower administration accepted that Britain wished to develop a new defence policy, and talks in Washington in October 1957, led to the establishment of two committees to oversee nuclear cooperation. The restrictions imposed by the McMahon Act were lifted and the exchange of information and technology began in earnest in 1958. Britain's European allies were angered by the intention to withdraw some British army and air force personnel from West Germany. This also added to the tension between Britain's service chiefs, who sought to resist cuts and were worried about NATO's strength and unity, and those government ministers who regarded retrenchment as the most urgent priority. The size and expenses of the British Army of the Rhine (BAOR) led to some wrangling between London and Bonn, and American army chiefs also disliked the projected shrinkage of Britain's conventional forces. They attributed the mania for cost-cutting to Eisenhower, and British defence policy became part of the debate surrounding the U.S. military's demand for more money. In Britain the Sandys reforms increased the armed services' competition for resources. The Royal Navy, vital for Britain's world role, continued to receive at least 25 percent of defence spending. The Americans objected when it was revealed that British participation in NATO's operations at sea would be scaled down, and the Macmillan government decided not to try simultaneously to withdraw troops from Europe and ships from the Atlantic. Therefore, the number of ships did not fall as sharply as had originally been envisaged.[12]

Britain's move towards a greater reliance on nuclear weapons did not find favour with some American strategists, but Eisenhower was sure that the British should have a credible deterrent. Eisenhower supported London on this issue because he wanted to restore Anglo-American relations after Suez and because he was worried about the rapid increase in the USSR's military strength. Washington was impressed when the British tested their hydrogen bomb in May 1957, and alarmed when the Soviets demonstrated their technological progress by launching Sputnik, the first earth-orbiting artificial satellite, in October 1957. All this made a closer defence relationship with Britain attractive. The Americans still needed their bases in Britain, moreover, if they were to maximise their ability to destroy targets within the Soviet Union. The French disliked Anglo-American nuclear cooperation and argued for a common foreign policy and security posture for Western Europe and a conciliatory approach to the Soviet Union. The British were willing to talk about a change, but Anglo-French discussions came to an end with Sputnik and the restoration of Anglo-American nuclear exchanges. To Macmillan, Britain's defence relationship with the Americans was far more important than that with the French could ever be. Direct requests from Paris for joint projects were turned down. Britain now had the hydrogen bomb, accepted intermediate range ballistic missiles (IRBMs) from the Americans under a dual-key arrangement, benefited from bilateral agreements with the United States concluded in July 1958 and May 1959, and went on to purchase new U.S. delivery systems on favourable terms.[13]

Sputnik indicated that Soviet technology was more advanced than the West had assumed. Macmillan eagerly used this to erode some of the remaining barriers to Anglo-American nuclear cooperation, but he was under pressure from Parliament and the public to promote disarmament and negotiate a test ban. He did not want to jeopardise a nuclear deal with the United States and could not press energetically for disarmament and a test ban until this deal was made. He also wanted to delay until Britain's development of the hydrogen bomb was assured. Another concern was the Soviet superiority in conventional forces in Europe, which meant that limits could not be confined to nuclear weapons. This made matters more complicated, as the prime minister was not slow to point out when his critics complained that he was not doing enough on disarmament. Macmillan stressed that the deployment of U.S. missiles on British soil would be highly advantageous, and that British sovereignty would be preserved because American control of the warheads would be combined with British control of the missiles. In fact, nuclear cooperation between Britain and America did not run smoothly. Political, strategic, financial, and technological problems arose, and there was a difference in motive: the British wished to maintain an independent deterrent whereas Washington viewed the missiles in Britain as a component of America's defence system. Of course, the Americans were not about to give away nuclear secrets and obtain nothing in return. They expected to influence British policy. They also made it clear that no control over warheads or bombs would be given to any ally, including Britain, unless this became necessary during a war. On testing, moreover, the Americans were not ready to compromise. In the spring of 1958 they rejected a Soviet proposal for the cessation of tests. Macmillan was attacked for failing to take up opportunities to arrange a test ban. He probably comforted himself with the reflection that, if Britain could gather all the information it needed from the United States, the need for British tests would diminish. Then he could gain credit by scaling them down and by speaking out more boldly for international disarmament.[14]

The British did not expect Blue Streak to be ready until the early 1960s and it was decided that, in the meantime, American Thor IRBMs would be deployed in Britain. In February 1958 it was arranged that the Thors would be provided free of charge. Warheads would be supplied by the United States and remain in U.S. custody until orders were received that the missiles should be readied for use. British and American officers had separate keys for each missile and both keys had to be inserted before the missile could be launched, which ensured that London and Washington would have to be in agreement before the missiles were fired. The British reserved the right to develop their own warheads and add these to the missiles. It was therefore possible that the control system would change because the U.S. firing key would no longer be needed, but this never happened. The dual-key arrangement remained in place and was a feature of later Anglo-American agreements. The Thors arrived in Britain in 1959. Meanwhile, there was joint planning and targeting by the two air forces and bombs were supplied for British aircraft. There was also closer contact in the intelligence and planning fields in general.[15]

Several historians have argued that it was the success of Britain's nuclear programme that convinced the Americans to opt for nuclear cooperation, that Eisenhower's pro-British attitude was also important, and that Macmillan's talk of 'interdependence' was not out of place. An alternative interpretation emphasises the impact of Sputnik and maintains that it was awareness of the USSR's advances that motivated Washington's commitment to Anglo-American nuclear exchanges. Macmillan did admit that Sputnik was important. As for Eisenhower's position, the main determinant might not have been a wish to repair the 'special relationship' after Suez or a personal preference for working with the British, but rather U.S. strategic interests. The British concept of 'interdependence' seems questionable, moreover, in view of America's huge and self-sufficient nuclear programme. Britain's was much smaller, and by itself it could not deter the Soviets. British nuclear forces mattered more when they were linked with those of the United States. The role of Sputnik can also be questioned. Sputnik featured prominently in 'Britain's Contribution to Peace and Security', a paper circulated by Sandys in February 1958, but perhaps the key point made therein was that 'invulnerable second-strike forces' could prevent war by increasing the likelihood of mutual destruction. Therefore, Sputnik had not really upset the balance of military power. Sandys suggested that the West's superiority would probably increase as it developed new medium-range missiles and enhanced its conventional capabilities.[16]

One of Eisenhower's central ideas was to withdraw U.S. troops from Europe and replace them with tactical nuclear weapons for battlefield use. British thinking was in line with this, for it would facilitate the ending of conscription and the downsizing of the British contingent in West Germany. London pressed for a review of NATO strategy. The Sandys reforms and the decisions taken by NATO, it was hoped, would not prove to be incompatible. The NATO review did not go as London and Washington wanted. A major war was deemed to be less likely than smaller conflicts in which nuclear weapons would not be used. Therefore, as the

FRG recommended and as NATO conferences in December 1956 and April 1957 agreed, conventional forces would have to be augmented. NATO strategy would now include multiple options. It would not have the nuclear focus that the British and Americans favoured. Macmillan and Eisenhower did not care for this outcome, for they still wanted to save money, and British and American service chiefs preferred not to plan for a limited, nonnuclear war with the Soviets. A compromise was worked out in March 1958. This entailed 'differentiated responses', which would include, but not be confined to, nuclear weapons.[17]

Britain's political and military leaders believed in nuclear deterrence and had long since decided that the hydrogen bomb was a necessity. It would deter the Soviets, prove that Britain was still a great power, and increase Britain's influence over the Americans. There was a time factor to consider as well, partly because of the suspicion that America would seek a reckoning with the Soviets before the latter caught up in military technology and hardware. Another reason for haste was the prospect of a test ban. The British wanted to try out various techniques and devices before testing was restricted. All this became increasingly controversial in Britain. The Campaign for Nuclear Disarmament (CND) was inaugurated in 1958. Some of its early demonstrations attracted 10,000 people. Soon its leaders claimed to have 100,000 active supporters. CND declined during the mid-1960s but questions were still asked about Britain's defence policy, even by those who approved of the deterrent. In the long run it was by no means clear that the nuclear option preserved Britain's great-power status in a cost-effective way. Weapons research became more and more expensive, a British missile system was never perfected, and there was still a need to station large conventional forces abroad. Nor was the nuclear deterrent an independent one: dependence on the United States could not be avoided. Blue Streak was cancelled in 1960, by which time Britain's bomber force was virtually obsolete. Both the United States and the USSR had now entered the space race and developed intercontinental ballistic missiles.[18]

Macmillan may have restored the 'special relationship', but this was not an all-encompassing panacea. The closer nuclear cooperation was very important, as was the influence of habit and culture that encouraged elites in Britain and the United States to focus on common goals and shared values. However, the relationship was so obviously an unequal one, especially on defence, that many British observers considered Macmillan's policies not to be in keeping with the national interests or indeed national pride. There was also the old problem, one that Churchill had not managed to solve, that the Americans tended to downplay the 'special relationship' while the British wanted to make it more binding and formal.[19]

Conversely, greater collaboration between American and British service chiefs probably made the British government less anxious about the loss of nuclear independence. The conferences and joint planning of the period gave each side the chance to influence the other. Even before the cancellation of Blue Streak, Britain's nuclear forces were becoming a feature in U.S. strategy. For their part, since the Second World War, British governments had wanted closer cooperation with the Americans on nuclear matters, and by the late 1950s there was satisfaction that Britain's success in developing weapons had so impressed Washington that the U.S. government was finally doing as London had been requesting. True, reliance on the Americans was frustrating in some respects, but the British needed U.S. technology if they were going to have the next generation of nuclear delivery systems. The cancellation of Blue Streak indicated that Britain could not afford an independent deterrent. As this stark reality dawned on Parliament, press, and public, the government maintained that Britain's sovereignty, power, and freedom of manoeuvre were unaffected. Purchasing weapons from the United States was nothing to worry about, Macmillan said, for foreign manufacture did not mean foreign control. Defence remained a contentious issue nonetheless. There were further efforts to cut expenditure, arguments about whether or not nuclear forces were really vital to Britain's security, and fears about the political consequences of relying openly on the Americans.[20]

Great-power status and independence were difficult to sustain, and it was recognised at the highest levels (if not often admitted in public) that in future Britain would have to combine more with allies. A planning paper of January 1957 had declared it 'implicit in the acceptance of forces at the level now proposed that foreign policy...will be severely circum-scribed by the United Kingdom's inability to follow even a relatively independent line'. Macmillan and Sandys both accepted that Britain could do little in the world without the help of allies. As in past times, the hope was not only that cooperation would maximise British influence, but that it would save Britain money. Yet it was also understood that Britain would often act alone. Macmillan wanted big savings but vetoed certain schemes because he opposed any significant weakening of Britain's posi-tion in the Middle East and Far East. The Sandys reforms had a politi-cally useful effect on the British press, Conservative MPs, and sections of public opinion. Britain could still be presented as a world power, and, at first, there was optimism about the new defence policy. The nuclear deter-rent and smaller, better-equipped and more mobile conventional forces seemed to promise much. Britain's interventions in Jordan, Oman, and Kuwait during the late 1950s and early 1960s demonstrated that despite Suez, Britain could still police the Middle East, and this was reassuring. Since the reduction of Britain's conventional forces and the operations in the Middle East were facilitated by the United States, however, and there was a possibility that the Americans would seek to push the British out of the region in a bid for dominance, Britain's leaders seized upon any American action or statement that would tell the rest of the world that this was not about to happen. Even so, by the early 1960s, Britain had narrower goals than before: securing oil supplies and protecting bases and clients in the Persian Gulf. Britain remained in the region, but in a weak-ened condition. The same was true of Asia and the Indian Ocean. Britain still had a chain of air bases, the garrison at Hong Kong, and a large naval base at Singapore, but Britain's regional influence was decreasing. Britain played little part, for instance, in the U.S.-Chinese dispute of 1958 over the offshore islands of Quemoy and Matsu. The Sandys reforms did not enable Britain to carry on as a major world power at a lower cost.[21]

Peter Thorneycroft, who was chancellor of the exchequer from 1957 to 1958 and subsequently served as minister of aviation and minister of defence, maintained that the economies were insufficient, whereas the service chiefs complained that Sandys had gone too far. They threatened to resign and managed to block some of his proposals. After the general election of October 1959, Sandys was moved from the defence ministry to aviation and thence to Commonwealth relations. The new minister of defence was the less assertive Harold Watkinson. Here was a sign that Macmillan did not want to compromise Britain's international position and wished to avoid alienating the service chiefs. Thereafter, although some measures were carried through, including the phasing out of conscription, overseas commitments were not greatly reduced. In fact, spending on them increased. Government and opposition continued regularly to clash on defence issues in Parliament. On June 22, 1960, Watkinson was asked to provide details about Britain's proposed purchase of Skybolt missiles from the United States. Labour MPs argued that the cost of missiles that did not yet exist could not possibly be estimated. The left-winger Sydney Silverman ridiculed Watkinson and claimed that 'what he has really done is to buy a pig in a poke with a blank cheque'. The *Guardian* argued that Blue Streak, a fixed-site weapon, would not have suited Britain, whereas the air-launched Skybolt missile would better enable Britain to respond to an attack. But why had it taken so long for the government to arrive at this 'commonsense' position? The *Guardian* suggested that ministers had badly misjudged the speed of Soviet weapons development. *The Times* condemned the continuing demand from some Labour MPs that Britain should give up nuclear weapons, and rejected the idea that NATO should not threaten to use nuclear weapons first in the event of a war.[22]

Macmillan remained anxious about both the domestic political and the international ramifications of changes in defence policy. The British military presence in Europe, he thought, should be as small as the government could get away with politically. This would mean that Britain's forces would continue to be spread thinly across the globe. Constantly in the background was the need to remain on good terms with America. Macmillan had decided that it might be possible to increase Britain's influence in Washington in one of two ways: either by moving closer to Europe, which would involve cutting down Britain's military presence outside Europe, or by maintaining the world role, which is what Macmillan preferred to do. It also accorded with the wishes of most Conservative MPs, so strengthening Macmillan as prime minister and party leader. The main problem was that he did not properly address underlying long-term issues, particularly the impossibility of remaining a world power while cutting costs.[23]

In the early 1960s Britain still spent a higher proportion of its national wealth on defence than did the other European members of NATO. Britain had more overseas obligations than they did. The situation was not helped by the selfish goals of the armed services, the needs of certain industries, and short-term political considerations, all of which diverted policymakers from thoughts of cost-effectiveness over the longer term. Although by 1963 the BAOR had been reduced to 51,000, from 77,000 in 1957, bases and personnel had to be maintained across the globe and in 1965 there were still over 60,000 British servicemen and eighty Royal Navy vessels East of Suez, safeguarding trade, keeping order, and improving security. These were tasks that benefited the *whole* of the West, not Britain alone. The strains were palpable. New quarrels broke out between the service chiefs as they vied for a bigger share of the defence budget. Dependence on the Americans caused more unease. One alternative would have been to combine with France, the fourth nuclear power from 1960, but the British and French defence establishments were never close, and in any case Britain could not risk losing U.S. help. The French caused considerable trouble within NATO from the late 1950s and were strongly critical of American policy, especially on nuclear matters.[24]

If defence planning and the nuclear relationship with the Americans were problematic, for Britain this was also a difficult period with regard to decolonisation. British leaders hoped for a smooth transition, with former colonies joining the Commonwealth. Some of them chose not to. Serious violence erupted at times, as in Kenya and Cyprus, which added further complications. In general, Britain was successful in making a peaceful withdrawal and public opinion at home was reconciled to the change (in time the necessary mental adjustment was made even in conservative circles, whereas in France the opposition to decolonisation was more obstinate). Nevertheless, the loss of empire had implications for

Britain's global influence and, as usual, whatever Britain tried to do was affected by the Cold War. It was hoped that if the colonies were treated well, as independent states they would side with the West. Oil, markets, raw materials, air bases, defence agreements, sea lanes, and global communications were all part of the equation, and policymakers concluded that Britain would gain more from friendship than from control. In addition, because the colonies were no longer such an asset by this time, there were advantages to be gained by freeing them. U.S. opinion would be mollified and more resources would be available to Britain for fighting the Cold War, whereas to retain the colonies would have been to take on massive expenses and increase the likelihood of wars and possible Soviet intervention. Much as Macmillan and his colleagues tried, decolonisation could not be supervised in such a way as to maintain intact Britain's world-power status, but the consequences of withdrawal from empire might have been much worse. Philip Hemming sees in decolonisation an attempt to exchange dwindling tangible assets for increased intangibles. This effort did not prevent a loss of influence and prestige, yet it was 'successful' in the sense that without it, Britain's relative decline would have been 'considerably more traumatic'.[25]

The Americans had been wary since 1945 of being drawn into those parts of the world where they would be obliged to prop up Britain's imperial position. Nevertheless, Washington was ready to cooperate with the British in strategically important regions, and disappointed when the British withdrew due to lack of resources. The Eisenhower administration was totally against the abandonment of Hong Kong, for example, and Macmillan was eventually able to treat Hong Kong as a defence problem that could be shared between Britain and the United States. Fortunately, the colony did not come under much pressure from Mao's China.[26]

During the premierships of Churchill and Eden, there had been a determination to uphold the empire, not dismantle it. A foreign office paper of mid-1952 had described nationalism in the colonies as an attempt 'by less developed nations' to undermine Britain's position as a world power. All such challenges were to be dealt with vigorously in order to safeguard Britain's strategic and economic interests and its status as 'a leader of the free world'. Before he became prime minister, Macmillan shared this view. He was a pragmatist, though, and when he took over as premier he asked his advisors to weigh up the costs and benefits of empire. When the costs outweighed the benefits, he had decided, it would be time to withdraw. Official thinking on the matter was clarified in September 1957 by a policy paper that listed the colonies that were ready for independence and likely to join the Commonwealth. There was an assessment of the economic and financial implications of aid to former colonies, and it was suggested that the net saving to Britain would probably be less than expected. If there were pressing reasons for granting independence to a colony that could not support itself, Britain would have to continue funding. These points were discussed, along with the probable impact upon trade, investment, and sterling balances, and the paper concluded that the economic arguments for and against decolonisation were quite evenly matched. By itself, therefore, Britain's economic interest would not determine policy. The same applied to strategic considerations. The paper also referred to political circumstances. It pointed out that in many colonies there was not yet a desire for independence and that 'any premature withdrawal would seem bound to add to the areas of stress and discontent in the world...The United Kingdom has been too long connected with its colonial possessions to sever ties abruptly without creating a bewilderment which would be discreditable and dangerous'. But the British government found that it was not in complete control of decolonisation: the pace quickened and could not be slowed.[27] Some of the provisos that policymakers originally had in mind were abandoned.

It would be wrong to exaggerate this abandonment, however, for Macmillan was determined to promote good Commonwealth relations, and his overseas tour of 1958 was both a goodwill exercise and an opportunity to find out more about what was going on in Britain's spheres of influence. He decided that Britain, and the West, had to do more to foster stability and prosperity across Africa and Asia and build up the Commonwealth as a barrier against communism. If he did not want to be hasty, Macmillan was also convinced that decolonisation had to proceed without undue delay, and between 1957 and 1960 his government doubled Britain's overseas aid.

Trade and finance loomed large in the government's calculations. Britain needed more export earnings to support the sterling area and invest overseas, and there was an expectation that the agricultural and mineral resources of the Commonwealth would command high prices. This optimism proved to be misplaced. Between the mid-1950s and mid-1960s, the terms of trade of most developing countries deteriorated and they became less valuable as markets. Trade between the major industrialised nations was much healthier, and this has prompted some historians to argue that Britain should have been trying to export more to the United States and Western Europe, not pursuing the Commonwealth option. At the time, however, it was not clear that this option would be damaging. The system of preferences and Britain's financial control were advantages that the government wanted to make full use of, and it was only later that the accusation about mistakenly neglecting Europe for the Commonwealth gained ground. Policy was never driven exclusively by economic considerations. The basic assumption was that colonies would become independent sooner or later; it was best for this to happen sooner because a friendly separation would have fewer ill effects than a rancorous rupture. Political and financial self-interest cannot entirely explain decolonisation. There was also a mood of progress and justice and an idea that empires belonged to a bygone age. Moral and intellectual influences pointed in the same direction as political and economic concerns, and there was some overlap between them. There were many contemporaries, for instance, who argued that the government should spend more on welfare provisions at home and that the withdrawal from empire would free up the necessary funding.[28]

The key decisions were probably those of 1957, which gave independence to Ghana and Malaya and created a (temporary) sense of multiracial optimism in the empire-Commonwealth. Macmillan had seen clearly that Africans and Asians had to be treated in a new way, and this was at the core of his global vision by the time of his 'wind of change' speech in Cape Town on February 3, 1960. The withdrawal from some colonies was too hasty, however, and not all local nationalist leaders were equipped to take over. Some of the newly independent states were far from stable. Before and after withdrawal there was uncertainty about the appropriate political arrangements, the rights of different racial and tribal groups, voting qualifications, and the status of the white settlers who stayed behind. Although Britain did manage to avoid major colonial wars, unlike the French and Belgians, disengagement was not unproblematic, and there were difficulties at home, notably within the Conservative Party, some of whose members and supporters opposed decolonisation. Right-wingers formed the Monday Club (the 'wind of change' speech was delivered on a Monday). Another cause for concern was the reaction of the older white Dominions. Canada hoped that the new Commonwealth would be an effective mediator in world affairs, but Australia preferred to focus on its defence relationship with the United States.[29]

Washington welcomed decolonisation but hoped, for Cold War purposes, that former colonies could be persuaded to retain some links with the European powers that had previously ruled them. The Eisenhower administration decided to work with the Europeans in arranging for their withdrawal from Africa, and new African governments were promised U.S. friendship if they looked to the West, not to the communist bloc, for aid and protection. Eisenhower was impressed by Macmillan's 'wind of change' speech and sent him a message of congratulation, but Macmillan had a growing sense that 'there were many threatening clouds on the horizon'. He was particularly worried about unrest across Africa and the apartheid policies of the South African government. Apartheid became a source of tension within the expanding Commonwealth, and it was not easy for Britain's political leaders and businessmen to reconcile their wish for good Commonwealth relations—such as would provide Britain with trade, security, and other benefits—with their closeness to a South African regime that was imposing apartheid. Nor was it clear that the Commonwealth, changed by the entry of numerous weak states, could provide lasting support for Britain's global position, and as an identity of interest within the Commonwealth became less likely, Britain struggled to promote inclusiveness and agreement.[30]

Soviet designs and the possible spread of communism in Africa represented a real danger and British leaders took this into account when contemplating decolonisation and overseas aid. In some of those newly independent states that embraced socialism, the Soviet model was not considered applicable, but this did not prevent the growth of Soviet influence in Africa. Still, important as this was in shaping the attitudes of British policymakers, the process of decolonisation was affected more directly by the strength of nationalism in the colonies. A more assertive nationalism had to be confronted in the Middle East, in Asia, and, increasingly, in Africa. The British withdrawal from Africa was speeded up from 1959 not so much because of the international environment or conditions within Britain, but because of pressure from the Africans themselves. After the Second World War, there had been few indications that the British commitment to empire was fading. In the ten years after 1947, recruitment to the colonial service increased by more than 50 percent. At the end of the war, no nationalist party existed in any of Britain's African colonies; colonial rule was returning to Southeast Asia and British leaders were certain that the empire was a necessary support for global power. Change was envisaged, but it did not entail the granting of independence except in a few special cases. In most cases, the intention was to improve colonial administration and promote economic development. By the late 1950s, the situation was different: African leaders were gathering local mass support and insisting on an end to British rule; a new kind of co-optive imperialism was impossible because Britain lacked the resources to make it work and the newly independent states would not have accepted it even had the British made the attempt.[31]

Decolonisation was not a sign that Britain intended to give up the global role and focus more on Europe. This was a period of adaptation. Some commentators might subsequently have liked to call it a retreat, but this is not how British leaders of the late 1950s to the mid-1960s saw it. To them, it was adjustment in order to *avoid* retreat. The policy was not always coherent or well organised, but it was a realistic response to the problem of limited resources. The fundamental elements of Britain's global position had to be retained and stabilised, which involved giving up some rights and commitments while seeking new allies, making new commitments, and exerting influence in new ways. It is important not to predate the 'end' of empire (as John Darwin has argued, this only came with the abandonment of efforts to retain 'some form of primacy in the external relations of old dependencies'). Decolonisation began for a combination of reasons—domestic politics, economic maladies, international pressures, change in the colonies—which became linked together in the aftermath of the Second World War. It was largely a matter of interest: preserving the empire was reckoned by policymakers no longer to be in Britain's best interests. But this was not a straightforward matter. Although relative economic weakness meant that Britain lacked the means to continue running a large empire, choice mattered as well as necessity, especially with regard to economic causes of decolonisation. The value of the empire as an exclusive zone of national exploitation faded and the granting of independence in return for continued economic contact was designed to benefit Britain. Previously, and most notably during the last ten to fifteen years of colonial rule, there was increased metropolitan involvement, not less, which suggests that British leaders wished to retain the colonies for their raw materials and dollar-earning exports. In addition, Labour and Conservative governments alike were determined to maintain sterling as a world currency. The protection of sterling was a priority and for a long time it was assumed that the empire would help with this. As the empire came to be seen as a liability in currency terms, opinion changed. There was more talk of the empire as a burden. Colonial development could no longer be financed from the sterling balances in London. When colonial produce was sold for dollars, these were retained in London and credited as pounds in the colonies' accounts. Prices fell, however, and the produce brought in fewer dollars. At the same time, the colonies were demanding the relaxation of financial controls while Britain went on spending considerable sums on development projects. The formation of the European Economic Community (EEC) added another complication, for this would be a common market that discriminated against British colonial commodities.[32]

The Macmillan government's preoccupation with American friendship, nuclear weapons, and the Commonwealth meant that less attention was paid to Europe, where the EEC was established by the Treaty of Rome of March 1957. Britain was an outside observer, apparently unworried, though there was concern about the consequences of being left out. At first British leaders refused to believe that the EEC could work well in practice, and they still entertained the notion that Britain, as a world power, did not necessarily need closer ties to Europe. Yet the Americans repeatedly urged Britain to work with Europe, and Macmillan and his colleagues did make proposals for a free trade area. In pursuing this aim, they were obstructed by Charles de Gaulle, prime minister (1958) and subsequently president (1959–1969) of France. The Americans were also frustrated by de Gaulle. He resented U.S. leadership of the West through NATO and America's economic and financial might, and considered that the British were too close to the Americans, so he tried to assert European independence of the United States by limiting British influence. De Gaulle was especially offended by the Anglo-American refusal to establish a joint British–U.S.–French directorate to control NATO, and by the United States' decision not to share nuclear secrets with France (Britain satisfied the formal requirements for this but the French did not). Moreover, the French were still angry about the Suez affair, and de Gaulle's policy was also bolstered by the developing Franco-German axis: Paris and Bonn cooperated closely, especially on European integration, and de Gaulle was able to use this relationship against Britain.[33]

De Gaulle opposed the British plan for a European free trade area because it was not in line with his vision for France and for Europe. At home he was trying to strengthen the French economy. As he saw it, domestically and externally the free trade area offered him nothing. To de Gaulle France and Britain were engaged in a struggle for control over the economic future of Europe, and hence of France, and friendship between Paris and Bonn would help the French to win this struggle. The FRG's chancellor, Konrad Adenauer, shared some of de Gaulle's suspicions about the British and Americans, but suggested that Britain ought not to be excluded from Europe's economic integration, and West German finance minister Ludwig Erhard was strongly in favour of a free trade area. De Gaulle therefore had to turn the EEC into a Franco-German alliance so as to destroy the free trade area. Paris and Bonn did not view the EEC in exactly the same way, and Britain tried to use this as a means to influence them both. Bonn argued against high industrial tariffs, wishing to create trade, not divert it. Nor did the FRG want the EEC to isolate itself from the rest of the world. The French, however, favoured high tariffs and a preferential system for the EEC. Paris hoped to shelter French industry from international competition and gain European customers for French farm products, which meant keeping out cheaper non-EEC imports. Whereas influential groups in the FRG welcomed Britain's plan for a free trade area, on the basis that it would bring some of the economic benefits promised by the EEC without the disadvantages, the French condemned the plan on political and economic grounds. Adenauer decided that in the long run the EEC would accord with his political goals: collaborating with France in the EEC would make possible an international role and influence for the FRG that would not otherwise be attainable. Macmillan tried to change Adenauer's mind, but the British overestimated their influence in Bonn and tended to delay concessions until they had little impact. Ludwig Erhard never sided with Britain, but briefly attempted to mediate between Britain and France. Had the British government pushed for an industrial free trade area much earlier, Bonn's doubts about the worth of the EEC might have increased. Instead, Adenauer could not be swayed and he moved the FRG closer to France. Macmillan and his colleagues were not converts to integration. They were responding to political and economic necessities and were more concerned about domestic circumstances than about building a stronger relationship with Europe. Throughout this period, in fact, British leaders failed to grasp the appeal of integration on the continent, limited themselves to what they thought domestic audiences would allow, and made choices that the Europeans knew were based on negative rather than positive motivations.[34]

For British leaders, the main problem with 'The Six' in the EEC (France, the FRG, Italy, Belgium, Luxembourg, and the Netherlands) was that they had accepted the principle of supranationalism. Britain had initially been involved in the discussions of the mid-1950s that led to the establishment of the EEC, but the Eden government disapproved of the course favoured by 'The Six' and British representation at the relevant talks was discontinued. The Treaty of Rome was ratified and acted upon while the Macmillan government was still trying to attract support for the nonsupranational free trade area, which by this stage had been under consideration for years. As sanctioned by the Eden government, it provided for continued imperial preference on food. British leaders expected the most industrialised parts of Europe to accept the plan, and they presented it as a means to increase international cooperation and promote collective economic progress. Leaders of 'The Six' were intent on a customs union, with supranational institutions, as envisaged at the Messina Conference of June 1955. They had no intention of abolishing tariffs against Britain and accepting British industrial competition when Britain could buy cheap food from the Commonwealth and enjoy a lower cost of living. It was and is asserted that the British should have taken the opportunities they had to negotiate with 'The Six' in a much more constructive fashion. They might thereby have joined the EEC and altered it from within. Yet this assumes that suitable arrangements could have been made with the Commonwealth, which is by no means certain, and that the leaders of 'The Six' were amenable to Britain's recommendations, which they were not. When Macmillan became prime minister it seemed that Britain still had options: some observers could not believe that 'The Six' would leave Britain behind, and quarrelling among 'The Six' encouraged London to think that support for a free trade area would grow. As these arguments were resolved, however, Britain's bargaining position became weaker.[35]

Macmillan was prepared to take a hard line with 'The Six', especially France and the FRG, as indicated by remarks he made to foreign secretary Selwyn Lloyd on June 24, 1958.

> I think sometimes our difficulties with our friends abroad result from our natural good manners and reticence. We are apt not to press our points too strongly in the early stages of a negotiation, and then when a crisis arises and we have to take a definite position we are accused of perfidy. I feel we ought to make it quite clear to our European friends that if Little Europe is formed without a parallel development of a Free Trade Area we shall have

to reconsider the whole of our political and economic attitude towards Europe. I doubt if we could remain in NATO. We should certainly put on highly protective tariffs and quotas to counteract what Little Europe was doing to us. In other words, we should not allow ourselves to be destroyed little by little. We would fight with every weapon in our armoury. We would take our troops out of Europe. We would withdraw from NATO. We would adopt a policy of isolationism. We would surround ourselves with rockets and we would say to the Germans and the French and all the rest of them: 'Look after yourselves with your own forces. Look after yourselves when the Russians overrun your countries'. I would be inclined to make this position quite clear both to de Gaulle and to Adenauer.[36]

De Gaulle and Adenauer stood firm and the British government found that neither the carrot nor the stick could make much difference.

The government was also misled on certain points. For example, the British ambassador in Paris, Lord Gladwyn, wanted the government to apply for EEC membership, advised that de Gaulle would help, and warned that the chance of success would decline if de Gaulle was replaced by another French leader. Another opinion that had to be borne in mind was that of Britain's leading entrepreneurs and industrialists, but there was no clear or united position on Europe among business leaders, and their relations with and influence over the government varied greatly in this period.[37]

Britain went ahead with the formation of the European Free Trade Association (EFTA). The founder-members, 'The Seven', were Britain, Switzerland, Austria, Norway, Denmark, Sweden, and Portugal. The EFTA treaty came into effect in May 1960 and provided for freer trade in industrial goods. EFTA was a loose association, intergovernmental in nature, dominated by a council of ministers, and little could be done without a unanimous decision. Members of EFTA had the right to withdraw from the body on twelve months' notice. From the outset, a merger with the EEC seemed very unlikely. Euro-sceptics in Britain probably supposed that matters could safely be left where they were. If the EEC did not need Britain, then Britain did not need the EEC, a self-evident truth when placed alongside Britain's 'independent' nuclear deterrent, links with the Commonwealth and unique friendship with the United States.[38]

It was unfortunate for Britain that the EEC turned out to be something other than what had been expected. The first secretary-general of EFTA, Sir Frank Figgures (1960–1965), saw a big difference between the Messina concept of 'a thoroughgoing customs union' and the framework created by the Treaty of Rome, which stopped short of this. In practice, none of 'The Six' had drastically to modify its economic relationship with any territory with which it previously had special links, but for political reasons it had not been possible to think or talk in these terms in advance. The union formed in the late 1950s was 'far from complete. Now, of course if we had been told that this was the sort of structure which was going to emerge, we would have been able to say, well, that's perfectly alright by us', for it was a structure in which Britain could have carried on importing cheap Commonwealth products. The Macmillan government had been unable to proceed in this way, however, because 'if we had said…we'll come in on the same basis as you, and that's what it means, the Treaty could not have been negotiated'. Imperial preference 'would have totally undermined all the concepts which were developed, both in the early stages and finally in the Treaty of Rome'. Had it not been for de Gaulle, perhaps, Britain and 'The Six' might have come to an understanding, though this is not to deny that there was still some distance between the two sides. The British were not against European integration, but they did not think that the united Europe should act as a single entity in its external economic relations. Britain wanted closer cooperation with 'The Six' but wanted also to have its own relationships with countries outside Europe. Talks on the free trade area did not bring forth a willingness on the part of 'The Six' to give up the common tariff to which Britain objected.[39]

In due course, speculation mounted that Britain would be willing to abandon EFTA in order to join the EEC. In the Commons on May 26, 1960, Labour leader Hugh Gaitskell asked if there was an intention to apply for membership of the EEC. Macmillan replied that it was government policy, 'having signed and agreed an association with six other countries, to act in conjunction with them, and only with them'. The prime minister did hope for useful links between EFTA and the EEC, but insisted that Britain would not make a separate agreement with the EEC. The EFTA project was well received in sections of the British press, but, as indicated by this Commons exchange, there was initially some confusion at the highest levels of government as to how to present it. Was it to be defended on its own merits, or treated as the means to obtain an agreement with the EEC? Macmillan told his colleagues that whatever they said, they should all say the same thing. He was also conscious of the signals emanating from the United States. Although U.S. leaders embraced free trade in principle, there were strong protectionist impulses in American government and society, and an aversion to any European arrangements that discriminated against the United States. American leaders were well disposed towards 'The Six' already, because they saw EEC-style integration as politically and strategically useful. Their attitude towards EFTA was less favourable, and they were alarmed by the prospect of a bargain between the EEC and EFTA.[40]

London and Washington had been arguing about European integration for years. At the time of the Messina Conference, the Americans had made it clear that they wanted the negotiations for an economic agreement to succeed, and they warned the British government not to stand in the way. Macmillan, when he was a member of the Eden Cabinet, thought that the Americans had an imperfect understanding of what was really going on in Europe. In Washington there seemed to be no appreciation of Britain's concerns about integration, and no awareness of the possibility that what might result was a high-tariff, inward-looking European economic association. Macmillan thought that the main reason why America was pushing Britain to join 'The Six' was U.S. hostility towards the Commonwealth. The Americans wanted a reorientation of British policy away from the Commonwealth and towards Europe: Did they not see that this would have wide ramifications? British coolness towards the EEC annoyed Eisenhower and Dulles. In addition, because they failed to recognise the importance Europeans attached to the EEC project, the British alienated 'The Six' and made the latter all the more determined to proceed without Britain, which in turn added to the complaints of those in Washington who had envisaged a leadership role for Britain in the EEC, as an insurance that Anglo-American interests would be properly respected in Europe. The American attitude did not assist Britain to persuade 'The Six' to opt for the free trade area rather than the EEC. British leaders had hoped that the free trade area would generally be seen as advantageous for Western Europe and for the United States. They had expected Eisenhower and Dulles to be pleased that Britain was ready to move closer to Europe. The Americans showed little enthusiasm for the free trade area, however, and Washington simply assumed that the British wanted to have too much their own way. In response, Britain tried to convince the Americans that the plan for a free trade area was not an attempt to weaken the customs union. The French, meanwhile, claimed that British schemes would block the political cohesion represented by the EEC, and it was the political cohesion that most appealed to Eisenhower and Dulles. The formation of an industrial free trade area in Europe would affect U.S. exports, they thought, and could not deliver a political compensation in terms of greater cohesion.[41]

Eisenhower and Dulles decided that the EEC should establish itself before any arrangements were made for Britain to join, in case the British ruined the whole enterprise. Henceforth, Washington's position was that the British should only be encouraged to join the EEC if they accepted the necessary elements of supranationalism. Yet some of the assumptions upon which U.S. policy was based soon proved to be unsound. It had been expected that 'The Six' would continue to respect America's wishes and that the NATO framework would remain intact, but once the EEC was formed it became clear that circumstances were changing. The economic relationship between the United States and Western Europe had to be reassessed. De Gaulle openly challenged U.S. leadership and began to pursue a more wayward and unilateral foreign policy. Sympathy grew in Washington for the British view of European integration. A related development was the appointment of Christian Herter as U.S. secretary of state in April 1959. Herter was more of an Atlanticist than Dulles had been.[42]

In time the EEC's economic success brought into sharper relief the relative weakness of the British economy, and despite the efforts of the government, its advisers, and Britain's entrepreneurs and manufacturers, Britain experienced periodic downturns and growth rates that were persistently lower than those of other industrial nations. The idea spread that membership of the EEC might be beneficial. Meanwhile, Britain fell further behind its main competitors. Government policy was partly culpable, for there was little consistency, though there certainly was an awareness of the problems associated with slow growth, inadequate investment, low efficiency, and outdated technology.[43] Efforts *were* made to turn things around, and it was by no means clear that joining the EEC was the answer. There was more to Britain's relative economic decline than complacency and error on the part of policymakers. Political and structural explanations do cast light on the problems experienced during the 1950s and 1960s, but some of these problems were not confined to Britain.

Notwithstanding the 'golden age' of prosperity in Europe, from the early 1950s to the early 1970s, 'catch-up growth' was not universal. Some countries fell behind. Growth was assisted by a move away from interventionist policies and the commitment to economic integration, and across much of Western Europe there were bargains between capital, labour, and government. The most remarkable economic growth after the Second World War was seen in the FRG, but in Western Europe as a whole advantage was taken of the favourable conditions created by American loans and technology, relatively high per capita incomes, the availability of skilled workers, the receptivity of businessmen and trade unions to mass production, and national and international institutional arrangements. During the 1960s it became more difficult to sustain progress, and growth rates dropped considerably in the 1970s. Britain did benefit from the 'golden age' but was not fully part of the integrated European economic order in the years when membership of that order might have had dramatic results. Britain did not join the EEC until 1973. Though EFTA brought down tariffs by about 80 percent between 1960 and 1967, for Britain this was of limited use. Membership of EFTA added only about thirty million people to Britain's domestic market, which was nowhere near the number of potential customers available in the EEC.[44]

In September 1960 *The Times* suggested that if 'The Six' and 'The Seven' were going to come together, the most promising method would be political rather than economic initiatives: intergovernmental bodies, perhaps, with members selected by national parliaments. Economic cooperation between 'The Six' and 'The Seven' was too difficult to arrange. Macmillan was willing to consider a closer relationship with 'The Six' on certain matters, which was encouraging, 'though not immediately practicable'. Many Europeans, meanwhile, thought that 'as European economic institutions of a sort already exist, the essential thing is that they should not be diluted. Any reconciliation between the common market and EFTA must therefore come from the strengthening of the latter rather than the weakening of the former'.[45] If this meant making EFTA more like the EEC, however, it would not be in keeping with Britain's idea of how European integration should proceed.

Questions about the future of Europe, and Britain's place within it, continued to puzzle British leaders over the following years, and there was ongoing concern also about the 'special relationship' with America, defence spending and planning, decolonisation and Commonwealth affairs, and tension in the Middle East, Africa, and Asia—especially in those areas that remained important to Britain's influence and status as a great power. The cardinal requirements remained the same: maximise influence and preserve status. As to the methods and the resources, there were shortcomings, disagreements, and obstacles that could not easily be overcome. Domestic and international circumstances were frequently unhelpful. Despite some disappointments, however, the British managed to sustain the attributes, position, image, and global reach of a major power, even while there was a creeping awareness of relative decline.

CHAPTER 2

COLD WAR, NO THAW

Despite the difficulties associated with decolonisation and restoring the 'special relationship', and the division of Europe into separate economic units, Harold Macmillan considered his foreign policy generally successful. He was particularly satisfied with his dealings with the Soviets, which raised his profile as a world statesman. While determined to uphold Britain's position and responsibilities in the Cold War, and to avoid betraying any signs of weakness, the Macmillan government also wished to explore opportunities for détente; when peace was jeopardised, the British preference was for diplomatic solutions even if provision was also made for military action. Rising tension in Europe prompted London to try to draw Moscow into talks, which in turn involved a complicated process of bartering and accommodation between Britain and its allies. In the West, unity was not easy to build or sustain, and this, along with Soviet machinations, hampered the British effort to promote stability and thaw.

In November 1958 Soviet leader Nikita Khrushchev declared that U.S., British, and French forces should leave West Berlin and that access to West Berlin must be negotiated with the government of the German

Democratic Republic. In this manner, he sought to coerce the western powers into recognising the East German state with a united Berlin as its capital city. Khrushchev announced that the USSR would sign a separate peace treaty with the GDR and called upon the western powers to end their occupation and make Berlin a 'free city' within six months. John Foster Dulles warned that West Berlin would be defended. Macmillan, with an eye on the Conservative Party's reelection prospects, saw a chance to relax the tension and raise his own reputation. He visited Moscow in February 1959 in a gesture that was meant to demonstrate Britain's great-power status and ability to act independently of America. Macmillan gained the publicity he wanted, and the six-month deadline was abandoned because he promised to arrange a top-level summit if Khrushchev first agreed that there should be a meeting of foreign ministers. The Soviets did not revive the Berlin ultimatum and Macmillan claimed that the talks in Moscow had helped, but his conduct had annoyed the FRG, France, and the United States, and they rejected his suggestion that the West ought to recognise the GDR and withdraw troops from West Berlin.[1]

Konrad Adenauer's misgivings about Macmillan's diplomacy increased. *The Times* was indignant, describing Adenauer as 'authoritarian' and suggesting that 'nearly ten years of undisputed power have set him in his ways and perhaps convinced him that he knows best'. Macmillan's visit to Moscow was simply 'a reconnaissance', but in Bonn and in Paris much was made of the upcoming election in Britain. Macmillan was accused by the French of sowing dissension within the West for the sake of domestic political advantage. France was willing to participate in negotiations with the USSR when the time was right, and on the understanding that the Soviets would not expect to gain anything without giving something in return. The view in Paris was that this position had not yet been reached. *The Times* approved of Macmillan's 'scouting expedition' in Moscow. The purpose was not to seek firm agreements but simply to find out if the Soviets were willing to negotiate. Britain's allies, commented the *Observer*, would take some convincing. They wanted to know what Khrushchev was prepared to offer, especially on the German question and disarmament, before they accepted Macmillan's assurances about the possibility of agreements, and Adenauer was likely to oppose any moves that obliged him to deal with the authorities in East Germany.[2]

Macmillan was sure that he had been right to visit Moscow, and his conversations with Khrushchev led him to conclude that a four-power summit was definitely needed. Without a summit, he thought, there would be no breakthrough in East-West relations. Macmillan also believed that he had gained concessions: the Soviets had agreed to participate in a foreign ministers' meeting and had implicitly abandoned the six-month deadline. On this latter point, however, Khrushchev was impressed more by U.S. military strength than by Macmillan's appeal, and it is possible that the Soviet leader had been thinking of relaxing the deadline before Macmillan's visit. Nevertheless, Macmillan's focus on the West's rights in Berlin, and his warnings about what could happen if the USSR persisted, probably helped to make Khrushchev more reasonable. Many British voters were impressed by Macmillan's bearing as a peacemaker and an important world figure, which is what he wanted, but the FRG, France, and the United States did not accept that he had gained much from Khrushchev. If there was more to Macmillan's policy than a bid for electoral popularity at home, there was also a limit to what could be achieved internationally, because the prime minister was not in a position to determine how the West would act. Bonn, Paris, and Washington did not treat him as he had hoped and he realised that he had little room to manoeuvre—hence his insistence on the West's rights in Berlin. The Soviets saw that the British, even if they argued with their allies, would not act independently on crucial matters. Despite the quarrelling within the western alliance, the Berlin crisis strengthened that alliance externally.[3]

Khrushchev wanted a summit. An East-West thaw was essential if he was going to divert resources, introduce domestic reforms, and improve living standards in the USSR as he wished. He made the necessary statements and Macmillan used these to persuade Britain's allies of the need for flexibility. The Americans remained cautious. The most they expected to gain was a limited short-term agreement with the Soviets, and this mood did not change when Christian Herter succeeded Dulles as U.S. secretary of state in spring 1959. France and the FRG, meanwhile, were even more cautious. They did not wish to fall in behind what they took to be Britain's flawed agenda.[4]

On Berlin Macmillan knew he had to sound firm, so he told the Commons on December 2, 1958, that rights and obligations there could not be 'unilaterally renounced or changed'. While Labour spokesmen blamed the government for not doing more about the German question, Macmillan declared that if talks became possible he would ensure that they took place. After his visit to Moscow he told MPs that cultural and economic links between Britain and the USSR would improve and that the Soviets had accepted that international problems—Germany, Berlin, nuclear tests, disarmament—should be settled by negotiation. He had not gone to Moscow to bargain, he said, but to prepare the ground, 'to seek a better understanding of our respective views on these grave issues and the reasons underlying them'. This had been gained. Government statements about the Geneva conference in July 1959 were rather vague, however, which indicated that progress was looking less likely. Arguments developed about the extent to which the West should compromise in order to secure a deal.[5]

Controversial at home, Macmillan's effort to facilitate an agreement between the West and the USSR continued to irritate other western leaders. Adenauer did not trust the British prime minister, another card that de Gaulle could play as Britain tried to draw closer to Europe. Bonn was offended by what it took to be London's arrogant presumption that the British were best qualified to communicate with the Soviets on the West's behalf. Adenauer's anti-Soviet predilections were as strong as ever. Any deal with the USSR had to be properly guaranteed, he insisted, and he doubted that satisfactory safeguards could be obtained. He claimed that the Soviets had broken nearly all of the treaties they had ever signed. Nor could he forget the 1.1 million German prisoners who had vanished into the Soviet Union during and after the Second World War, of whom less than 10,000 had been accounted for. Soviet proposals of 1952, 1955, and 1959 for German reunification were all regarded by Bonn as attempts to deceive, and Adenauer continued to advise the German people to look to the West for freedom, jobs, and the rule of law. By the late 1950s,

Adenauer had accomplished his basic aim of binding the FRG to the West economically, militarily, and politically. He believed that peace and prosperity could be built on the foundation of Franco-German cooperation. Adenauer and de Gaulle had different views about international affairs. De Gaulle wanted the FRG to act as France's partner and provide the necessary support that France needed to remain influential, whereas Adenauer was more interested in the political cohesion of Western Europe and in its links with the United States, and he sought an equal role for the FRG in all the relevant discussions. Despite this difference, however, the two leaders were determined to work together.[6]

Macmillan's attempt to take the lead in dealing with the Soviets was criticised abroad, but at home *The Times* backed the prime minister on the grounds that nobody else was up to the task. Eisenhower was 'a declining force', Adenauer 'an old unhappy man', and de Gaulle was 'preoccupied with other problems', which meant that it was Macmillan's responsibility to take the initiative. Macmillan did not win over de Gaulle or Adenauer. He had expected the latter to be more forthcoming, but Bonn did not want anything to interfere with NATO's evolving defence posture and the FRG's full involvement in Western Europe's economic and security arrangements, and there was strong opposition to anything like even a de facto recognition of the East German state by the West. Adenauer was also concerned about the Americans. He suspected that rather than risk a confrontation with the Soviet Union, Washington might choose to deal with the GDR and retain America's rights in Berlin by making compromises that would legitimise the partition of Germany. Adenauer urged Britain and America to resist Soviet pressure. He had de Gaulle's support in this, for which he was grateful. The French leader took advantage. He had already challenged the United States on nuclear matters and the future of NATO. Now he warned the Americans not to make concessions to Khrushchev. In reply Dulles told him that it would be unwise to act provocatively. If Dulles was worried about the French, however, he was even more concerned about British efforts to conciliate Moscow. Eisenhower saw that the American public would not support a war over Berlin, while Dulles advised that concessions were unnecessary. All that was needed was a demonstration that America was prepared to fight. Then the Soviets would draw back and force would not be needed. De Gaulle's position was useful to Dulles in this respect, because they were both insisting that the allies must stay together and give Moscow no reason to think that it could prevail. Dulles does not appear to have realised that de Gaulle had other ends in mind besides resisting Moscow. One of these related to the Paris-Bonn relationship. De Gaulle wanted Bonn to be closer to Paris than to Washington, so he exploited Adenauer's fear that an agreement might be reached with Khrushchev at the FRG's expense.[7]

Although the postwar division of Germany had not been intended, the integration of East Germany into the Soviet bloc certainly had been. By the mid-1950s, the 'two Germanys' approach was very much a part of the Kremlin's imperial and ideological disposition. This did not mean that the Soviets gave up on the idea of bargaining with the West for a thaw. Indeed, some historians contend that détente remained a constant Soviet priority. This is not entirely true, for détente was only in the ascendancy intermittently and all Soviet leaders viewed it within the context of the ongoing struggle between socialism and capitalism. The competitive elements of détente usually mattered more to Moscow than the cooperative elements.[8] Soviet leaders tied the consolidation of the GDR with the need to strengthen and protect the USSR, and a related motive was their wish to secure their own personal positions at home and internationally. There was also a desire to control inter-German relations. Khrushchev's German policy was marked by assertiveness and brinkmanship. In part this was because of his revolutionary commitments. He wanted to facilitate the ultimate victory of the communist system. A German settlement, he thought, would usher in a long period of stability and make possible the peaceful transformation of the world from capitalism to socialism, with the nuclear arsenals of the USSR and the West deterring aggression on both sides. His Berlin ultimatum of November 1958 was in line with this. Yet it was a clumsy manoeuvre that alarmed the western powers and prompted them to consider a military response. Some of Khrushchev's colleagues thought him rash to push for an agreement on Berlin in this manner, but he had decided that something had to be done about the East German regime's lack of political legitimacy, the country's economic failings, and the exodus to the West (which increased in 1958). In October 1958 the GDR's leader Walter Ulbricht declared that the western powers had no legal basis for their presence in Berlin and that the whole city should be incorporated into his state. Khrushchev had long been accusing the West of obstructing a German settlement. If it refused to join the USSR in resolving this matter, he announced, the USSR would consider itself obliged to make alternative arrangements. In November 1958 he spoke of West Berlin becoming a demilitarised 'free city' in whose affairs neither the FRG nor GDR would be allowed to interfere, and of all existing regulations, occupation zones, and administrative bodies being null and void. Khrushchev hoped to enhance the domestic stability and international position of the GDR, to limit the influence of West Berlin as a showpiece for democracy and capitalism, and to make West Berlin vulnerable by weakening its link with the FRG. He also wanted to obtain a general acceptance of the post-1945 order in Europe and remove the threat to this order that emanated from Bonn, which was refusing to recognise the GDR or its frontiers. Khrushchev felt able to put pressure on the western powers because the Soviet Union had been gaining strength. Sputnik proved that the Soviets could develop effective missiles and that the United States was not invulnerable; America's economic growth was slowing down whereas the USSR's was gathering pace; and the West's problems with internal divisions, decolonisation, and financial pressures were also encouraging. Another concern for Khrushchev was his personal power base. He had to keep important groups in the USSR satisfied, which explains the mixture of confrontational gestures and a readiness to negotiate with the West if the terms were acceptable.[9]

Hoping to win general acceptance for the existence of two German states, Moscow knew that Bonn would offer strenuous opposition. Khrushchev was worried that Adenauer would persuade the Americans decisively to take up German reunification, and that Bonn might make agreements with some of the governments in Eastern Europe, which could cause military and economic complications for the Soviet Union and undermine Moscow's authority in the eastern bloc. The biggest fear of all, though, was that the FRG would acquire nuclear weapons, and Khrushchev told Adenauer that he would enter into no talks about German reunification if the FRG made any such move. Yet Bonn showed no signs of drawing back from its rearmament programme and its full participation in NATO. Ulbricht's regime in the GDR did not help, meanwhile, for it was intent on eradicating capitalism in its territory, and in all of Berlin, and Ulbricht insisted that it was Khrushchev's duty to help him take control of West Berlin. Khrushchev wanted communism to work in East Germany and the USSR provided massive aid to this end. For propaganda reasons, it could not be admitted that the GDR was lagging behind the prosperous FRG. Traditional unease about the prospect of a Germany turned against the East resurfaced in Moscow, where it was believed that the FRG might rise, with U.S. support, to dominate Europe. The idea that this was no time for the Soviet Union to appear weak was reinforced by its problems with China. Khrushchev was worried about Mao, whose willingness to accept Soviet leadership of the communist world was diminishing. Mao was pressing Moscow to get tough with the Americans.[10]

Mao wanted to stir up the Chinese people, to prepare them for revolutionary sacrifices, economic development, and the 'Great Leap Forward'. Washington assumed that the Chinese bombardment of Quemoy and Matsu between August and October 1958 represented a desire to annex them as a prelude to the invasion of Taiwan, but Mao was thinking more of 'active defence', which was meant to strengthen China strategically so that Mao could put pressure on Taiwan and the United States as and when he wanted. Mao also wanted to encourage antiwestern interests in other regions, especially the Middle East. The Soviets opposed Mao's policy on Taiwan, and his pressurising of the Americans, and were annoyed that he had not been consulting them. In Moscow it was feared that Mao would provoke a local war against the United States, into which the Soviet Union might be drawn; the Kremlin also disparaged Mao's domestic reforms, believing that economic chaos would be the result. Suspecting that China was intent on becoming a competitor rather than remaining an ally, Khrushchev had an added reason for the Berlin ultimatum. If he was going to solve the German question and make sure that the FRG did not acquire nuclear weapons, he thought he had to do it before the split between Moscow and Peking became obvious to the West. Although the West did not give the constructive side of his policy the attention he expected, Khrushchev did speak of reducing the threat of war and of new arrangements for stability, especially in the Far East and Pacific, where he thought there should be a ban on nuclear weapons. The Kremlin did not want China to become a nuclear power, and in pursuing détente Khrushchev was probably trying to warn the West of this danger. If the message was lost, one of the reasons was the continuing Soviet aid to China. Even while trying to contain Mao, the Kremlin hoped to keep him happy with a seven-year assistance programme involving services, goods, technology, training, and finance, with a particular focus on heavy industry. The programme was announced early in 1959.[11]

The West was struck less by Khrushchev's talk of peace than by his threats regarding Berlin. He desperately needed a victory on Berlin if he was effectively to address his problems at home and abroad, but the West would not cooperate and he grew vulnerable not only because of his handling of China and the German question, but also because of problems in the Middle East. The USSR was funding the Aswan Dam project in Egypt, for instance, and yet Gamal Abdel Nasser had condemned communism and was trying to weaken Iraq's ties with Moscow. Although the Berlin crisis did not give Khrushchev exactly what he wanted, he thought his boldness had paid off because it made the Americans more willing to talk.[12]

The Soviets did not stick to their ultimatum of November 1958, but this was not the end of the matter. The status of Berlin remained one of the most contentious issues in the Cold War. Whenever the Soviets wanted to get the West's attention, they simply put pressure on West Berlin. If this situation was to be transformed Khrushchev would have to be consulted, and on this point Macmillan was correct, but the Soviet leader was unpredictable. If he favoured a moderately reformist line within the USSR, in foreign affairs he was proving to be a gambler. Believing that the Soviet Union was losing ground to the United States, particularly on the economic front, Khrushchev decided to redirect resources from conventional forces into social and economic improvements. He wanted more consumer goods for the Soviet people, and a higher standard of living. This diversion of resources would not pose a security risk, he decided, because possession of nuclear weapons ensured a rough parity with America. Khrushchev's concept of 'peaceful coexistence' rested on a dynamic global competition between the two superpowers that stopped short of war. The main goals were to keep the Soviet bloc together, to demonstrate equality with the United States, to establish a more positive relationship with the Americans, and to increase Soviet influence in the developing world. In truth these aims did not fit well together, and another problem was that Khrushchev desperately needed a foreign policy success in order to convince the Soviet generals and his political opponents of the wisdom of relying on nuclear weapons. He had to show that he could make America respect the USSR.[13]

The renewed emphasis on Berlin necessitated negotiations. Eisenhower, while declaring that the West would not give way, invited Khrushchev for talks once the Soviet leader had removed his six-month deadline for a settlement. Berlin happened to offer Khrushchev a chance to achieve his wider goals. Perhaps he was not really bothered about its status. Certainly he hoped to take advantage of quarrels within the western alliance. Macmillan was still urging the U.S. government to be more flexible on Berlin and the GDR, whereas the Americans, the West Germans, and the French were insisting that Britain's compromise proposals were inappropriate. Macmillan wished to avoid a stalemate. He was sure that an agreement could be reached with the Soviet Union that would not undermine the West's security. His talks with Khrushchev in February 1959 were not easy. Still, Macmillan improved his standing in an election year and although his visit to Moscow brought no immediate change in East-West relations, he thought it had gone well. He yielded nothing, blocked Soviet efforts to divide Britain from the other western powers, and, he told Washington, Bonn, and Paris, opened the way for a thaw. Adenauer and de Gaulle were sceptical, Eisenhower had no wish for an early summit, and Dulles advised strongly against it before retiring on health grounds in April 1959. It was agreed that, on Moscow's suggestion, there should be a conference of foreign ministers in Geneva in June and July 1959, but Macmillan wanted more. Since the Soviets were intent on a great-power summit, he reasoned, they would not make any concessions at Geneva, while the Americans were unlikely to agree to a summit *unless* something was achieved at Geneva. 'It would be on the horns of this dilemma', Macmillan later wrote, 'that I felt sure I should soon be impaled'. He assured Eisenhower that, for all their apparent stubbornness, the Soviets were willing to bargain. Eventually Eisenhower suggested that a summit could be arranged for August 1959, whether or not anything was accomplished at Geneva. Then he changed his mind, much to Macmillan's disgust. The prime minister was relieved, but not entirely happy, when Eisenhower invited Khrushchev for bilateral talks in the United States.[14]

Macmillan considered Eisenhower's conduct unhelpful. It prompted the Soviets to harden their position at Geneva, annoyed the FRG and France, and made it difficult for western leaders to explain to their people why Khrushchev was going to the United States despite the lack of progress at Geneva. It also removed the need for a summit at which Macmillan could further enhance his reputation. Now it would be widely assumed that the Americans and Soviets could bargain by themselves, which showed Britain up as a second-rate power and undermined Macmillan's core policy of close cooperation with the Americans. Macmillan was worried, but his mood improved as the press gave him some credit for the proposed Eisenhower-Khrushchev meeting. The Conservatives were quick to put this to good use in their election campaign and in due course, Macmillan was pleased to find that the Americans were willing to go ahead with a great-power summit after all. These developments assisted de Gaulle, however, in his effort to convince Adenauer that the FRG should rely more on France. De Gaulle predicted that the Americans would conclude an agreement over the heads of their European allies, which was what Moscow had been wanting for years.[15]

Throughout the Berlin emergency Eisenhower was careful. He did not want to overreact or be pushed into making snap decisions. He tried to minimise risks and checked the hardliners among his advisers and

U.S. service chiefs. He rejected the suggestion that more U.S. troops should be sent to Europe. He gave Khrushchev an opportunity to retreat and eventually expressed a willingness to meet the Soviet leader face to face. Eisenhower's invitation was greeted by Khrushchev as a sign that, owing to Soviet pressure, a deal with the West had been brought much closer. The Soviet leader relaxed, believing that the FRG was not about to obtain nuclear weapons from the United States, that a German settlement could be worked out, and that China would have to admit that the USSR was still the leader of the communist world. Eisenhower and Khrushchev met at Camp David, Maryland, in September 1959. They reached no agreement on Berlin but planned to continue their dialogue at the scheduled four-power summit in Paris in the following spring. The prospects for a thaw seemed to be improving. In January 1960 Khrushchev announced that the Soviet army was to be reduced in size, which made the USSR more reliant on strategic missile defences. All this was condemned by Mao, who accused Khrushchev of giving in to the West. Then the Paris summit of May 1960 proved to be a fiasco. Just before it opened the Soviets shot down an American U2 spy plane and in Khrushchev's first speech at the conference he denounced the Americans. Détente was suspended.[16]

Khrushchev had been pleased with the Camp David talks because he thought he had at last made the Americans recognise that they must deal directly with him. He envisaged an interim arrangement on Berlin, as had been discussed by the foreign ministers in Geneva: the postwar division and occupation of Berlin would continue for a designated period during which a peace treaty would be worked out involving both East and West Germany. Khrushchev considered this an important concession to Eisenhower, for it would avoid any appearance of the Americans being chased out of Berlin. After Camp David, in fact, Khrushchev thought he got the better of Eisenhower. The American president agreed to go ahead with the four-power summit, while Khrushchev had agreed only temporarily to lift his Berlin ultimatum. As for Paris, Khrushchev decided before he arrived there that he should wreck the summit. He was angry about the U2 incident, and his mood was not helped by the rapid deterioration in Soviet-Chinese relations.[17]

These were tense times. After the Sputnik shock of 1957, Eisenhower had been pressed to respond. He was reluctant to increase U.S. defence spending but could not resist, especially as reports circulated that the USSR was spending more on arms and had a faster rate of economic growth than the United States. The Soviets had also stepped up their supply of arms to friendly nations, including Syria and Egypt in the Middle East. Eisenhower's administration provided for a bigger defence budget and encouraged the development of space technology. April 1958 saw the establishment of the National Aeronautics and Space Administration (NASA). Eisenhower wanted to limit expenditure and escalation, however, and hoped for a test ban and disarmament deal with the Soviets. The Paris summit represented a welcome opportunity, therefore, and its collapse was doubly embarrassing for Eisenhower, who was already being criticised at home for allowing the Soviets to take the lead in armaments. In fact, Khrushchev had by now decided that the Berlin problem could not be solved and that a test ban would favour America and reveal the true state of Soviet defences. Eisenhower was deeply disappointed by this train of events. He was sure that the Camp David meeting had been worthwhile, and as preparations were made for the Paris summit his optimism grew. Macmillan shared his commitment to disarmament and de Gaulle and Adenauer were willing to help. Eisenhower consulted them all, as well as his secretary of state, Christian Herter, who was notably less hawkish than Dulles had been. The Americans were convinced that Khrushchev wanted a thaw. The U2 incident changed the mood immediately. Eisenhower decided not to admit to anything. He hoped that a cover-up would work. In truth the Soviets had known about the U2 missions for some time (as had those allies of the United States that facilitated the flights over Soviet territory—Britain, France, Turkey, Norway, and Taiwan). Eisenhower, Macmillan, and de Gaulle met before the Paris summit opened and decided that there should be no 'crawling' to Khrushchev (as Eisenhower termed it) and that there would be a military response if the Soviets attacked U2 bases. They still wanted the summit to go ahead, though, and were hopeful that some useful progress could be made there. The portents were hardly positive. Khrushchev had resumed his practice of making public demands, especially with regard to Berlin, and the U2 incident prompted a wave of anti-American propaganda. The Soviets also argued that the discussions in Paris should be open rather than secret and that full details should be given to the press, which suggested that they intended to use the summit for propaganda purposes. On the eve of the summit, Khrushchev assured Macmillan that agreements were still possible. Macmillan wanted to believe this, but he must have had doubts. The atmosphere changed after Paris. Hopes for a thaw had been disappointed, yet again, and East-West confrontation was extended, notably in the developing world.[18]

Eisenhower later reflected that the summit would probably have failed anyway, even without the shooting down of the U2 spy plane, and that Khrushchev wanted an excuse to take back the invitation he had given Eisenhower to visit Moscow. The president's main regret with regard to the U2 affair was the attempted cover-up, which he considered a mistake, but he maintained all along that the U2 programme was essential to U.S. security. Macmillan and de Gaulle both thought that the Soviet leader broke up the summit in order to prevent Eisenhower's visit to Moscow. Khrushchev's previous visit to the United States and American vice president Richard Nixon's visit to the USSR had contributed to an exchange of information and a greater awareness of U.S. wealth and power. Khrushchev was disturbed by the exposure of the Soviet people to western ideas and evidence of western progress. If Eisenhower visited the USSR this trend would continue, Khrushchev realised, for the visit would entail enormous publicity.[19]

After the Camp David talks, and in the final stages of the general election campaign in Britain, Macmillan had looked forward to a significant change in the diplomatic climate. Some of his suggestions were rejected by Eisenhower, however, because the president did not want to give the impression that the United States and Britain were working independently of their allies, and though Macmillan and the Conservatives won the election of October 1959, and increased their parliamentary majority, concern about the tension within the western alliance continued to grow. Bonn and Paris were more suspicious than ever that the Americans would make a deal on Berlin and Germany that did not suit the FRG or France, and the resentment created by Britain's closeness to America complicated London's pursuit of improved economic links with Western Europe and stronger collective defence. Macmillan failed fully to appreciate the confidence that had arisen between Bonn and Paris, not least on Berlin and the German question, and he continued openly to treat the 'special relationship' with America as more important to Britain than relations with Western Europe. He expected the Paris summit to produce an interim agreement on Berlin. Thereafter, he envisaged military disengagement in central Europe.[20]

There was amazement in sections of the British press about Khrushchev's behaviour in Paris. *The Times* admitted that the U2 affair was 'a bad business', but denied that this gave Khrushchev any excuse for disappointing 'the millions of people everywhere who had hoped that the heads of four great nations could behave like responsible men when they met with the world's destiny in their hands'. Why had he done this? Perhaps Eisenhower's refusal to dissociate himself from the U2 flights had led the Soviet leader to conclude that it would be better not to bargain with a tainted U.S. administration, but to wait for the election of a new American president in November. *The Times* considered this foolish. There had to be something else behind Khrushchev's conduct, perhaps a struggle in Moscow that had weakened the advocates of thaw. Instability in the world was bound to increase. The only consolation was that Britain, France, and the United States had made clear their willingness to resume contact with the Soviets if the opportunity presented itself.[21]

Macmillan hoped that events in Paris would not put off an agreement between the West and the Soviets for too long. In the Commons on May 30, 1960, he speculated about the motives behind Khrushchev's conduct. He said that too much had been made of the U2 incident: it was not as if the Soviets did not engage in similar infringements of national sovereignty in order to gain intelligence. The whole experience, Macmillan went on, had reminded leaders in the West of the need to stand together. He referred to economic cooperation, Britain's relations with EFTA and the EEC, and the question of tariff reduction and the promotion of trade. The West had to maximise its economic strength, Macmillan declared, and military power had also to be maintained, which made Britain's nuclear deterrent essential. Only time would tell what Moscow intended. Meanwhile, the West had to prioritise unity and preparedness. A willingness to negotiate was also important, however, and Macmillan was pleased to report that talks on disarmament and nuclear tests would continue. He believed that Khrushchev still wanted a thaw and that the Soviet people did too: 'I saw myself, when I was in Russia, a greater freedom of movement, discussion and argument than I expected. I realised how the common people had their hearts set on peace and prosperity. All this cannot fade in a day'.[22]

Although he tried to sound positive, the collapse of the Paris summit was a blow to Macmillan. For months he had been pushing for a summit and there was no meaningful role for him now as an honest broker between East and West. The limits on British influence became clearer as Eisenhower decided against a prompt resumption of communication with Khrushchev. De Gaulle and Adenauer refused to help Macmillan, who had probably been overoptimistic about what summitry could accomplish. Macmillan concluded that another four-power meeting would not be feasible for at least a year. In order to be ready, he wanted a stronger NATO and an agreed, definitive allied plan for Berlin. Since Eisenhower was not seeking reelection, Macmillan focused on de Gaulle, but as the basis for a closer bond between Britain and France Macmillan proposed an agreement on economic matters, whereas de Gaulle was more interested in military and strategic matters, especially with regard to the future development of NATO and nuclear strategy. Against foreign office advice, the prime minister began to welcome and encourage friction within NATO and within the EEC, because he thought this would give Britain more influence, and he decided that it would suit Britain to side with the Americans on some issues and with de Gaulle on others. Macmillan spoke confidentially in September 1960 about the EEC. He was happy for 'The Six' to quarrel with each other, he said. They had joined together to injure Britain economically and yet expected Britain to defend them at enormous expense. Macmillan would not seek to cause arguments in

Europe, he added, but if they happened, Britain should let them happen and not get involved. By the end of 1960, Macmillan had made up his mind that Britain should apply to join the EEC, not only for the sake of the country's finances and export trade but also because the route to British leadership of Europe lay through the EEC. The foreign office agreed that discord among 'The Six' was useful, but advised that the best course for Britain would be to combine even more closely with the Americans while promoting opposition to de Gaulle within the EEC and NATO. Any hint that Britain was willing to sacrifice NATO to de Gaulle in the hope of concluding an economic agreement with him, Macmillan was told, would cause enormous difficulties.[23]

In John Gearson's account, Macmillan comes across as clumsy and deluded. He lacked a clear design, annoyed Britain's most important allies, overestimated his own influence and Britain's international standing, and combined 'arrogance and myopia' with 'compromise and weakness'. He was anti-German—'he actually made a virtue of discriminating against Germany'—and all he really achieved in seeking to mediate between the West and the USSR was to encourage both sides to regard Britain as the weak link in NATO.[24] This condemnation is excessive. Much depended on the domestic and international contexts. Britain had already accepted the FRG's membership of NATO. This was not compatible with Macmillan's wish for a security agreement between the West and the Soviet Union. Although Churchill had for a while explored the idea of a united neutral Germany, Macmillan doubted that reunification was possible, but he did not say so publicly for he knew it would embarrass Bonn. Macmillan thought that a united Germany, instead of leaning towards the West, might seek to recover power in Europe by turning East and West even more perilously against each other. In his suspicion of Germany, moreover, Macmillan was in line with British public opinion. The British people evinced little warmth for Germany. Few were really bothered about the fate of Berlin. The prime minister also had party politics to consider. The Labour Party and the Liberals both favoured a compromise on Germany and advocated formal recognition of the GDR in 1960, and Gearson notes that Macmillan's idea of military disengagement in central

Europe was partly motivated by a desire to outmanoeuvre the parliamentary opposition. As for Macmillan's view that détente was more important than good relations with Adenauer, most contemporaries agreed with this.

It would not have been easy for any British leader at this time to decide what was in the nation's best interests, if it meant choosing between several eligible scenarios. Economic needs seemed to be pointing Britain more towards Europe. Culturally and historically Britain had an affinity with the United States. The legacy of empire and determination to remain a world power, meanwhile, indicated a more independent foreign policy. Gearson thinks that Macmillan was indecisive and that he would have done better to prioritise Europe. The implication here is that Macmillan should have realised sooner that Britain's future lay in Europe. He might then have followed de Gaulle's example in working more closely with Adenauer. But it cannot be assumed that Adenauer would have been won over, even had the British government acted differently on Berlin. The construction of the Paris-Bonn axis was vital to both de Gaulle and Adenauer. Though the latter was annoyed by Macmillan's effort to draw Khrushchev into a thaw, it is not likely that Britain could have done anything to induce Adenauer to go against de Gaulle on a matter like British membership of the EEC.

John F. Kennedy assumed the U.S. presidency early in 1961. Khrushchev still needed a foreign policy success and sought to manipulate the young and relatively inexperienced Kennedy, while the new American leader made plain his assertive disposition and promised that America would support liberty all over the world. Soon Kennedy announced large increases in military spending, which alarmed Khrushchev because he was trying to make further cuts in the Soviet armed forces. Tension in Berlin rose again when the U.S. garrison there was augmented. Moscow had to respond by sending reinforcements. The Soviet leader and the new U.S. president both saw an urgent need for a further summit. This took place in Vienna in June 1961. Khrushchev had repeated his threat to establish closer links between the USSR and GDR and to push the Americans out of Berlin. The U.S. government's blundering attempt to overthrow the communist regime in Cuba, by the Bay of Pigs invasion of April 1961, made Moscow think that Kennedy was weak and vulnerable. Khrushchev told Kennedy that the Soviet Union and its allies had the right to develop as they wished and would help any country that wanted their assistance. He also issued another ultimatum on the status of Berlin: the matter had to be settled by the end of the year or the Soviet Union would break from the four-power procedure and sign a separate treaty with the GDR. Khrushchev was bound to talk tough, under pressure as he was from hardliners in the USSR and GDR, but this meant that the summit was a disaster for Kennedy, who regretted his inability to convince the Soviets of his serious intent to defend American interests.[25]

If Khrushchev was responsible for the resumption of the confrontation over Berlin so were Kennedy and his aides, for they believed that the Kremlin only respected force and that the United States should make no concessions. There was a determination to back up bold talk with robust actions, particularly in the U.S. state department, and this preference for a hard line was supported by the experienced Dean Acheson (U.S. secretary of state from 1949 to 1953), whom Kennedy drafted in as a special adviser on NATO and the German question. When Macmillan and British foreign secretary Lord Home visited Washington in April 1961, they were disappointed by the inflexibility they encountered there. Historians have long disagreed about whether Kennedy was a hardliner, or reckless, or shrewd, or a visionary, and about the extent to which he wanted to work with allies and make agreements with Moscow. What is clear is that before going to Vienna the president received conflicting advice. On the one hand, it was suggested that he should stay relaxed and good-humoured, that he must get to know Khrushchev and not be drawn into quarrels. On the other hand, Kennedy was urged to be resolute and assertive, in order to compensate for his relative youth and the Bay of Pigs affair. Then Kennedy met with de Gaulle on the way to Vienna and realised that the French leader would go on challenging the United States on nuclear matters and NATO strategy. De Gaulle indicated that he did not trust the Americans to defend Western Europe. Kennedy arrived in Vienna in a less than positive frame of mind, therefore, and Khrushchev's behaviour during the summit made him even more uncomfortable.[26]

The Soviet leader insisted that there should be a final German settlement. In Britain Macmillan's government came under pressure to clarify its position and there were many Labour MPs who accepted the Soviets' point that a united Germany should not be part of the western military alliance. In the aftermath of the Vienna summit, the parliamentary opposition contended that the government should not simply fall in with American policy. On June 19, 1961, a response was made by lord privy seal Edward Heath, the government's main spokesman on foreign affairs in the Commons (the foreign secretary, Home, sat in the House of Lords). Heath upheld the principle of self-determination and declared it to be the essential condition for a German settlement. He called upon the USSR to respect the freedom of West Berlin and reaffirmed Britain's determination to act in accordance with its rights and responsibilities in the city. Heath was challenged about Kennedy's remarks after the Vienna summit, to the effect that America would take any risk for the sake of the West's interests in Berlin. Was this also the British government's intention? Had it nothing more constructive to offer? Heath said that Britain would consult closely with the Americans and the French, for these were not matters that should be settled unilaterally by any government. As for the possibility that a united Germany would side with the West, this was not the problem. Agreement was being blocked primarily because the Soviets would not accept the need for self-determination.[27]

The Americans and Soviets both described the Vienna meeting as useful. 'Useful to whom?' asked *The Times*. 'The Russians, who believe in hammering away with their arguments, will be glad of the promise of further contacts. Mr Kennedy may hope that his warnings have sunk in', but in truth the summit ended 'with world affairs neither any worse nor any better'. The neutrality and independence of Laos had been recognised, but on nuclear testing, disarmament, and the German question there had been no progress. The *Economist* was a little more optimistic. Dialogue between the Americans and Soviets had been restored and a 'delicate balance of trust' established. Negotiation would be given another try. Although U.S.-Soviet relations could easily break down, as they had done before, the *Economist* argued that problems associated with Laos, Berlin, Cuba, and other issues could in time be resolved. It would take focused effort, but Kennedy and Khrushchev both wanted diplomatic successes. They had to keep their conversation going.[28]

By the summer of 1961, Khrushchev had decided that communism was losing prestige because so many East Germans were crossing to the West. They tended to be the most educated and economically productive people in the GDR, and it seemed that the very viability of the East German state was in jeopardy. Khrushchev could not back down. His domestic critics were waiting to act and he needed a victory. The U.S. government made further increases in military expenditure and promised to send more troops to Europe: it wanted to make Khrushchev realise that America would not abandon Berlin. At the same time, however, American leaders accepted the division of Germany. Since the exodus from East Germany (now about a thousand a day) created instability and danger, they suggested that the Ulbricht regime would be within its rights to close East Germany's borders. This situation led to the erection of the Berlin Wall in August 1961. Ulbricht gained prior approval from Khrushchev and the Warsaw Pact. Although the Soviets took account of East German views, Ulbricht did not have the final say. Khrushchev agreed that the wall offered a means to rescue the GDR, but he was not pushed into anything. Ulbricht probably saw the Berlin Wall as a means to coerce the West into negotiating a German settlement, and in Moscow there was some fear that he would go too far. Therefore, the Soviets were keen to restrain him even while they allowed the construction of the wall. Khrushchev was also hoping to save face. The Soviet leader declared that the GDR gained more from the Berlin Wall than might have been gained from a treaty; however, one of his advisers, Oleg Troyanovsky, considered the wall a silent acknowledgement that the Western powers could not yet be persuaded to recognise the GDR.[29]

Was the erection of the wall a sign of Soviet confidence or anxiety? In 1961 the Kremlin's impression was that the global balance of power was shifting to the USSR's disadvantage. Soviet missile capabilities were not all that had been expected, the rift with China was becoming more open and bitter, decolonisation was not greatly increasing Soviet influence in the developing world, and economic and security cooperation in the West was proceeding apace. The Ulbricht regime was constantly complaining, warning, and demanding. The Kremlin was told that the West intended to take measures against the GDR, that the economic strength of the FRG gave the West a huge propaganda triumph, and that the EEC would leave Eastern Europe economically far behind. Soviet leaders agreed that the stability of the GDR was vital if the eastern bloc was to develop as they wished. Above all, Khrushchev wanted a German peace treaty. Once the treaty was settled, he intended to address the GDR's economic weakness. Ulbricht, meanwhile, prioritised economic rather than political concerns. He eventually convinced Khrushchev that the economic situation had to be tackled without delay. Poland and Czechoslovakia protested about the special treatment received by the GDR, but Khrushchev declared in August 1961 that the Warsaw Pact needed the GDR as its first line of defence, and that living standards there had to be improved even if this took resources away from the USSR and the rest of the eastern bloc. Khrushchev was still hoping that a treaty could be agreed within the four-power framework. During the summer of 1961, however, he came around to the view that unilateral action was necessary, to close the borders and thereby ensure the survival of the GDR and the bloc. Having hoped that the Vienna summit would confirm an interim agreement on Berlin, Khrushchev was annoyed when Kennedy refused to consider changing Berlin's status. He could not believe that the Americans would really fight over West Berlin, but he was worried that Kennedy's policy would make war more likely. The Berlin Wall was therefore a useful stopgap. Moscow thought that the Americans would tolerate the wall and that it offered stability in East Germany with a minimal risk of war. But as Khrushchev was aware, the wall settled nothing. He still wanted a German agreement and had to keep open the possibility of talks, which in turn meant that he could not stick to his ultimatum. He wondered if the Kennedy administration might offer a de facto recognition of East Germany in return for guarantees on West Berlin. Khrushchev abandoned the deadline he had announced in June 1961, on the grounds that negotiations were in progress. His enemies in Moscow took advantage. Some criticised him for giving way to the Americans, others for risking war over a relatively unimportant matter while reducing the USSR's military strength.[30]

In Britain the erection of the Berlin Wall was greeted with dismay. *The Times* commented that 'the solid division of Berlin is a fact', expressed sympathy for the people of the city, and called for careful analysis rather than hasty reaction by the West. There was no communist design to 'obliterate' West Berlin and the building of the wall was an understandable move by the East German authorities, for they were worried about the economic and political problems associated with the constant stream of refugees passing over to the West. The western powers had to find a middle way: doing too little would be pointless and would damage their prestige, while doing too much would cause the crisis to escalate. *The Times* argued that British, American, and French governments should focus on upholding their rights and duties in Berlin. The leaders of the FRG were demanding more because they could not accept the division of Germany, but although the prospects for further talks with the USSR were not good, a period of stability would improve them and the FRG would then have less to complain about.[31]

Edward Heath told the Commons on October 17, 1961, that the West would not try to settle the matter by force no matter how 'unpalatable' recent events were 'to all decent people everywhere'. The construction of the wall had 'revealed both a lack of humanity in the East Berlin government as well as the weakness of the East German regime'. Khrushchev was making threats but there were certain fundamentals upon which the British government had to insist: the liberty and viability of West Berlin, the presence of western troops there, and freedom of access to West Berlin. Danger was growing, talks were urgently needed, and Heath was encouraged by reports that Khrushchev had described his deadline of December 31 as 'not necessarily firm'. But the Soviets had to understand that they would not be permitted to 'consolidate East Germany so as to be in a position later to undermine West Berlin and thus threaten West Germany and the countries of Europe'. Labour leader Hugh Gaitskell, while condemning the Berlin Wall, suggested that the whole crisis was attributable to the West's previous policy and especially the failure to communicate with the Soviets more assiduously. Gaitskell thought that the West's response to the wall was confused and disjointed: instead of promoting unity, hardliners and 'appeasers' were attacking each other and wasting precious time.

On October 18, 1961, Macmillan informed MPs that the government was willing to be flexible in order for negotiations to take place. He admitted that the French attitude was not all that it could be, and that political developments in the FRG (where a new government was being formed) were also hindering the attempt to arrange talks. 'We must get accustomed to anxiety and not let ourselves drift or be pushed into panic', the prime minister said, and above all 'we must keep our alliance together... We must not lose any chance of agreement, even if it be over a restricted field. But we must not be led too soon into too extensive a negotiation; nor must we shirk discussion of wider issues than Berlin at the right time'. The Soviets knew that the West would not give way. At the same time, the West had made clear its eagerness to talk, and Macmillan was sure that Moscow would prefer to talk rather than fight.[32]

Soon after its erection, it was widely recognised that the Berlin Wall had reduced tension. It eased the pressure on Khrushchev for more risky action. According to the British minister in Berlin, Geoffrey McDermott, the wall meant that Khrushchev did not have to keep to the ultimatum he had issued in June 1961. Senior Soviet leaders, including Khrushchev, left Moscow for their holidays just before and after the wall was erected, which suggests that they did not expect any new emergency. The Americans realised that they could do little about the Berlin Wall, although they felt obliged to make gestures. Kennedy promised to protect West Berlin and sent 1500 U.S. troops by road from the Federal Republic of Germany into West Berlin, but the president and his defence secretary, Robert McNamara, insisted that war could and should be avoided. Khrushchev declared that the USSR was not planning to blockade Berlin and would not deny the western powers their rights in the city. The British counselled restraint, which had some effect, and in the U.S. Senate, too, there

were calls for a diplomatic solution. The president decided that agreeing
to talks would not be seen as a sign of weakness. New negotiations on
Berlin commenced and went on for years, without making much progress. Like Macmillan, Kennedy responded to the wall cautiously. He saw
that Khrushchev had to do something to preserve Moscow's sphere of
influence, and expected also that the wall would have a negative effect on
the reputation of the USSR and the appeal of communism.[33]

The Americans wanted stability. So did the British. Bonn complained
that the West's response to recent events was too restrained, but Macmillan told audiences at home and abroad that although efforts to negotiate a settlement would continue, the West's rights in Berlin would not
be given up. Britain did not consent to the division of Germany and of
Europe, Macmillan declared. In practice, though, the existence of two
German states was accepted, even if the British government refused
formally to recognise the GDR. Demands from Bonn and Paris for
more proactive measures inconvenienced Macmillan and Kennedy, and
Macmillan decided that this problem could be circumvented if the future
of Berlin and Germany was dealt with primarily through bilateral U.S.-
Soviet talks. This made Bonn and Paris even angrier, because there was a
risk that the Americans would make concessions that damaged the interests of the FRG and France. Macmillan took up a more rigid position
on Berlin in order to mitigate their suspicion of Kennedy's intentions.
He also put some distance between himself and Kennedy, making objections whenever the U.S. authorities in West Berlin acted in a unilateral or
provocative fashion. But none of this brought closer a bargain on Berlin
and Germany. The British urged Bonn to accept the Oder-Neisse line as
the frontier between Germany and Poland and to give up any claim to
nuclear weapons. Not only did Washington disagree, but in late 1961 de
Gaulle told Macmillan that he could not promise never to give the FRG
nuclear weapons. Macmillan thought that these matters could be used as
bargaining tools, along with issues like recognition of the GDR and the
relationship between West Berlin and the FRG, but Kennedy objected
that more must be done to satisfy Adenauer. Britain's plan to apply for
membership of the EEC added a complication. At a NATO meeting in

December 1961, the French opposed the reopening of negotiations with the USSR. The Americans became more concerned about the possibility that the FRG would seek its own nuclear capability. Interallied friction increased. The British proposed a reduction of troop levels in Europe in order to see what the Soviets would offer in response, and London was confident that a breakthrough on the Berlin question would make possible the resolution of such other matters as Germany's borders, the status of the GDR, the FRG's nuclear aspirations, and general disarmament. Washington found this overly optimistic.[34]

Negotiation, not escalation, was Macmillan's line, and though some elements in Washington considered the British government unduly fearful, Kennedy himself wished to avoid a confrontation with the Soviets. Berlin had come to matter more to the Americans than it did to the British, in part because U.S. and British public opinion diverged. In Britain people were more concerned about the economy and relations with Europe. In the United States, the president's words and actions made Berlin more significant and there was considerable support for military action to protect the West's interests there. According to a report in the *Daily Mail* of July 21, 1961, opinion polls suggested that 71 percent of Americans were willing to fight over Berlin, compared to a British figure of 46 percent. In France only 9 percent of those polled were prepared to support military action. Macmillan and his colleagues were adamant that an effort should be made to conciliate Khrushchev, but they were ready to side with the United States if a serious emergency arose. Britain's approach helped Kennedy to stand up to the hardliners in Washington, and the British also helped when it was necessary to put on a show of unity and firmness. By keeping up appearances, Washington and London dissuaded Moscow from pressing them harder.[35]

Kennedy was encouraged by Khrushchev's abandonment of the deadline for a Berlin deal, and relieved when Khrushchev withdrew his demand that the office of secretary-general of the United Nations should be divided into three and shared between nominees of the West, the communist states, and the neutral bloc, a suggestion that had been rejected by the Americans as a recipe for confusion and paralysis. Less welcome was the Soviets' resumption of nuclear weapons tests. Still, Kennedy and his advisers accepted the Berlin Wall because it stabilised the situation, was clearly defensive, and suggested that the Soviets would not try to take West Berlin. Kennedy enjoyed an important public relations victory because the wall, he said, proved that Germans would not freely choose communism. Kennedy's detractors accused him of weakness, but he reaffirmed the U.S. commitment to protect West Berlin. Inevitably, Adenauer continued to protest about the wall, but he had no jurisdiction in Berlin and was happy for the wider question of German reunification to be sidelined. There was a brief furore in June 1963, when Kennedy made his strongly anticommunist 'Ich bin ein Berliner' speech, but the Soviets let it pass. As before, neither the USSR nor the United States wanted or expected a war over Berlin. An insight into Kennedy's thinking has been provided by John C. Ausland, who was a member and then deputy director of the Berlin Task Force, which consisted of officials from various U.S. government departments. Ausland stresses Kennedy's wish for détente. As the anxieties caused by the Cuban missile crisis and Berlin Wall faded, Kennedy thought that a genuine thaw was possible. He was irritated by arguments within the western alliance, by de Gaulle's veto on British membership of the EEC, by Bonn's sensitivities concerning Berlin and related matters, and by the objections that had been raised about the Polaris deal between the United States and Britain. Kennedy was determined to improve U.S.-Soviet relations and one of the reasons for his visit to Europe in June 1963 was to tell America's allies that this was the right course to pursue. The 'Ich bin ein Berliner' speech was the speech of a hardliner, but Kennedy made it at a time when he was working towards a nuclear test ban treaty with the British and Soviets. Committed to a thaw, he was also making provocative public statements that were designed to reassure sections of U.S. public opinion. Moscow chose to focus not on Kennedy's hawkish remarks but on his commitment to peace, and Khrushchev himself wanted a test ban treaty, and stability, because he could not afford to risk collisions with the West and with China at the same time.[36]

Kennedy arrived in London for talks with Macmillan at the end of June 1963. *The Times* suggested that there were two pressing issues that needed close attention: 'how to keep Britain as close as possible to Europe until she can actually join it' and 'how to develop between Britain, the United States and Europe a greater degree of trust and agreement on the broad strategy of the Cold War'. European complaints about U.S. policy had been growing for some time. *The Times* cited the troubled history of the plan for a multilateral nuclear force (MLF) as an example: 'it is partly European distrust of American intentions that has produced make-believe solutions such as the multilateral force', to which Britain and France were opposed and about which the FRG seemed equivocal. Kennedy also faced a difficulty in that he wished to promote a thaw with the Soviet Union, while for political reasons, he had to rule out compromise and acquiescence. Now was the time for Macmillan and Kennedy to make plans, asserted *The Times*. Britain's views on the EEC could be clarified and British membership brought closer. Stronger links between the United States, Britain, and Western Europe could be promoted. In addition, now that Kennedy had reaffirmed his desire for a German settlement, 'it should be possible to seek broader cooperation on reaching hard, controlled and practical agreements with the Russians'.[37]

The *Guardian* pointed out that it would take more than Kennedy's speeches and charisma to counteract the divisions in the West caused by de Gaulle's veto of the British EEC application and to reassure NATO members about U.S. security guarantees. The future of NATO was an especially urgent matter. The alliance needed stronger institutional props if it was going to work properly, and reorganisation was desired by its European members in order for them to have a greater role in decision making. Their resentment on this score had been repeatedly exploited by de Gaulle. Something had to be done or he would continue making trouble for Washington and London. Yet the Americans were reluctant to give their allies more influence within NATO. The *Guardian* urged U.S. leaders to reconsider and suggested that a sharing of control over nuclear weapons was the place to start.[38]

Kennedy and Macmillan issued a joint communiqué on June 30, 1963, and on July 2 Macmillan reported on their talks to Parliament. He did not say much about Berlin. Instead, the prime minister strongly reaffirmed his commitment to a test ban treaty, which, he insisted, would lead to the resolution of other problems. Macmillan was sure that 'great opportunities will open up'.[39]

Berlin had been the place where the Americans and Soviets tested each other's nerve. There was relief on both sides when the danger receded. The Kennedy administration felt bound to show that it would not give way, and the same was true of the Soviet leadership. For the latter, the added goal of restraining the Ulbricht regime in East Germany was also important. Some of Kennedy's advisers feared that the 'Ich bin ein Berliner' speech was a step too far and that it would undo the work that was being done to promote détente. It was fortunate that Khrushchev did not take the speech more seriously. Different audiences heard what they wanted to hear in Kennedy's speech and were not put off by remarks that did not accord with the preferred interpretation. For all his bluster and talk of victory, Khrushchev did not emerge from the Berlin struggles of 1958–1962 with his position at home or his influence abroad greatly enhanced. The Berlin Wall was a gift for western propagandists, and, though the Soviets resumed their nuclear weapons tests and tried in other ways to exude confidence and strength, the ultimatum of June 1961 had to be dropped. Khrushchev's actions strengthened western unity and helped President Kennedy to justify increases in U.S. defence spending. His rivals in the USSR stepped up their efforts to remove him. According to the Americans, meanwhile, the existence of a free and democratic West Berlin within East Germany was close to being accepted by all parties, which made possible a real easing of Cold War tensions in Europe. In Bonn, however, this claim was contested. The Adenauer government resisted all talk of recognising the GDR, even though the Americans argued that détente could not proceed unless such obstacles were removed. Increasingly, Kennedy opted for bilateral U.S.-Soviet discussions.[40]

The British government shared Washington's wish for stability in Europe and hoped that more flexibility on both sides would moderate the rivalries and friction engendered by the Cold War. Macmillan had tried repeatedly to promote agreement in the West and fresh approaches to the Soviet Union. He had made his own overtures to Moscow, and was criticised for this at home and especially abroad. The status of Berlin and the division of Germany preoccupied Britain and its allies throughout these years, but international circumstances prevented a settlement, and quarrels within the West became more heated not only on Berlin and Germany but also on economic relations, security, nuclear weapons, and the future of NATO. The British influenced and participated fully in all these debates. London frequently clashed with Bonn and Paris. There were also disagreements with Washington. Britain's capacity for independent action was still significant, but was limited, and it remained to be seen if the outstanding issues of the period could be resolved in accordance with British goals and interests.

CHAPTER 3

STAYING NUCLEAR AND GOING EUROPEAN

KEEPING BRITAIN GREAT

Among the most pressing unresolved problems for the British were those involving nuclear strategy, NATO, and Britain's relationship with the EEC. Disputes went on within NATO, and increased within the EEC, which did not make for calm and steady diplomacy in the West. The MLF plan, for an international nuclear force under a joint command, was divisive. The British had their own nuclear weapons and did not wish to share control with anyone else, and the French position was the same. For Harold Macmillan's government, it was important to maintain Britain's deterrent and to make sure that it was seen at home and abroad as an independent deterrent, so as to impress allies and enemies alike. This seemed to rule out a compromise on the MLF. The pros and cons of interaction with Western Europe had to be addressed, meanwhile, and discussions about the EEC and EFTA continued. The government's determination to hide and slow down Britain's decline relative to the world's other great powers was constantly in the background. Macmillan and his colleagues wanted to get the maximum benefit from the 'special relationship' with America and to shape what happened in Europe, hoping thereby to advance British interests and safeguard Britain's international status.

Believing that the Soviets had more missiles than they did, the Americans were keen to close the gap and proposed that their European allies should build up conventional forces while the United States focused on the upgrading of its nuclear arsenal. European governments refused on the grounds that they lacked the resources to build their conventional forces up to the level that the United States deemed satisfactory. Strained personal relations added to the acrimony: Kennedy did not get on well with Adenauer and de Gaulle and much preferred Macmillan. The quarrel about the nuclear-conventional balance proved that the 'differentiated responses' compromise worked out by NATO in spring 1958 had settled nothing. American service chiefs had continued to place their trust in strategic nuclear weapons. European members of NATO wished to stick to those parts of the previous agreements that most suited them. Only the British advocated a further review of NATO strategy, and this was partly because they wanted to sideline the MLF proposal, which was dropped and taken up again several times and necessitated some careful manoeuvring. From the outset, London and Washington did not see the MLF in the same way. For London it represented a challenge to Britain's independent deterrent. For the Americans, the multilateral force offered a way of dealing with difficulties inside and outside NATO that related to the FRG's nuclear aspirations. The Soviets maintained that the MLF would mean nuclear proliferation, and the British agreed. They wanted a nonproliferation treaty in order to prevent other states from acquiring nuclear weapons. The dissemination of tactical nuclear weapons in NATO was a related concern, and by August 1962 Macmillan had decided that some means had to be found to limit their number. Designed for battlefield use, tactical weapons interposed a stage between response to small-scale aggression and a strategic nuclear strike, but Macmillan doubted that there could be a limited war without the use of strategic nuclear weapons.

The Americans had similar reservations, but this was a sensitive matter because the rest of NATO was committed to tactical nuclear weapons. Macmillan did not want to accept more of these weapons for British forces in West Germany, irrespective of whether or not NATO members could be persuaded to accept Britain's views.[1]

Lack of resources continued to hamper the British as they tried to dispel the sense of post-Suez retreat. Economic problems mounted at the end of the 1950s. Nuclear independence had finally to be given up, and the hope of reducing defence costs by developing nuclear as opposed to conventional forces was dashed. An unsuccessful bid to join the EEC was also a blow: de Gaulle vetoed British membership early in 1963, claiming that Britain was not really a 'European' power but an American pawn. His view had been confirmed by the Nassau Agreement of December 1962, whereby Macmillan and Kennedy arranged for Britain's purchase of Polaris missiles from the United States. Britain's nuclear programme proved disappointing. Exchanges with the Americans had revealed that British technology was out of date. The emergency in Jordan in 1958 showed that there was still a need to deploy British troops abroad, and the crises of 1961 in Kuwait and Berlin led Macmillan's government to extend the period of service for the last intake of conscripted troops and call up the reserves. A confrontation between Malaysia and Indonesia in 1963 meant that more British troops were required in the Far East. Defence estimates for 1963 were £150 million higher than in 1962. The lesson was that nuclear defence did not mean cheaper defence. Blue Streak was abandoned because of the cost. The government appeared to retrieve the situation by leasing a submarine base near Glasgow to the Americans in return for Skybolt missiles. Britain could still claim to be an independent nuclear power because these missiles would be carried by British bombers under British control, but in 1962 Kennedy's administration scrapped Skybolt. Macmillan, worried about Britain's and his own reputation, was determined to obtain Polaris.[2]

The Polaris sea-to-air missile system necessitated the construction of nuclear submarines and some strategic and financial adjustments on Britain's part. These were hotly debated, not least because nuclear submarines did not quite suit the East of Suez responsibilities to which Britain was still wedded. Britain's Canberra bombers had first gone nuclear with American weaponry in West Germany in 1958. American help was also needed in the development of fission bombs for the V-bombers, which had been operational since the mid-1950s. There were three types, the Valiant (1955), the Vulcan (1957), and the Victor (1958). The Valiant initially carried American nuclear weapons under the dual-key arrangement. Later, all three types carried British weapons, and by 1961 they could carry hydrogen bombs; however, by this time improved Soviet air defences had increased the need for up-to-date missiles. The Valiant was withdrawn in 1965 owing to metal fatigue. The Victor was converted into a tanker aircraft and remained in service into the 1990s. The Vulcan was withdrawn in 1982. Plans to develop a new British aircraft were abandoned for financial reasons in 1965. The first Polaris submarine was launched in 1967 and the system became operational in 1969. The tactical role (nonstrategic) was later taken over by Tornado aircraft, developed jointly by Britain, the FRG, and Italy and ordered in 1970, and by short-range U.S. nuclear weapons. The commitment to nuclear weapons was repeatedly questioned in these years, and policymakers had simultaneously to contend with pressure to save money, the growth of antinuclear sentiment among the British people, and interservice rivalries.[3]

Arguments about Skybolt, the Nassau Agreement, and Polaris were inseparable from concerns about Britain's economic performance. The British did enjoy increased national wealth, more private affluence, and higher living standards, low unemployment, low inflation and high rates of growth. The problem was that Britain's competitors, especially the FRG and Japan, were doing better. Historians generally agree that the 'stop-go' policies of the period did not help. In key sectors of the economy, caution and restriction were followed by expansion, which in turn gave way to intervention and controls again. In 1960 British productivity was about 14 percent higher than it had been in 1955, and output per head was 12.5 percent higher, but the largest economies of Western Europe had rates of growth that were twice as high. Paradoxically, the global economic environment was quite favourable to Britain in the 1950s, and although the empire and the world role imposed psychological as well as economic burdens, and affected policy, the British *did* prosper during the 1950s. Nevertheless, their foreign competitors moved further ahead. The Conservatives, in office from 1951 to 1964, took a bipartisan approach, moderate rather than bold, which probably meant that economic problems were not analyzed or tackled as effectively as they might have been. Certain policy areas were neglected, especially industrial relations, training, management, and efficiency in the use of labour.[4] There was a delay in moving research closer to industry and a failure to concentrate technological effort in areas that would most benefit Britain domestically and internationally. In addition, huge sums were lost on cancelled defence projects. Blue Streak cost £84 million, for instance, and Skybolt £27 million. Despite all this, Macmillan insisted that Britain was still great. He stressed continuity. He told the people that the economy would improve and that Britain still mattered in the world.[5]

The decision to abandon Blue Streak was made in February 1960. The project was going to cost hundreds of millions of pounds to complete and the chiefs of staff had advised that by the time Blue Streak was ready it would be 'obsolescent and unsuitable'. Little value could be placed in weapons fired from a stationary position when the necessary technology was coming together to develop mobile systems, and the life of Britain's bomber aircraft could be extended by the purchase of Skybolt air-to-ground missiles. Macmillan took this course for strategic and financial reasons and by April 1960 he had an assurance from the United States that Skybolt would be provided. He also saw political and moral grounds for the abandonment of Blue Streak. To opt for fixed rockets in a small country like Britain, he later wrote, would be to increase alarm, especially if the rockets were placed near towns, whereas bombers stationed in air bases were more acceptable. Mobile weapons had an added attraction, too, in that they could be kept out of sight. A particularly controversial part of the Skybolt agreement was that the Americans would be allowed to use a submarine base at Holy Loch on the Clyde, not far from Glasgow, one of Britain's largest cities, which, as Labour MPs, CND protesters, and others pointed out, was bound to be targeted by the Soviets. On November 1, 1960, Macmillan assured the Commons that the Americans would not do anything involving their bases and weapons in Britain without the proper consultation. Protests against nuclear weapons went on and there was wide dissatisfaction with what were regarded as negative aspects of Cold War culture. This was seen on the continent, especially in the FRG, as well as in Britain. Many people believed that nuclear weapons did not make them safe.[6]

The initial preference of the Kennedy administration was for America's NATO allies to build up their conventional forces. Some of Kennedy's advisers also wanted to push for greater European unity and thought that the sharing of nuclear technology with Britain should cease, in order to encourage the British to cooperate more with Europe. One of the most significant points about the Cuban missile crisis of October 1962 is that Kennedy only told America's allies about his decisions *after* they had been made, which suggests that he did not regard them as nuclear partners. Nevertheless, Kennedy's personal friendship with Macmillan and belief that the 'special relationship' with Britain was worth strengthening opened the way for the Nassau meeting at the end of 1962. The cancellation of Skybolt caused a crisis in Anglo-American relations that, according to some observers, was comparable to Suez. Kennedy's adviser Richard E. Neustadt compiled a report in which he explained that Eisenhower and Macmillan had made the Skybolt deal as part of a cluster of Anglo-American nuclear, defence, and intelligence arrangements. By 1962, however, some of these were no longer required by the U.S. government. Skybolt had gone over budget and the necessary technology was proving difficult to perfect. Even so, in Washington there was a desire to avoid controversy and a concern that if the Macmillan government fell in Britain, Labour might get into office, and the Labour Party was regarded as neutralist, antinuclear, and anti-EEC in outlook. Neustadt also noted that nuclear cooperation with the British was becoming more sensitive at a time when the international community was worried about nuclear proliferation, when the United States was trying to control the West's arsenal and preempt the FRG's bid for nuclear weapons, and when any new deal between the Americans and British would encourage de Gaulle to block

Britain's application to join the EEC. Further difficulties arose because of misunderstandings between the United States and Britain. The main point for the British was not the quality of their deterrent, nor its military capability, but its independence. The Americans did not fully appreciate this. The main point for them was that Skybolt was not cost effective and had been rendered unnecessary by new strategic plans and long-range weapons. Robert McNamara, the U.S. secretary of defence, told Kennedy that the cost factor had become more important than the question of whether or not Skybolt could actually be made to work. The U.S. state department advised that the British should not be offered Polaris and that their security worries should be used to push them into a closer relationship with Europe. Nobody in the American government realised how badly the British would take the cancellation of Skybolt.[7]

As these matters were being discussed in Washington, and disagreements arose there on the importance of Britain's deterrent, British membership of the EEC, and the 'special relationship', Macmillan assumed that the Americans would persevere with Skybolt. London had recognised that reliance on an American missile that was still in its experimental stages was far from ideal. Yet no contingency plans were made in case Skybolt was cancelled, despite all the problems and delays in the project. Gradually it dawned on Macmillan and defence minister Peter Thorneycroft that cancellation was likely and that it would weaken them politically and reveal to the world that Britain had no independent deterrent. Macmillan was loath to raise the nuclear issue with the Cabinet, or Parliament, or the service chiefs, because he did not want to face the same old questions about the cost of nuclear weapons and dependence upon the United States, and he did not wish to provide more sustenance for the antinuclear protest movement. Nor did he want to upset the British weapons programme, for Britain would soon be producing its own nuclear warheads. Macmillan needed private, face-to-face talks with Kennedy. In autumn 1962, before the Nassau meeting, he wondered if the Skybolt deal could be kept alive for another year or so, to avoid political problems at home. This delay before cancellation could be used to work out a bargain on Polaris. Then McNamara indicated that Polaris might indeed be made available in place of Skybolt. The Cuban missile crisis subsequently sidelined all other matters. Its peaceful resolution brought much relief and Macmillan decided that the time had come to act. He was losing popularity, his government was beset with difficulty on Europe and other issues, and the newspapers were increasingly drawing attention to Britain's declining influence abroad (it was alleged, for instance, that Britain had not been consulted at all by the Americans during the Cuban missile crisis).[8]

It is probable that Kennedy made up his mind to offer Polaris before going to Nassau.[9] He did not commit himself to anything in advance, however, and he thought that various options might be tried. Perhaps Britain would take over the Skybolt project with the United States paying half the cost. This was discussed at Nassau, and only when Macmillan refused did Kennedy agree to provide Polaris, on condition that Britain's nuclear forces would be linked with NATO. In response, Macmillan wanted it understood that Britain would have the right to use these forces independently should the nation's security be threatened. Even McNamara, who favoured U.S. control over the West's nuclear arsenal, accepted that this point had to be conceded to the British. In the state department there was much opposition, but Kennedy saw no way forward unless he allowed the British to preserve some semblance of nuclear independence. As Thorneycroft had emphasised to McNamara, Britain had to have this. It was really a matter of politics, not strategy, diplomacy, or the financial costs involved.[10]

The Polaris missiles would be fitted with British warheads and carried by British submarines, which would be part of a NATO force (the MLF, never in fact formed). However tenuous it was becoming, the claim to nuclear independence lived on. But Macmillan came in for some hostile press coverage, the Labour Party announced that it would renegotiate the Nassau Agreement when it came into office, and Labour leader Harold Wilson dismissed the 'independent British deterrent' as a myth. Macmillan was annoyed by all the criticism and maintained that Nassau was a major coup. He had obtained Polaris from the Americans, at low cost, and ensured the survival of a British deterrent that could still be called 'independent'. Some of his colleagues focused more on the continuing American support for the MLF and the fact that Britain's Polaris force and some British bombers would have to be given over to NATO purposes, but Macmillan declared that, under the agreement, Britain would make an appropriate contribution to 'interdependent' defence while retaining the rights of a sovereign state. 'This', he remarked, 'accepts the facts of life as they are'.[11]

In *The Times* it was argued that the Nassau conference and the deal on Polaris would have been much less important had the Skybolt decision been delayed, had the Conservative Party not been 'in such deep water at home', and had such a fuss not been created by the recent remarks of Dean Acheson (who, in a speech of December 5, 1962, on the subject of 'Our Atlantic Alliance', declared that Britain 'has lost an empire and has not yet found a role'). Nassau had clarified the nature of the 'special relationship', argued *The Times*, and this would help to correct 'some complacent assumptions about Anglo-American relations'. A system based on Skybolt would not have been truly independent, as was shown by 'the way in which it collapsed', and a system based on Polaris 'will not be greatly different in kind. It will be equally geared to American production, though with an additional political string that Britain's Polaris missiles are at some stage and in some way to become part of an Atlantic arrangement'. Although friendship with the Americans was important, this friendship now had to be seen more in the context of NATO. Anglo-American cooperation would go on, but Nassau did not remove Britain's need to feel that it had a say on matters directly affecting its own interests, and 'if the relationship is special it will survive for reasons more enduring than choice of a particular make of missile'. *The Times* was disappointed that no new initiative in East-West relations had come out of the Nassau talks and that although progress on Berlin, Congo, Cuba, nuclear testing, and international aid was not impossible, there was a 'note of marking time on the other leading question, Britain's entry into Europe'. That the Polaris deal presaged the end of Britain's nuclear independence was the point stressed by the *Observer*, which dismissed Macmillan's claims to the contrary and argued that Britain was losing the ability to use its weapons without approval from others—principally Washington, but also the rest of NATO should the multilateral force be established.[12]

The Nassau Agreement is a testament to the determination of Macmillan and Kennedy to preserve a joint approach to strategy and defence. On the British side, Thorneycroft argued strongly against reliance on the United States. As for Kennedy, he had to overcome colleagues and advisers who considered that offering Polaris to the British would be a mistake. There was a preference in Washington for nuclear cooperation to proceed on a U.S.-European basis, not a U.S.-British one, which is why the MLF plan gained such support. There was also the abiding opinion that Britain should give up its deterrent and join more closely with Western Europe militarily, politically, and economically, which meant that it would be counterproductive to encourage the British to stick to their 'special relationship' perspective. The president knew that Macmillan's government was in trouble at home, however, and that the Skybolt crisis was partly to blame. He did not want to be held responsible for the fall of Macmillan's government or to see Macmillan forced to adopt a cooler line towards the United States in order to stay in office. Kennedy wanted to help, though he had no wish to annoy the rest of NATO or undermine the MLF plan. He was impressed by the argument that some American newspapers were presenting, to the effect that Britain's friendship was worth having, and felt that he had inherited a commitment to nuclear cooperation with Britain from his predecessor, Eisenhower. At Nassau he was moved by Macmillan's appeals for justice and assistance and by Macmillan's concessions: the latter agreed to assign British bombers to NATO as the core of the MLF and to increase Britain's conventional contribution to NATO. The Americans thought they could limit controversy within NATO by offering Polaris to France on terms that were similar to those agreed at Nassau. It did not matter that the French nuclear programme was not sufficiently advanced to make use of the offer: this was a ploy to reassure the Europeans and calm their concerns about America's relationship with Britain.[13]

Kennedy was relieved to get through the Skybolt crisis. It had created an awkward situation, linked as it was to issues concerning Europe,

NATO, and the MLF, and the offer of Polaris to France made sense in these circumstances. Macmillan understood this. De Gaulle, however, was not to be won over by Kennedy's gesture, for he rejected Polaris, vetoed Britain's EEC application, and made it clear that France would not be a party to America's European intentions. The Skybolt crisis exhausted Macmillan, but to his way of thinking the Nassau Agreement represented a skilful recovery. Polaris was the boost he needed to shore up his personal prestige and could be used to strengthen his government in Parliament and the nation. At Nassau the prime minister employed a combination of pleas, offers, requests, and threats. He exaggerated certain problems. He misled Kennedy. He warned, for instance, that if Polaris was not provided, Britain would have to arrange for nuclear cooperation with France. This alarmed Kennedy and his aides, for they saw that this would complicate their nuclear discussions with the FRG and probably cause a split in NATO. Macmillan was well aware by now that de Gaulle would almost certainly block Britain's bid to join the EEC, but he could not admit this to the Americans. He had to pretend that Anglo-French relations were better than they really were. In addition, he and his colleagues never believed that the government would fall over the Skybolt issue. The British still had control over their own national defence, and they interpreted the undertakings they made about the MLF and NATO as loose and general rather than specific or binding. Indeed, the Nassau Agreement was quite ambiguous on certain matters. It had to be, so that both sides could claim that they got most out of the bargain.[14]

Macmillan's policy was approved in the Commons on January 30 and 31, 1963, but some Labour MPs were incensed. George Brown, a future foreign secretary, declared that the Commons could have

> no confidence in a government whose defence policy has collapsed and which, at Nassau, entered into an agreement which, by seeking to continue the illusion of an independent British nuclear deterrent, imposes further economic burdens upon the nation and makes more difficult the solution of Great Britain's defence problems.

Harold Wilson made it clear, to audiences in America as well as Britain, that if he became prime minister he would abandon the concept of a unilateral deterrent. He did not openly repudiate the Nassau Agreement, but said he regretted it and wished to alter Britain's defence policy. Labour went into the general election of 1964 promising to reconsider Britain's commitments, though there was no pledge to disarm, and, once in office, Wilson did not eschew nuclear deterrence, not least because voters approved of it.[15]

De Gaulle's opinion was that the Nassau Agreement threatened British and perhaps European sovereignty. Still nurturing his vision of an independent Europe led by France, he denounced Britain's close relationship with the United States, stepped up France's nuclear programme, and raised objections to British membership of the EEC. Kennedy had been encouraging Macmillan to join the EEC, arguing that European unity was essential to NATO and good for trade. Talks on British entry during 1962 did not get far. Macmillan tried to divide the FRG from France, stressing that the needs of West German industries were not the same as those of French agriculture. He also assured de Gaulle that there would be no U.S. domination of Europe and made new suggestions about European political cooperation, but de Gaulle thought that the British were trying to trick him. Adenauer did not back Britain's bid because he considered Macmillan too soft on the Soviets, resented Anglo-American acceptance of the Berlin Wall, and did not want to jeopardise the FRG's understanding with France. On January 14, 1963, de Gaulle vetoed Britain's EEC application and rejected the U.S. offer of Polaris. He explicitly linked together the Nassau Agreement and Britain's bid to join the EEC.[16]

The supposition that de Gaulle would respond well to a nuclear bribe had been part of Macmillan's calculations since the application to join the EEC had been definitely decided upon in 1961. The matter had to be kept secret and the prime minister did not even tell the Cabinet, but in the event the Americans would not allow him to provide what de Gaulle was thought to want. Macmillan could not admit to the French leader that there would be no nuclear deal because this would certainly have wrecked the EEC bid, and there could be no public discussion of possible nuclear cooperation in case this damaged Macmillan's position at home and alienated other members of the EEC. Macmillan told Kennedy that de Gaulle's main demands related to the EEC's rules on agriculture, not nuclear cooperation: Macmillan did not want anything to spoil the Nassau Agreement.[17]

From the outset, Britain's application to join the EEC was beset by delays, disagreements, and behind-the-scenes dealing. The Commons approved of the government's decision to make an application on August 3, 1961, but the resolution stated that Britain would negotiate in order to find out if satisfactory terms of membership could be agreed, that British sovereignty and the special interests of Britain, the Commonwealth, and EFTA would be protected, and that no agreement would be made with the EEC until there had been full consultation with Commonwealth leaders and the Commons had been given the opportunity to vote on the final arrangements that were being proposed. The government was not seeking endorsement for a straightforward application to join the EEC, therefore, but only for a process that would determine whether or not terms could be agreed. Macmillan stressed the political as well as the economic importance of what the government was trying to do, and he pointed also to the global implications. 'In this modern world', he said on July 31, 1961, 'the tendency towards larger groups of nations acting together in the common interest leads to greater unity and thus adds to our strength in the struggle for freedom'. When it was suggested that Britain ought not to seek full membership of the EEC, but an associate status, because this would involve no loss of sovereignty and no impact on the Commonwealth, the prime minister dismissed this as pointless. Mere association would give Britain little influence in the shaping of EEC policy, and it would not make it easier for Britain to reconcile its need for European markets and cooperation with the ongoing connection with the Commonwealth. Although Macmillan stated that the membership application related purely to economic matters and did not directly involve defence and foreign policy, he kept telling the Commons that if the talks failed there would be danger for the 'free world'. He issued a warning to the EEC governments, pointing out that there would have to be a major reassessment of Britain's international responsibilities if the bid to join the EEC failed. On August 2, 1961, Macmillan told the Commons that it was not consistent to object to EEC membership while accepting closer links with Europe in other spheres, notably security. 'I think', he concluded, 'that most of us recognise that in a changing world, if we are not to be left behind and to drop out of the mainstream of the world's life, we must be prepared to change and adapt our methods. All through history this has been one of the main sources of our strength'.[18]

That de Gaulle was not ready to let Britain join the EEC, and that Britain was not really prepared for the necessary adjustments that would have to be made, became obvious during 1962. Macmillan met de Gaulle for crisis talks on December 15 and 16, 1962, at Rambouillet (one of the French president's official residences, south-west of Paris). De Gaulle made it clear that he did not want Britain in the EEC. According to French foreign minister Maurice Couve de Murville, Macmillan was 'very sad', 'almost broke down', and could not appreciate that the fundamental issue for the French was the lack of flexibility on Britain's part: Macmillan 'could not imagine that Britain could change'. Jean Monnet, one of the chief architects of European integration and president of the ECSC from 1952 to 1955, made a similar remark. The British were slow to turn to Europe, said Monnet, because they had deluded themselves into thinking they could maintain what they had without changing.[19]

This meeting in December 1962 followed an earlier, apparently more promising meeting between Macmillan and de Gaulle at the Chateau de Champs, east of Paris, in June 1962. Nuclear matters featured prominently at Champs. Macmillan and his advisers were sure that de Gaulle wanted Anglo-French nuclear cooperation, for it would be in line with his bigger plans for the security of Western Europe and he needed a partner to share the costs (London attributed some of France's economic problems to the cost of de Gaulle's nuclear programme). Macmillan was not too worried about de Gaulle's statement that the nuclear question and EEC membership were unconnected, or about his insistence that France wished to remain an independent nuclear power. Despite opposition from the foreign office, unfavourable coverage in the press, and warnings from the

Americans, Macmillan made offers to de Gaulle on nuclear cooperation. At Champs, de Gaulle did speak of an Anglo-French force that, though linked to NATO, would not be under NATO's control. It would represent a European centre for decision making that was not dependent upon the Americans. Macmillan made similar remarks and said that an enlarged EEC would be the equal of the two superpowers. He subsequently told the Americans that Britain would not share confidential information provided by the United States and that the nuclear issue had nothing to do with Britain's EEC bid. He misled Kennedy about the Champs talks and refused to provide details to Parliament on the grounds that the negotiations were still at a sensitive stage. Macmillan had to fend off searching questions from the Americans while the foreign secretary, Home, advised that it would not be in Britain's interests to work with the French in developing nuclear forces and that the Americans would not allow this anyway. The prime minister had a rude awakening at Rambouillet in December 1962 when he realised how much de Gaulle's position had changed since June. De Gaulle's confidence had been boosted by the French elections, which had brought significant gains for his party, and by the rapidly improving relations between France and the FRG. At Rambouillet the French leader went back on many of the things he had said at Champs. In particular, he told Macmillan that Britain's EEC application had to be treated purely as an economic matter.[20]

Was Macmillan to blame for the failure of Britain's application for membership of the EEC? In fairness to him it should be remembered that there were many circumstances over which he had little control. Those things he could influence, he did influence. Once he had resolved that Britain should move closer to Europe Macmillan set about building up support for this endeavour, but the EEC bid was widely judged to be an acknowledgment that Britain's international influence was waning. The government tried to make the best of things but the initiative usually lay elsewhere, in Europe, and British proposals regarding the course of European integration generally met with cynicism on the continent. Macmillan was not a keen Europeanist. Moreover, although he might initially have had reason to think that he could win over both de Gaulle and

Adenauer, he indulged this fancy for too long and should have accepted that the ties between Paris and Bonn, and the ongoing Berlin crisis, made it more than likely that Adenauer would side with de Gaulle on EEC matters. The economic context did not help. Britain's economic position was getting weaker, relative to 'The Six'. De Gaulle knew that others in the EEC would complain when he used his veto, but he also believed that they would rather not jeopardise the smooth running of the common market, which was by now delivering considerable benefits. Had Macmillan shown more enthusiasm for the EEC, and offered more in his dealings with 'The Six', things might have been different. But de Gaulle would probably still have blocked Britain's application, and there were good reasons for Macmillan's equivocation. The British government, Parliament, press, and public were not united on Europe, and Commonwealth interests had to be respected.[21]

It was not just the prime minister's fault that the EEC application was vetoed, but Macmillan was partly to blame. He allowed the process to become sluggish. Matters could not be rushed, he thought, because of the opposition to EEC membership at home and because it was important to take repeated soundings in Washington and throughout the Commonwealth. Delay, however, made the government seem less than committed, and de Gaulle took advantage. The latter's conduct was hardly open, fair, or constructive, but de Gaulle did have some grounds for his suspicion about British goals. For example, Macmillan was continually trying to detach the FRG from France. He had been doing so since 1957, when the Treaty of Rome was readied for signing. Disagreements between Paris and Bonn gave some encouragement to the British as they looked for ways to recover from the failed EEC application. The government took comfort from the fact that it had not had to choose between the 'special relationship' with America and the desire for closer links with Europe: both could still be useful. In the FRG, consolidation of the EEC was not considered to be inconsistent with a close security relationship with the United States. De Gaulle's idea of independence was not very appealing to the rest of 'The Six', and he exaggerated the independence that 'The Six' could achieve in a divided continent. After all, it was the Cold

War that made the Americans influential in Western Europe, not so much the 'special relationship' between Britain and the United States. As for Anglo-French relations, there was common ground on EEC matters even if the differences were stressed for domestic political reasons. Like the British, de Gaulle preferred intergovernmental to supranational bodies. On institutional change it was probably Macmillan, not de Gaulle, who was the more flexible, and Macmillan was also willing to make agricultural concessions. What was really at stake was political leadership in Europe. The lesson of the early 1960s was that in this competition the French, already inside the EEC, had opportunities and advantages that the British lacked.[22]

Matters were complicated by U.S. policy and by Britain's need for American friendship. The Kennedy administration wanted Britain to join the EEC as part of a 'grand design' that would reshape Europe in a way that helped America to deal with its own problems, especially nuclear strategy, slow economic growth, and a trade deficit. Kennedy and his advisers looked at the growing prosperity and nuclear aspirations of Western Europe and tried to make more use of America's allies financially and strategically. It was suggested that the allies should join the United States in sending aid to developing nations and pay more towards the cost of U.S. troops stationed in Europe. In the longer term, Washington had in view the reduction of tariffs and expansion of America's exports, and the elimination of instability from Europe so as to focus more on resisting communism in the developing world. The Americans knew that their 'grand design' would run up against French and West German hostility. This obstruction could be overcome, it was thought, if America's principal ally, Britain, joined the EEC, a solution that would also enhance Western Europe's unity and bring strategic advantages, as well as enlarge the market for U.S. goods. Trade would be liberalised, NATO bolstered, and a stable, prosperous, unified Western Europe could then take on a greater share of world responsibilities. Macmillan's priority was to obtain Polaris, however, and de Gaulle was unwilling to admit Britain to the EEC. Kennedy hoped that the Nassau Agreement would not rule out British membership of the EEC. Washington tried to coax

Paris in various ways, and the offer of Polaris on 'similar' terms to those agreed with Britain was one such attempt. Yet the French lacked the necessary warheads and submarines, and the Americans wanted eventually to bring French weapons under NATO control. De Gaulle saw no reason to do America's bidding.[23]

In attempting to shift Britain's relationship with Western Europe onto a new basis, Macmillan had to bear in mind Britain's other, extra-European interests, and, of course, the need to maintain the 'special relationship'. Anglo-American cooperation took precedence over Britain's involvement with Europe, as de Gaulle had recognised. Macmillan was attacked at the time and afterwards for failing to downgrade the 'special relationship'. Had he done this, however, it would have been harder for Britain to go on acting as a global power. Suez may have been a sign of decline, but the full extent of this decline was masked for another ten years or so, which allowed people at home and abroad to think that Britain was still strong. Perhaps Macmillan believed in the early 1960s that he could get what he wanted from both Europe and America. Historians of a Euro-sceptic disposition have sometimes condemned him for deceiving the British Parliament and public. The potential benefits of EEC membership were misrepresented; different arguments were used on different audiences; certain points were exaggerated and others glossed over. It is true that the case presented by Macmillan and by lord privy seal Edward Heath, who had special responsibility for the EEC bid, was selective, but it is also true that government policy remained equivocal. The application for EEC membership was conditional upon the terms that could be agreed with 'The Six'. Macmillan has also been criticised on the grounds that, in settling for the *appearance* of a 'special relationship' with the United States, Britain lost the chance to assume a leadership role in Europe. Macmillan's stress on the Anglo-American link, it is assumed, made it more difficult for Britain to negotiate entry into the EEC. That Britain gained significant benefits from the 'special relationship' is undeniable, however, and Macmillan used American help to considerable effect at key moments.[24]

Macmillan's mistakes and the nature of Anglo-American relations might have mattered less than the conduct of de Gaulle, although on this point there is also disagreement. Perhaps Macmillan ought to have offered economic arrangements that would have left no doubt as to Britain's commitment to the EEC application, and perhaps entry into the EEC remained possible until as late as November 1962, when de Gaulle's supporters unexpectedly gained an absolute majority in the French national assembly. Before this de Gaulle was politically vulnerable at home, and he had yet to cement his alliance with Adenauer and was under pressure internationally to let Britain into the EEC. Conversely, it could be argued that even if de Gaulle was relatively weak before November 1962, the British were not to know that the French elections would change things so dramatically, and they could not bank on pushing him into a decision on their EEC bid before he was ready. Such were his fixed ideas about Europe, Britain, and America, moreover, that he might not have allowed Britain to join the EEC—on terms that Britain could accept—even had the political context not been transformed late in 1962. There is something to be said, however, for the view that the negotiations took too long. The response of 'The Six' to the British application affected and was affected by their policy towards each other. The EEC's members found it impossible to resolve all of the economic and political issues involved, and Britain's application remained conditional, which overshadowed the whole process. 'The Six' had always to settle things prior to discussing them with the British, which made for further delay and uncertainty.[25]

'The Six' had different, sometimes conflicting, motives with regard to the negotiations for Britain's entry to the EEC. British officials appear not to have assessed these thoroughly or accurately. Belgium, the Netherlands, and Luxembourg wanted to admit Britain, largely because of their concern about the animosity between France and America. In Italy as well as in Belgium, the Netherlands and Luxembourg, people wondered if the EEC was a worthwhile project after all. De Gaulle used his veto in January 1963 not only to block what he took to be a British challenge to French leadership of the EEC, but also to reassert that leadership. Bonn complained about Britain's unwillingness to accommodate the FRG's interests, meanwhile, and viewed the EEC bid in the light of the Berlin question. Britain's application was not necessarily doomed from the outset, but there were always going to be problems. The Macmillan government had little room for manoeuvre and was unable to win much public support for a pro-Europe policy. It was being urged forward by the Americans, who at the same time ruled out the nuclear sharing that Macmillan thought would satisfy de Gaulle—although on this matter it is not easy to tell what, if anything, would have been sufficient to persuade de Gaulle to let Britain join the EEC. Agriculture was also a stumbling block. All this suggests that de Gaulle did not use his veto because the British bid was on the point of succeeding. Rather, there was still much to be settled.[26]

Britain had also to consider the Commonwealth. The EEC application failed in part because of Britain's concern for Commonwealth interests, though the problem might not have been in the details but in the delay caused by the necessary consultations. In the spring of 1962, convinced that EEC and Commonwealth interests were incompatible, the French warned Canada, Australia, and New Zealand that their trade would be damaged if Britain joined the EEC. Britain, meanwhile, had to reassure Commonwealth leaders repeatedly. If the success of the EEC bid depended on speed, the prospects of success must have been reduced by this prolongation of the negotiating process. Even had 'The Six' been willing to tolerate the ambivalent nature of Britain's application, tactical errors during the negotiations caused trouble and 'The Six' also came to realise that British membership would entail great disruption, including fundamental legal and institutional changes for both the EEC and Britain.[27]

The Kennedy administration wished to promote European unity. EEC enlargement was an attractive proposition and Washington gave priority to the political aspects. The Americans were frustrated that Britain seemed not to appreciate the political importance of the EEC and that Macmillan stressed the economic reasons for Britain's application for membership. When the negotiations stalled on matters like Commonwealth preferences and the subjection of British agriculture to EEC rules, Washington thought that these issues were being used by Britain as an excuse for equivocation. The Americans recommended more than once that Macmillan should simply go ahead and join the EEC and leave such difficulties to be resolved at a later date. Yet this was never a serious option for Britain, and there was no guarantee that big concessions would placate de Gaulle or be accepted by British public opinion. Retreats would also have weakened Britain, and weakness within the EEC would hardly have enabled Britain to push for the kind of unity and policy that the United States wanted.[28]

De Gaulle's vetoing of British membership of the EEC and construction of a Paris-Bonn axis frustrated various long-term aims of both Britain and the United States. This exacerbated the confusion of the time. In U.S.-European relations, in Britain's bid to join the EEC, in NATO deliberations, and even in the closer collaboration between Paris and Bonn, there were many incongruities and little was straightforward. The FRG's willingness to go along with de Gaulle, for example, was limited by Bonn's desire to retain U.S. goodwill. Before approving the Treaty of Friendship between France and the FRG in May 1963, the West Germans inserted a preamble that referred to cooperation between Europe and the United States, the need for a strong NATO and integrated armed forces, and the unification of Europe involving Britain and any other countries that wished to join in. Certainly Bonn wished to work closely with Paris; but Bonn also wished to take its own path as appropriate, a tendency that was reinforced at this time by American proposals for the MLF. Bonn's liking for aspects of the proposed multilateral nuclear force brought into sharper relief its doubts about de Gaulle's veto on British membership of the EEC and his ideas about Franco-German cooperation, because there was a danger that de Gaulle would build on these further to irritate Washington. The Americans realised that the FRG's position would greatly influence the nature of their future dealings with Europe, and the MLF project was in part a means of strengthening the FRG's commitment to NATO and preventing Franco-German nuclear coalition under de Gaulle. Kennedy assured NATO's European members that they could rely on the United States, and he put pressure on Bonn to make sure that the preamble was added to the Franco-German Treaty of Friendship. As the MLF talks proceeded, the project took clearer shape. The force was to consist of twenty-five vessels, manned by international crews and armed with Polaris missiles. It would be jointly financed and controlled by those allies who chose to participate. Each participant could veto the use of the missiles, which meant that they could not be used unless there was unanimity, and Washington kept hinting that the Europeans could expect in time to have more say in nuclear strategy and the way the MLF operated. Bonn wanted to go ahead with the MLF but the British did not want or need a collective deterrent, and neither did the French. Other European members of NATO also had misgivings. They were worried that if the Americans eventually withdrew from the MLF, it would come under Bonn's control. The difficulties surrounding the MLF in particular and U.S.-European relations in general continued to grow. Kennedy lost interest in the MLF. He decided that militarily it was unnecessary, that the United States could not expect its European allies to spend the huge sums the MLF plan required, and that the preamble to the Franco-German treaty had reduced the MLF's political importance as a tool for binding the FRG into NATO and countering de Gaulle.[29]

The MLF plan was revived by Kennedy's successor, President Lyndon B. Johnson, but little was accomplished and at the end of 1964 it was again shelved. Nevertheless, the nuclear issue frequently dominated international relations in these years. Eisenhower had come to think that the FRG should be supplied with nuclear weapons in order to facilitate U.S. military withdrawal from Europe. From late 1961, Adenauer made a nuclear agreement one of his priorities, and Soviet diplomacy was heavily influenced by the desire to prevent the FRG from acquiring a nuclear capability.[30] If the Soviets were so worried about Bonn's nuclear aspirations, however, it might be asked why they did not take the opportunities they had to negotiate a German settlement, and why a thaw was deemed to be possible even though the MLF plan—which provided for West German participation in NATO's nuclear force—was being pursued by Bonn and, periodically, by the Americans. In addition, Adenauer did not subordinate everything else to the nuclear question. When he pretended otherwise he was presumably hoping to put pressure both on the Soviets and on the FRG's allies, in order to improve his negotiating position on other matters. It did not take long for Bonn to revise its earlier opinion of the MLF plan.

The failure of the talks in Brussels for British membership of the EEC put Macmillan on the back foot, at least temporarily. In the Commons on February 5, 1963, he was asked about the economic alternatives to EEC membership. On the possibility of boosting trade with the Commonwealth, or perhaps with the Soviet bloc, the prime minister was noncommittal. On February 11 and 12 the Commons debated the EEC application and a resolution was passed expressing 'full confidence' in the government. Macmillan blamed the French for what had happened. He said that the negotiations had not been floundering but were going to succeed, which had frightened de Gaulle and led him to use his veto. In response to Macmillan's remarks, Labour leader Harold Wilson was scathing. The prime minister had 'got a lot off his chest' about de Gaulle, but had offered not 'a breath of justification for his policies over the past eighteen months'. He appeared not to know what to do next, and the people of Britain, on considering Macmillan's statements, 'will find nothing but defeatism, a certain amount of peevishness, and a complete policy vacuum'.[31]

The Times claimed that de Gaulle's action had provoked 'shock and disapproval' across Europe. The French leader had made much of the fact that 'The Six' were united and did not want to admit Britain to the EEC, yet, almost immediately, there had been denials from Bonn and elsewhere. A desire had been expressed for the negotiations in Brussels to continue. De Gaulle must have known that this was the attitude of his EEC partners, and some commentators had suggested that his purpose was to force the British to give way on crucial points before lifting his veto. *The Times* dismissed this possibility, considering de Gaulle 'a fundamentalist rather than a tactician'. If anything, his remarks about the British application made it harder for compromises to be made at Brussels. He objected not merely to the details of Britain's application, but stressed 'Britain's geography, national character and history—matters that are outside negotiation'. It was not likely that de Gaulle would change his mind. He knew that enlargement would change the EEC. French influence would be reduced, and he had acted to prevent this, but Britain should not give up. To abandon the application would be to discourage those in Europe who were prepared to resist de Gaulle. The *Economist* made similar remarks, emphasising the rush by other members of the EEC to distance themselves from French policy, de Gaulle's exaggerations with respect to Britain's unsuitability for EEC membership and the homogeneity of 'The Six', and the likelihood that if he persisted he would encourage other EEC leaders to block his proposals for its future development.[32]

The abortive effort to join the EEC added to the impression that Macmillan's government had lost its way. By-elections were going against the Conservatives, their opinion poll ratings were falling and there had been controversy over ministerial changes (Macmillan had sacked a third of his Cabinet on July 13, 1962, in an effort to restore the government's fortunes). The premier himself was regarded in some quarters as old, weak, and no longer fit to lead. For all this, however, the British application for EEC membership had some favourable results. The willingness to move closer to Europe impressed the Americans and helped Macmillan in his pursuit of U.S. assistance on defence issues. Macmillan had decided that even if the EEC bid failed, the attempt was worth making in order to shore up Britain's influence in Washington and indeed in Europe, and it was not thought that the failure of the application would be deeply damaging. Tariffs were already coming down, Britain's exports to the EEC were increasing, and it was not clear that membership of the EEC would do much to solve Britain's long-term economic problems. Economically, therefore, it did not seem so bad to remain outside the EEC for the time being. Politically, it was convenient to condemn de Gaulle and Macmillan gathered more sympathy for the EEC bid by stressing that de Gaulle only used the veto because the negotiations were close to succeeding. The Conservatives rallied while the EEC application divided the Labour Party (although Europe was not a major issue at the general election of October 1964, which Labour narrowly won). Another consideration is the wider purpose behind the application. If the basic goal was to maintain for Britain an international status that was higher than that of France and West Germany, this was achieved. De Gaulle was resisted in the EEC when he pushed for structural reforms. He had to settle for more limited arrangements. This removed a potential threat to Britain's influence in the world because it meant that 'The Six' would not replace Britain as America's main ally.[33]

Macmillan continued to think that his triumph in obtaining Polaris from the Americans mattered more than other aspects of British foreign policy. Britain's deterrent probably made the Soviets think that a second centre of command existed in the West, but it was of limited military importance and its main value was as a symbol of Britain's status. Relative economic decline mattered less when Britain had up-to-date nuclear weaponry. The promise to apply for EEC membership may have increased Macmillan's influence over the Americans, and de Gaulle's veto enabled him to argue that it was French policy that was frustrating U.S. goals in Europe. De Gaulle's confrontational approach to transatlantic relations assisted Britain while also, by angering others in the EEC and contributing to their disagreements about institutional reform, slowing down European integration. Another useful result of the EEC application to Britain concerned EFTA. As 'The Six' argued amongst themselves, the members of EFTA became more enthusiastic about the alternative body to which they belonged and Britain won approval for its proposal that all internal tariffs should be abolished by January 1967.[34]

The failed application was helpful to Britain, therefore, in various ways, but it was a defeat and upset the government's foreign policy in important respects. Given that Britain was becoming increasingly dependent on the Americans, an attempt to restore British prestige by taking on a leadership role in Europe seemed a good idea. This role, however, was not available. Macmillan feared that the world would soon be divided up into separate units: an American sphere, the Soviet bloc, and a united Europe of which Britain was not a part. In the meantime, the Test Ban Treaty of July 1963 offered some compensatory indication that Britain was still a great power. The U.S., Soviet, and British governments agreed to stop nuclear testing underwater and in the earth's atmosphere (though not underground) in what was probably the most notable sign of a thaw in the Cold War for many years.[35]

Before the Paris summit of May 1960, the Americans had been ready to go ahead with an agreement on atmospheric tests and underground tests above a certain explosive yield. They also wanted a fixed number of on-site inspections each year. Initially, the Soviets were receptive. Eisenhower and Macmillan intended to settle some of the details at Paris, but after the collapse of the summit the president decided not to revive the issue of nuclear testing for the remainder of his term. When Kennedy succeeded Eisenhower he made it clear to Macmillan that he was in favour of a test ban. The view in London was that the Americans should relax their demands regarding on-site inspections and the use of nonmilitary research and technology for military purposes, and guarantee the Soviets an equal role in control arrangements. In April 1961 the United States and Britain issued a draft test ban treaty. In May they suggested that the number of inspections per year, instead of being fixed, could vary, depending on the frequency of unexplained seismic events. Hopes for an agreement were dashed, however, by the Vienna summit, which led Kennedy to think that Khrushchev was not willing to bargain. Macmillan urged Kennedy not to give up. The Cuban missile crisis in October 1962 seemed to vindicate the American insistence on the need for a thorough inspection regime, but the crisis was ended, war was averted, American and Soviet atmospheric test cycles were coming to an end, and the Kennedy administration became more flexible after the U.S. mid-term elections of November 1962. Nevertheless, because neither the Americans nor the Soviets were willing to take the initiative and press ahead with the test ban negotiations, Macmillan decided that it was up to the British. In the spring of 1963, he made another determined effort to convince Kennedy and Khrushchev that a treaty could be agreed.[36]

Kennedy referred to Macmillan's role in arranging the treaty as 'indispensable' and congratulated the prime minister for doing so much for world peace, but Macmillan also had other reasons for pursuing a test ban. Conservative MPs were overwhelmingly in support of it, opinion polls indicated public approval, and the government had long since linked disarmament with the need to reorganise Britain's defences. Macmillan had been disappointed by the lack of progress in disarmament negotiations and by American and Soviet nuclear tests. He had welcomed Moscow's acceptance in 1961 of the necessity for on-site verification, but then the Americans complained that Moscow was trying to limit the scope of this and the talks stalled. In March 1962 Macmillan found that Kennedy was unwilling to put his full weight behind a test ban. The president's advisers were telling him not to negotiate with the Soviets on nuclear matters. There was a risk that Paris and Bonn would be further alienated, they said, and Macmillan's campaign for a test ban was primarily a manoeuvre in British party politics. In time, though, Kennedy decided to find out if Khrushchev was really prepared to sign a treaty. The Soviet leader raised the old problem—that the Americans were demanding too much in terms of inspection and verification because they wanted to spy on Soviet technology—but Kennedy began to speak more about peace and détente and in June 1962 he met Macmillan for detailed discussions. Macmillan was keen to build up momentum. He managed to obtain certain undertakings from Kennedy on the test ban while delaying action on the MLF, and in July 1962 Moscow announced that a partial ban on testing might be arranged. Underground testing was dropped because the inspection arrangements could not be settled. Macmillan kept guiding Kennedy forward, praising his courage, and offering support when the negotiations were condemned in the U.S. Congress or newspapers. When the treaty was signed Macmillan was widely praised. He had hoped for a more comprehensive measure, but at least, he reflected, an important step had been taken. Later he suggested that Kennedy had let a fine opportunity slip away. Kennedy's difficulties in Congress had obliged the president to be cautious, but he was satisfied with the Test Ban Treaty of 1963 because he expected it to make possible other agreements.[37]

The treaty marked a success for British persistence and showed that Britain could still influence U.S. policy on key international issues. Yet it also underlined, once again, that the wish for close relations with the United States limited Britain's ability to act independently in the Cold War. During the period that led up to the signing of the treaty, Macmillan was motivated largely by domestic political considerations, international opinion (especially that of the nonaligned states), and a desire to stop the arms race. Macmillan's strategic and moral arguments had some effect in Washington, but Kennedy and his advisers thought that it would be better to continue the arms race than to lose it, and the White House had also to listen to military and industrial leaders who wanted to go on testing and developing weapons. The Test Ban Treaty did not cover underground tests and the nuclear arms race did not end. For the Americans, this represented an appropriate political compromise: atmospheric testing would be banned and underground testing accelerated (in fact, testing in the atmosphere continued—France and China did not stop atmospheric testing until 1974 and 1980, respectively). Khrushchev's treatment of Kennedy at the Vienna summit led the latter to resist Macmillan's proposals for a comprehensive test ban, and Washington's reservations only increased when the Soviets unilaterally ended a voluntary moratorium in August 1961. This made the Americans more insistent on the need for inspection and control arrangements that Moscow considered excessive. Macmillan, meanwhile, came under pressure from the antitest lobby at home, grew more concerned about the possible alienation of developing countries, and tried to persuade Kennedy that a test ban would not only prevent nuclear proliferation but also speed up the process of East-West détente. Macmillan also made good use of humanitarian arguments that were reinforced by the growing concern about nuclear fallout. At the same time, his desire to moderate the arms race was intimately connected with the intention to maintain a credible British deterrent. The Test Ban Treaty was signed because the British persuaded the Americans to adopt a specific goal and made sure that the effort was kept up until that goal was reached. Nevertheless, a temporary convergence of U.S. and Soviet interests after the Cuban missile crisis was also a key determinant, and to claim that the treaty was as much a British as an American and Soviet achievement is probably to exaggerate. Though Macmillan had been working hard for the Test Ban Treaty, and was proud of it, it did not guarantee that Britain would continue to have a decisive say in international nuclear matters. The Cuban missile crisis confirmed that the main issues would have to be resolved by the two superpowers. The treaty was signed not simply because Macmillan willed it, but because Kennedy and Khrushchev were ready to make a deal.[38]

Macmillan only pursued a test ban vigorously *after* the British had tested their hydrogen bomb and the Cuban missile crisis had demonstrated their limited influence during a superpower confrontation. A test ban was certainly in Britain's interests, for Britain could not possibly compete in a quickening nuclear arms race, and Macmillan also realised that in arguing for a test ban he could garner support domestically. The pursuit of a test ban went hand in hand with securing Polaris from the Americans. Macmillan thought that he would be better able to justify maintaining the British deterrent if he also made an effort to slow down the arms race. The signing of the Test Ban Treaty was a personal success for the prime minister. He had overcome the reluctance of some of his colleagues and resistance from Kennedy's advisers; he had raised his own standing as a world statesman; and he had apparently been able to deal with the Americans and the Soviets as an equal.[39]

Macmillan believed in talking to the Soviets, much as Churchill had, and he also accepted Churchill's 'three circles' idea. Britain must try to balance the three, Macmillan had decided, for to focus only on one might damage British interests in the other two. Yet attachment to the Americans frequently took priority at a time when Britain could not do without U.S. friendship and nuclear weapons. British attempts to promote thaw and play a bigger role in global events were sometimes unrewarding. Macmillan helped to organise the Paris summit of May 1960, but it collapsed over the spy plane controversy. Britain was not invited to join in other important meetings, such as the Camp David talks of 1959 between Eisenhower and Khrushchev and the Vienna summit of 1961. Macmillan's own efforts at détente, especially his visit to Moscow in 1959, were condemned in NATO. As for the Test Ban Treaty of 1963, it did promote thaw and proved to be a useful environmental measure, but it did not stop the arms race and Britain did not have the money and technology to keep up with the United States and Soviet Union in this race. Reliance on the Americans complicated Britain's dealings with France, the FRG, and the rest of continental Europe. The application to join the EEC was based on mixed motives and had mixed results. On one hand, it was a mark of confidence, a bid for primacy, a sign that the British had recognised that mutual economic, political, and security advantages might come out of greater coordination and integration. On the other hand, the application indicated anxiety about the condition of the British economy and jealousy about the growing prosperity of 'The Six', a search for new opportunities to exercise influence as other options were being lost, and a desire to be more useful to the Americans in order to get favourable treatment from them in return. The British attitude towards Europe remained equivocal. De Gaulle's veto was a setback, but not a disaster. Britain had opened the way for closer links with Europe, impressing elements in the EEC and in Washington in the process. Britain had not had to choose between the United States and Europe, and had ensured the ongoing credibility of its nuclear deterrent—the essential basis of British defence planning.

CHAPTER 4

CHANGING CONTEXTS

The need to balance the 'three circles' and the danger that in its involvement with one of the three, Britain would damage its standing in the
others, added greatly to the Macmillan government's problems with the
Commonwealth. In trying to keep the Commonwealth happy, Britain ran
the risk of annoying the United States and Western Europe—the Americans because of Britain's inability to change the antiwestern stance of
such Commonwealth countries as India and Ghana, and the Europeans
because of the commercial preferences for Commonwealth products.[1]
These considerations reinforced the prime minister's notion that to focus
too heavily on one circle would hamper Britain's dealings with the other
two. The extension of Cold War rivalries into Africa affected Britain's
links with the Commonwealth. In Europe, meanwhile, the nature of the
enemy seemed to be changing. The Cold War was transformed as economic, social, cultural, and political developments intensified the competition between East and West and reshaped some of the military, strategic,
and diplomatic relationships that had been established since the Second
World War.

Difficulties with the Commonwealth constantly troubled the British government in this period. Ethnic, tribal, and religious divisions in the colonies sometimes led to violence as independence was granted and the British withdrew. The Commonwealth prime ministers' conference of March 1961 was a stormy affair, mainly because of apartheid in South Africa; South Africa left the Commonwealth in May 1961. The conference of September 1962 was overshadowed by Britain's bid to join the EEC: members of the Commonwealth were concerned that Britain could not be relied upon to safeguard their economic interests. Britain's immigration policy was also impugned in this period. New limits were imposed in July 1962. Anti-immigrant feeling was growing in Britain and the influx had been causing anxiety for some time, but as former colonies joined the Commonwealth in the early and mid-1960s it became truly multiracial and Britain had to take more account of its members' sensibilities.[2]

In their efforts to manage decolonisation, the British faced similar problems to those of the French, Belgians, and Portuguese. Political change in Africa, for example, did not come in the form of an orderly, planned process controlled by governments in the imperial capitals. Rather, it came for a variety of local, metropolitan, and international reasons, and it came more quickly than many contemporaries expected, whether African nationalists or colonial rulers. Between January 1957, when Macmillan asked the Cabinet's colonial policy committee for a 'profit and loss' assessment of each colony, and October 1964, when a Labour government took office in Britain for the first time in over thirteen years, about half of Britain's formal dependencies became independent or had dates set for independence. Decolonisation gathered momentum but was complicated by domestic party politics, the Cold War, anticolonial sentiment in the UN, controversy over apartheid, Britain's application to join the EEC, war in the Congo, the confrontation between Malaysia and Indonesia, and disorder in Aden and Southern Arabia. Many observers assumed that decolonisation was economically necessary and that the abandonment of empire would enable Britain to take advantage of better financial and commercial opportunities in Europe and the United States. Yet decolonisation was itself expensive. Former colonies expected and received generous financial settlements and Britain continued to fund their economic development. In 1961 the colonial secretary, Iain Macleod, argued that these costs could not be avoided if Britain's influence was to be preserved and communism kept at bay (he was talking specifically about Tanganyika). That decolonisation was not simply a matter of saving money is further indicated by the debates surrounding withdrawal from particular territories after 1964. Financial motives appear to have mattered less than concern about Britain's reputation and pressure from the UN. Britain's turn to Europe was prompted largely by economic considerations. Geopolitical needs were also important, and British leaders repeatedly declared that they would not take the country into the EEC if it meant cutting ties with the Commonwealth. Despite the decreasing importance to Britain of trade with the Commonwealth, the Cold War and Britain's strategic interests made it important not to turn away from Africa and Asia completely. A smooth transfer of power, it was thought, was the way to turn a former colony into a useful friend, and Macmillan maintained that nationalism could be harnessed to prevent the spread of communism. Local and regional conditions also shaped British policy. The pace of change in East Africa owed a lot to the Congo crisis, and the creation of the Federation of Malaysia in 1963 was dictated largely by defence needs (this federation brought together Malaya, Singapore, Sabah, and Sarawak). In these cases, economic and financial interests might have been important but they do not appear to have been decisive.[3]

Concerned as the government was to maintain advantageous links with the Commonwealth, it is not surprising that ministers had misgivings about limits on immigration. Domestic political pressure and the widespread notion that housing, welfare services, and even British culture would be detrimentally affected unless controls were imposed helps to explain the legislation of 1962, but Macmillan and the colonial secretary at the time, Alan Lennox-Boyd, were worried about the likely impact on Commonwealth unity. For several years, ministers had debated immigration without any consensus emerging, and along with the reluctance to alienate the Commonwealth there was uncertainty about the electoral consequences for the government. Within the Conservative Party there was a strong attachment to the colonies and the Commonwealth. This bond was partly emotional and symbolic and partly also a legacy of the party's traditions. Commonwealth enthusiasts complained that the government was failing to provide a lead and that more practical and constructive measures were needed to maximise the benefits of the Commonwealth for all concerned. As immigration became a more pressing concern, though, Conservative right-wingers grew uneasy. Empire lost some of its appeal to them, which probably helped the government to accelerate the pace of decolonisation. In the Labour Party, meanwhile, decolonisation was an issue on which there was general agreement. The party leader between 1955 and 1963, Hugh Gaitskell, had to deal with internal discord on the Labour Party's constitution and the nuclear deterrent, but on decolonisation and immigration there were few clashes. Most Labour MPs were committed to a multiracial Commonwealth, opposed discrimination, and were quick to exploit the difficulties that immigration posed for the Conservatives, although by 1962 there were some murmurings against excessive immigration both within the Labour Party and the trade unions.[4]

The Commonwealth needed structural reform and a new secretariat was established in 1965. Although British leaders were not initially keen on this proposal, they recognised that change was unavoidable. The Commonwealth was growing, there were complaints that it lacked direction and meaning, its newer members wanted more influence, and in London it was decided that it would be better to guide than to resist reforms. While there was concern that administrative adjustments would reduce Britain's role as leader of the Commonwealth, it was hoped that the secretariat would facilitate cooperation and provide a useful forum for addressing economic inequality and racial antagonism. Britain paid 30 percent of the secretariat's costs, by far the largest share. Britain, Australia, and Canada together paid more than half of its costs.[5]

Economically, the Commonwealth and sterling area were becoming less important. This had ramifications for Britain's global position and prompted further reassessments of Britain's international priorities. In 1950 the Commonwealth had taken 47.7 percent of Britain's exports. In 1960 it took 40.2 percent, and only 24.4 percent in 1970. The proportion of imports that came from the Commonwealth fell from 41.9 percent in 1950 to 34.6 percent in 1960. By 1970 only 25.9 percent of Britain's imports came from the Commonwealth. In the same period, Britain's trade with the United States and the EEC increased: they took 16.3 percent of Britain's exports in 1950 and 33.3 percent in 1970, and they provided 20.8 percent of Britain's imports in 1950 and 33 percent in 1970. British overseas investment was shifting as well. About 60 percent went to the sterling area in 1960, and only 38 percent in 1970.[6]

For a while, there was a desire to foster close relations with developing countries in Africa, the Middle East, and Asia, especially former colonies, because these were seen as a means of counterbalancing other relationships. Some British leaders disliked the growing dependence upon America, did not want to be locked into NATO, and opposed European integration. The concern was that Britain's capacity for unilateral action was being eroded. To these political concerns were added financial motives: the sterling area was still considered an asset and worth protecting. After Suez had demonstrated that Britain's ability to act independently in the world was limited, and circumstances at home and in the empire pointed Macmillan's government towards quicker decolonisation, it seemed that the best course would be to seek more influence within the West. This entailed closer cooperation with the Americans rather than with numerous developing nations across Africa and Asia, and the bid to join the EEC was a related matter. For Britain to focus on the least dynamic sectors in world trade would be disastrous, it was believed, and the government set about reducing Britain's most disadvantageous commitments around the world and improving Britain's position politically and economically in the West. Withdrawal from the colonies proved to be troublesome, but probably less so than such other tasks as obtaining nuclear assistance from the Americans, easing East-West tension, defending sterling as a major currency, and securing entry to the EEC.[7]

The spread of the Cold War into Africa and Asia created problems for Britain and the West. The antiwestern rhetoric of 'racism' and 'imperialism' was one of the most negative aspects of Cold War ideology and was not without impact on newly independent states. Their ill feeling towards the former colonial powers increased, exacerbating the violence and instability to which many of them succumbed. Wars broke out, notably in Congo in the summer of 1960. Congo shared borders with the British territories of Uganda, Tanganyika, and Northern Rhodesia. The political situation in these territories was becoming very delicate and the turmoil in Congo was bound to affect them. With the French and Belgians quitting Africa, Macmillan was sure that it would be unwise for Britain to remain, and what happened in Congo increased his eagerness to prepare Britain's African colonies quickly and thoroughly for self-government. He did not want the British to be accused of leaving a mess behind when they departed. The Congo crisis drew in the two superpowers and the UN. Macmillan feared a great power conflict, for the international situation at this juncture looked ominous owing to the U2 incident and the unproductive Paris summit of May 1960, and ongoing anxieties over Berlin, the German question, and disarmament. An incident in July 1960 did not help. Operating from a base in Britain, an American survey aircraft on a mission over the Arctic Ocean was shot down by a Soviet fighter. Washington insisted that the U.S. plane had not entered Soviet air space, while in Britain there was a revival of the controversy surrounding the presence of American bases.[8]

Congo had been a Belgian colony. Disturbances there prompted Belgium to grant independence, but a civil war began as Congo's new government was challenged by secessionists in the mineral-rich province of Katanga, in the south of the country. Congo's prime minister was Patrice Lumumba, who favoured central control and was widely regarded as a communist. An opportunist in foreign policy, he was willing to accept help from both sides in the Cold War. Congo's size, strategic location, and mineral wealth attracted Moscow's attention and the Soviets, seeking influence in Africa as the European colonial powers pulled out, established close ties with Lumumba's regime. Khrushchev wanted to open a new front in the Cold War by recruiting allies among the newly independent states of Africa. Congo was too far away for the use of combat troops, but the Soviets sent planes, vehicles, and guns, and provided diplomatic support at the UN. Khrushchev was sure that he could buy Lumumba's allegiance.[9]

The Belgians intervened to protect their assets in Congo and sided with the Katangan rebels. The country descended into anarchy. Europeans were murdered and other atrocities abounded. To African nationalists, Belgium's intervention was unacceptable. Lumumba appealed to the United Nations, which ordered Belgium to withdraw and arranged to send in a peacekeeping force. The Americans disliked Congo's government and covert action against it was stepped up when Lumumba sought Soviet aid in August 1960. The overriding goal was to prevent Soviet gains in Africa. The Eisenhower administration had been trying to make friends there, hoping to contain communism and gradually to build up a neutralist buffer. During the war in Congo the Americans worked mainly through the UN. A 10,000-strong force was sent in, heavily reliant on U.S. money, personnel, and advice. When western hostages were seized in Stanleyville, the Americans assisted a Belgian rescue attempt that provoked an outcry from African leaders, who condemned what they saw as the revival of colonial ventures on their continent. Khrushchev became a noisy critic of the UN secretary-general, Dag Hammarskjöld, who was killed in a plane crash in September 1961 while on a mission to Congo. The war continued into the early weeks of 1963, when the Katangan rebels accepted that there would be no secession. UN forces stayed on, but financial pressures necessitated their withdrawal in June 1964.[10]

In 1960 Eisenhower had sanctioned a plot to kill Lumumba because he was persuaded that Congo might become another Cuba. Before the Central Intelligence Agency (CIA) had the chance to carry out the intended assassination, however, Lumumba was murdered by a rival faction in Congo. This occurred early in 1961, just after Kennedy's inauguration as U.S. president. Kennedy allowed CIA involvement in Congo to increase. While his administration backed the UN peacekeeping operation, it was also pulling strings behind the scenes. Kennedy put American influence and resources behind right-wing groups as Congo descended further into chaos. Congolese politicians were bribed. Funding and weapons were provided for supporters of the central government. Before long the CIA placed its own mercenaries in Congo. Some were Cuban exiles, veterans from the Bay of Pigs, and they included pilots who were instructed to carry out bombing raids against the Katangans. Kennedy wished to create a stable regime in Congo that would be friendly to the West and protect foreign investments.[11]

The situation was not improved by the increasing number of foreign military advisers and mercenaries in Katanga. The UN's envoy, Irish diplomat Conor Cruise O'Brien, insisted that there could be no settlement until they were removed, for they were encouraging Katangan resistance. O'Brien advocated vigorous UN action. Soon the Americans, British, and Belgians were complaining about his confrontational approach. In September 1961 Kennedy agreed that Belgian personnel should leave Katanga as soon as possible, but he also called for restraint and reconciliation. As UN forces made progress against the secessionists in Katanga, Kennedy argued that the UN's task was not to defeat secession militarily, but to persuade Katanga's leaders to cooperate with the government of Congo. The United States, Britain, and Western Europe hoped for negotiations that would allow Katanga a measure of autonomy and preserve their economic interests, but the Soviets and many of the new nations across Africa and Asia argued that the Katangan secession should be ended by force. Macmillan feared that the UN would go too far and that a war to restore the Congolese government's control over Katanga would open the door for extremists to take power. They would rely on Soviet backing and the USSR could then step in and seize the resources of Katanga. Though Macmillan was not in favour of Katanga's secession, nor did he want a united Congo to be a communist Congo. He was also frustrated by the quarrelling at the UN. There was no explicit Security Council authorisation to end the secession by force, but O'Brien wanted a quick solution to what he regarded as a local problem.[12]

Instability in Congo had consequences for the plans Britain was putting together for its colonies in Africa. The Conservatives were already divided on such issues as majority rule, and economic considerations had also to be taken into account. During the summer of 1960, Macmillan was pressed to accept Katanga's declaration of independence. British businessmen, Conservative MPs, and colonial administrators in Africa all wanted Katanga to be peaceful and amenable, and when the secessionist leader Moise Tshombe was arrested in April 1961 they urged the government to work for his release. Macmillan became concerned about division within his party as UN forces advanced against the Katangans in the autumn of 1961. A group of Conservative MPs protested on Katanga's behalf, and did so again at the end of the year when the government announced that Britain would supply the UN forces with arms. Why, it was asked, should Britain assist in the destruction of a friendly government on the borders of British territories, especially when such action would also endanger British investments? British companies were heavily involved in the region. Tanganyika Concessions had an interest in Katanga's copper mines, for example. Its members and backers favoured paternal rule and opposed political change in Africa. The Joint East and Central Africa Board, which represented businessmen and settlers, also stood against decolonisation and the Macmillan government's decision on Katanga. Many Conservative MPs sympathised. A range of political and economic groups combined together in the 'Katanga lobby' and tried to undermine the government's policy of assisting the UN to suppress the Katangan rebellion.[13]

The government felt itself bound to support the UN but knew it had to be careful. There was more behind the sympathy for Katanga than economic self-interest. Tshombe and his colleagues were would-be allies of the West and they were close to members of the administration in Northern Rhodesia. Macmillan supposed, however, that any blatant sign of partiality would push Congo's leaders completely over to Moscow, and thinking of the Korean example he envisaged a dismembered Congo with a large part of the country under communist rule. Macmillan had no wish to annoy African and Asian opinion, which was sensitive about colonialism, but at the same time he could not simply stand by and see the Katangans defeated, for the likely result would be a burgeoning of communist influence across central Africa. The crisis helped to accelerate Britain's preparations for the handover of power to its colonies in the region. It was hoped that the promise of independence would stop disorder from spreading, even if this hope ran up against the growing opposition to majority rule. Katanga's leaders were hailed as exemplars, for they were willing to cooperate with white Europeans and had rejected extreme nationalism. White settlers, especially in Northern and Southern Rhodesia, condemned the UN's military action against Katanga, blamed the UN for the anti-European mood in Africa, and claimed that Congo showed what could happen when black rule was established without white guidance. Unrest in Northern Rhodesia appeared to confirm that bloody conflict was indeed beginning to extend into British areas.[14]

Macmillan could not expect much help from the Americans. He and Kennedy regularly discussed the situation in Congo during 1961 and 1962, and there were disagreements between them. In 1961 the Americans insisted that Britain should support UN action to bring down Tshombe and in March 1962 Kennedy urged Macmillan to provide money to pay for the UN operation. Macmillan argued that Tshombe should not be removed while Britain was still engaged in awkward conversations about the future of the Central African Federation. Formed in 1953, this federation consisted of Northern and Southern Rhodesia and Nyasaland and would be dissolved in 1963. Washington had little sympathy for Britain's colonial troubles, however, and accused London of encouraging Tshombe to obstruct a peace settlement that would reunify Congo. Tshombe did accept a federal constitution for Congo, but then in October 1962 he repudiated it. At Nassau two months later, Kennedy and his aides argued that Tshombe would never keep to any agreements he made, and Macmillan could not defend him any more in view of Britain's need for Polaris. Tshombe was ousted early in 1963 and went temporarily into exile. American influence over Congo's central government had been increasing, and once the country was reunited Soviet personnel were expelled. The British had their own economic and political interests in central Africa, and although Anglo-American cooperation was indicated by the common desire to prevent the spread of communism, after that danger had passed there were obvious differences between London and Washington. The conduct of U Thant, Hammarskjöld's successor as secretary-general of the UN, brought further confusion. As UN forces advanced in Katanga and it became clear that Tshombe—though he alternated between accepting and rejecting terms for a settlement—would soon have to capitulate, U Thant became inflexible, would not listen to the western powers, refused to offer concessions, and announced that the UN's intervention would not be ended prematurely. U Thant simply waited for Tshombe to accept defeat. Officials of Congo's central government were brought in by the UN to administer Katanga. By now the British were urging Tshombe to work with the UN, but the Congolese government condemned Britain's link with the secessionist leader and threatened to sever diplomatic relations. Finally an agreement was worked out between January 15 and 17, 1963.[15]

Apart from the wish to prevent Soviet interference, Washington was also motivated by a general concern for peace and order. As the former colonial powers moved out of Africa, it had been decided, America should make sure that viable and stable states were left behind. In this context the secession of Katanga had to be ended, otherwise chaos might spread through the whole region. Yet Tshombe was regarded in the West as a reliable anticommunist, and several of America's European allies wanted access to Katanga's minerals. Tshombe's insistence that he was willing to cooperate with the UN in finding a settlement encouraged London and Paris to oppose the measures favoured in Washington, and although African and Asian members of the UN demanded more direct and robust intervention against the secessionists, the British repeatedly declared that the UN should not use coercive methods or seek to impose agreement. Britain's reluctance to support the UN's military operation angered the Americans. Unlike the United States, Britain was willing to accept a loose federated system in Congo on the grounds that to demand Tshombe's participation in a more integrated system would be to ensure future instability.[16]

When the war in Congo came up for discussion in the Commons, fiery altercations resulted. On March 15, 1961, Labour MP Denis Healey complained that British policy was frustrating the UN effort. It was offending African and Asian states and associating Britain too closely with the ill-considered Belgian intervention on Katanga's side. Healey urged ministers 'to realise that continued conduct of this kind by any western government will throw the whole of Africa into the hands of the Russians.

We have a duty to support the United Nations…even though Belgium is our ally'. For the government, Edward Heath protested that Britain *was* assisting the UN effort. Africans could hardly question Britain's motives, he added, at a time when colonies were being freed and aid was being provided to help the continent advance economically, socially, and politically. Heath stressed that African nations were themselves divided about the UN's involvement in Congo and that it was far too simplistic to claim that they were suspicious of Britain or hostile to the West. Some of them wanted the UN to pursue a different course altogether. As for the government's position, 'our responsibility in the Congo has been limited to our share in sustaining the effort of the United Nations and also in trying to ensure the safety of our nationals'. There was 'no desire of any kind to intervene in the affairs of the Congo. Our only interest has been in its development, in the maintenance of its independence, and in allowing the Congo to have its individual liberty and law and order restored and to be able to make progress'. As the conflict in Congo continued, many Conservative MPs became more vocal in their opposition to the UN operation, whatever the claims of the government front bench. In February 1963, when it was announced that Britain would be providing more money for the UN, a demand was made for a full and impartial investigation into the military action in Congo. Accusations were made about looting and other outrages, and it was said that the conflict would not have escalated had UN forces not entered Katanga. The undersecretary of state for foreign affairs, Peter Thomas, replied that the government supported the UN operation and wished to ease the UN's financial problems (caused mainly by the failure of members to pay their subscriptions). Labour MPs were appalled by the attacks on the UN, took Thomas's unwillingness energetically to repudiate them as further proof that the government had never been in sympathy with the UN's actions in Congo, and insisted that it was in Britain's interests to support the UN and that the government's policy during the Congolese crisis had cost Britain a lot of goodwill and prestige around the world.[17]

This was also the view of *The Times*, which lamented the government's inability—despite the help it had given to the UN operation—to convince its critics at home and abroad that it was doing enough. Ministers had 'incurred concentrated odium for their stand for negotiations rather than a settlement imposed by force'. They had given no unconditional support to Tshombe's regime, but had sought 'a reconciliation that would do justice to Katanga's claim to a fair measure of self-determination'. The policy 'was a gift to Britain's enemies, however, and the fruit of it may be sour'. *The Times* argued that Tshombe had made a mistake in not abiding by the proposals made to him through the UN. The Katangans would have benefited from a general amnesty and a measure of autonomy within the federal Congolese state. Tshombe had forfeited all this by his vain effort 'to bankrupt the UN into pulling out of Katanga'. UN personnel would now have to remain in Congo to oversee a settlement. Economic recovery and efficient administration were needed, and relations between the federal government and the different parts of Congo would have to be sorted out, all of which entailed 'a vast salvage operation' for which 'no end is in sight'. The *Guardian* had noted with concern the British government's embarrassment as Tshombe went on rejecting proposals for a settlement. Foreign secretary Lord Home had declared that the British government did not regard coercion as an appropriate way to promote a solution, yet he admitted that if the UN approved sanctions there was 'nothing we could do'.[18]

Although the end of the war brought some relief to the government, it did not remove those political and colonial problems that had been highlighted and exacerbated by what was happening in Congo. Britain's backing for the UN intervention had been combined with efforts to restrain the UN and discourage moves to bring down Tshombe. The Katangans were defeated, however, and this outcome prompted black African leaders in the British territories to be more assertive. The presence in the region of UN forces boosted the cause of anticolonialism, created an expectation of imminent freedom, undermined the authority of the British government and of local white elites, and weakened the appeal of Britain's political proposals. White fears of African nationalism, meanwhile, increased as a result of the atrocities committed in Congo, sometimes by UN forces, and many whites accused the

Macmillan government of weakness and prevarication. In Southern Rhodesia, white leaders were adamant that they would not share power with blacks. The violence in Congo prompted many white people living there to flee beyond its borders, and this had a wider impact because many of the whites in British areas decided to leave Africa altogether. Britain's plans for decolonisation were partly based on the assumption that people of British and European stock would remain, but it was too late to reverse schemes that were being implemented. Non-African involvement in African affairs was becoming much more difficult. For instance, Lumumba had taken Congo into the Union of African States, formed in 1958. This body was led by Ghana, which had been granted independence from Britain in 1957. Ghana's president Kwame Nkrumah, a vocal advocate of African self-rule and socialism, urged the independent nations of the continent to cooperate for their mutual benefit. He sent troops into Congo to help Lumumba's regime and tried to deal with the Katangan crisis through an African joint command. For Britain, and indeed for other outsiders, the lesson was clear: Africans wished to solve African problems in their own way.[19]

Events in Africa showed that it would not be easy for Britain to continue to act like a great power. The Cuban missile crisis had a similar tendency, as did the Berlin question and the disputes over European integration. Britain's role in Europe and beyond was directly affected by the course of the Cold War. The communist adversary was changing. There were important developments in the Soviet Union and eastern bloc during the late 1950s and 1960s. Moscow began to relax its control over satellite governments, although the intervention in Hungary in 1956 suggested that change would have its limits. Reform was seen mainly in economic affairs. There was a gradual retreat from rigid planning and before long market forces were tolerated. At the end of the 1950s, economic growth slowed down. In order to rectify this, more freedom was allowed. These developments were most obvious in Hungary (and in the more independent Yugoslavia). The GDR, Poland, Rumania, and other states did not experience the same level of economic improvement, and even in Hungary it was a slow process.

Planning remained the norm, which discouraged innovation and meant that trade within the bloc was vital. Policy was guided by Comecon. Moscow's original intention was to use economic union to effect an international socialist division of labour: manufacturing would be boosted in East Germany and Czechoslovakia, for example, while Rumania was to remain primarily agricultural. This dictatorial approach had to be given up as unrealistic. In time, each member of Comecon aimed for 50 percent of output to be industrial. The attempt to alter the balance between industry and agriculture caused problems, but Comecon did stimulate trade within the bloc. During the 1950s, the volume of trade between countries in Eastern Europe was double what it had been in the 1930s. The USSR remained the most important trading partner for the satellite states. Trade with Western Europe declined dramatically, because the Soviets and their allies concentrated on Comecon as the answer to the economic integration that was under way in the West.[20]

Moscow usually dealt with each satellite on a bilateral basis, but Comecon's role expanded quickly during the mid-1950s as new committees were established and more attention was given to joint planning, investment, transportation links, and other structural improvements. Trade remained mostly bilateral, but it increased and it was encouraged in other ways. In 1954 the Soviet Union restored economic relations with Yugoslavia, for instance, and in the same year there was an economic and financial agreement with China. As part of the latter deal, Moscow handed over mixed Soviet-Chinese companies to Peking. In due course, Soviet-controlled enterprises in the GDR and Rumania were placed under the regimes in East Berlin and Bucharest, respectively, and in 1956 the USSR provided cheap credit for Bulgaria. Unrest within the bloc also resulted in economic agreements as the Kremlin sought to make loyalty worthwhile. After the troubles of 1956, for example, Poland benefited from debt cancellation and Hungary was granted a new aid package. The Soviet Union also established closer economic links with developing countries outside Europe in these years, notably Argentina and India. As a result of détente, meanwhile, trade between East and West increased. The USSR's imports and exports more than doubled between 1950 and 1958. Within the bloc there was accelerated expansion for selected industries, especially in Hungary, which benefited from access to the vast Soviet market and an increased volume of trade with Comecon members.[21]

A relaxation of economic controls in certain parts of the eastern bloc was matched by greater freedom in social and cultural spheres, although these changes should not be exaggerated because the party line was still dominant. Objectionable books were banned. Many writers and scientists left the bloc or were sent into exile. In spite of this, attempts to Sovietise the areas under Moscow's control were mostly unsuccessful. Soviet culture had no popular basis in the bloc and was often seen as an imposition. The same was true of government authority, and this lack of a popular basis made it easier to blame the state for social, economic, and other problems. The powerful central state apparatus was designed to ensure discipline, but its use of force and terror was a gift to critics and propagandists in the West who condemned the Soviet system, the crackdowns, executions, purges, and persecution.[22]

In the GDR, protest was developed and sustained by groups that mostly believed in socialism but tried to alter it from within. Strikes and revolts had not worked, for the state had crushed them, and it was clear that the West was not going to intervene militarily. Therefore, the aim was peaceful change. Throughout the bloc, indeed, various groups focused on the possibility of reform and made sure that the aspiration was never entirely suppressed. Yugoslavia had managed to break away from Moscow, but though the West courted Yugoslav leader Josip Broz Tito, his independence did not cause the Soviet bloc to collapse. Later there was another break, when Albania left Comecon in 1961 and the Warsaw Pact in 1968, but Albania did not turn to the West. An isolated and economically backward state, Albania began to draw closer to China. During the 1970s, Rumanian leader Nicolae Ceausescu appeared to take a more independent line in foreign policy, and in the West it was thought that his quarrels with Moscow might lead to Rumania's detachment from the bloc. This did not occur, and in any case Rumania's economic underdevelopment and human rights abuses hardly endeared Ceausescu to the West. At the same time, however, the large private sector in Polish agriculture and ongoing development of a market economy in Hungary did confirm that the eastern bloc was far from monolithic.[23]

The response to Yugoslavia's defiant stand against Moscow gives some idea of what the West might have done, had the eastern bloc broken up. Tension had developed between Tito and the Soviets during the Second World War. This continued as Tito refused to follow Moscow's instructions in the postwar period. The West offered economic and military aid and in the early 1950s Yugoslavia's imports from the United States and Western Europe rose from 25 percent to 65 percent of Yugoslavia's overall trade in just three years. The United States spent $2.3 billion on aid to Yugoslavia, including $719 million on military supplies. Washington hoped that 'Titoism' would affect the wider region and that at least some of the communist states in Eastern Europe would separate from Moscow. The goal of dividing adversaries influenced U.S. attitudes towards the USSR's satellites for several years. Yugoslavia remained open to the West during the 1950s and this orientation in Tito's foreign policy was reinforced by the 'Programme of the League of Communists of Yugoslavia' of 1958. By this time, the relative openness to the West was closely linked with Yugoslavia's commitment to nonalignment. Tito wanted the benefits of friendly relations with the West and sought at the same time to avoid conflict with Moscow. The combination of openness and nonalignment suited his purposes. The Soviets were worried that nonalignment would attract support among their satellites and weaken Moscow's influence outside the bloc, but they did not directly challenge Tito's stance for fear of making matters worse.[24]

Tito's friendly gestures probably mattered less to the West, especially the Americans, than Yugoslavia's strategic position. The western powers knew that their own security could be enhanced if they built Yugoslavia up as a barrier against Soviet expansion. Indeed, the former head of the policy planning staff at the U.S. state department, George Kennan, had stressed in the early days of the Cold War that the West needed a militarily uncommitted area in Europe, an area in which political authority could develop independently of Soviet control, because this would minimise Soviet influence. Yugoslavia's economic frailties represented a lever that could be used to good effect, and Britain joined the Americans in this endeavour. London agreed to aid Yugoslavia to the tune of tens of millions of pounds in the early 1950s. France also made a contribution. Tito needed this help and goodwill, but he never intended to become a formal ally of the West or make Yugoslavia a democracy, and he occasionally stood up to the West in order to satisfy hardliners at home. Tito moved towards an understanding with Khrushchev in the late 1950s. Yugoslavia's economic links with the Soviet bloc improved, and in order to preserve Tito's independence the western powers continued to send aid, provide credit, and cancel debts. Tito's statements to the effect that no strings should be attached to the West's assistance did not go down well in Washington, and the American attitude hardened under Kennedy. Nevertheless, a wave of reforms in Yugoslavia during the mid-1960s led to further loans and trade agreements and in 1970, with détente the order of the day, Yugoslavia concluded an agreement with the EEC. Tito continued to steer a middle course between East and West.[25]

Washington had decided that Yugoslavia was not an enemy because it was not a tool of Soviet expansionism. In the mid-1950s the British accepted this analysis, but there remained some distance between London and Washington on the matter of relations with Yugoslavia. They did agree that they should make the most of Tito's rift with Moscow, but the British were always more cautious. They disliked the 'liberation' rhetoric of the Americans, had less faith in the West's ability to draw satellites away from the USSR, and remained sceptical about the advantages that aid for Tito would deliver. London thought that Tito should offer more in return for what he was getting, and that the best policy in Eastern Europe would be to let the satellites quarrel amongst themselves. Crucially, the British advised, these satellites should not be promised a level of support that the West could not give. At the same time, if Yugoslavia really could be used as a wedge to break up the Soviet bloc the British were ready to help, with aid, propaganda, trade, and diplomatic contact. Yet Britain persistently refused to make economic sacrifices for Yugoslavia. The preference was for the type of trade that would benefit the British economy, and London thought that aid should be limited so that Tito received just enough to allow his regime to survive. This would show the world that a communist state did not have to rely on Moscow. The Americans were more generous: they wanted Yugoslavia's economic success to be exemplary, to demonstrate the full benefits of cooperation with the West. After the Korean War increased western fears about possible Soviet aggression in Europe, and the idea spread in NATO that Yugoslavia could be a strategic barrier, military aid was increased. Again, the Americans gave Yugoslavia far more than the British did, which embarrassed London, but in time the military links had to be scaled down because Tito did not wish to commit himself and the Americans could not be sure how the West's aid would be used. Within NATO there was also a concern that sensitive information about the alliance might inadvertently be revealed. The British and the Americans realised that Tito's main goal was nonalignment. He would keep his distance from Moscow but he was also determined not to become too reliant on the West.[26]

In the 1950s and 1960s Yugoslavia was an exceptional case. Other threats to unity and order in the Soviet bloc, and to its ruling elites, were dealt with more easily, and the danger receded as economic growth improved the standard of living. During the 1960s, the more backward areas of Eastern Europe began to industrialise. In fact, the USSR lagged behind other parts of the bloc in industrial output and social conditions. East Germans, Czechs, and Hungarians were relatively better off, as they had been before communism was forced upon them. In the bloc, a striking disparity existed between actual and potential growth, which meant that Eastern Europe never matched the prosperity of Western Europe. On one hand, some historians have assumed that the problem was institutional and that the disparity was due to the nature of state socialism. On the other hand, the gap between East and West can be placed in a longer time frame, for it was clear before the Second World War as well as after. Long-term patterns in trade and investment and East-West interaction made Eastern Europe the 'periphery' that was always likely to stagnate as the supplier of the more dynamic 'core'. Such explanations are problematic, but they do cast light on the differences between Eastern and Western Europe and on why the bloc found it difficult to catch up with the West.[27]

Between 1950 and 1973, the annual average rate of growth in Gross Domestic Product (GDP) for the USSR was 3.4 percent. For Eastern Europe as a whole, the figure was 4 percent. Over the same period, the British growth rate was 2.5 percent, the French 4 percent, and that for the FRG 5 percent. The figure for Western Europe as a whole was 3.8 percent. GDP growth statistics for 1973 to 1992 are also revealing: the USSR's rate of growth was –0.4 percent, and Eastern Europe's was –0.8 percent. Their GDP shrank while the growth rates in Britain, France, the FRG, and Western Europe as a whole were 1.4 percent, 1.7 percent, 2.1 percent, and 1.8 percent, respectively. Statistics for output, employment, and productivity suggest that the USSR and Eastern Europe had impressive growth during the 1950s. Although the rate of growth fell slightly in the 1960s, the USSR and bloc were still outperforming Western Europe and the United States. But the growth could not be sustained, which had a lot to do with the arms race between the superpowers. The Soviets diverted technology and resources from civilian to military uses and this began to affect the USSR's economy in the 1960s.[28]

During the growth period of the 1950s and 1960s, the Soviets were ready and able to utilise their strength, improve their position in the Cold War, and extend the Cold War beyond Europe. In the Middle East, their links with Egypt, Syria, and Iraq countered America's relationship with Israel. In Asia, they promised to help new nations in the struggle against 'imperialism', and although no Soviet troops fought in Korea or Vietnam, communist leaders there and elsewhere enjoyed massive assistance from the USSR. The Soviet Union's strategic preoccupations in Asia continued, not least because of the long border with China. Quarrels with China over political ideology, foreign policy, and nuclear cooperation became increasingly bitter. By the end of the 1950s, it was becoming difficult to sustain even the pretence of friendship. Peking wanted to project an image of strength. Self-assertion was needed in order to gain respect, and the bigger aspiration was to become the leading revolutionary influence in world affairs. After a brief war in 1962 between China and India, the Soviets drew closer to India. The Chinese then protested about the Test Ban Treaty of 1963, which they regarded as an attempt to slow down their nuclear programme and exclude China from future discussions involving the nuclear powers. There were several border clashes involving the USSR and China. By 1969, the Soviets were threatening to use nuclear weapons, and both sides were building up their naval strength.[29]

Developments across Africa and Asia between the mid-1950s and mid-1960s in some cases inconvenienced Britain and in others provided opportunities to exercise influence, alleviate danger, and solve problems. Preserving status and protecting interests became harder when circumstances were unfavourable and resources limited. Disputes within and concerning the Commonwealth were embarrassing and even inhibiting. This was a situation with which Britain would have to contend long after Macmillan's premiership, and in his time there were many disagreements about decolonisation, Commonwealth affairs, immigration, and the contribution that colonies and former colonies could make to Britain's political and economic strength, prestige, and global reach. Britain's other relationships continued to be debated, too, particularly those with America and Western Europe, and very rarely could policymakers deliberate without taking into account the exigencies of the Cold War both in Europe and beyond. Changes in the Soviet Union and eastern bloc presented challenges even when they potentially improved the prospects for negotiation and agreement. If the communist countries became stronger economically and more assertive in the international arena, what would be the consequences for Britain? The USSR and its allies might feel more secure and seek to bargain with the West, but they might also choose to threaten and confront. Increasingly, Britain was responding to events, not controlling them. The other great powers still respected and treated Britain as one of their number, however, and the Macmillan government and its successors hoped to keep this going for as long as possible.

CHAPTER 5

TO THE BRINK

CUBA

The Cuban missile crisis of October 1962 brought the world—however briefly—closer to a nuclear war. The British were involved, though their role and influence during the crisis continue to be disputed. This was an international emergency that affected both the course of the Cold War and the Anglo-American 'special relationship'. At a time when Sputnik made American leaders fearful about a 'missile gap', when they realised that the Soviets had the technology for long-range attacks, and when the Soviets were making threats about Berlin and involving themselves militarily in Africa, it is not surprising that U.S. foreign policy became more nervous and more assertive. President Kennedy and U.S. secretary of state Dean Rusk believed in boldness, to reassure the American people and America's allies, and to remind the Soviets that they would not go unanswered. The president committed the United States to action overseas and declared that it had obligations as leader of the free world. Concern grew in London about U.S. policy and intentions. There were disagreements between Britain and the United States in the early 1960s, but the friendship and mutual respect of Macmillan and Kennedy helped to smooth over some of the problems that arose. This process was aided by David Ormsby-Gore, who was close to the Kennedy family and served as Britain's ambassador in Washington.[1]

Khrushchev had decided that Soviet success would come not through nuclear or conventional forces, but through wars of national liberation in Africa, Asia, and Latin America. Kennedy promised to defend freedom everywhere, and, confident that the United States had the resources to overcome Soviet efforts, his administration sought to make friends by aiding developing nations and spreading liberal democratic values. Counterinsurgency methods were also used. Kennedy's proactive agenda caused trouble, for if the two superpowers were to avoid confrontation they needed to respect a delicate balance. They had to be selective and flexible. Kennedy's foreign policy was designed to establish U.S. primacy and it disturbed and destabilised international affairs. The fixation with Cuba is best understood in this context. Fidel Castro had taken power in Cuba in January 1959. Domestic and U.S. opposition to his measures of social revolution made him more radical in his policies and rhetoric. The United States wished to dominate the Caribbean, he claimed, and in order to gather support for his reforms he linked Cuba's freedom with the need to frustrate U.S. designs. Pressed to discountenance communism, he declared that it would be dishonourable to persecute communists just so that he would not be called a communist. Washington's aversion to Castro increased, which was inevitable in view of Cuba's proximity to the U.S. mainland. Previously there had been no strong anti-U.S. sentiment in Cuba, but the opposition to Castro changed this and made a future accommodation between Washington and Havana less likely. Castro had to weaken U.S. influence in Cuba for his own political survival, while Washington was sure that no Cuban government could survive without its approval. As U.S. political and business leaders became obsessed with proving that Castro had communist links, he was able to use Cuban nationalism for his own ends.[2]

In Washington, there was little doubt that Castro was creating a communist dictatorship and would make Cuba heavily reliant on the USSR.

Cuba had formerly been an ally of the United States. Now Castro was turning it into a Soviet satellite. Although plans were made under President Eisenhower to topple Castro, no firm decisions were taken. Eisenhower was later accused of passivity, but he was receiving incomplete information and inconsistent advice from the state department, military chiefs, and the CIA. When Kennedy assumed the presidency early in 1961, he found the Bay of Pigs scheme already in place: CIA-backed anticommunist Cuban exiles would invade the island and remove Castro's regime. The invasion was a terrible failure. Kennedy refused to provide full U.S. air support because he did not want to be seen as an aggressor, yet Washington was already tied in morally and politically. After this fiasco, the CIA plotted in various ways to get rid of Castro. It was a policy of vendetta and part of a wider programme of plots, coups, and covert action against international communism. Washington's perspective was determined mainly by Cold War imperatives and the wish to maintain regional hegemony. According to the CIA's deputy director of operations at this time, Richard M. Bissell, it was Kennedy who ensured the failure of Bay of Pigs operation by ruling out open intervention. Subsequently it was the president and his brother Robert Kennedy, the attorney general, who put the CIA under increasing pressure to find a way of removing Castro. The president and his closest advisers were embarrassed by the Bay of Pigs affair and sought quickly to recover, despite the likelihood that this determination would lead to greater danger in the future. Historians have differed in their assessments of Kennedy's attitude towards Cuba. Some regard him as an imprudent interventionist. Others stress the motives and concerns created in Washington by the Cold War, the nuclear threat, and the unpredictability of Khrushchev. Some point out that the White House found it hard to restrain U.S. military, intelligence, and bureaucratic chiefs. Kennedy's decision to abandon the Bay of Pigs operation had a lot to do with his fear that the Soviets would intervene to defend Cuba. He weighed up the pros and cons of continuing and realised that it would be better to pull out. He saw that the removal of Castro would require a substantial commitment of U.S. forces and probably a war, the duration of which could not easily be predicted.[3]

British newspapers were not impressed. Whatever was happening in Cuba, declared *The Times*, the United States should keep out. Direct interference in Cuba's affairs would provoke the Soviet Union and make enemies in Latin America. As *The Times* put it, 'the whole strength of the U.S. thesis is that the Castro system has become a perversion and alien to the spirit of the Americas. It will have to lean over backwards to prove that from this point on it is doing no more than cheering on the touchline'. The Bay of Pigs operation was an unfortunate miscalculation. Kennedy had apparently inherited a confused situation, for which he could not be blamed, but it was hardly wise politically to identify himself and his country with failure. What would come of it? *The Times* linked Cuba with Laos, where the United States was assisting the Laotian army to combat Soviet-backed insurgents. Though containment of communism was necessary, Kennedy would have to find an alternative method, negotiation rather than military force, and settle for 'a workable form of neutrality' for both Cuba and Laos. He would have to think again about 'the picture the United States has been presenting to the world'. According to the *Observer*, the Bay of Pigs 'fiasco' would be widely regarded as a 'disastrous blunder' on Kennedy's part, whereas Castro, who posed no military threat to the United States, would be seen as the victim of U.S. aggression. If communism had to be resisted, this was not the way to do it. Washington had to pay more attention to the advice of America's allies, show neutral nations that it respected their opinions, and abandon its misguided efforts to impose its wishes on others.[4]

Macmillan considered the Bay of Pigs invasion a bad mistake. Kennedy had opted for an awkward combination of what Eisenhower had envisaged—a small guerrilla landing—and the large invasion favoured by the U.S. joint chiefs of staff. British leaders grew alarmed about Washington's scheming against Castro but there was little they could do. The United States wanted British cooperation in areas where British power could make a difference, principally in Europe, the Middle East, and parts of Asia. Cuba was too close to the United States for Washington to allow London to meddle. When the British Parliament considered the Bay of Pigs affair, several speakers condemned the United States for an act of aggression and urged the government to dissociate Britain from it and denounce it openly. On April 18, 1961, Edward Heath argued that hasty action was best avoided. The scope of the invasion and its point of origin were not yet clear, he said, and Washington had denied that U.S. forces were involved. On April 20, Labour MPs asked if there had been any communication between the prime minister and President Kennedy. Would the government not act to deter the Americans, who seemed willing to trigger off a major war? The home secretary, R. A. Butler, declared that the whole matter was under consideration at the UN, which was the place to deal with it, and when Labour MP Michael Foot argued that 'the best service we could have given to the Americans as our allies was to have warned them beforehand of the consequences which might follow from the act of folly and crime on which they were embarking', Butler dismissed this as 'a presupposition of the situation which we cannot accept'.[5]

To President Kennedy and his inner circle of advisers, the administration could not rest idle but had to make things happen because, as time passed, Castro's regime would consolidate its position and move closer to the Soviets. Robert Kennedy headed an inquiry into the Bay of Pigs invasion, which concluded that the plan had really been Eisenhower's and that it had not failed because of the lack of air support because air support had never been a central part of the plan. The inquiry blamed the CIA and joint chiefs for what had happened. To Moscow, the attempted invasion proved that the Americans would not leave Cuba alone. The Soviet Union had to act. 'We had an obligation to do everything in our power to protect Cuba's existence as a socialist country and as a working example to the other countries of Latin America', Khrushchev later explained. The Bay of Pigs provided valuable propaganda material for the Soviets, whose prestige was also boosted at this time by the first manned flight in space (April 1961). Khrushchev tried to take advantage of supposed American weaknesses at the Vienna summit in June 1961, but on all the urgent international issues of the time Kennedy refused to make concessions. Khrushchev gave more attention to the possibility of placing missiles on Cuba. He wished to take the initiative in his dealings with Kennedy and show the world that the Soviet Union was America's equal. He probably thought that he could also use Cuba to gain a bargain on Berlin.[6]

These developments reinforced the Kennedy administration's interest in Latin America. The president was determined that the Cuban revolution should not be replicated elsewhere in the region. Washington had always accused Castro of being a communist, and in what could be described as a self-fulfilling prophesy Castro's regime moved quickly to the left after the Bay of Pigs, in terms of both policy and personnel. Castro expected the United States to try again to remove him from power. He needed Soviet protection. Yet it was not clear that Moscow would be willing to forge a closer alliance with Castro. Cuba was near to the United States, far from the USSR, not easy to defend, and there were doubts in the Kremlin about Castro's reliability and about the extent to which reforms could be carried out in Cuba. Khrushchev told Kennedy at the Vienna summit that the United States had pushed Castro into the Soviet camp, which suggests that a different policy would have led to a different outcome. It is also possible that Castro might not originally have intended to implement a full communist revolution in Cuba. However, it must be recognised that Castro's associates were devoted communists, that Castro was an authoritarian, and that in seeking to govern and improve an underdeveloped Cuba he favoured radical agrarian reform and the nationalisation of foreign property. He needed economic, political, and military support from the USSR and the Bay of Pigs affair strengthened the bond between Havana and Moscow. Castro seized foreign assets and signed a trade treaty with the Soviet Union. Continuing U.S. harassment and the prospect of another invasion soon presented Khrushchev with an opportunity to station missiles just forty miles from the U.S. mainland.[7]

Placing missiles on Cuba offered Khrushchev a way out of his own problems. He was facing opposition at home, and in order to shore up his personal authority he had to accept the advice of Moscow hardliners (whom he had previously defied) and demonstrate that he was truly committed to preserving Soviet power. Troop reductions were suspended, the nuclear arsenal was expanded, and Khrushchev offered help to liberation movements in the developing world. He had wished for the stability abroad that would enable him to focus on economic progress at home, yet he was obliged to uphold Soviet influence and continue the ideological struggle against capitalism. He had tried to negotiate. He had tried threats and coercion. The USSR's relative strategic weakness meant that he could not compel the West to give way, however, and the Kennedy administration was similar to Eisenhower's in that retreat was deemed impossible on account of the likely reaction of U.S. domestic opinion and America's allies. Khrushchev decided that the placing of missiles on Cuba would ensure that Cuba could not be lost to the Americans, secure Castro's regime, and advertise and protect the Soviets' global interests. Khrushchev was still in search of a spectacular foreign policy success. Indeed, the need seemed greater than ever. The Sino-Soviet split was now more visible to the West; Albania was refusing to cooperate with Moscow; there was tension within the USSR after a run of deficient harvests; the United States had based Jupiter missiles in Italy and Turkey; and Soviet intelligence had confirmed that the United States was winning the nuclear arms race. Kennedy was clearly committed to further expansion, whereas the Soviet Union could not afford to build more long-range missiles. Khrushchev's previous efforts to make the United States treat the USSR as an equal had not achieved a great deal, but the alliance with Cuba meant that he could continue the Berlin confrontation in another location, and sending missiles to Cuba would save the USSR perhaps ten years in its pursuit of nuclear parity with the United States.[8]

Long after the event, Khrushchev claimed that his priority had been to prevent a U.S. invasion of Cuba. His goal was to deter, not to threaten or alarm: the missiles would both defend Cuba and balance the American bases that surrounded the USSR. Some historians do not accept Khrushchev's explanation, contending that the real purpose was to force the Americans to make a bargain on Berlin. Another goal, perhaps, was to exploit divisions in NATO by showing its European members that Washington could not be relied upon in an emergency. Evidence that became available after the end of the Cold War, however, indicates that Khrushchev was not planning to use the Cuban missile crisis to make a deal on Berlin or to use pressure on Berlin as leverage in his dealings with Kennedy on Cuba. Nor did the strategic nuclear balance feature prominently in his thinking. He did not intend to use the Cuban revolution to close the nuclear gap on the United States. Instead, his primary concern was to protect Cuba in order to promote the spread of communism across the world and reinforce Soviet leadership of the communist camp. The motive was ideological. Some commentators maintain that the crux of the matter was Khrushchev's desire for a significant gain at Kennedy's expense. This developed into a battle of wills, and, having failed to make a breakthrough on the Berlin question, the Soviet leader looked outside Europe for a place to continue the struggle. He had taken risks in Berlin, and the risks he was willing to take with regard to Cuba could only be justified in the context of the prize he had in mind: improving the Soviet Union's international position relative to the United States. So there was at least some linkage between Berlin and Cuba. Nevertheless, it appears that Khrushchev was genuine in his support for the Cuban revolution, more so than Washington appreciated, and also that he was worried about a possible deterioration in Soviet-Cuban relations. The Kremlin was sensitive about Chinese allegations that the USSR was not doing enough to resist the West and fearful about what might happen if China drew closer to Cuba.[9]

Kennedy thought that what Khrushchev really wanted was to test U.S. resolve, in which case the main motive for placing the missiles on Cuba was to see how much Kennedy himself was willing to endure. The president also decided that Khrushchev had two other, but lesser, aims in mind. These were to shield the Castro regime and to establish missile bases close to the United States and thereby compensate for the American lead in ICBMs.[10]

As for Castro, he decided that the missiles would make his regime safer, though he preferred to speak not about Cuba's own security but about Cuba's willingness to share responsibilities with the Soviet Union and assist in defending international freedom and socialist revolution. He probably had no choice in the matter. The Soviets wanted to base missiles on Cuba, and without their massive aid Castro's regime would collapse and Cuba would sink into chaos. Although Castro had not asked for missiles, he could hardly refuse to accept them when Khrushchev put the matter to him. It might be the case, however, that Castro had been hoping to get Soviet missiles for some time. According to this line of argument, Castro really believed that the Americans were going to invade Cuba, persuaded Moscow that an invasion was coming, and used the threat of invasion to obtain the missiles he wanted. Conversely, Castro's ability to guide Soviet decision making was not great. Moscow did not trust him fully, and Khrushchev's sense of the ideological sympathy between Cuba and the USSR was accompanied by certain reservations. Perhaps the ideological bond mattered less than the USSR's superpower rivalry with the United States.[11]

Khrushchev's idea of a bold move, to gain an advantage over the United States and shift the Cold War balance, had the same flaw as Kennedy's similarly proactive approach: destabilisation was dangerous. Moreover, Khrushchev made matters worse because he deliberately lied to Kennedy, assuring him that only short-range surface-to-air missiles were being sent to Cuba. In fact, the Soviets provided medium-to-long-range nuclear weapons, along with 22,000 troops and technicians and twenty-four antiaircraft missile groups. Since a build-up of armaments of this magnitude could not be concealed, Khrushchev and his colleagues must have realised that the Americans would react. Kennedy's administration was initially split between those who advocated a decisive air strike against Cuba, and in due course an invasion, and those who preferred a blockade in the hope that this would make the Soviets relent. The president wavered between the two positions and finally decided on a blockade, which was announced on October 22, 1962. Blockade was the option favoured by the president's brother Robert Kennedy and by secretary of defence Robert McNamara, who emphasised that the missiles on Cuba did not really change the nuclear equation because the United States still had a clear lead in terms of warheads capable of reaching the Soviet Union. McNamara was annoyed by the attitude of the joint chiefs of staff, for they were set on military action. Kennedy grew in confidence on October 23 because of clear indications of international approval. These exceeded his expectations, and those of the Soviets. Khrushchev hoped that the British could be persuaded to arrange negotiations and secret overtures were made to this end. In his public statements, the Soviet leader adhered to a hard line, at the same time stressing that the crisis could be ended if the blockade was lifted. Kennedy made sure that the blockade was implemented in a restrained manner and U.S. vessels were specifically ordered not to open fire. Though Kennedy was slow to rule anything out, including an invasion of Cuba, he was not unwilling to make concessions, and by October 25, according to a report submitted to London by Britain's representative at the UN, he saw a possible linkage between the Cuban missiles and U.S. missiles in Turkey.[12]

In Britain, as the foreign office issued statements accusing the USSR of 'deception' and 'deliberately opening up a new area of instability', and confirming that the British and American governments were working together, *The Times* supported the official line and declared that Kennedy had no option but to blockade Cuba. The Soviets had pushed him into it. True, past U.S. mistakes in dealing with Cuba, Washington's aversion to the Castro regime, the Bay of Pigs, and the president's 'sudden display of toughness now during a mid-term election campaign in which he has been accused of softness' might lead one to be sceptical. But the main point to bear in mind was that the Soviets intended to station offensive weapons on Cuba despite their previous assurances to the contrary. They probably 'counted on catching America napping until the bases were complete and western hemisphere defence was indisputably breached'. Obviously the blockade was dangerous, but to his credit Kennedy had made clear its limited purpose: there was no desire to topple Castro or strike a blow against communism, only to have the missiles removed. The Soviets did not want war. If they went too far, however, a war might begin accidentally. This is why they had to be resisted, and why the confrontation could not be allowed to drag on. Many nations would dispute the legality of the U.S. blockade. Nor was it likely that Castro would permit UN observers to enter Cuba and supervise the dismantling of Soviet bases. The friction over Berlin added another complication. Nevertheless, a deal could be worked out, especially if both the United States and the USSR agreed to give up a number of their 'forward bases' situated close to each other's borders.[13]

Kennedy and Macmillan communicated often in these days, and when the latter made a statement to the Commons on October 25 he had already informed Kennedy of the line he was going to take. The prime minister told MPs of the discovery of missiles on Cuba, with a range of over a thousand miles, which contradicted Soviet statements that Castro would be provided only with defensive weapons. Kennedy had no choice but to insist on the removal of these missiles, Macmillan said, otherwise doubt would be cast on America's pledges and commitments all over the world. The prime minister expressed support for the attempts that were being made at the UN and in other ways to end the crisis. Labour MPs warned that the U.S. blockade would set a damaging precedent: What was to stop the USSR or China from doing the same thing when they chose? Urged to restrain the Americans, Macmillan repeated several times that he hoped for a negotiated solution and that the Kennedy administration, like the British government, wanted a disarmament treaty as soon as possible. On Cuba and on disarmament, Macmillan added, words and promises would not be enough. A system of independent verification would be needed for agreements to be truly worthwhile.[14]

The Times subsequently reported that the United States 'pledges Berlin firmness' and that progress at the UN seemed likely. In these circumstances, it was not advisable for Britain to seek a more active mediatory role. Rather, Kennedy and Khrushchev should be encouraged to talk directly to each other. A summit might be arranged, although in view of what happened at Vienna eighteen months earlier this was probably not a good idea. Still, the prospect that U.S. missiles in Turkey could be used to strike a bargain on the Soviet missiles in Cuba offered some hope. The *Economist* took seriously the prospect that Khrushchev would order a blockade of Berlin. War was not impossible: Khrushchev had spoken of 'liquidating' the West's military presence in Berlin, and if he had to back down on Cuba he would not do so on Berlin.[15]

In a letter to *The Times* dated October 25, 1962, historian J. B. Conacher, an associate professor at the University of Toronto, complained about those British commentators who opposed the U.S. blockade of Cuba. Their 'plague on both your houses' attitude towards the superpowers ignored the threat posed by the USSR and the reasons why the United States had abandoned isolationism to become the leader of the West. Conacher asserted that the bases in Turkey were not to be viewed in the same way as the bases on Cuba and that the Cold War was not to be conducted by the rules of 'fair play' that some in Britain still seemed to cherish. The plan to place missiles on Cuba posed a threat to the West as a whole, and the Americans had to take action. They could not wait for the UN, because the Soviets would use the delay to make their missiles ready for use. No state would allow this to happen if there was a way of preventing it. Would London not act to stop missiles from being based in the Republic of Ireland and pointed across the Irish Sea?[16]

The British government's public position did not reflect its misgivings about what Kennedy was doing, which was fortunate for him, although he would probably have made the same decisions during the Cuban missile crisis even had he not enjoyed backing from Macmillan. Had Britain been less supportive, Kennedy's policy would not have been different, but it is also the case that an unhelpful British attitude would have added to his difficulties.

Kennedy and his advisers gambled that Khrushchev would draw back rather than go to war, and on October 26 the Soviet leader agreed to remove the missiles in return for a pledge that the Americans would not invade Cuba. The next day he added another condition. He demanded the withdrawal of U.S. missiles from Turkey. Kennedy ignored the second condition and agreed only that Cuba would not be invaded, and Khrushchev accepted this as the basis of a settlement on October 28. Castro was furious because he had not been consulted about the withdrawal of the Soviet missiles, though he later accepted that war had to be avoided. Peking accused Moscow of a shameful surrender.[17]

Both the Soviet and U.S. leaderships claimed victory. Although Khrushchev was blamed by some of his colleagues for taking risks and then backing down, and he would be replaced as Soviet prime minister and first secretary of the communist party in October 1964, from the outset his options had been limited. Cuba was too far away from the USSR to gain the full benefit of Soviet protection. Yet Khrushchev's brinkmanship was not entirely fruitless. Despite Kennedy's undoubted skill in the public relations aspects of the Cuban missile crisis, U.S. missiles were withdrawn from Turkey, the Castro regime survived intact, and Cuba remained a military ally of the USSR. Yet, the missiles in Turkey were obsolete and would soon have been withdrawn anyway, and in the long run the link between Cuba and the USSR did not prevent the Americans from doing the important things they wanted to do in the world. Eisenhower had approved the stationing of Jupiters in Turkey at the end of 1957 and when Kennedy became president he decided that they should stay there even though more advanced submarine-launched weapons, for which IRBMs were a stopgap, were about to come into service. Kennedy made this decision in order to enhance America's standing with its NATO allies and contribute to the containment of the USSR. Although the Turkish missiles did feature in the arrangements Kennedy made with Khrushchev, Washington was bound to deny it. The United States could not be seen to be withdrawing these missiles in response to Soviet pressure. In addition, the government of Turkey wanted to keep them, and the Americans knew that a quarrel on this matter would open up a serious rift in NATO. Kennedy therefore declared that he would never bargain away western security. In this he had Macmillan's full approval.[18]

Khrushchev later expressed respect for the way Kennedy had handled the crisis, especially his refusal to order an attack on Cuba despite pressure from hardliners. To Khrushchev the outcome was 'a triumph of common sense'. It was also 'a great victory' for Moscow, because Kennedy had promised that Cuba would not be invaded, which guaranteed the existence of a socialist Cuba and added to the strength of the communist camp in its global contest with capitalist and imperialistic states. Even within Moscow, however, it was thought that the real victor was Kennedy and that Khrushchev had drawn back, humiliated Castro, and given up on some of the wider revolutionary aims he had long been enunciating.[19]

During the crisis, questions had been raised in Washington and London about who was really in charge of Soviet policy. It was assumed that Khrushchev was being swayed at times by moderates and at times by hardliners, and that another struggle for ascendancy was developing in the Kremlin. Kennedy was certain that the USSR had submitted in the face of American firmness; however, Khrushchev had reason to think differently. Khrushchev might have made concessions in order to keep the peace, but he had also prevented an invasion of Cuba. He had stopped a would-be aggressor and saved the Cuban revolution. If this was really his main goal, and he was not really out to alter the strategic balance, the tactic of placing missiles on Cuba can be seen as shrewd and effective. But we cannot be sure that the removal of these missiles was part of the plan, and it is clear that criticism of Khrushchev increased in Moscow as a result of the Cuban missile crisis and subsequently led to his downfall. The Cuban missile crisis ended Khrushchev's efforts to coerce the West. He realised that threats would not work and that confrontation was dangerous when the USSR's power did not match that of the West.[20]

What had Khrushchev really accomplished in Cuba? He claimed he had safeguarded the Castro regime, but many historians doubt that the Americans were likely to invade. If Khrushchev's goal was to compel the western powers to leave Berlin, he failed. If his main concern was to close the strategic gap between the USSR and the United States, here, too, he failed. In the immediate aftermath of the Cuban missile crisis, the U.S. nuclear arsenal was eight times larger than the Soviet Union's, taking all weapons into account. The United States had 180 to the USSR's 20 ICBMs. When Khrushchev fell from power, taking all weapons into account, the American nuclear arsenal was still much larger than that of the Soviet Union. Yet Khrushchev did get the Jupiters removed from Turkey and he did ensure that the USSR would have an ally close to the U.S. mainland. These were strategic gains. Khrushchev was concerned that these depended too heavily on Kennedy's promises, and that a leadership change in Washington would ruin everything. In order to make a deal, Kennedy might have gone much further in reassuring Khrushchev on these points than some historians have appreciated.[21]

Historians continue to debate the strategic, nuclear, political, intelligence, personal, leadership, organisational, and bureaucratic aspects of the Cuban missile crisis, and to investigate policy errors and unintended consequences. It has been suggested that Khrushchev's principal gains—the end of the blockade, the promise that the Americans would not invade Cuba, and the removal of U.S. missiles from Turkey—were of lasting importance. Although he had to withdraw the missiles from Cuba, there had not been any there before the crisis, so in this sense he did not lose anything, and he had obtained a guarantee of Cuba's security, which had not been assured before the crisis. Nevertheless, the Kennedy administration did not put an end to covert action against Castro's regime. There was no attempt to mount another CIA-supported invasion, but there were sanctions, threats, and harassment, all designed to prevent Castro from gaining influence in Latin America. There was still talk of 'freeing' Cuba. Kennedy maintained that his pledge not to invade Cuba depended on the removal of the Soviet missiles under UN supervision. Since Castro subsequently refused to allow observers into Cuba, Kennedy considered the bargain null and void, in which case the United States could quite properly go on pressurising the Castro regime. Moreover, if Khrushchev gained more from Kennedy than many observers believed at the time, there was also a serious defeat, with long-term consequences, in the sense that it now became impossible for the USSR quickly and cheaply to gain strategic parity with the United States. In addition, the Turkish Jupiters were going to be decommissioned anyway, and only six months after the Cuban missile crisis a new U.S. Polaris submarine, with sixteen missiles, began patrols in the Aegean Sea. Some historians contend that the crisis should have been used by Kennedy to conclude a comprehensive agreement with the USSR. For example, more might have been made of a proposal made at the UN by Brazil for Latin America to be completely denuclearised. A related idea was that neither the United States nor the Soviets should have a military presence in Cuba (in 1903 the United States had been granted a perpetual lease for the base at Guantanamo, on the south-eastern tip of Cuba). Kennedy, however, did not wish to negotiate with Castro or legitimise his regime. Therefore, Cuba remained an ally of the USSR and the Soviets continued to station forces in Cuba, support the Cuban economy, and devote huge resources to the nuclear arms race.[22]

How important was Britain's role in the Cuban missile crisis? As America's main ally, Britain had some influence, though this had to be used from the sidelines and, understandably, the core elements of U.S. policy were decided by the Americans themselves. Kennedy's advisers stressed that Cuba was a long way from Britain and Europe: their perspective was bound to be different because their interests were not directly affected. Therefore, it would not be wise to involve them in the decision-making process, and specifically, the views and wishes of the European members of NATO had to be blocked out because of the nuclear context. Washington had never wanted them to have independent control over nuclear weapons, in case the United States was dragged into a nuclear war to defend interests that were not vital to it. The Cuban missile crisis turned this situation around: now the European members of NATO were worried that they would be involved in a nuclear war caused by decisions taken by Washington alone.[23]

A number of historians have argued that Britain's influence during the Cuban missile crisis was negligible. Although Kennedy and Macmillan spoke regularly on the telephone, contends David Reynolds, the British did not shape U.S. policy at all. Macmillan and his advisers were 'valuable as a sounding board' but otherwise 'impotent'. This is also the view put forward by Christopher Bartlett. John Dumbrell points out that Macmillan opposed the removal of missiles from Turkey and that Kennedy rejected Macmillan's suggestion that Thor missiles in Britain should be used as a bargaining tool, to get the Soviets to talk. Dumbrell thinks that Kennedy became increasingly doubtful about Macmillan's advice as the crisis unfolded. John Baylis emphasises that although Britain did make important contributions, all the significant decisions were taken by Kennedy and his advisers. For Baylis, the crisis demonstrated the imbalance of power between Britain and the United States. When there was a direct confrontation between the two superpowers, neither the Americans nor the Soviets had to pay the British much attention.[24]

This is too harsh a verdict. As Richard Aldous stresses, no other leader had the close relationship that Macmillan enjoyed with Kennedy or the direct and regular communication with the U.S. president during the Cuban missile crisis. Alistair Horne has argued that Macmillan *was* genuinely consulted by Kennedy and that the crisis marked 'a new peak' of intimacy and trust between them. The British ambassador in Washington, David Ormsby-Gore, was also an important participant. British influence at this juncture might not have been decisive, and should not be exaggerated, but neither can we discount it entirely. Macmillan saw that Britain had a role to play. He urged others to remain calm and avoid hasty responses. In his dealings with Kennedy and with NATO and Commonwealth leaders, he set an example of firmness and restraint. After the crisis, he insisted that the British government had done its part, sharing in U.S. decision making and keeping Western Europe together so that complications from that direction were minimised. Macmillan thought that Khrushchev backed down primarily because his adventurism lacked support from other elements in the Soviet leadership. As for the question of why Khrushchev had risked so much in the first place, Macmillan supposed that there were several motives: to alter the strategic balance, to take attention away from domestic problems, to discourage U.S. interference in Eastern Europe, to offer a bargain on Cuba as the means to obtain one on Berlin. Macmillan admired Kennedy's conduct, especially the way the president ordered a rapid mobilisation to show Moscow that Cuba would be invaded unless a resolution was found. Although it is clear that Kennedy and his closest colleagues made the key decisions, and Ormsby-Gore later admitted that British advice reassured Kennedy but did not change his policy, it is also true that the president listened to Macmillan, took to heart Macmillan's counsel to combine firmness with calmness, and was very grateful for Britain's support. Kennedy and Rusk, the U.S. secretary of state, knew that the British had done invaluable service in preserving NATO's unanimity and reassuring the governments of Western Europe. Kennedy and Macmillan were both annoyed by press reports that the Americans had not consulted their allies during the Cuban missile crisis and by claims that the United States did not need a 'special relationship' with Britain and that Britain's position as a nuclear power brought with it no real influence. Macmillan was sure that he had played an important role, and this was also the view of senior figures in the Kennedy administration.[25]

It was Macmillan, backed strongly by Ormsby-Gore, who pressed Kennedy to publish photographic evidence of the Soviet missiles on Cuba. Kennedy was initially reluctant, but Macmillan and Ormsby-Gore persuaded him that proof was necessary to sway international opinion. When Kennedy confided that pressure was building for air strikes against Cuba, or even an invasion, Macmillan pointed to the risks involved and urged caution. When Kennedy decided to impose a blockade, Ormsby-Gore suggested that the 'quarantine' line should be five hundred instead of the proposed eight hundred miles off the Cuban coast, so that Moscow would have more time to reflect and Khrushchev could save face. Macmillan agreed with Ormsby-Gore. So did Kennedy. Another useful contribution was the intelligence provided by Oleg Penkovsky, a Soviet spy who had been recruited as a double agent by the British. Penkovsky gave details about the missiles on Cuba and suggested that Soviet weaponry was less advanced than Khrushchev claimed. As the tension mounted, and Kennedy asked Macmillan what he thought about a U.S. invasion of Cuba, the prime minister replied (October 25, 1962) that the time for an invasion had passed and that other means should be tried.[26]

The release of photographic evidence was absolutely vital in generating support for the United States during the Cuban missile crisis, especially in Europe, just as Macmillan and Ormsby-Gore had counselled. Penkovsky's role was probably less important. The information he provided was only attended to after the photographic evidence had been assessed. Nevertheless, Kennedy and his advisers trusted Penkovsky, particularly on the matter of when the Soviet missiles would become operational. The president believed that he could buy time with the 'quarantine', and use this time to negotiate with Moscow. Had the intelligence indicated that the missiles were close to operational status it would have been even more difficult to resist the pressure for immediate air strikes and an invasion. Kennedy benefited because he could draw out the crisis and keep options open. Decisions did not have to be rushed. This was very much in line with what the British wanted. In a number of ways, therefore, the information and advice offered by Britain did contribute to the course and outcome of the Cuban missile crisis. The conversations between Kennedy and Macmillan had much more to them than simply the president telling the British prime minister what he had already decided to do.[27]

There was a limit to Britain's helpfulness. The government was far from passive and it was not slow to criticise those U.S. decisions with which it did not agree. This robust approach was most evident in the foreign office, where it was thought that the Bay of Pigs episode and Washington's vendetta against Castro had nothing to recommend them. Instead of trying to topple Castro, the preference was to do nothing drastic and allow his experiments with communism to fail by themselves, and whatever happened, the view was that Britain should not get involved. The foreign office was also concerned about the possible ramifications of U.S. policy towards Cuba. What would happen if the Soviets used the American 'quarantine' as an excuse to blockade Berlin? At the foreign office the legality of the U.S. blockade was questioned, and the advice tendered to Macmillan was that he should leave it to Kennedy to justify the blockade at the United Nations. When the Americans suggested that NATO forces should be placed on alert, it was Macmillan himself who took the lead in resisting. He feared that such a move might precipitate war. The British also insisted that the blockade must not be extended to cover items other than weapons: they were sensitive about Britain's maritime rights and the free movement of British shipping. Some of Kennedy's colleagues complained about Britain's attitude on these points, but the foreign office countered by suggesting that the blockade should not continue without the approval of the UN Security Council. In public, government ministers tried to avoid making specific statements, so there were no pronouncements on whether Cuba was a threat to the United States or whether the placing of Soviet missiles on Cuba really altered the global strategic balance. On both these matters the foreign office entertained doubts. For the foreign secretary, Home, the main point was not to take sides against the Americans and to steer clear of the most sensitive issues for as long as possible. Anglo-American friendship was preserved in public, while privately, the British government's complaints and suggestions challenged U.S. policy.[28]

The government was worried about the possible consequences of the crisis, but there was also an idea that the crisis could be used, particularly to promote a deal on Berlin. If the UN guaranteed an agreement to demilitarise Berlin, it was thought, the Soviets would respect the inviolability of West Berlin and in tandem with this the Americans might be persuaded to leave Cuba alone. Ormsby-Gore championed a deal along these lines because it seemed to offer so much: security for West Berlin, the involvement of the UN in an uncontroversial way, and a test of Moscow's good faith, for if the Soviets really cared about the safety of Castro's regime they would no longer cause trouble over Berlin. In London's calculations, peace in Europe mattered more than Cuba. If there was a wish to exploit the Cuban missile crisis to achieve political goals elsewhere, however, the snag was that little could be done in Europe without U.S. cooperation, and pressure from Washington would also be needed to persuade the Soviets and the Cubans to participate in the desired arrangements. Macmillan regarded Berlin as the priority. He thought that the Soviets were using Cuba to get what they wanted in Berlin, and that Cuba itself had little to do with British interests. Berlin was far more important to Britain.[29]

After the Cuban missile crisis, Macmillan and his colleagues liked people to think that they had been more active and influential than they really were, and this accorded with the continuing desire to present Britain as a great power. In this sense, the whole affair was helpful to Britain's leaders. They had not shaped U.S. policy, but at least they were able to *pretend* that they had, and on matters that directly affected Britain's international commitments they took the opportunity to persuade the Americans to take British interests into account. For Kennedy's administration, it was important not to alienate Britain. The British could not greatly influence U.S. policy on Cuba, but they had no need to, except in so far as Britain's wider interests might be affected. The EEC application, disputes within NATO, and problems associated with decolonisation and Commonwealth relations were all causing trouble, which meant that the government was determined not to weaken the 'special relationship' with America, because it was an essential prop for Britain's great-power status. Macmillan's determination to stay close to the Americans is also illustrated by his reaction to information he received from the intelligence services. Through various intermediaries it was indicated that if Britain arranged a summit, Khrushchev would accept the invitation and discuss the withdrawal of the missiles from Cuba. Macmillan was sure that this was a genuine proposal, but after discussing it with Home he decided not to respond. He thought that Moscow was trying to drive a wedge between Britain and the United States.[30]

There has been some speculation that Britain became more involved in the crisis than was realised at the time and afterwards. It is possible, for instance, that Britain's strategic nuclear forces were secretly placed on alert. Parliament and public were not informed and even ministers were unaware, because what happened was disguised as a training exercise. As such, it was supervised by the British and U.S. strategic air commands. Macmillan had decided against mobilisation, in case it led to war, and the foreign secretary apparently knew nothing of the emergency manoeuvres that were taking place. The prime minister did agree that precautionary moves were necessary, but he seems not to have been aware of their full extent. On a related point, it has generally been assumed that the Americans did not bring any of their European-based IRBMs to operational readiness during the Cuban missile crisis. Yet the Thor IRBMs based in Britain possibly *were* made ready. Since these were deployed under the dual-key arrangement, and could not be used unless both Britain and America agreed, the impression of close cooperation between the relevant senior personnel in the two air forces becomes even stronger. So does the sense of secrecy, for the dual-key process, if it really was set in motion, must have involved top-level political and military conversations between Britain and America, and the full details have never been divulged. Another related matter is the worldwide alert upon which U.S. forces were placed, and the implications not only for the American bases in Britain but also for NATO, because the alert was apparently ordered without any consultation between the United States and its allies. Certain duties were transferred from U.S. tactical air squadrons in Europe to those in Britain, freeing up the Europe-based units in case of a new Soviet threat against West Berlin.[31]

Questions also remain with regard to the nature of the bargain Kennedy made with Khrushchev in order to end the Cuban missile crisis: the withdrawal of Jupiter missiles from Turkey in return for the removal of Soviet missiles from Cuba.[32] According to Robert Kennedy's account, published in 1969, the U.S. leadership had long been thinking about withdrawing the Jupiters, the Soviets were informed that the missiles would soon be gone, and this was not part of any bargain with them. Macmillan maintained that President Kennedy had been unwilling to make an accommodation with Moscow at the expense of America's allies and would not have made a deal involving the Jupiters because of the possible damage this would do to the strength and unity of NATO. While counselling restraint and flexibility during the crisis, Macmillan had insisted on firmness with regard to the Jupiters. Thereafter, he could hardly claim to have influenced the outcome of the Cuban missile crisis if he accepted that Kennedy had made a private deal with Khrushchev, but this is exactly what Kennedy did. The Soviet ambassador in Washington said so, and Dean Rusk later confirmed that Kennedy had been determined not to allow the Turkish Jupiters to prevent a settlement on Cuba. Macmillan had apparently been kept in the dark about the details, which is not surprising. The Americans could not let anyone know.[33]

There were also good reasons for them to conceal the true extent of their consultation with Britain. For instance, Washington downplayed its discussions with London in order to avoid offending Paris. De Gaulle was informed about U.S. decisions during the Cuban missile crisis but he was not consulted, and in view of his fractious nature Kennedy did not want him to think that Macmillan had been treated any differently. Nevertheless, Macmillan *had* been treated differently, and, largely because of the precrisis closeness between Kennedy and Macmillan and between Kennedy and Ormsby-Gore, the British government knew much more about what the president and his advisers were hoping, thinking, and considering than did all other governments. It should be remembered, though, that in asking for advice Kennedy was not committing himself to act upon it. His conversations with Ormsby-Gore were frank and open. Kennedy would try out ideas, think aloud, seek comments and make suggestions. This was the way he liked to reach decisions. His eagerness for a diplomatic solution to the Cuban missile crisis was shared by British leaders, and on October 21 the president left Ormsby-Gore in no doubt that he wanted to negotiate with Khrushchev. He wondered if the Soviets would agree to a reciprocal closing of bases and added that he could see no good reason for keeping the Jupiter missiles in Turkey. In a similar fashion, Kennedy liked to test ideas and invite responses in his phone calls to Macmillan, as on October 25, when he suggested that the Soviets might agree to withdraw their missiles from Cuba in return for an international guarantee that Cuba would not be invaded.[34]

The cumulative effect of Macmillan's written and verbal communications with Kennedy during the Cuban missile crisis must have been considerable. The transcripts have been published. Not only do they give an impression of the mounting tension of the time and reveal details about the options that were available and how they were evaluated, but they also indicate the nature and extent of the interaction between the two leaders. Kennedy and Macmillan repeatedly referred to the blockade and its legality, how to handle the UN and NATO, Berlin, opinion in Western Europe, and the likely U.S. response to various potential Soviet moves. Kennedy promised not to resort to force without discussing it with Macmillan. The prime minister recognised that Kennedy was under enormous pressure and assured him that he could count on British support, especially at the UN. Macmillan's main concern was that the crisis would drag on—'we've always found that our weakness has been when we've not acted with sufficient strength to start with'—but he accepted that the situation was dangerous and confused and that much would depend on Khrushchev's actions. When UN secretary-general U Thant called upon the USSR to send no offensive weapons to Cuba, in return for which he wanted the Americans to suspend the 'quarantine' for two weeks, Kennedy complained that this would allow building work on the missile bases on Cuba to continue and Macmillan was disappointed to learn that U Thant intended to make his proposal public: 'that's rather tiresome of him, because it looks sensible and yet it's very bad'. Macmillan wanted U Thant clearly to understand that the main priority was to have the missiles removed, but he agreed with Kennedy that the immediate task was to ensure that the Soviets respected the blockade. On October 26 Kennedy informed Macmillan of unconfirmed reports that the Soviets were willing to withdraw their missiles in return for a promise that there would be no invasion of Cuba. Macmillan asked about the possibility of an international guarantee of Cuba's security. He also suggested that Britain's sixty Thor missiles could be immobilised as part of a bargain on Cuba (they had already been scheduled for dismantling). Kennedy was reluctant to go down this road for fear that the Soviets would bring up the missiles in Greece, Turkey, Italy, and elsewhere. He preferred to focus on the construction of the missile sites in Cuba and to wait and see what the Soviets would expect in return for stopping this work. Macmillan understood Kennedy's viewpoint, adding that any hasty moves would probably provoke another crisis over Berlin. The prime minister subsequently emphasised that Moscow should be given the opportunity to make a dignified retreat and that it would be better if the Thor missiles were used as a lever rather than missiles elsewhere, especially those in Turkey: 'This has, of course, the disadvantage that it brings in the concept of bargaining bases in Europe against those in Cuba. Nevertheless if it would turn the scale I would be willing to propose it to U Thant and it might be less invidious for us to take the lead rather than place the burden on the Turks'. On October 27, Macmillan assessed Khrushchev's two messages to the Americans. The first message, 'unhappily not published to the world, seemed to go a long way to meet you'. Khrushchev's second message, 'widely broadcast and artfully contrived, adding the Turkey proposal, was a recovery on his part. It has made a considerable impact'. Macmillan continued to favour a cautious and unhurried approach and agreed that 'the use of any initiative by me is all a matter of timing'.[35]

Although he was not privy to the discussions between Macmillan and Kennedy during the Cuban missile crisis, the leader of the opposition, Hugh Gaitskell, gained the impression that Anglo-American consultation had been totally inadequate. After the crisis, Gaitskell told the Commons (October 30) that much better communication would be needed if another such emergency arose, and that it was up to the prime minister to make appropriate arrangements. The lack of consultation in this case, Gaitskell opined, had been unfortunate and dangerous. Still, he was prepared to pay tribute to Kennedy, who had offered Khrushchev something substantial (the promise that there would be no invasion of Cuba) and had the good sense not to claim that the outcome was a U.S. victory and an embarrassment for Moscow. As for the Soviets' breach of faith regarding the basing of missiles on Cuba, Gaitskell thought this indefensible, for there could be no peace or stability if governments were unable to trust each other.[36]

Whatever Gaitskell may have thought, there had been regular and significant consultation between British and U.S. leaders. Taken together, the Bay of Pigs affair in April 1961 and the Cuban missile crisis of October 1962 pushed Kennedy closer to Macmillan than would otherwise have been the case and thereby strengthened the 'special relationship'. The difficulties Kennedy encountered in his dealings with Cuba increased his sense of the need for British cooperation. The Bay of Pigs had been a serious blow. Subsequently, he was glad of Macmillan's support during the missile crisis. Kennedy wanted and valued British advice at that time, and this advice gave him more options. It helped him to follow his instincts, which pointed towards caution rather than bellicosity, and it helped him to stand up to the hawks in Washington, who were pressing for air strikes and an invasion. Anglo-American cooperation in October 1962 also ensured the survival of a common front against the USSR. The 'special relationship' was probably stronger in the later months of 1962 than it had been at any time since the end of the Second World War, and the Cuban missile crisis was quickly followed by the Nassau Agreement. Anglo-American cooperation continued into 1963, and the Test Ban Treaty was one concrete result. Circumstances changed, as did the personnel involved, for by the end of 1963 Kennedy and Macmillan were no longer in office. The two leaders had developed a remarkable rapport but their successors did not get on nearly so well.[37]

The Cuban missile crisis had lasting consequences. American and Soviet leaders agreed to establish a 'hotline' between Washington and Moscow and to work for limits on missile development and proliferation.

Tension over Berlin receded, and although the USSR concluded a separate treaty with the GDR in June 1964, Moscow stressed that this would not affect the rights of the western powers in West Berlin. Another result of the crisis, albeit an informal one that did not grab the headlines, was that each side accepted the other's use of spy planes for the gathering of information. This mutual tolerance and greater transparency also covered satellite reconnaissance. In various ways, the threat of war in October 1962 opened the way for détente, though this did not mean that serious disagreements did not continue. Indeed, Khrushchev briefly tried to restore friendly relations between the Soviet Union and China, apparently in preference to détente with the West. The Chinese were unreceptive and by June 1963 Khrushchev's patience was exhausted, so he switched back to the idea of a thaw between the USSR and the western powers. The United States and Soviet Union both wanted to be safe, and their interaction began more clearly to reflect this, but the thaw was limited and it was driven by self-interest. The two sides did not really become closer. They just made sure that their disagreements did not get out of hand. Indeed, in some respects superpower rivalry became even more intense, notably in the 'space race'. Kennedy was keen to outdo the Soviets in this field, whereas his predecessor Eisenhower, notwithstanding Sputnik, had resisted calls for a dramatic expansion of the U.S. space programme because he was worried about the economic and financial effects. But Kennedy wanted action, especially after the spring of 1961 when the Soviets put the first man in space and when Kennedy's presidency and America's reputation were dented by the Bay of Pigs invasion. Space missions were planned and executed from 1963, at an enormous cost, and eventually an American set foot on the moon in 1969. By 1972 the United States and the USSR had launched over 1200 satellites and probes. There was no end to the build-up of armaments. Khrushchev's successors in the USSR increased the number of ICBMs on Soviet territory and expanded the Soviet Union's conventional forces. Enhanced military capability made the Soviets feel secure enough to go for détente. The removal of missiles from Cuba, meanwhile, made U.S. leaders overconfident, and they grew all the more eager to oppose communism elsewhere, most notably in Vietnam.[38]

CHAPTER 6

INTERNATIONAL CONSEQUENCES
OF THE VIETNAM WAR

Much to the eventual regret of British leaders, the Kennedy administration's interest in Vietnam grew quickly in the aftermath of the Bay of Pigs disaster. Kennedy was convinced that America had to regain the initiative and block the spread of communism, and that U.S. power would be more credible if South Vietnam could be 'saved'. The Geneva accords of July 1954 had provided for the temporary division of Vietnam, to be followed by elections within two years and reunification. At the time, Eisenhower's advisers suggested that even if communists won the elections, U.S. security would not be at risk. Had he wished to, Eisenhower could have persuaded South Vietnam's leaders to accept the terms agreed at Geneva, but he believed in the domino theory, according to which the loss of Vietnam to the communists would be followed by the loss of Indochina as a whole. Eisenhower rejected the Geneva terms and approved massive aid to South Vietnam. There were no elections and reunification was postponed indefinitely. The Vietcong emerged, and a war to unite the country under the communists began in 1957. By the time Kennedy became president, Vietnam was one of America's largest and costliest overseas commitments. Kennedy's critics called upon him to go back to the Geneva arrangements, but Kennedy and his advisers did not wish to give the impression that they were weak, or willing to retreat in Asia, and it was clear that the Vietcong would not wait for elections. The Vietcong's aim was to take control of the whole of Vietnam by force. Kennedy increased the U.S. military presence in South Vietnam in December 1961. The aid continued and in October 1963 U.S. strategists were predicting that the war would be won before the end of 1965.[1]

Under the rules of SEATO, established in 1954, South Vietnam was entitled to ask its members for help as the security situation worsened, and given that the Eisenhower administration had already linked U.S. prestige to the survival of the noncommunist South Vietnamese state, American aid was bound to increase. There were financial and economic reasons for this, as well as political and ideological motivations. The Americans were drawn in as part of their effort to solve some of the problems created by decolonisation in Asia. The Cold War reinforced this trend, and the regional situation was also seen in the context of a world view in which the U.S. model of liberal capitalism was pitted against international and revolutionary socialism. Another consideration is that involvement in Vietnam would present opportunities for the United States to boost Japan's economy, for Japan could find in Southeast Asia the trade it was denied with China as a result of the American embargo. The larger vision was of a world in which the United States would create, manage, and lead a liberal bloc that embraced Western Europe and Japan. In other circumstances, perhaps, Kennedy would not have thought of extending the U.S. commitment in Vietnam, but he and his administration wished to live up to their anticommunist rhetoric and anticommunism remained strong in the newspapers and public opinion, especially with regard to Asia. Before he became president, Kennedy had accepted the principles of containment and the domino theory. Early in his presidency he intervened in Laos to forestall a communist takeover, and he approached the question of Vietnam as a test of American strength and resolve. There was an agreement for the neutralisation of Laos, which, it had been decided, was not a promising place in which to fight communist insurgents, whereas South Vietnam offered better prospects because its government and army were stronger than those of Laos. Kennedy's wish to demonstrate American power only grew as Khrushchev continued to promise the Soviet Union's support for wars of 'national liberation'. There were frequent quarrels between Washington and the regime in Saigon, as the Americans pressed for reforms in South Vietnam and its government instead became more authoritarian, but U.S. support increased and had to go on increasing in order to get the results to justify it.[2]

Initially, Kennedy did not desire or expect a substantial U.S. military presence in Vietnam, and even during the summer and autumn of 1963, as the situation in Saigon became chaotic, he wanted to explore all options. From May 1963, in fact, he appears to have wished to withdraw from Vietnam, but he could not see how to arrange a settlement that would be politically acceptable. Kennedy's success in averting war at the time of the Cuban missile crisis possibly made him think that he could control the trouble in Vietnam. The inducements and threats that were used to influence Ngo Dinh Diem's government in Saigon did not have the desired effect, however, and another miscalculation was the increasing use of covert diplomacy and action. The ramifications of this were not properly considered. In practice it was easier to approve covert efforts than overt military moves, which *were* subjected to long and detailed analysis. Robert McNamara later admitted that the decision to get more involved in Vietnam was based on two premises that turned out to be contradictory: that the fall of South Vietnam would endanger the security of the West, and that the U.S. military role would be limited to training and logistics. Political conditions in South Vietnam did not help, for they quickly deteriorated, but Kennedy did not have the chance to strike out in a new direction. He was assassinated on November 22, 1963.[3]

By attaching U.S. involvement in Vietnam to American patriotism and credibility, the Kennedy administration raised the costs of withdrawal. Pressing for reforms in South Vietnam helped to disrupt peasant society there. Allowing the South Vietnamese army to police the countryside and root out enemies of the Diem regime helped the communists to recruit supporters. Acquiescing in Diem's fall increased political turmoil in Saigon. Publicly downplaying America's role in Vietnam hindered a serious debate about U.S. policy. By committing the United States to the survival of an anticommunist South Vietnam, the president and his advisers made it more difficult to blame the Saigon government for its own mistakes. By insisting that there could and should be a military victory, they closed off the possibility that negotiation could provide an acceptable way out.[4] This situation caused arguments between the United States and Britain, where a Labour government took office in October 1964 after thirteen years of Conservative rule. Macmillan had resigned as prime minister in October 1963 through ill health. His successor was Sir Alec Douglas-Home, formerly (as the Earl of Home) foreign secretary, but the Conservatives narrowly lost the general election of 1964 and Harold Wilson took over as premier. During the election campaign, Home focused on defence and foreign policy, and this proved to be an unlucky tactic. Just a day after polling, news came through that Khrushchev had fallen from power in the USSR and that the Chinese had exploded their first atomic bomb. Had this news come earlier, Home's campaigning on international issues might have had more impact, as might his warning that Labour intended to dismantle Britain's nuclear deterrent. Realising that defence policy and foreign affairs had been opening up divisions within their party for some time, senior Labour figures had said little about these matters at the party conference of 1963 and during the 1964 election campaign Wilson (who had taken over as Labour leader in February 1963) hardly mentioned them at all. It was to Labour's good fortune that most voters considered social and economic matters to be the most important of the day. The foreign secretaries in the Labour government of 1964–1970 were Patrick Gordon Walker (1964–1965), Michael Stewart (1965–1966 and 1968–1970), and George Brown (1966–1968), but it was primarily Wilson who shaped policy.[5]

Despite protests from Labour left-wingers, the Wilson government for the most part followed the example of its Conservative predecessors and prioritised close relations with the United States. As in previous years, the British presence and Britain's contacts across Africa and Asia would be used to benefit the West and contain communism. British power would remain operative in regions where the Americans were relatively weak, substantial forces would be committed as necessary to restore order (as during the confrontation between Malaysia and Indonesia), and in all these ways Britain would share the burden with America, in return for which the United States would treat Britain as its chief ally, cooperate closely on nuclear matters, and offer financial help. Unfortunately, matters were less settled and straightforward than this picture suggests. The 'special relationship' was damaged by the war in Vietnam. As communist infiltration of South Vietnam increased, the presidency of Kennedy's successor Lyndon B. Johnson (1963–1969) saw a rapid extension of the U.S. commitment in the region. Following the Gulf of Tonkin incident in August 1964, when U.S. vessels came under attack, Johnson ordered air strikes against North Vietnam. Then Congress approved the deployment of a large contingent of U.S. combat troops. Australia, New Zealand, and South Korea also sent troops. The USSR threatened to allow 'volunteers' to support North Vietnam and the Chinese warned that they also would respond to any further U.S. attacks on North Vietnam.[6]

There has been great controversy over the escalation of the conflict in Vietnam. In February 1965 Johnson was told that the war would be lost unless the American effort increased, that there was still time to avoid defeat, and that, having taken responsibility for the survival of South Vietnam, the United States had to discharge this responsibility in a manner that left the world in no doubt of America's reliability. Johnson realised that the involvement in Vietnam would have to continue for several years. The most important point was that America could not fail there, for this would have potentially disastrous consequences elsewhere. Johnson had pressing concerns at home too: he wished to frustrate his political opponents and his determination not to suffer defeat in Vietnam had much to do with his need to build support for his domestic policies. The rights and wrongs of these reasons for escalation continue to be debated among historians. It is clear that the wish to keep as free a hand as possible in Vietnam led the White House to evade or even block the mediation efforts of others. The UN was marginalised. Johnson and his aides were incensed by some of the comments and proposals made by UN secretary-general U Thant. According to Dean Rusk, who remained as U.S. secretary of state under Johnson, U Thant never kept the Americans informed about what he was doing, misrepresented North Vietnam's willingness to talk peace, and for a time relied on an intermediary who turned out to be a Soviet spy.[7]

Some of the most serious arguments between Britain and the United States in the past had concerned Southeast Asia, and there remained a conflict of opinion about how best to respond to regional crises. During the Korean War, the British and Americans had not seen eye to eye, and on Indochina Eden had worked hard to limit instability and restrain the Americans. Macmillan had also had reason to urge the Americans to be more cautious, as when Kennedy became involved in Laos. In London, there was a continuing fear that communist gains in the region might provoke hasty U.S. retaliation, the wider impact of which would be unfortunate. There was a fundamental difference between the American and British view of regional security, one that had become increasingly obvious from the late 1940s. The American priority was to resist communism and rarely did Washington make a clear distinction between communism and nationalism. In the opinion of the British, the West had to come to terms with nationalism and provide for peace and order in the whole region. London had reservations about SEATO because it tended to reinforce rather than remove divisions. The Cold War and British decolonisation in Asia created circumstances that were often unhelpful, however, and the spread of anti-imperialist sentiment increased the need for caution. Sometimes Britain tried to use India or the Commonwealth as surrogates. British leaders had long since decided that an attempt to preserve the territorial empire in Asia would be unwise and that economic links mattered more than political control. The wish for economic success overtook the residual attachment to imperial primacy.[8]

Although Macmillan did try to restrain the Americans in Southeast Asia, he also thought that U.S. military intervention there might not be inappropriate, in which case, he reasoned, Britain could gain more influence by supporting U.S. policy. With regard to the communist insurgency in Laos, for example, Macmillan hoped for a negotiated settlement but was prepared to send in British forces if the Americans asked for assistance. Kennedy did not ask. As for South Vietnam, Macmillan agreed that it was strategically vital and that its loss to communism would start the dominoes falling. He doubted that negotiation was a valid option. Without any prompting from the Americans, indeed, Britain established an advisory mission in Saigon in September 1961 to help with the counterinsurgency effort. Britain also persuaded the Commonwealth representatives on the International Commission for Supervision and Control in Vietnam (Canada and India) to exaggerate North Vietnamese infiltration into South Vietnam in violation of the 1954 Geneva accords. This enabled the Americans to increase their active support for South Vietnam. The policy of the Macmillan government was based on several goals and concerns. In restoring Anglo-American cooperation after Suez, for instance, the British believed that it was incumbent on them to demonstrate their usefulness. There was also a desire to maintain influence in Southeast Asia at a time when Britain's commitment to regional security was being questioned. This had implications for Commonwealth unity because Australia and New Zealand suspected that Britain was unwilling or unable to meet its regional responsibilities, and the application for EEC membership reinforced their impression. Another reason for British support for the Americans in Vietnam in the early 1960s was linked with Britain's own experience in dealing with the insurgency in Malaya (from 1948 to 1960 British and Commonwealth troops had fought Chinese-backed communist forces in Malaya). British leaders genuinely believed that guerrilla wars could be won in Southeast Asia. They also looked at the wider context and decided that U.S. intervention in Vietnam was a Cold War necessity and that by supporting the Americans Britain could help to contain China. Had Kennedy pushed for a SEATO operation, it is likely that British forces would have participated. The British attitude began to change, however, late in 1963. The foreign office decided that the reliance upon military means to bring a settlement in Vietnam would lead to a bigger war involving the USSR or China and possibly both. This was not a war that the United States could win. Britain, therefore, advocated negotiation and compromise.[9]

There was opposition to increased American involvement in Vietnam even at the highest levels in the U.S. government, but key figures could not or would not try harder to stop the escalation. Perhaps the British would have found it easier to facilitate a settlement had the dissenters in Washington done more to help. Such cooperation never materialised. President Johnson and his aides did consider nonmilitary options in Vietnam, but they never accepted that retreat would be less damaging to U.S. interests than escalation, and they believed that it was possible to preserve the noncommunist state of South Vietnam. Some historians have argued that the war in Vietnam was not inevitable or necessary, that it had nothing to do with U.S. security, and that policy was determined by domestic politics and the fear of personal humiliation. Incremental decisions were taken for short-term gains. These led to war, but in this process there were opportunities to change direction. The problem was that to change direction would have been to undermine the credibility Kennedy and Johnson wanted as leaders, and the credibility they wanted for the United States on the world stage. In the summer of 1963, the British and French governments urged Washington to work for a political solution in Vietnam, and there were signs that both Hanoi and Saigon were ready to talk, but the Americans decided that the time was not right and Britain and France did not complain very strongly. If the Kennedy and Johnson administrations are to blame for the escalation in Vietnam, the allies might have been less quiescent and exerted themselves more to make recommendations or ask questions. Conversely, if the Americans really believed that their own credibility was at stake, they were unlikely to listen to any ally that objected to the measures upon which this credibility was thought to depend.[10]

Disappointed by the situation in Vietnam in the early 1960s, Macmillan did suggest that the Americans were not giving enough in return for British assistance. Britain's position in Southeast Asia became a greater concern as Indonesia moved towards a confrontation with the Federation of Malaysia. London requested U.S. backing for military action against Indonesia but Washington equivocated, fearing that Indonesian leader Ahmed

Sukarno might seek allies in the communist camp. This made Macmillan turn more towards Western Europe as a complementary platform for British influence. From 1963 to 1967, British forces resisted Indonesia's effort to undermine the Federation of Malaysia. This commitment was difficult to sustain. Wilson's government decided that there could be no question of sending British forces to fight in Vietnam. Money and manpower were limited. Moreover, many Labour backbenchers opposed the U.S. intervention in Vietnam and threatened to revolt against the government if Britain joined in. Yet Wilson and his colleagues had to support U.S. policy publicly, anxious as they were to retain American friendship. Wilson hoped for a quick end to the war and tried to arrange peace talks. In June 1965 he proposed a Commonwealth peace mission. An envoy arrived in North Vietnam in July. Nothing was achieved, however, and the North Vietnamese rebuffed all peace efforts at this time.[11]

Wilson was attacked in some quarters for not doing more to alter U.S. policy and not combining with those leaders in the West who openly opposed escalation. It might have been possible for Britain to take a firmer line in the weeks before and after the U.S. presidential election of November 1964, when the involvement in Vietnam was subjected to close attention. Wilson had to be careful, however, for his government enjoyed only a small parliamentary majority, and the worrying balance of payments situation—which was bound to affect sterling and Britain's role overseas—suggested that Britain might soon need to ask for American help. The government was also conscious of Britain's obligations in Asia. As a member of SEATO, Britain was partly responsible for the integrity of South Vietnam, and to wriggle out of this would be to jeopardise British influence in the region. The British involvement in Malaysia was also significant. Wilson was worried that if he objected too strongly to U.S. policy in Vietnam, the Americans would not support Britain's military effort in Malaysia. Wilson was sure he could persuade President Johnson that in view of the emergency in Malaysia there were no British troops to spare for Vietnam.[12]

For the Labour left, criticism of U.S. foreign policy was normal. Wilson did not wish to alienate left-wingers in his party. Nor was he on good terms personally with Johnson, who became resentful as his demand for a token British contingent in Vietnam was resisted. British and American interests were diverging and Washington was not slow to condemn the scaling down of Britain's commitments around the world as well as the British refusal to help out in Vietnam. That the Americans did not react more strongly suggests that Washington still thought that British cooperation or at least acquiescence was worth having on other matters. The rapport that had developed between Kennedy and Macmillan made more obvious the ill feeling between Johnson and Wilson, but the wider, impersonal context for Anglo-American cooperation was changing as well. Washington viewed Britain as one of several important allies and ignored British claims to precedence whenever these looked like complicating America's dealings with other states.[13]

Wilson knew that Washington was uneasy about Britain's wish to give up important overseas responsibilities. From 1965, as the Americans poured more men and resources into Vietnam, Britain decided to leave Aden, suffered a serious sterling crisis, became embroiled in difficulties with the Commonwealth, and eventually announced an almost complete withdrawal from East of Suez, all of which revealed both the limits on British power and differences between the British and American view of intervention in the developing world. Although Wilson wanted to act as a peacemaker in Vietnam, moreover, his attempt was doomed. Some of his colleagues, notably Denis Healey (defence secretary 1964–1970) and Richard Crossman (minister for housing and local government 1964–1966, lord president of the council and leader of the House of Commons 1966–1968, and secretary of state for health and social security 1968–1970), insisted that Britain could not mediate because Britain could not denounce the Americans; however, Wilson was sure that Britain could help and should do so by standing with the United States. Johnson did not appreciate or understand this stance. What he wanted was not a peace initiative but a contribution to the military effort. Johnson did not believe that Britain would be able to bring peace, and the actions that Wilson thought helpful were dismissed in Washington as unwanted interference. The president told Wilson in one particularly heated exchange that if the Americans were not telling the British what to do in Malaya, then the British had no business telling the Americans how to run the war in Vietnam. At the time and afterwards, Wilson played down the division and insisted that his conduct on Vietnam was welcomed by the U.S. government. Yet Johnson angrily rejected the suggestion that Wilson should visit the United States for crisis talks in February 1965. When Wilson did go to America, in April 1965, he said he would press the Soviets to support a peace effort. He recorded that the president was willing to give negotiations a chance. This was an exaggeration, but it suited Wilson's political purposes to talk and act as if Washington approved of what he was doing.[14]

In April 1965 Johnson and his aides expressed the hope that Britain's economic problems would diminish. They commended Wilson for his government's determination to strengthen sterling and avoid devaluation. They said they were grateful for whatever signs of support the British could offer for U.S. involvement in Vietnam. Johnson probably wished to avoid alienating Wilson in case the latter decided to pursue peace in Vietnam unilaterally. Equally, the Americans did not want to push the British into cooperation with de Gaulle or U Thant. If peace was going to be pursued, the Americans wanted to make sure that their interests would be respected. Therefore, it made more sense to accept Wilson's peace initiative than to reject it. Wilson knew that the U.S. military operation in Vietnam would continue. He emphasised, however, that for domestic political reasons he would have to play an active role in the arrangement of peace talks. This Anglo-American understanding came under increasing pressure. Sterling grew weaker, Wilson had to attend to the future of Rhodesia, and in Washington it was feared that Britain would decide massively to scale down its responsibilities in the Middle East and Far East. A new sterling crisis coincided with the arrival of many more U.S. troops in Vietnam, raising London's concerns about escalation, and Wilson's longing to be seen as a peacemaker became problematic. If he was genuine, it was argued, he would not have insisted on leading the Commonwealth mission because it would be impossible for the Soviet Union, China, and North Vietnam to believe that he was acting independently of the Americans. By the time Wilson returned to Washington in December 1965, he seemed not to be focusing so much on peace plans, which gratified Johnson and Rusk. The prime minister complained that he was under constant pressure at home to distance himself from U.S. policy in Vietnam and scale down Britain's military commitments East of Suez. Johnson and Rusk told him that if he wished to make further moves for peace, they would understand. As for Britain's world role, they urged him not to make too many cuts and Wilson promised to consult them before making any final decisions.[15]

The diary of Richard Crossman provides some insight into the suspicions and disagreements generated by Wilson's conduct, especially in the government and the Labour Party. In June 1965 Crossman confessed that he did not trust the prime minister or the new foreign secretary, Michael Stewart, who was '100 per cent Anglo-American in a prim and proper way'. Labour MPs were becoming tense and 'not only left-wingers are beginning to organise letters and stage protests in their constituencies'. Wilson and his confidants were saying that the Commonwealth peace mission would be a great success, but Crossman called it 'gimmickry'. Wilson simply wanted 'to calm the left wing of the party'. Rather than 'going away on a Vietnam stunt', Crossman wrote, Wilson should stay at home and deal with the ailing economy.[16]

When Wilson explained his peace plan to the Commons on June 17, 1965, MPs were angry because he had already spoken about it on television. Wilson claimed that an earlier statement to the Commons would not have been appropriate, owing to the terms under which he had been negotiating with Commonwealth leaders. He spoke of the urgent need for 'a permanent and honourable peace settlement' in Vietnam. To do nothing would increase the danger, Wilson said, and given that it was not possible 'in present circumstances' to work through the UN or to act with the co-chair of the Geneva conference on Vietnam of 1954, the USSR, it was up to the Commonwealth to take the initiative. This was accepted by Home for the Conservatives and by Jo Grimond for the Liberals (Grimond was pleased that a Commonwealth initiative would mean a multiracial approach to the Vietnam question), but then MPs challenged the prime minister on several points. Would U.S. bombing be stopped in order to assist with the organisation of a conference? Would Vietcong action be suspended, too? Would all the governments interested in Vietnam receive the peace mission? What mattered more, the good of the Vietnamese people or the wishes of outside powers? Would Britain continue to cooperate with the Americans? How had the composition of the Commonwealth peace mission been decided? Wilson's supporters thought that he should not be required to go beyond generalities, in view of the delicacy and seriousness of the matter, but he did respond to some of the questions put to him. He warned of 'a serious poisoning of the world atmosphere' and stressed that the prospects for détente and disarmament were worsening. The war also had to be ended because it was a 'terrible human tragedy'. The composition of the peace mission had still to be finalised, Wilson continued, and it would not be helpful to get into 'invidious questions of selection', but the mission would be led by Britain and would probably include two African members of the Commonwealth and one each from Asia and the West Indies. The intention was to arrange a conference that would be attended by representatives from North Vietnam, China, the Soviet Union, South Vietnam, and the United States. Nobody outside the Commonwealth had been consulted in advance. Now every country knew what was intended, had a chance to offer approval, and 'the world would form its own judgement of those who did not'. Wilson agreed that it was important for hostilities to cease in order to give the mission a good chance of success. This was a sensitive issue, however, and he could give no details. Perhaps it would be impossible to arrange a conference. Nevertheless, 'I believe it better to have tried and failed than at this historic, critical moment for us not to have made the effort', and the plan showed that the Commonwealth had a key role to play in world affairs and that it was committed to peace.[17]

Such confidence as there was in Wilson's plan when it was announced, and there was not a great deal, quickly faded. On July 5, 1965, Michael Stewart confirmed in a written answer to parliamentary questions that North Vietnam had made its response: the peace mission would not be received. The *Guardian* pointed out that the North Vietnamese had never indicated a willingness to talk to the Commonwealth envoys. Wilson tried to justify his actions. He had not insisted on leading the peace mission, he told the press, but had been duly appointed as its chairman by the Commonwealth, and he was not 'slavishly following' the Americans. *The Times*, which maintained that the situation in Vietnam called for a political rather than a military solution, had suggested that the communist regime in Hanoi would probably receive the mission in return for Britain's diplomatic recognition, and much was made of a speech delivered by Wilson in Wolverhampton on July 2 in which he declared that 'we cannot afford and the world cannot afford to take "No" for an answer in this vital issue'. The North Vietnamese line was that Wilson was an agent of Washington and that the only way to end the war was for U.S. troops to leave Vietnam in order for its people to determine their own future. *The Times* was subsequently disappointed to learn that U.S. troop numbers in Vietnam were going to be increased: 'the more American military power is deployed to the exclusion of political initiatives, the more it gives all the political arguments away to its opponents'.[18]

Vietnam ranked below Europe in importance to Britain, and in London it was hoped that the Americans would not overcommit themselves in Asia and allow themselves to be distracted from the NATO area. This concern had previously influenced British policy on Korea and Indochina in the 1950s, and now it resurfaced. These considerations of strategy and security suggest that there was more to Wilson's refusal to send troops to Vietnam than personal authority, party politics, international criticism, and lack of resources. If British forces were sent in the war in Vietnam would be intensified and further internationalised, which would probably reinforce the U.S. commitment to the region. The British government wanted to avoid this. Many Labour MPs, meanwhile, expected Wilson and other ministers to speak out against U.S. policy. Anger grew as members of the government made no such remarks. Wilson did like to pose as a restraining influence on the Americans, however, and sometimes he made the appropriate gestures. He dissociated himself from the U.S. bombing of North Vietnam in mid-1966, for example, and the government also suspended the sale of weapons that might possibly be used in

Vietnam. In November 1967 the foreign secretary, George Brown, told the Cabinet that Britain must adhere to its 'committed detachment' and could not fall in uncritically behind U.S. policy. Although Washington went on complaining, Johnson had already chosen not to exert full pressure. In 1965 and 1966 his advisers suggested that U.S. loans and support for sterling could be used to compel the British to send troops to Vietnam, but Johnson decided that this would be too extreme a measure.[19]

The British did not remain entirely uninvolved in the war. They provided a medical team, supplied intelligence, gave advice on counterinsurgency, sent weapons (sometimes disguised) and possibly also an elite special unit, and offered South Vietnam economic aid. British personnel trained U.S. and South Vietnamese troops in jungle warfare. Britain also made available the port at Hong Kong and maintained airfields in Thailand. Johnson wanted more, but Wilson argued that Britain was already stretched by the military action in Malaysia and would be most useful to Washington as a mediator. On this latter point, the prime minister's view accorded with that of the foreign office, which advised that the Americans could not defeat the communists in Vietnam and would eventually need Britain to broker a peace deal. After the Commonwealth peace effort of 1965 stalled, Wilson took up other plans, annoying the Americans and trying to get the Soviets involved. The prime minister overestimated Moscow's influence over the North Vietnamese. Little progress was made and Wilson accused Johnson's aides of undermining Britain's peace policy. The Americans blamed North Vietnam. Wilson appreciated that there was a limit to their patience, and he tried to stop short of this limit because of Britain's need for U.S. help, but he would not abandon his peace initiatives. He persisted in part because of personal vanity and a belief that he knew best. He also acted as peacemaker to deflect American demands for British troops, to raise his own international profile, and to mollify the many Labour MPs who opposed the U.S. intervention in Vietnam. Johnson could not openly oppose the peace efforts, which played into Wilson's hands, and difficulties in the Commonwealth help to explain why Wilson preferred to work through that organisation when he was able. Some Commonwealth countries were outspoken in their criticism of U.S. policy, whereas Australia and New Zealand both had troops in Vietnam. The Commonwealth seemed to be in danger of falling apart, peace offered a unifying cause, and Wilson also saw a chance to divert attention away from an equally divisive Commonwealth issue, Rhodesia. In addition, he wanted to show the Commonwealth that Britain was for peace and that Britain was willing to act independently of the United States, and he calculated that peacemaking was a matter on which it would be difficult for his opponents—Conservative and Labour—to attack him.[20]

British strategists and advisers had decided that America could not win in Vietnam, but Wilson was also repeatedly told that Britain had an interest in the containment of communism in Southeast Asia and that backing U.S. policy would give the British government opportunities to influence the Americans. Wilson continued uncomfortably in much the same vein as before. He continued to resist pressure from the Labour left and refused publicly to oppose U.S. policy, even though this did not improve his standing in Washington. There were times when the conduct of Labour MPs was acutely embarrassing. The government had a Commons majority of only four after the October 1964 general election, and although the majority rose to over ninety at the election of March 1966, backbenchers could still make life difficult for ministers. When Wilson was in Washington in December 1965 to address the UN and discuss the Rhodesian crisis with American leaders, he received a message from sixty-eight Labour MPs demanding an end to the U.S. bombing of North Vietnam. During 1966 and 1967 he was urged by party conference, the trade unions and Labour backbenchers to condemn U.S. policy. Such was the growing rebelliousness among Labour MPs, indeed, that forty-nine of them voted against the government on Vietnam in December 1969. Outside Parliament, the government had to contend with popular protests and movements such as the Vietnam Solidarity Campaign. There was a mass demonstration in London in October 1967 and opposition to the Vietnam War and to Wilson's pro-U.S. stance continued to gather strength. After inconclusive talks with Soviet premier Aleksei Kosygin, who visited London in February 1967, Wilson stopped pursuing new peace initiatives for a time. In fact, he lost confidence across the board at the end of the 1960s, weighed down with political problems at home as well as abroad.[21]

Wilson had alienated sections of the Labour Party and the British media and public opinion, and damaged Britain's relations with the Commonwealth, many of whose members opposed the war in Vietnam, and with Western Europe, where antiwar sentiment was strong. De Gaulle's argument that Britain was too close to America was reinforced, which had implications for Wilson's intention to apply for membership of the EEC. In view of all these disadvantages Wilson might have hoped for more sympathy from the U.S. government, but although the Americans allowed him to portray himself as someone to whom they would listen, in order for him to withstand domestic criticism, there was little consultation. Indeed, Wilson and his colleagues resented the lack of prior warning whenever America made a new move in Vietnam, for this made it harder for them to deal with the fallout in Parliament and the press. The Americans did not take the British into their confidence.[22]

One of the central figures in the peace effort of late 1966 and early 1967 was the foreign secretary, George Brown. He later recalled the huge difficulties he had faced. The Americans were demanding that Britain put off the withdrawal from East of Suez, and doubted that Britain could end the war in Vietnam, and it was not clear that the Soviets could or would persuade Hanoi to negotiate. Brown saw that a way had to be found for the Americans to leave Vietnam, but also that it could not look like surrender or retreat, and Brown thought that the Americans should stay until conditions in the region were such that the further spread of communism would be impossible. He went to Moscow in November 1966 to talk to the Soviets. The Americans and Wilson had agreed on a formula for a ceasefire: U.S. bombing raids would be suspended if North Vietnam stopped sending troops into South Vietnam, and in due course America would halt the build-up of its own forces in South Vietnam. Brown did not get far in Moscow, but discussions continued when Kosygin was in London in February 1967. By this time, Wilson was desperate for a breakthrough, and Brown was worried that if the Americans were pushed out of Southeast Asia, they might decide to quit Europe as well.

During the London talks it became clear that Washington had been in touch with the Soviets through Italian and Polish intermediaries. Therefore, the proposals that Brown and Wilson wished to put to Kosygin and Soviet foreign minister Andrei Gromyko had already been put to them by others. 'The Americans had not told us what they were doing with anyone else', Brown later wrote, 'so our attempt to act as mediators ultimately put us in a ridiculous position'. Wilson was still optimistic. Brown was not. He tried to convince Washington that the war had to be fought on the ground (as the British had done in Malaya) and that air cover was relatively unimportant. Bombers did not win jungle wars. Brown had 'intense difficulty in getting any of these ideas through', in part because 'many Americans, regrettably, think that the only thing that matters is the weight of power—they honestly believe that if you flood the world with enough Coca-Cola you are bound to win in the end'. Nothing changed. Johnson and his advisers decided that it was not yet possible to announce the end of U.S. bombing. Brown wondered if the Americans really had reliable contacts in Moscow, as they claimed, and he began to suspect that the Soviets could not influence Hanoi. He thought that the Soviets said they could help primarily because they wanted to embarrass China. When the Americans indicated that they would offer firm undertakings in order for peace talks to be arranged, Brown informed Kosygin and Gromyko, but then the Americans changed their minds. Instead of urging them to reconsider, as Brown advised, Wilson immediately told the Soviets that the position had changed. The peace effort collapsed. Wilson and his colleagues had been too anxious to broker a deal and failed to check everything out with Washington. The U.S. government was itself divided, with hawks and doves struggling to control policy. There was no consistent line, which meant that the British picked up mixed signals. The peace process was also hindered by the Soviets, who did not really have the influence they claimed to have over North Vietnam. Brown also considered that there were too many special advisers and interests seeking to sway Wilson and Johnson.[23]

Senior U.S. officials had been suggesting in public that America was willing to make the first move and would stop the bombing if North

Vietnam promised to make a constructive response. But the U.S. military effort made notable gains early in 1967, leading Washington to think that the war could be won. Attitudes hardened. In return for a ceasefire the Americans made new demands, having decided, apparently, that they could get more by fighting than they could by negotiating. Wilson was furious. He asserted that a real opportunity for peace had been wasted. Though North Vietnam had asked the Soviets to find out more about U.S. intentions, however, the Americans never took the London talks very seriously. They saw the talks as another bid by Wilson to gain credit for himself and boost Britain's international prestige. There was more to Wilson's conduct than this, for he was also responding to his critics in the government and the Labour Party, and he had concluded that the Americans could not win militarily in Vietnam. His wish for peace was genuine. If Hanoi proved willing to make a deal, though, Johnson wanted the political benefits for himself, not Wilson. The president supposed that Wilson might offer too much to Kosygin and did not want to be bound by promises made by anyone else. Wilson and Brown blamed the United States for the failure of the London talks, but nobody in Washington wanted Britain to act on America's behalf, and Hanoi's willingness to negotiate had yet to be established. The shift in the U.S. position with regard to the terms that Wilson and Brown put to Kosygin might not have been as sharp as the British claimed. Some of the details had not been settled and there had never been any question of an unconditional American bombing halt. Perhaps Wilson and Brown ignored information from Washington that did not suit them. Matters also appear to have been confused by deliberations within the U.S. government, and it is possible that Johnson and his advisers did not intend to be duplicitous. Rather, they were reacting to events, including North Vietnamese troop movements. At the same time, there was no eager push for peace from the White House, and Wilson and Brown carried on even though they must have known about the American objections. The prime minister gambled. He thought he could see a way to deal with political problems at home and demonstrate British influence and his own statesmanship, but the White House could not be sure that Hanoi would listen to Kosygin, realised that the Soviets were competing with China, and knew also that Moscow was pleased to see American resources and attention devoted to Vietnam. The Soviets did not want an outcome that benefited the United States (or the Chinese).[24]

Though irritated by the Wilson government's attitude on Vietnam, the Americans still valued Britain's contribution to security arrangements in those parts of the world where the British had traditionally been strong—especially the Indian Ocean and Persian Gulf—and they were willing to cover some of the costs of Britain's global role in order to prevent its further shrinkage. They reacted badly to indications from London that the East of Suez presence might have to be abandoned and they hoped that Wilson would be able to avert the devaluation of sterling. It is possible that Wilson agreed to support U.S. policy on Vietnam and to postpone devaluation in return for American loans. For many people in Britain, and especially the Labour left, the prime minister had gone too far in doing what the Americans wanted. Some Conservative MPs also began to take up this argument, complaining that the government had made Britain a subservient nation, although the leader of the opposition from August 1965, Edward Heath, thought that Wilson was not backing the Americans strongly enough. The devaluation of sterling in November 1967 and confirmation of the withdrawal from East of Suez in January 1968 deeply frustrated the Johnson administration, and when Wilson arrived in Washington in February 1968 he could not have expected an easy time. Johnson and his advisers complained about the East of Suez decision and the president was offended by Wilson's assertion that there could be no military solution in Vietnam.[25]

Wilson repeatedly denied that he was supporting U.S. policy on Vietnam in return for American financial help. He told the Cabinet in February 1966 that the Americans had never suggested that their financial assistance was conditional upon any such arrangement. What Wilson did say, however, was that Britain's position in the Far East *was* a determinant of America's attitude. Indeed, much was said in public both in Britain and the United States about Britain's role in keeping order and defending freedom in the Far East. In May 1966, as Wilson came under growing pressure to distance himself from U.S. policy on Vietnam, he insisted that he could not do this 'because we can't kick our creditors in the balls'. Clearly, Britain's financial predicament did oblige the prime minister to use all the political tricks at his disposal to hold back difficulties at home and minimise the damage that was being done to Anglo-American relations. Britain could not do without American money, but reliance on it, as members of Wilson's own government recognised, could not solve a basic problem. The United States was helping Britain in order for Britain to meet its overseas commitments, but the very reason why the British needed American assistance was the insupportable burden of the commitments that Washington wished Britain to maintain. Although some historians accept that American financial support was not dependent on Britain's promise not to devalue the pound or withdraw from East of Suez, if some such understanding existed it could hardly have been expressed in a formal or explicit way. This does not mean that the British and the Americans had any doubts about what they each required, or that they declined to conduct their relations accordingly. Wilson knew that the Americans wanted Britain to remain East of Suez. He told them in December 1965 that he would consult them before any major decisions were taken, and in return Wilson probably hoped that they would accommodate his refusal to send British troops to Vietnam. Perhaps he led them to attach too much importance to what he said, for when the withdrawal from East of Suez was announced the Americans were indignant. They thought Wilson had agreed that America would not be left alone in Southeast Asia, which meant that British withdrawal would not happen while the United States was involved in Vietnam.[26]

Some of Johnson's advisers argued strongly that U.S. financial aid should not be used as a lever to obtain British troops for Vietnam, that it was in America's interests to support sterling regardless of what was happening in Southeast Asia, and that helping the British to remain East of Suez was much more important than getting them to fight in Vietnam. The understanding between London and Washington may have been political rather than financial: the Americans backed Britain up on Malaysia and the British backed the Americans up on Vietnam, as had been agreed by Johnson and Home in 1964. When Johnson did explicitly link financial help with the request for British troops to fight in Vietnam, in April 1967, Wilson insisted that any such arrangement would bring down his government.[27]

In 1965 Johnson's top aides had admitted that the firmest public support from *anyone* for U.S. policy in Vietnam was coming from the British. The Americans kept London informed about the course of the war and made suggestions with regard to Wilson's mediation efforts. Nevertheless, Johnson's more hawkish advisers, and the hardliners in the U.S. military, accused Britain of defeatism and of wishing to abandon the worldwide struggle against communism, and the fact that ships flying the British flag were stopping off in North Vietnam also led to serious quarrels. The difficulty was that many of these vessels were registered in Hong Kong and it was not legally possible to prevent them from visiting North Vietnamese ports. Most were used by Chinese businesses based in Hong Kong. In May 1966 the navy minister, Christopher Mayhew, pointed out that if the ships were not subjected to firmer control, Britain could not expect American help in imposing sanctions against the white regime in Rhodesia (formerly Southern Rhodesia), which was defying British authority. The government moved to stop the trade with North Vietnam in case the Americans made more of it. British strategists and planners, meanwhile, persisted with their advice to the government that U.S. policy in Southeast Asia was misguided, and in the foreign office it became a fixed idea that Johnson was neglecting Western Europe's security. In Washington, awareness of Britain's economic problems and inability to sustain the global role meant that the 'special relationship' was downgraded and the need to listen to British advice reduced.[28]

The quarrelling between British and U.S. leaders became even worse after July 1967, when Wilson's government announced its plans for the withdrawal from East of Suez. Johnson pressed Wilson to reverse this decision and suggested that the least Britain could do was remain in the Persian Gulf. Britain's decision had obvious implications for the U.S. involvement in Vietnam because Britain's withdrawal from Southeast Asia would make the Americans more exposed there. In fact, Washington was coming to realise that America's own role in the Far East needed to be reassessed. Johnson did not seek reelection in 1968, largely because of Vietnam. In London there was relief that the Americans were finally looking for a way out of Vietnam. There was also fear, however, because of the possibility that a scaling down of U.S. commitments in Asia might lead to a scaling down in Europe, and because Britain could not easily appeal to the Americans to remain in Europe after having refused to help in Vietnam.[29]

At the same time, there seemed to be little point in trying to curry favour with the Americans when the 'special relationship' mattered less to them than it once had. Anglo-American defence talks continued, and there was diplomatic cooperation during the Arab-Israeli War of July 1967 and Czech crisis of August 1968, but the ill-feeling prompted by disagreements on Vietnam and East of Suez did not quickly fade away.

In its wider impact, moreover, the war in Vietnam wrought significant changes in the international order. America's allies rejected Washington's claim that intervention in Vietnam was essential for western security and credibility, and complained about the consequences for trade and finance. The war had important effects domestically—not just in Britain but also in Italy, the FRG, and elsewhere. Political and social life in certain countries would never be the same again owing to the ideas and emotions that the war in Vietnam had stirred up.[30]

Although he was angry about Britain's decision to withdraw from East of Suez, Johnson encouraged another of Wilson's peace efforts early in 1968. Wilson was hopeful, as he had been with previous proposals, but he made no progress in 1968 because Moscow refused to put pressure on Hanoi. Nevertheless, Johnson's decision not to stand for reelection and the scaling down of U.S. bombing indicated that circumstances were changing. The British government wanted to help the Americans to leave Vietnam, while minimising communist gains in Asia and protecting Britain's commercial and political interests there. In the foreign office, there was also the ongoing concern that any hint of western weakness or an American defeat should be avoided. Wilson's peace initiatives remain contentious. Perhaps he was never bothered about whether they worked or not, for they were the means to other ends. Wilson wanted to take attention away from Britain's pro-American stance, appease Labour MPs, avoid a split in the Commonwealth, and establish himself as a world statesman. However, much went on behind the scenes and this part of Wilson's activity cannot merely have been for show, and there were good reasons why Britain should have wanted peace and stability in Southeast Asia. Whatever Wilson did, he could not ignore the fact that Britain needed American financial help and could not do without U.S. support in the confrontation between Malaysia and Indonesia; even had Wilson opposed the Americans more openly on Vietnam, they would probably have taken no notice. British policy was not unsuccessful. The Commonwealth did not break up, there was no serious breach with Australia and New Zealand, and Wilson did not irreversibly alienate the Americans while parrying Johnson's demand for British troops. Domestic opposition was formidable, but rarely unmanageable. Britain kept out of an expensive and controversial war. Britain was still committed to containment in Southeast Asia, and did not want the Americans to be defeated there, but Vietnam was less important to Britain than other problems. The cardinal requirement was to avoid a rupture with the Americans because U.S. help was needed with some of these other problems.[31] Western security, Commonwealth affairs, decolonisation, relative economic decline, Polaris and national defence, and the contracting range of options for Britain East of Suez all had to be addressed if Britain was to remain a great power.

CHAPTER 7

BRITAIN IN RETREAT

From the mid-1960s, Britain had less influence in Washington because of the quarrels over Vietnam, the scaling down of Britain's overseas commitments, and the weakness of the British economy. Maintaining the global role had less appeal when it seemed that the effort would make little difference in Britain's dealings with the Americans. The Johnson administration's refusal to listen to advice on Vietnam strengthened the idea that the British government should ignore U.S. wishes when it came to doing what Britain's economic well-being required—withdrawing from East of Suez. Britain's focus in defence and foreign policy had been shifting towards NATO and Europe for some time. Relationships and responsibilities elsewhere were not peremptorily discarded, however, and Commonwealth links and a range of economic, strategic, and other interests across Africa and Asia meant that Britain still played a role outside Europe. The British tried to have a say in what happened in every part of the world where they were involved, but economic and military rivals appeared to be getting stronger as the British became more conscious of the difficulties they faced in seeking to preserve status and influence, both in Europe and beyond. Much depended on Britain's economic performance and on the timing and extent of changes in British activity East of Suez.

Britain had been attempting to reinvigorate NATO when the French decided in 1966 to pull out of its military arrangements (on the grounds that the Americans were using NATO to control Western Europe). The French action caused alarm, for other members of NATO were reducing their forces and the quality of U.S. personnel based in Europe fell as the most effective units were sent to Vietnam. In 1967 Britain's defence secretary, Denis Healey, argued for coherence and reform in NATO and helped to persuade its council to adopt the strategy of 'flexible response', which allowed each member to decide on the type of forces that it would contribute to the alliance. When the Czech crisis broke out in 1968 the NATO council required all members to increase the size of their armed forces. Healey confirmed that the BAOR would be reequipped. America's failure to consult its allies about the Strategic Arms Limitation Talks (SALT), which began in Helsinki in November 1969, raised the concern that Western Europe's security would be detrimentally affected by any deals that the Americans made with the Soviets. The 'Euro-group' emerged within NATO. America's allies wanted more information about SALT and complained that Vietnam had prompted the United States to pay less attention to Europe.[1]

The Wilson government's reluctance to send forces to Vietnam was reinforced by opinion in the Commonwealth. Among Commonwealth members, only Australia and New Zealand sent troops, and they had existing military links with the United States through the ANZUS Pact and SEATO. Some other members of the Commonwealth openly condemned U.S. policy. Australia welcomed American involvement in Asia and the Pacific, while Britain was committed to decolonisation and turning more towards Europe. The confrontation between Indonesia and Malaysia complicated matters. There were disagreements about how to handle Indonesian leader Sukarno. Was he an aggressor who had to be restrained, or could he be conciliated and prevented from befriending the USSR and China? Attitudes shifted, largely because of the course of the war in Vietnam. The British and Americans had contradictory views of Sukarno, and Australia and New Zealand were unsure about how to respond to the advice emanating from London and Washington.[2]

Wilson's government invested a great deal of time and effort in the Commonwealth. There was economic aid for the poorest members and improvements in Commonwealth administration, yet the idea that the Commonwealth could be made into more of an asset, and buttress Britain's great-power status, proved to be mistaken. Some former colonies were not economically viable and needed heavy subsidies, notably Gambia from 1965. Controversy developed over Gibraltar, whose inhabitants wished it to remain a British dependency while the UN and Spain pressed for a change. London wanted to retain the naval base in Gibraltar, maintained that the wishes of local people had to be respected, and asserted that it would be morally wrong to hand the territory over to the Spanish dictator, Francisco Franco. In September 1965 the Kashmir dispute between India and Pakistan led to a brief war. Peace talks were arranged in January 1966 by the Soviets, not by Britain, the former imperial power. The unilateral declaration of independence (UDI) by white leaders in Rhodesia, who intended to deny the black majority equal rights, placed the Wilson government in an awkward position. The Commonwealth demanded military intervention, as did the Labour left, but Wilson opted for economic sanctions against the illegal regime established in November 1965, in the hope that it would agree to a new constitutional settlement. The sanctions were evaded. Negotiations failed in 1966 and again in 1968. Britain gave up the demand that there should be majority rule before independence, but insisted upon social reforms and at least some demonstrable move towards majority rule. White Rhodesian leaders refused and made their own constitutional arrangements. Another controversy related to arms sales to South Africa, whose system of apartheid continued to provoke the bitter hostility of Commonwealth members. Wilson's government decided to cancel the relevant contracts, but this decision was attacked by the Conservative leader, Edward Heath (who also criticised the policy on Rhodesia), as a damaging blow to Britain's finances, trade, and defence industries. Ministers were also condemned when Britain provided support for the Nigerian government during the Biafran war of 1967 to 1970.[3]

Despite these problems, Wilson and his colleagues were loath to accept that Britain could not go on acting as a global power. They chose to focus on the successes that Britain had: the protection of Kuwait from 1961, the interventions in East Africa in 1964 to assist new governments that were facing military coups, the operations in Malaysia from 1964. It was politically necessary to draw attention away from failures, and Labour also had a principled attachment to overseas aid and made much of Britain's attempts to help poorer nations. The record here, though, was mixed. There were a lot of idealistic promises but Britain's economic condition meant that many of these could not be kept. Prompting from Washington affected British policy. The Americans favoured decolonisation, although after the secession crisis and civil war in Congo they realised that it would be better not to force the pace. Macmillan's mostly peaceful withdrawal from empire made Washington more willing to defer to the British on decolonisation. For example, Kennedy's administration had helped to deflect some of the criticism levelled against Britain at the UN, and as the Rhodesian situation worsened the British were determined to handle it without UN interference. Unfortunately, the wish to move slowly and avoid confrontation, although pleasing the United States, led the white minority in Rhodesia to think that Britain was unable or unwilling to prevent them from setting up the kind of government they wanted, which set in motion a train of events that culminated with UDI. The changing nature of the Commonwealth, and the problems this posed for Britain, led many people to question the value of the link with former colonies around the world. Popular misgivings were matched by the anxiety that was growing at elite levels in British politics and society.

Decolonisation was far from trouble-free in practice or entirely positive in its consequences. Even so, the claim that Britain's experience was not so different from that of France (in Indochina and Algeria), Belgium (in Congo), and Portugal (in Angola) is questionable. Although British decolonisation was problematic, there was nothing like the bloodshed, bitterness, and domestic political division that arose as a result of the policies pursued by the other colonial powers. It cannot be denied, however, that British policy did to some extent produce grave and negative results.[4]

On issues like aid to Gambia there was considerable discord. Official British aid in 1966 was about £840,000. A four-year package worth £3.2 million was announced in the spring of 1967, along with grants for specific purposes. The government reckoned that the need for these additional grants would gradually diminish. British money was intended to improve education and agriculture; Britain also provided loans and technical assistance. Many British experts and volunteers went to work in Gambia. Exports to Gambia did not show a marked increase. In 1965 they were worth £2.1 million. By 1967 they had risen to only £2.5 million. Some important contracts for British companies were announced in the spring of 1968, but they were financed from British funds. Aid to African members of the Commonwealth was designed in part to counter communist influence, and much of it was distributed under the Commonwealth African Assistance Plan adopted in 1960. Canada, Australia, and New Zealand made contributions, and from the mid-1960s small amounts were also given by India and Pakistan.[5]

On Gibraltar, the government had to steer a middle course between upholding British rights and making conciliatory gestures. Foreign secretary George Brown told the Commons in October 1966 that Gibraltar was British and that 'recent Spanish actions, including the Spanish government's activity in imposing new restrictions at the frontier, and the mob attacks on our consulates, which I deplore, cannot affect this fact'. The British government would not abandon its responsibilities in Gibraltar and the interests of its inhabitants would be safeguarded, but at the same time Britain was ready to negotiate.[6]

During and after the war over Kashmir, there were complaints that the government had not done more through the UN and the Commonwealth. On December 22, 1965, the secretary of state for Commonwealth relations, Arthur Bottomley, insisted that the government was 'very distressed' about the conflict between two Commonwealth members, had done everything possible to help the UN broker a ceasefire, and had decided not to act through the Commonwealth for fear of cutting across the UN's efforts. He promised that Britain would assist the UN to address the problems that had caused the war, and engage in relief efforts. Bottomley welcomed Soviet mediation, but on January 25, 1966, when he was asked why Britain was not taking the lead, he merely repeated that the government would continue to play a part through the UN and if necessary the Commonwealth.[7]

White Rhodesia's UDI, the sanctions, and the failed negotiations of 1966 and 1968 prompted sustained criticism of the Labour government. Summing up the situation in May 1969, foreign secretary Michael Stewart insisted that 'if the door is now being slammed it is not by us, but by the regime. We have made repeated attempts to reach an honourable settlement'. Britain had made concessions that many in the Commonwealth disliked, but had to insist on 'unimpeded progress within a reasonable time towards majority rule', which the illegal Rhodesian regime flatly refused to accept. Some MPs thought that sanctions should be lifted. They claimed that sanctions had made the regime less—rather than more—cooperative. Stewart denied this. The regime had long been intransigent, he said, and sanctions should continue as a sign that its racist principles and denial of equal rights were unacceptable. Stewart could not convince the opponents of sanctions, however, and they continued to insist that government policy was harming Britain, that other countries were not observing the sanctions, and that coercive means were unlikely to bring about a settlement.[8]

On the arms sales to South Africa, the government was condemned both by those who thought that its policy was not stringent enough, and by those who opposed the arms embargo and claimed that it was damaging British trade. In some quarters it was argued that Britain should have pressed for a mandatory embargo at the UN, but the foreign office decided that no case existed for this because the situation in South Africa did not threaten international peace. The supposition that Britain's overall trade with South Africa had declined was firmly rejected in July 1969 by the parliamentary secretary to the board of trade, Gwyneth Dunwoody. South Africa was still the fourth largest market for British exports, she declared. It was true that Britain's share of the South African market had declined (from 34 percent in 1958 to 24 percent in 1968), but South Africa's economy was growing and Britain still had a substantial share of a rapidly expanding total volume of trade. Despite intense competition, indeed, no country invested more in South Africa and none of Britain's main economic rivals could match the value of Britain's exports to South Africa. Though Dunwoody acknowledged that in 1968, Britain's balance of trade with South Africa favoured the latter for the first time, she did not think it essential that Britain's trade with South Africa should balance: 'in terms of balance it is our trade with all countries which is important'. The changes that had taken place began before the arms embargo and were not caused by it. The South Africans disliked it but there was no evidence that it was affecting the wider trade, and it was important to remember that the embargo was being observed by most of the West, that it was in line with the decisions of the UN Security Council, and that it only covered a limited and specific set of items.[9]

Controversy over the Biafran secession and civil war in Nigeria increased because Britain supplied weapons to the federal government of Nigeria. A humanitarian crisis in Biafra added to the furore. In October 1968 Wilson denied that British mediation efforts were being hampered by the arms sales and rejected the claim that Britain had lost moral authority. He told the Commons that African members of the Commonwealth approved of Britain's position, as did members of the Organisation of African Unity (the OAU had been established in 1963 to give African countries a collective voice and to eradicate colonialism and build up a neutral force in world affairs). Wilson regretted that some governments had recognised Biafra as an independent state and supplied it with arms. This was not the way to promote a ceasefire. The British government would continue to press for a settlement, he said, on the basis of the established federal system in Nigeria and 'adequate safeguards' for the people of Biafra. Meanwhile, Britain's relief efforts would go on, although Wilson had to admit that much of the aid was not getting through to the needy. He attributed this to the unhelpful actions of both the Nigerian government and the Biafran authorities. When MPs urged him to organise an international ban on arms sales to both sides, he insisted that such a ban, even if it were possible, would make no difference. The priority had to be a ceasefire, he said, and his efforts would be devoted to this end. MPs objected that Britain should at least stop its own arms sales, but Wilson upheld 'the traditional role of Her Majesty's Government in supplying the federal government. I cannot accept the doctrine of neutrality in this matter because here we have a Commonwealth country facing a secessionist revolt'.[10]

For some of Britain's difficulties in these years, there were many observers who thought that the prime minister was chiefly to blame. On Kashmir, Wilson called for negotiations and made a direct plea for the avoidance of war, but India invaded nonetheless. Wilson's condemnation of Indian aggression meant that Britain could not act as mediator, though the government was not too worried when the USSR stepped into this role. The resulting settlement brought no great change to the prewar situation. The affair was a blow to British prestige, however, and it may have prompted Wilson to think more about Britain's relationship with Europe, because Commonwealth ties were not proving to be very useful. There was probably little that Wilson could have done about the dispute over Kashmir. On Rhodesia he was more culpable, at least in the opinion of Richard Crossman, who wrote in November 1965 that the prime minister 'has judged it completely wrong'. Wilson regarded the dispute as 'his Cuba', a test of his statesmanship and his ability to deal with a crisis. Party politics also shaped Wilson's conduct, for he wished to prevent the Conservatives from taking advantage and to convince the public that the British government could not be held responsible for UDI. Unfortunately, Wilson had failed to put together a plan in case UDI happened, and when it did happen the government was unprepared. Wilson believed that a resort to force in Rhodesia would be politically disastrous. The Labour government's slim parliamentary majority from 1964 to 1966 obliged him to be cautious, and he remained cautious even when the majority was increased at the 1966 general election. Public opinion polls indicated an approval rating of just 2 percent for the use of force against the white Rhodesian regime in October 1965. A year later this figure had risen to only 16 percent. Wilson opted for sanctions. These were not strictly enforced; members of the Commonwealth stepped up their attacks on British policy; and Wilson could do little more than attempt to buy time by insisting that sanctions would eventually have an impact.[11]

The Labour government condemned racism but was reproached abroad and at home for failing to do more to end white rule in Rhodesia and South Africa. Domestic quarrels about immigration and discrimination added to the discomfort of Wilson and his colleagues. The Rhodesian policy was confused and ineffective. Having been unable to prevent UDI, Wilson did at least manage to keep the Commonwealth together and attach the blame for what had happened to the white elite. The British government could not impose itself on events, however, and neither threats nor concessions brought nearer an end to the crisis.[12]

George Brown took strong exception to the prime minister's conduct on the arms sales to South Africa. Britain had agreed to supply items that were vital for South African security, Brown argued, and the contracts were in keeping with the Simonstown Agreement of June 1955. Under the terms of this agreement, Britain transferred control of the Simonstown naval base and the South African navy to the government of South Africa, in return for which the Royal Navy could continue to use the base. Britain had to help South Africa to perform those tasks in the region that had formerly been Britain's; the need to protect sea routes and keep the Soviets out of the Indian Ocean was as strong as ever. Britain also needed the export revenue, and Brown stressed that the weapons in question were not of the type that could be used for internal repression, which meant that Britain could not be accused of supporting apartheid. To stop the arms sales would be to damage Britain's relations with South Africa and to invite French weapons manufacturers to step in and steal Britain's trade and earnings. Wilson seemed to accept these arguments but late in 1967 succumbed to pressure from the Labour Party and suggested that the arms sales should be stopped. Within the Cabinet there was a majority in favour of this move. The minority, led by Brown and Healey, argued that the party should be properly consulted, to see if it really wanted the contracts cancelled, but the proposal was blocked. This was one of the reasons why Brown eventually resigned as foreign secretary. As for the

South African government, it needed British equipment and was quick to put pressure on the Wilson government. The last contingent of British personnel left Simonstown in the spring of 1967. Then the Arab-Israeli war of June 1967 and the closure of the Suez Canal increased Britain's need for support facilities on the Cape route. As South Africa now reminded Britain, the Simonstown Agreement implied that continued access to the base would be linked to the supply of arms. South Africa added to the existing contracts by placing a further order worth £100 million.[13]

Britain's relations with South Africa had long been complicated by arguments over apartheid, by attitudes in the Commonwealth, of which South Africa, from 1961, was not a member, and by British party politics. Labour was solidly against apartheid and when in opposition had committed itself to end the arms sales. Once in government, though, Wilson and his colleagues had also to take into account Britain's trade with South Africa, the security relationship, and South Africa's regional strength. There was heavy British investment in South Africa, which was a source of raw materials and an important customer for British goods, and there was no wish to jeopardise the Simonstown arrangement or alienate a firm ally against communism. In the Commonwealth and the UN there was support for sanctions against the apartheid regime. In Britain there was some equivocation, and despite a UN resolution of 1963 the Conservative government had not stopped arms sales to South Africa. When Labour took office, its leaders decided to end the sales in line with their previous pledge, but there were exceptions, and Wilson and his colleagues were attacked for an abandonment of principle. Quarrels about this, and the devaluation of sterling in November 1967, brought on a Cabinet split. Devaluation was a blow to Wilson's prestige because he had fought so hard to prevent it, and some ministers and advisers took advantage by recommending the resumption of arms sales to South Africa. They said this would help to boost the economy. They also argued that defence cooperation with South Africa had to be preserved as part of the withdrawal from East of Suez. Wilson was wary of antagonising the Labour left and the Commonwealth. He manoeuvred well, obtaining an agreement that Cabinet unity must be preserved in public. The policy on arms sales remained unchanged. So did the position on apartheid, although Britain did not back new moves in the UN against South Africa's interests. Wilson preferred to let matters lie.[14]

Britain's policy on Nigeria was one of nonintervention, yet it clearly favoured the federal government of Nigeria. Britain was the former colonial power, had set up the federal system, and wanted Nigeria and other former possessions in Africa to be stable. Territorial integrity was an important principle to uphold. Britain wanted Nigeria's friendship and wanted also to increase trade with and investment in the country. The decision to supply weapons to Nigeria caused uproar. Wilson and his colleagues stressed that some of these had been ordered before the civil war. They also insisted that Britain would only send defensive weapons, and that refusal to help a fellow Commonwealth government would be like siding with the rebels. Britain had a duty to assist the federal government, Wilson argued. This would increase Britain's influence, whereas failure to help would prompt Nigeria to look to the Soviet Union. Similarly, other states would provide weapons if Britain did not, and it would be better for everyone if the civil war was ended quickly, so that the Biafrans would not be encouraged to hold out. Popular protests developed in opposition to the government's policy. The moral and humanitarian aspects of the crisis received increasing attention and in 1968 pressure built up for an end to the arms sales. Newspapers, churches, Labour MPs, and some Conservatives joined in. Wilson promised to change course if it became clear that by doing so he could bring closer a settlement. Britain continued to engage in relief work to ease the suffering in Biafra and in diplomatic efforts to end the war. By such means, Wilson hoped, the public might tolerate the arms supply for a while longer. Crossman wrote in his diary on December 5, 1968, that attacks on the Labour government were unfair, because serious efforts *were* being made to end the war. The USSR was sending in weapons for the Nigerians, the French were arming the Biafrans, and, meanwhile, the British public was demanding that food and medical aid should be provided for Biafra. Crossman thought that if the government's actions were put to a vote in Parliament it would lose, yet Britain alone could not stop the war and suffering. Above all, what was needed was a joint Anglo-French-Soviet agreement that no more weapons would be supplied. Crossman thought that Britain should set an example and stop arms sales in the hope that others would follow suit, but Wilson would not risk offending Nigeria's leaders. The Biafran army finally collapsed in March 1970. Wilson's efforts at mediation had come to nothing, as had peace efforts made by the Commonwealth secretariat. In fact, division within the Commonwealth was another of the impediments that imposed limits on what Britain could do. Although Britain never recognised Biafra's independence, Commonwealth members Zambia and Tanzania did.[15]

Wilson had his own interpretation of events, and when he published his version a few years later, his goal was to justify what he had done and counter the claims of his critics. Wilson contended that his foreign policy had been consistent and successful. He had resisted the 'needling' of the UN with regard to Gibraltar, for instance, and in September 1967 the people of Gibraltar voted by a massive majority to retain the connection with Britain. On Kashmir, Wilson pointed out that his options had been limited, not least because the Commonwealth was divided over Rhodesia. He complained about being misled by advisers, some of whom were sympathetic to Pakistan. According to Wilson's account of the Rhodesian crisis, the real villains of the piece were the extremists in the white Rhodesian elite, who ensured that genuine chances for a settlement were lost, and the Conservative opposition in the British Parliament, who did nothing to help, but rather tried to score political points at a time of national difficulty. On the question of supplying weapons to South Africa, Wilson maintained that he had been 'irrevocably opposed' to these arms sales but that he was obliged by Cabinet colleagues and by economic considerations to allow time for deliberation. On Nigeria, Wilson stressed that he had no choice but to help the established government when it applied for Britain's help in the autumn of 1967. Britain was the traditional supplier of weapons to Nigeria and had trained Nigeria's army. To have turned the Nigerians down would have been a hostile move against a Commonwealth nation whose friendship and integrity were important to Britain. Refusal would also have opened the door for the Soviets, who would have taken the opportunity to extend their influence in the region. More-over, the British had many interests in Nigeria and 17,000 British citizens were there, and most African states wanted Nigeria's unity to be pre-served. 'Balkanisation' would have meant 'anarchy and chaos throughout the continent far transcending anything experienced in any other part of the world'. During the war, Britain had to remain involved in order to prevent atrocities and send in aid.[16]

Whatever he said or wrote at the time and afterwards, Wilson was more equivocal than he liked to admit. Although he hated apartheid and opposed the arms sales to South Africa, for example, he also needed a solution to the Rhodesian crisis and came to decide that the best way to pressurise Rhodesia's white leadership was through South Africa. There-fore, he wanted to conciliate the regime in Pretoria, and it was certainly the view in Washington that he was out to appease the South African gov-ernment. As for Nigeria, again Wilson had to be careful. A complicating factor here was oil. The war in the Middle East in June 1967 had created the need for an alternative supply of oil, and all of Nigeria's oil was in Biafra—that is, in the eastern part of Nigeria. Wilson also had to contend with a schism in his party, for many Labour MPs sympathised with the separatists and considered them to be innocent victims of an oppressive federal government.[17]

On all of these matters there were deep divisions in British politics and society. Sometimes political and economic influences pointed in different directions, as on Rhodesia. For those companies that had a lot at stake in both Rhodesia and Britain, UDI was unwelcome and dangerous, for Rhodesia's prosperity was largely dependent on international trade and especially on economic links with Britain. For the Conservative right, decolonisation was regrettable and white settler rights in Africa had to be respected. UDI in Rhodesia and war in Nigeria were very challenging for Britain because they directly affected what had long been regarded as British spheres of influence. Critics of the Wilson government have asserted that it descended into timidity and error. Perhaps it is true that other measures should not have been ruled out. Perhaps a show of mili-tary force would have brought the illegal white regime in Rhodesia into line. The public did not oppose economic sanctions against the Rhodesian government, had not opposed other shows of force in the region, and Labour had won a clear victory in the general election of March 1966, which further reduced the need to fear a popular reaction to a firmer policy on Rhodesia. The use of force there would not have greatly hastened or worsened the sterling crisis of July 1966. Military action would also have been justifiable, because Queen Elizabeth II was the sovereign of Rhodesia. Instead of acting boldly, however, the Wilson government went in for sanctions that were never strong enough to make much difference. This damaged Britain's reputation across Africa and Asia and the more Wilson conceded to the white Rhodesian leader Ian Smith, the more Smith thought that his followers would remove him if he accepted Britain's terms. As for Nigeria, the critics accused the Labour government of half-heartedness and half-measures. In an effort to safeguard the federal structure Britain had created for the independent state, arms and assistance were provided for the federal government, but not enough was done to prevent weapons from reaching Biafra and to end the civil war much sooner. Britain felt responsible for the stability of Nigeria, but did not act decisively on that sense of responsibility. During this period, there were frequent reassessments of the value of the Commonwealth to Britain. What emerged was an approach that was not entirely consistent. On the one hand, the government was disillusioned with the Commonwealth and ministers were determined, as difficulties arose, to put British interests first. On the other hand, the government never thought of breaking up or abandoning the Commonwealth and was ready to stand firm against the pressure of threatened departures from it.[18]

This was also a period in which Britain's ongoing economic problems made for a more acute awareness that the global role could not be paid for and would probably collapse without a major rearrangement of commitments and priorities. The Wilson government had several key decisions to make—about the position East of Suez, about the possible abandonment of expensive weaponry, about the expediency of another bid to join the EEC—and none of the implications was very welcome. The FRG was becoming a more valuable ally to the United States, moreover, and there were fears that the West Germans would surpass Britain in this respect. If the gradual British withdrawal from overseas activities saved money, it also weakened Britain's influence over the U.S. government. Those areas of the world in which Britain had been the West's policeman, and necessary to the Americans, were still among the most strategically sensitive and politically unstable of regions, but now the British presence was to be scaled down. Britain did not lose all influence in the Middle East and Far East, but its role in these regions was decreasing. Meanwhile, the FRG took advantage of its growing importance to the Americans: it became the strongest European member of NATO, with larger armed forces than Britain, and was strategically vital as the West's front line against the Soviets. The FRG also had a leadership role in the EEC. Britain was still outside the EEC, with an economy that had fallen behind West Germany's. Indeed, by the end of the 1950s, the FRG had overtaken Britain in trade and industrial output, and by the end of the 1970s Britain's GDP would be only half that of the FRG. In addition, Britain had persistently higher inflation and slower economic growth than West Germany, France, and Japan. The politics, culture, society, and economy of the FRG bore clear marks of U.S. influence. The French were always more resistant to the American way of life, and there were some commentators in the FRG who condemned American dominance, but the Cold War tended to focus attention more on the positive than the negative aspects. The United States and the FRG grew closer, a fact that the British could not fail to notice.[19]

The rise of the FRG would have been less alarming had the British economy been stronger, for economic success was an obvious contributor to political weight, diplomatic influence, and military power. The Wilson government's economic record was disappointing. Ministers inherited a large trade deficit and had only a small parliamentary majority. They were reluctant to manipulate the exchange rate, even though other countries had found this an effective way to eliminate deficits. The general election in the spring of 1966 gave the government a bigger Commons majority. Instead of promptly devaluing the pound in order to facilitate economic recovery, however, the government delayed until late 1967. Meanwhile, inflation was rising and levels of productivity, investment, demand, and employment did not improve. Eventually, there was a balance of payments surplus, which suggests that devaluation was helping and that, so some commentators believe, it should have happened earlier. Moreover, the delaying of devaluation probably helps to explain the failure of the government's incomes policy and the rise in industrial unrest by 1970. According to its advocates, earlier devaluation would have ensured faster growth and enabled ministers more effectively to pursue other objectives, such as full employment and higher public spending. At the same time, it is not clear that earlier devaluation would have brought greater financial stability or better industrial relations.[20]

When they came into office in 1964, Labour ministers decided that the first task was to restore some order in the economy. One result was a tax on manufactured imports, which was controversial at home and annoyed Britain's EFTA partners abroad. Other measures also caused trouble, notably the increase in pensions, the abolition of prescription charges, and the introduction of capital gains tax. These early changes disturbed the financial markets and led to a run on sterling. For several years, the Wilson government struggled to bring the budget under control and tried to stabilise sterling. External events did not help, as in 1966 when France insisted that sterling would have to be devalued if Britain was to join the EEC. The balance of payments deficit continued to defy all remedial efforts at a time when Britain's economic rivals enjoyed an annual surplus. Finally the pound was devalued in November 1967, which helped to improve the payments situation, but not for long. The collapse of the Bretton Woods system in 1971 led to freely moving exchange rates (Bretton Woods had fixed these to the U.S. dollar). Sterling was floated in June 1972, which effectively put an end to the sterling area. The pound continued to fall against the U.S. dollar. Its fall against the Japanese yen and West German deutschmark was even more pronounced. Britain's balance of trade also deteriorated. Alec Cairncross, a senior economic adviser to Conservative and Labour governments in the 1960s, did not look upon the Wilson years very favourably. He noted tensions in policy making (especially on the macroeconomic side). The prime minister acted purely on tactical impulses, Cairncross and other officials were sceptical about the government's planning for faster economic growth, and too much effort was misdirected.[21]

As the world economy expanded and recovered after the Second World War, there had been many opportunities for Britain to benefit. Britain's competitors also enjoyed economic growth. Britain's share of global trade decreased, but the key problem was the balance of payments, not market share, and it proved to be very difficult to make British goods and services more competitive. By the 1960s, the structure of the British export trade was changing, with the focus more on Western Europe, and there was a strong upward trend in imports. Between 1964 and 1967 there was a surcharge on imports. Demands for protection had risen in the context of industrial decline and balance of payments crises. Devaluation was one response.[22] Yet structural problems and long-term trends could only be affected by specific policy choices in a limited way. Recurring payments crises were inevitable. The British were not as competitive as they had been in world markets, supply side weaknesses promoted inflation, wage demands were not in line with productivity, and in time these wage demands and attempts to curb inflation led to unemployment. Historians have long debated the deficits, inflation, unemployment, and related problems; some have noted that policy was constrained by social influences. People wanted higher living standards, but the economy did not grow at a rate that was sufficient to deliver all that was demanded. Low productivity has been blamed on restrictive practices and overmanning, a lack of market discipline, and inadequate training and education. Sidney Pollard thinks that the main flaw was low investment, although to be more specific, the actual level of investment probably mattered less than the question of how productive it was.[23] According to Cairncross, Britain's relatively poor economic performance resulted not only from a lack of competitiveness but also from an excessive attachment to extra-European trade. In connection with this, external conditions meant that Britain's choices were limited. Britain alone could not reshape global markets or control measures devised at the international level.[24]

To the extent that some problems could be mitigated by state action, the government did have choices. It is widely thought that the government made the wrong choices, but Cairncross doubts that policy alone retarded Britain's economic growth. Fluctuations in demand, for instance, were also seen in the faster-growing economies of Western Europe. At the time and subsequently, Cairncross did not share the 1960s faith in planning and denied that governments could greatly influence the growth rate. Conversely, it is clear that certain issues could have been handled differently. Worried about the balance of payments, the Wilson government repeatedly rejected advice to devalue the pound until devaluation could no longer be avoided. Cairncross does not claim that earlier devaluation would have solved all of Britain's problems, and he accepts that political and administrative considerations had to be taken into account by ministers, but he does criticise the policy-making process and regards sterling as vitally important. By the mid-1960s sterling was vulnerable. Without the backing of a strong monetary policy and positive balance of payments it did not inspire the confidence it once had and it was hit hard by changes in the global economy. All this was disconcerting because the exchange rate was intimately bound up with British prestige and status. Wilson spoke of 'dying in the last ditch' to defend sterling, but November 1967 saw a 14.3 percent devaluation. A stringent policy of deflation was not politically advisable. Nor was it likely to provide much relief, owing to the lack of competitiveness abroad at the existing exchange rate. Therefore, deflationary measures could only have a temporary impact, whereas devaluation was thought to promise more, particularly if accompanied by international assistance. Foreign governments agreed not to alter their policies in response to devaluation. Had they acted differently, the benefits of devaluation to Britain would have been much reduced.[25]

Nevertheless, shrinking resources prompted compromises regarding military strength and the global role. Wilson and his colleagues faced a balance of payments crisis because of high government spending, especially abroad: defence took one third of a total outlay that was still growing. Expenditure overseas had gone up from £50 million in 1952 to £400 million in 1964. To cut this spending was an urgent task, all the more so at a time when the economy was relatively weak. The retreat from East of Suez was a matter of economic necessity, and the devaluation of sterling in November 1967 was an admission to the world that Britain was in trouble. Since the exchange rate was widely regarded as a symbol of national power, British governments had tended to focus more on protecting sterling than promoting economic growth. Now the combination of difficult circumstances at home and abroad forced an undisguised withdrawal from the global role. For the most part, this was a gradual retreat, and naturally British leaders put the best possible spin on it, but saving money was the order of the day. In 1965 the government cancelled plans for a new bomber, and from 1968 there was a further downsizing of infantry battalions. By 1967, in fact, the personnel in Britain's armed forces numbered 400,000, significantly down on the 700,000 ten years earlier. Attempts were also made to cut costs by reorganising departments and controlling procurement. These measures led to more quarrels between Britain and other NATO members, especially the FRG, whose government complained whenever it seemed likely that troops would be withdrawn from the BAOR. At the end of the 1960s, the need to send troops to Northern Ireland added yet another straw to the camel's back. Just as the Macmillan government had done, Wilson's government hoped that by relying more on nuclear forces Britain's defence needs could be met in a cost-effective way. Although the Labour Party manifesto of 1964 had condemned the Nassau Agreement, Wilson decided that purchasing Polaris missiles was probably the best option after all.[26]

In October 1964 Wilson met with foreign secretary Patrick Gordon Walker and defence secretary Denis Healey to examine the Polaris question 'in the light of the information now available to us'. Wilson later wrote that the Polaris programme 'was now well past the point of no return' and could not be stopped 'except at inordinate cost'. The decision to proceed was of lasting importance. Britain continued to be a nuclear power and influenced the course of the Cold War accordingly. The leaders of the Labour Party, despite their past statements and their sympathy for disarmament and détente, not only accepted Polaris but went on to make it the mainstay of Britain's defence posture. There was nothing inevitable about this. Wilson misled the Cabinet when he informed it that the pro-gramme was past the point of no return. Navy chiefs told Healey that the submarines could be modified for other purposes at no extra cost. Some of them even doubted the value of Polaris and advised that the money could be better spent on other things. When Healey passed this on to Wilson and Walker, they told him not to let the Cabinet know. He agreed with them that Britain needed Polaris, because of the international situation and the influence it would give Britain in Washington and in NATO. In the Cabinet, the main opponent was George Brown, then the secretary of state for economic affairs, who thought that if the Polaris submarines had to be built, their number should be limited to three. The Conservatives had planned for five. The Cabinet accepted Healey's suggestion of four, the minimum required if Britain was to have one stationed permanently East of Suez.[27]

The Labour government appointed in 1964 intended to put off retreats and preserve Britain's great-power status for as long as possible. Arguments in favour of devaluation were continually resisted, precisely because Wilson and his closest colleagues believed in the world role and regarded devaluation as a sign of weakness. As for the nuclear deterrent, Wilson was aware that his party was divided on the issue but he maintained that Britain could not do without Polaris because it was vital for national defence and the world role. The announcement that the Polaris arrangement with the United States would be honoured also prevented the Conservatives from making more of the matter. In order to mollify Labour's antinuclear left-wingers, however, Wilson eschewed the Conservatives' rhetoric about Britain's *independent* deterrent. He said he considered the Polaris submarines to be part of NATO's defence forces. On the British presence East of Suez, the government did not wish to depart from established policy. The idea that Britain had a responsibility to remain was accepted. These aims and professions were to be sorely tested as the resource gap became more obvious. The need to save money forced a reappraisal and there were gloomy predictions about what could happen if Britain did not pull back and had to deal with challenges in far-off places. Since there was no way greatly to increase the resources available for the East of Suez role, that role could not continue. In addition, Wilson and his colleagues could not ignore the fact that the pattern of British trade was changing. Although exports to the sterling area increased between 1955 and 1965, exports to Western Europe and the United States increased more quickly and brought in more revenue. Trade and consumption were turning Britain away from Africa and Asia. So was decolonisation, though, as in the 1950s, British leaders made the best of it and sought to adjust to changing circumstances in a way that did the minimum damage to Britain's status and prestige. For the Wilson government, as for its Conservative predecessors, there were to be no surrenders except where the pressure was irresistible.[28]

Resources and opportunities that might have been available in the 1950s were gone by the 1960s and the Labour government had less room to manoeuvre. The 1960s saw a genuine transformation: Britain ceased to be an imperial state. Yes, the British had been withdrawing from empire for many years, but the assumption had always been that this could be managed in a way that would not greatly reduce British power and, in particular, that it would not affect Britain's position in the West. By the end of the 1960s, it was clear that these expectations were not being fulfilled, and outside Europe Britain was no longer able to use military protection and economic aid to retain influence, even in former colonies. Economic weaknesses, sterling crises, industrial disputes at home, and the loss of dollar reserves that had to be spent on oil as a result of the war in the Middle East in 1967 were among the clearest indicators of Britain's predicament.[29]

From the late 1950s, there was a growing sense that excessive defence spending was harming the economy. After resigning as chancellor of the exchequer in 1958, Peter Thorneycroft declared that the enhancement of Britain's nuclear capability was unwise and irresponsible. Prestige depended not on the size of the defence budget, Thorneycroft argued, but on Britain's ability to contribute to the West's economic strength and solvency. The 'National Plan' issued by the Labour government in 1965 made a similar point. If too much was spent on defence, it stated, economic performance would suffer. Despite these concerns, however,

Conservative and Labour governments of the 1960s were never able to effect a real reduction in defence spending. All they could do was slow down the increase. The British continued to spend more on defence, as a share of the national wealth, than all of their main allies and economic competitors except the United States. Among the many reasons for the relative weakness of Britain's economy, the military burden continued to loom large. Other countries did not feel the need to spend so much on defence. They were willing and able to specialise in their military commitments. They did not have to protect widespread global interests. They did not require a capacity for long-range intervention. Britain's retrenchment efforts in the 1950s and 1960s were prompted by the belief that high defence expenditure would impinge on the nation's prosperity, but there was little specific knowledge about the direct impact. Defence spending was only one of many factors that affected economic growth, and the financial effects of the world role cannot be assessed by looking solely at military expenditure. If defence was financed from reduced levels of consumption, living standards would have suffered but investment might not have, in which case economic growth need not have been greatly affected. Defence spending would also have had technological spin-offs that would have facilitated growth. Alternatively, if defence was financed by reduced levels of investment, living standards and welfare services would not have been badly affected in the short term, but economic growth might have been impeded. Malcolm Chalmers has shown that in Britain, the trend was for investment to suffer rather than consumption. This was because governments were worried about losing public support. They took the easier, less unpopular options.[30]

Efficiency drives, cost-cutting exercises, and structural changes went hand in hand. In 1964 the ministry of defence was reorganised and its political head became secretary of state for defence rather than minister of defence.[31] Five departments of state had previously been responsible for the tasks that now fell to the unified defence ministry: the admiralty, the war office, the air ministry, the ministry of aviation, and the ministry of defence itself. In 1964 the first three and the ministry of defence were amalgamated. The defence functions of the ministry of aviation supply (as it had by then become) were absorbed in 1971, when the ministry of defence took over responsibility for supplying military aircraft and guided weapons.

Economic concerns had a huge impact on the Wilson government's thinking on defence. As Duncan Sandys had done in the late 1950s, Labour's defence secretary, Denis Healey, tried to find a way in which Britain could remain a great power while bringing down the cost. The government's position was clarified in the 'Statement on the Defence Estimates' of February 1965, which stressed that 'the present government has inherited defence forces which are seriously over-stretched and in some respects dangerously under-equipped' and that it was necessary 'to review our strategy, taking into account not only the economic position, but also new or reaffirmed political objectives which our strategy must be designed to implement'. The desired end was a defence system that the country could afford. One early decision was to aim at an expenditure of £2000 million, at 1964 prices, for 1969–1970. Healey admitted that this was an arbitrary figure. The point was to set a limit. Ministers feared that expenditure would continue to rise unless quick action was taken and Healey recognised that Britain was spending far more on defence than any other nation of similar size and wealth. This was because Britain was still trying to do three things at once: maintain the overseas role, contribute to Western Europe's security, and pay for the nuclear deterrent. The 1965 white paper was designed to clear the way for change. Wilson and other senior Labour figures were still committed to the world role, however, and it was a long time before they reconciled themselves to the abandonment of responsibilities East of Suez. One of the reasons for this was the importance they attached to the 'special relationship' with the United States. To continue a British presence East of Suez was regarded as a duty. It was one of Britain's main contributions to the partnership with the Americans. For Wilson, the priority was to find a balance. He was under pressure from those ministers and Labour backbenchers who wanted to reduce Britain's overseas commitments, and from the Americans and those of his own colleagues who wanted Britain to remain East of Suez. To the Labour Party he tried to justify the world role by pointing to U.S. demands, and he tried to explain to the Americans why that role had to be downsized by pointing to opinion in the Labour Party. By the spring of 1966, it was obvious that Britain could not remain East of Suez. From then on, the debate was not about whether or not to withdraw but about how fast Britain should pull out.[32]

When the Wilson government had taken office in 1964, Washington was concerned about its willingness to continue the world role, and gratified by early indications that the prime minister had no intention of withdrawing British forces from East of Suez. The Americans made it clear at the end of 1964 that they considered Britain's security contribution in Europe to be much less important than the contribution outside Europe, especially in Hong Kong, Malaya, and the Persian Gulf, but the Johnson administration had soon to face up to the fact that Britain could not afford a world role. Even while scaling down its overseas commitments, though, Britain needed to maintain its military, financial, and political links with the Americans. Although the Wilson government decided not to buy new submarines from the United States, it did arrive at what was thought to be a cheaper alternative, the Chevaline project for updating Polaris. Secret cooperation with the Americans on this project began in 1966 (and Parliament was not informed until 1981, by which time its cost had reached £1 billion). Healey also announced in December 1965 that Britain would be purchasing new aircraft from the Americans. This followed the cancellation of the British aircraft programme and statements about the need to develop aircraft as inexpensively as possible.[33]

The defence review commenced in 1965 was overtaken by events. The general election of March 1966 returned many new Labour MPs to the House of Commons, and they were quick to demand economies; scepticism about British interests East of Suez was also prevalent in the Europhile lobby led by the home secretary, Roy Jenkins. In the summer of 1966, there was a sterling crisis and the government, preferring not to devalue, had to cut spending, raise taxes, and freeze wages. Labour's popularity plummeted and it became clear that economic growth targets would not be met. Overseas expenditure was a prime target for retrenchment. The withdrawal from Aden had implications for Britain's presence in the Middle East, while the end of the confrontation between Indonesia and Malaysia (following a U.S.-backed coup in Indonesia, which installed an anticommunist regime) offered an opportunity for savings. The prospect of stability in the wider region also led to suggestions that there was no need to maintain British bases there. The government came under increasing pressure from business leaders who argued that the world role had become untenable and that resources should be diverted into industry and exports. Healey understood that defence spending was too high, but he doubted that overseas commitments could be quickly reduced. As he later wrote:

> My problem was to extricate our forces from their commitments East of Suez with the least possible damage to Britain's influence in the world, and to the stability of the areas where they were present. The United States, after trying for thirty years to get Britain out of Asia, the Middle East and Africa, was now trying desperately to keep us in; during the Vietnam War it did not want to be the only country killing coloured people on their own soil. Moreover, it had at last come to realise that Britain had an experience and an understanding of the Third World, which it did not possess itself. We were under Commonwealth pressure to remain in Asia—not only from Malaysia and Singapore, but also from the governments of Australia and New Zealand, which regarded it as their forward defence zone.

Initially, it seemed that the withdrawal could be selective and gradual and that, despite the urgent need to save money, some commitments would continue. The situation changed quickly, however, and Healey was repeatedly asked to make further cuts. While insisting that Britain's security should not be jeopardised for the sake of party interests or penny-pinching, Healey came to accept that Britain's survival depended on NATO, not on the military presence East of Suez.

When planning and announcing changes in defence policy in 1966, Healey tried to bring responsibilities into line with resources. If savings were to be made, commitments would have to be cut, but it was important not to cut them too far. It was hoped that some commitments could be shared, and that the military tasks associated with the commitments that remained could be limited. Healey was sure in 1966 that Britain could and should remain East of Suez in some form, but he knew that Britain could not defeat a major military power outside Europe, and he was embarrassed when Wilson declared that Britain's frontier ran along the Himalayas. That this was not a realistic assessment of Britain's place in the world was made clear when India and Pakistan accepted Soviet mediation after their war of 1965, and when they ignored Wilson's subsequent offer of nuclear protection. The trend of events made Healey less attached to the military role East of Suez. He saw that the growth of nationalism made the British presence objectionable to the peoples and governments of the region.[34]

During 1965 and 1966, for all the talk of the need to withdraw from East of Suez, the government's line was that Britain would definitely stay. Cutbacks were made and the world role was viewed increasingly in the context of economic means and political needs. To some historians, though, the idea that Britain could remain East of Suez even on a greatly reduced scale was nonsensical. British leaders would not admit this to themselves or to the world outside. In September 1966 Wilson stated that the approved programme of defence cuts was adequate and that Britain could afford to meet its remaining commitments. This optimism lasted into the spring of 1967, but there were fears that another financial crisis was approaching and that the deflationary policies of 1966 had only delayed the devaluation of sterling, not ruled it out entirely. Arguments about whether or not Britain should try again to join the EEC added to the instability.[35]

In February 1967 the chancellor of the exchequer, James Callaghan, took up an American proposal that Britain should apply for a large ('and possibly irredeemable') twenty-five-year international loan in order to cover existing debts and end the 'inhibiting' concerns about sterling. The Johnson administration attached 'political conditions' to the deal, however, insisting that Britain must remain East of Suez. The British government could not accept this. Callaghan was himself in favour of close defence links with Commonwealth countries, but he knew that overseas expenditure had to be reduced and 'it was not sensible to maintain a worldwide influence on borrowed money'. The question of EEC membership had also to be resolved. Any attempt to carry on a global role would have undermined the government's claim to be genuinely committed to Europe. As for Healey, he was obliged to accept that the withdrawal might be quicker and more substantial than he had envisaged. He advocated a continuing British presence East of Suez, but on a smaller scale. The chiefs of staff also wished for at least a limited role East of Suez, and in early 1967 this is what they and Healey were still expecting.[36]

Continuing financial worries led to the supplementary statement on defence policy of July 1967. In the crucial divisions in the Commons at the end of July, the government's proposals were approved by votes of 321 to 231 and 297 to 230. Healey presented the policy as necessary and sensible. It would 'enable the present government and future governments to keep every aspect of our defence policy permanently under review' and ensure 'that we are getting the best possible value for every pound we spend for military purposes'. Healey criticised the Conservative governments of the past for their unrealistic approach to the question of balancing resources and commitments. He said he had inherited a plan that involved 'spending seven per cent of our national product on defence for the following ten years. It took no account of the impact of this rate of spending on our economy over a period when none of our European allies envisaged expenditure on anything like this scale'. The cost factor featured prominently in the prime minister's remarks in this same Commons debate (July 27, 1967). Insisting that 'we cannot police the world on the basis of far-flung military stations', Wilson explained that the government would make adequate financial provision for the armed forces and their equipment, and would contribute to efforts to keep the peace, but with the proviso that 'the strength of a nation's resources can never be greater than the strength of its economic base'. Therefore, 'the whole policy—defence, foreign and economic—must represent a conscious unity based on priorities'.[37]

'Many of you will be spending much more time at home with your families in Britain', Healey told British troops in Singapore in a broadcast of July 18, 1967. He continued: 'In a few years' time we shall have a lot more men in Germany, and this will be the most important theatre for the British army. There will be a lot more men in Britain than there are today'. To the troops and their families this might have been welcome news, while *The Times* carried reports that Washington, 'obviously distressed' by the prospect of a British withdrawal from East of Suez, thought that the defence statement of July 1967 'left the door open to persuasion'. Labour left-wingers had other ideas. They pressed Healey to speed up the withdrawal. Conservative defence spokesman Enoch Powell condemned the government for its muddled defence policy, which seemed to change every six months or so. Powell claimed that the latest statement offered no intelligible picture of Britain's future defence posture: 'It is to be simply the death by a thousand cuts'. *The Times* argued that withdrawal from the Middle East would be inadvisable, in view of the instability there. Britain still had vital interests in the region. Withdrawal from the Far East might be relatively easier, but would still need careful consideration. Domestic political considerations, emphasised the *Economist*, should not take precedence over real defence needs. The proposed cuts would *not* boost the British economy. The main problem was the balance of payments, and the savings expected within the next three years amounted to less than 1 percent of the sum Britain was spending on imports. The *Economist* argued that defence policy had been reduced to a shambles because Wilson was worried about his own position as prime minister. The policy had little to do with the condition of the economy or the state of Britain's international relations. The government would alienate the United States, Australia, Malaysia, Singapore, and other countries if it persisted in this vein, and the Labour Party would still be divided. The timing was all wrong as well. Cuts were being announced just as problems were multiplying in Asia owing to Chinese pressure on India, Hong Kong, and Burma. Britain's actions were bound to undermine the causes of peace and democracy in the Middle East and Far East: Wilson and his colleagues were taking 'a big chance, at a bad time for taking chances'.[38]

The supplementary statement on defence policy of July 1967 suggested that it was unnecessary for British forces to remain East of Suez in large numbers. Instead, Britain would help its allies in the Middle East and Far East to do more for their own security and prosperity. The bases in Singapore and Malaysia would be abandoned and the total number of personnel in the armed forces reduced. Decisions about the Persian Gulf were less clear, and the possibility that British forces might have to return to the Far East in an emergency was also recognised. The chiefs of staff were comforted by this, and by the realisation that a future Conservative government might reverse Labour's decisions. Another financial crisis in November 1967, however, plunged Wilson and his colleagues into deeper political trouble and led to the devaluation of the pound and further cuts in defence spending. Attacked for its failed economic policy and the inconclusive defence reviews, the government could no longer temporise. Though Healey, Callaghan (now home secretary), George Brown (foreign secretary), and Michael Stewart (secretary of state for economic affairs) advised against hasty action, Wilson and Jenkins (now chancellor of the exchequer) prevailed and early in 1968 the government confirmed that there would be a complete withdrawal from East of Suez by 1971 and that the order for American aircraft would be cancelled.[39]

In less than six months, therefore, the defence statement of July 1967 had to be revised. If 1966 had been a difficult year for the government, 1967 was even worse. Oil supplies were affected by the Arab-Israeli War of June 1967 and by the civil war in Nigeria. Britain had to buy oil in the West at higher prices, and by the autumn there was panic about the trade deficit and the impact of a prolonged dock strike. Then another sterling crisis, more serious than that of 1966, resulted in devaluation. Wilson and several of his senior colleagues had steadfastly opposed devaluation, but the rest of the Cabinet thought that it could not be put off. There was some talk of applying for a large loan from the United States, but America's own economic problems closed off this option, and for the pro-Europeans in the government devaluation was a step on the road towards membership of the EEC. Devaluation weakened Wilson, for he had staked his reputation on avoiding it, and he had also been in favour of a continuation of the East of Suez role. Doubts grew about his leadership and he became more passive in Cabinet. There was a ministerial reshuffle in November

1967, because it was agreed that Callaghan, the chancellor of the exchequer, could not stay in that post after repeatedly stating that the pound would not be devalued. Wilson did not want Callaghan to leave the Cabinet, in part because he wished to check Callaghan's leadership ambitions, and the prime minister also thought that he could revive the government by promoting Jenkins, a rival of Callaghan, who had done well as home secretary. The answer was for Callaghan and Jenkins to exchange offices. Neither of them would support the other in a bid to replace Wilson as prime minister, and this may have been uppermost in Wilson's thoughts at this time, but if he expected the change to bring stability to the government he was mistaken. In fact, the balance of forces in the Cabinet was disturbed. Jenkins, relatively untainted by devaluation and the confused defence policy, was in a much stronger position than before, and he took advantage of this to press for an end to the global role and an attempt to join the EEC.[40]

Concerned above all for the survival of his government, Wilson accepted that Britain's overseas commitments should be substantially pared down. He backed Jenkins in Cabinet and the quicker withdrawal was approved early in 1968 by a narrow margin. Wilson and Jenkins also stood up to pressure from the chiefs of staff and from officials in the ministry of defence, foreign office, and Commonwealth relations office, all of whom insisted that it would be a catastrophe for Britain to give up the world role. In the Cabinet, it was Brown and Healey who objected most strongly to the timetable for withdrawal and wanted it to be drawn out over a longer period, but Healey decided that this was not a resignation matter. He stayed in his post, and, in order for Britain to retain some capacity for far-off operations, he tried to protect the Royal Navy from what he considered to be excessive cuts. Residual commitments East of Suez continued: naval training went on in the Far East and there were regular exercises to demonstrate that Britain still had the ability to intervene there if necessary. In fact, this ability to intervene was inconsequential. Further savings were needed and resources had to be diverted into trade and investment to take advantage of devaluation and improve Britain's balance of payments. Strategic flexibility was lost. In 1968 Wilson confirmed that there would be no special capacity for military action in the Middle East or Far East, just a general capability, based in Europe, which might facilitate a deployment overseas in an emergency.[41]

January 1968 marks an important turning point in that the government was accepting that Britain's status and role in the world had changed. Savings did result, yet Britain continued to spend more on defence than the countries of Western Europe, as a proportion of national income, and the British economy still underperformed relative to its main competitors. The targets set by Healey in the defence white paper of 1968 were not met. As before, defence spending was impossible to reduce in any great measure. The rate of increase was addressed, but defence still took the same share of the nation's resources, and because the relative economic position did not change Britain fell further behind the other advanced economies. Some commentators have suggested that there was a clear opportunity in 1967–1968 to restructure defence policy radically. It was not taken, despite the widespread belief that high defence spending had harmed the economy. Most of the forces withdrawn from East of Suez were given roles in NATO. Reorganisation did not go further because British strategy was still influenced by military and industrial interests that were dependent on high defence spending. Another reason was the entrenched attitude among Britain's political leaders that Britain was still a great power. The East of Suez decision was not based purely on economic necessity. It was shaped also by political and strategic considerations, many of which had influenced but not been effectively addressed by the Wilson government's Conservative predecessors. A lot depended on external events. The confrontation between Indonesia and Malaysia, for example, affected British thinking about the base at Singapore. In addition, the withdrawal policy did not mean that all of Britain's responsibilities outside the NATO area were suddenly given up, for Britain could still act in many parts of the world.[42]

Wilson confirmed that British forces would leave the Far East and Persian Gulf by the end of 1971 in his speech to the Commons of January 18, 1968. About 10,000 troops had recently returned following the end of the campaign in Borneo, and the British had pulled out of Aden in late

November 1967. The context had also been changed by the devaluation of sterling. The prime minister contended that the government's policy was correct because it was realistic. Britain would 'make to the alliances of which we are members a contribution related to our economic capability, while recognising that our security lies fundamentally in Europe and must be based on the North Atlantic Alliance'. On January 25, 1968, Healey told MPs that British forces could still be sent outside Europe if necessary, particularly in UN operations, but that defence policy would now have a European emphasis. If Britain henceforth cut a rather less ambitious figure on the world stage, the motives were sound and reasonable. Alternative courses had to be rejected because they were too expensive, more difficult politically, and possibly less useful in terms of security and strategy, and for Britain to live within its means made sense. Defence spending had stood at 7 percent of the national wealth in 1964 when the Wilson government took office. In 1968 it was down to 5.3 percent, about the same as the French figure, which was some achievement in just five years.[43]

   Limited resources forced a change in policy, yet relative economic decline cannot entirely explain the withdrawal from East of Suez. British leaders had been aware of the decline for years, and it did not stop them from thinking of Britain as a global power. Short-term political and domestic causes played their part, and the shift in Wilson's Cabinet and the influence of the pro-European Jenkins had a direct bearing on what happened, as did the financial crises of the period. There had been financial problems before, but they had not led to the ending of Britain's overseas role. The big difference in 1967–1968 was that there was a willingness to take this step. Faith in the world role was weakened by the continuing financial problems and the Cabinet changes of the late 1960s, combined with Britain's relative economic decline. Why had the consensus behind the world role lasted so long? It had lasted because it was a master rationale of the foreign policy establishment, in all its strategic, political, bureaucratic, and diplomatic sections, and also because of continuing military operations around the world, the tendency not to treat the overseas role as a whole but to look at different regions separately, and

U.S. pressure to remain East of Suez, which grew as the Americans were drawn into Vietnam. By the late 1960s, the Americans had concluded that Britain's usefulness East of Suez was not what it had been, but at this stage the Wilson government was moved more by domestic factors than by the attitude of the United States. Wilson and his Cabinet, after years of defending the global role, decided quite abruptly that it could no longer be sustained. A related matter was the influence of Labour backbenchers. Many of them were sceptical about the global role, ministers were worried about possible revolts on various issues as the government's prestige was damaged by the financial difficulties of the time, and for Wilson himself there was the added desire to remain as prime minister and nullify any rival claimants to this office. Meanwhile, in the Conservative Party and in the press and the country generally, doubts had arisen about the wisdom of trying to maintain a global presence (perhaps a legacy of Suez) and the government did not expect too negative a reaction from these quarters. This facilitated the presentation of alternative ideas about Britain's future, with more emphasis on economic recovery and Europe.[44]

At the mercy of various pressures and demands, the government managed to give the impression that it was weathering the storm. Nevertheless, it did not do enough to convince its critics that Labour's record in office from 1964 to 1970 represented anything other than, as one of them calls it, a 'breach of promise'. The merging of economic and strategic problems proved too much. The Americans tried to help, for their own reasons, but their offer of a large loan early in 1967 made Callaghan uneasy about paying for the world role with borrowed money, and Wilson did not think that the Cabinet and the Labour Party would accept loan arrangements that were public and formal in nature. Previously, in September 1965, Washington had promised to support sterling in return for Britain's promise to remain in the Far East. That deal had not been made public. Subsequently, in December 1966, there had been some discussion in Cabinet about confining cutbacks to the Middle East, leaving the Far East unaffected, and some senior ministers preferred a thinning out of British forces all round rather than a dramatic reduction in specific theatres. Then, in July 1967, a mental adjustment was made: there would definitely be a withdrawal from East of Suez. This ended the 1965 deal with the Americans. It was plain from the loan negotiations of early 1967 that U.S. assistance would not be available on what Wilson and Callaghan deemed to be acceptable terms. This removed a barrier to withdrawal from East of Suez. The British presence in the Far East had become a bargaining counter, which put off a thorough reassessment of military commitments, and between 1964 and 1968 there were last-gasp attempts to stick to these commitments. In 1968 the schedule for withdrawing from East of Suez had to be amended. This came too late to have a decisive impact on defence expenditure. Despite the mental adjustment and the withdrawal from East of Suez, there was still a reluctance to admit that Britain was no longer a major power. Wilson made much of the nuclear deterrent, for instance, and continued to spend huge sums on it.[45]

The decision to withdraw from East of Suez might reasonably have been made long before 1967–1968. Had the loss of India in 1947 been followed by a gradual scaling down of the imperial defence system in line with political and economic needs, it might have been easier to preserve influence and status—albeit on a more modest scale. There would have been no embarrassing change in the late 1960s: the appropriate reappraisal of strategy would already have been made. Yet it cannot be denied that policymakers thought they had good reasons for taking the options that seemed best to them before 1967–1968. In addition, it is important to go beyond the metropolitan perspective. For example, no understanding of Britain's position in Southeast Asia is possible without some appreciation of the circumstances in the region itself, and there are wider considerations to examine too, related to the Cold War, trade, and colonies. There *were* changes in the imperial defence system after the Second World War. Until 1957, the tendency was to treat Southeast Asia as a discrete unit. The same was true of the Middle East. There was no uniform approach to some larger entity called 'East of Suez'. This altered as a result of the Suez crisis of 1956. Different units were brought together and were all covered by East of Suez planning as a whole. The merging of hitherto discrete units probably made it easier to justify general withdrawal in the late 1960s, although with regard to the Persian

Gulf the opposition to withdrawal was considerable. Britain had commitments to Bahrain, Kuwait, Qatar, the Trucial States (later United Arab Emirates), and Oman. The British military presence in the Persian Gulf only cost about £12 million a year, and because local states met almost half of Britain's energy needs, and had been promised that British protection would continue, it seemed inappropriate to think about leaving the area. The Labour government, however, had to think in these terms because of economic and financial problems and because Arab animosity towards Britain was increasing, due largely to British policy before, during, and after the Six-Day War. In late 1967 British troops had to leave Aden after a long and fruitless campaign there. Saudi Arabia and the Arab rulers in the Persian Gulf looked upon Britain as seriously weakened. This influenced the government's deliberations. So did a ministerial bargain, whereby limits on social welfare would be accompanied by cuts in the defence budget, and the widespread opinion that valuable resources should no longer be used to prop up oil-rich rulers in the Middle East. The Americans warned that stability in the region depended on a continued British presence and in London there was concern that communist influence might grow. The struggle in Aden had resulted in the establishment of the People's Democratic Republic of Yemen, which was receiving aid from the USSR and China. London trusted Saudi Arabia and Iran to step in, so that there would be no vacuum, but this meant removing restraints from the two states whose ambitions had long disturbed the small states of the Persian Gulf. Then Britain agreed to sell weapons to them, which aroused much negative comment at home and abroad.[46]

The East of Suez decision did not go down well in the Commonwealth. Australia accused Britain of grossly disregarding its obligations. The government of Singapore threatened to withdraw its sterling balances from London and injure Britain's commercial interests. Some of Britain's allies in the Persian Gulf offered money to help the British to remain. In Washington, there was huge disappointment. President Johnson told Wilson in January 1968 that if Britain did pull back, the United States would no longer regard the British as useful or reliable allies in any vital part of the world, including Europe. Wilson explained that it was impossible to change course. Britain could no longer sustain a world role and had to focus on doing only what the available resources permitted. Perhaps Wilson had previously misled the Americans by suggesting that a final decision could be postponed. Some of Johnson's advisers thought that the president ought simply to accept Britain's withdrawal on the grounds that Wilson would now have a better chance of doing the other things that the United States wanted, such as boosting the British economy and gaining entry to the EEC, but Johnson did not agree. He had repeatedly warned Wilson against the abandonment of commitments East of Suez. Now he argued that the withdrawal must be put off. He reminded Wilson of all the assistance the United States had given Britain in the past, insisted that America would not take up the responsibilities Britain wished to relinquish, and pointed to the damage that was being done to the West's interests and security. Wilson was no longer able to approach these wider questions in the way he had done earlier. He looked to Europe for an opportunity to construct a more impressive foreign policy. Believing that de Gaulle's veto of 1963 was based on the idea that Britain preferred the United States to Europe and still thought of itself as a world power rather than primarily a European one, Wilson thought that the changes his government was making would remove the main obstacle to EEC membership. Wilson also wished to appease the pro-Europe members of the Cabinet. Given that the Americans wanted Britain to join the EEC, moreover, he probably thought he could find a way of compensating them for the East of Suez decision.[47] To some contemporaries, the focus on NATO and the EEC was appropriate and represented more of a reorientation than a retreat. To others, talk of another bid to join the EEC was related to a premature surrender of the world role and marked the end of Britain's greatness.

CHAPTER 8

EUROPEAN TROUBLES

The reevaluation of Britain's role and responsibilities East of Suez became inextricably linked with attempts to improve Britain's relationships with Europe. Eventually, there was a second application to join the EEC. Like the first, this application and the goals behind it were questioned and frustrated primarily by the French: de Gaulle's agenda for France and for Europe did not take in British membership of the EEC. The Paris-Bonn axis remained intact and operated against Britain not only with respect to the EEC but also, frequently, on NATO matters. Concerns about the future of the alliance and disagreements about its strategy and function became more serious, and NATO affairs were further complicated by measures of thaw in Europe. Of particular importance were the diplomatic initiatives of Paris and Bonn, the responses of London and Washington, and changes in Soviet policy and the external dealings of the eastern bloc.

The Labour prime minister, Harold Wilson, was less enthusiastic about European unity than the Conservative leader, Edward Heath, whose thinking was in line with that of some European politicians. Heath saw economic integration as the beginning. Cooperation would in due course spread into other areas, he thought, especially defence and foreign policy, which would mean changes in NATO. Western Europe could thereby make itself a centre of power linked to, but also more independent of, the United States. Wilson seemed not to care much for this process, but his views were evolving. He could not be open about his intentions in case he annoyed Europhile and Europhobic sections of the Labour Party or weakened his bargaining position in Europe. In time, he decided that Britain could not afford to remain outside the EEC. Though he would have preferred an EFTA-type relationship, the fact that de Gaulle had obstructed federalist proposals in Europe removed some of Wilson's concerns about applying to join the EEC. Moreover, some members of the government were insisting that membership of the EEC would strengthen the British economy and increase Britain's international influence. The prime minister had his doubts but saw no alternative method of achieving these ends.[1]

Economic difficulties and the resource gap had been pointing Britain towards Europe for some time, and the reassessment of defence policy and the global role proceeded alongside discussions about another application to join the EEC. Labour had never been keen on the EEC and Wilson had previously declared that he would only consider entry if it involved no surrender of essential British interests. As he stressed in a speech in Bristol on March 18, 1966, 'suitable' arrangements would have to be worked out with the EEC: 'So: Negotiations? Yes. Unconditional acceptance of whatever terms we are offered? No'. There was no sign that French objections to British membership had been assuaged since de Gaulle's veto of January 1963, yet the Wilson government grew more eager to make its bid. This was partly because the Commonwealth was not the asset that had been expected. Britain, it was claimed, had much to offer the EEC. The body could be enhanced on the economic side and Britain would also be better able to boost European security as the French ended their military involvement in NATO. On May 16, 1967, however, de Gaulle announced that Britain was not ready to join the EEC.[2]

The Times looked forward to a time when de Gaulle was no longer president of France, trusting that his successor would be more flexible.

In the meantime, it was important for the British government to satisfy the other members of the EEC that Britain's adherence would be mutually advantageous. As for de Gaulle, his opinion had not really changed since 1963. He was not interested in the details of Britain's second application. He liked the EEC as it was, with France dominant, and he opposed enlargement because he expected this to make the EEC weaker, less cohesive, and more vulnerable to U.S. influence. Other members of the EEC wanted Britain to join, noted *The Times*, but they did accept de Gaulle's point that the EEC should not be radically altered. Britain would therefore have to accept the EEC's rules and convince its members that Britain's purpose was to build economic and political unity 'so that the old continent can stand up to the Americans and to the Russians; and that, by putting membership of the Community first, Britain can ensure that her historic relations with the Commonwealth and the United States can be brought as a dowry, not as a liability, into Europe'. The *Guardian* suggested that Britain's application might yet succeed if the 'sour and sceptical' de Gaulle could be made to realise that his obstinacy worried the rest of the EEC far more than the prospect of British membership did.[3]

Wilson did not accept de Gaulle's announcement of May 1967 as a final answer, and when the two held talks at Trianon in June 1967 he was struck by the French leader's low morale and sense of political weakness. This led Wilson to believe that persistence would pay off and that de Gaulle would relent: 'I feel paradoxically encouraged. He does not want us in and he will use all the delaying tactics he can. But if we keep beating firmly at the door and do not falter in our purpose or our resolve I am not sure he has the strength finally to keep us out'. In fact, de Gaulle confirmed his veto of Britain's second EEC application on November 27, 1967.[4]

British attitudes towards Europe, and the Commonwealth and developing world, were still shaped by the Cold War and the perceived Soviet danger. The Wilson government's EEC bid cannot be understood apart from Cold War calculations. Washington continually pressed for greater European unity, and as the EEC grew stronger the British were conscious of being left out. It could be argued that, because Britain lacked the will, allies, and strength to break the EEC up, an attempt had to be made to influence it from within. This was certainly the view of George Brown, Britain's foreign secretary from August 1966 to March 1968, who revived the 'third force' idea of a more integrated Western Europe that would be able to stand up to both the United States and USSR. Brown regarded British membership of the EEC as a step in this direction. Like Wilson and other ministerial colleagues, Brown also anticipated that EEC membership would help Britain to remain a major power. That they all knew of de Gaulle's position, but went ahead anyway, probably shows how desperate they had become as the Commonwealth waned, as Britain's position East of Suez was effectively given up, as the British economy continued to underperform, and as Britain's importance to the United States declined.[5]

When the Cabinet came to its decisive vote on the EEC bid, in May 1967, there were ten ministers in favour 'without qualification', seven strongly opposed, and six 'maybes'. These six thought that if the application was to go ahead it should be quick and unequivocal. Richard Crossman, one of the six, advised the prime minister to proceed in a way that would please Europe, irrespective of the effect this might have on members of the Cabinet. Crossman wanted there to be no suggestion that Britain was attaching too many conditions to its application. Brown, having formerly hoped that many of Britain's wider global responsibilities would not be given up and that Britain would not be reduced to a European focus, resolved as foreign secretary that Britain should participate more actively in European institutions. He saw merit in political integration and pushed for much closer cooperation on economic and security matters.[6]

Brown's strategic arguments and his notion of an expanded EEC that would halt the polarisation of the world around the two superpowers, although important, were not the primary motivations behind Britain's second application for EEC membership. The condition of the British economy provided the main stimulus. Britain's rate of growth was below that enjoyed in the EEC, and closer links with the Commonwealth offered no solution because Britain's trade with the Commonwealth was in decline while the need for European markets had become more urgent. Given that de Gaulle preferred intergovernmental arrangements to supranational ones, moreover, British concerns about political integration had been at least partly allayed. Slowly but surely, government ministers and sections of the Labour Party had warmed to the idea of EEC membership. There was a fear of economic stagnation and a desire for resources and markets. Wilson's government was no different to Macmillan's government in that there was no conversion to the ideals behind the EEC or to some 'European vision' (by which many continental politicians claimed to be guided). Labour's bid was a pragmatic affair and was presented as such to the British people. National identity and interests were not to be given up, nor was the 'special relationship' with America. Once Wilson had decided to seek EEC membership, he worked hard to keep the government and Labour Party together and to secure public support. He knew that French opposition would not be easy to break down. Wilson apparently thought that it would be overcome by others in the EEC who wanted Britain to be admitted, but they were swayed by de Gaulle's opinion that Britain's economic weakness was a barrier. They did not want their comparatively rude economic health to be impaired by closer association with Britain, and however difficult the French had been in the past, France was still more important to the EEC than Britain was.[7]

If Britain's second EEC bid was largely motivated by economic concerns, political goals played a significant part as well. Indeed, the economic reasons for joining the EEC at this time were debatable, and nobody could be sure in advance about the impact on industry or food prices or anything else. If the application was politically motivated, the potential economic costs must have been considered by Wilson to be worth paying in order for Britain to remain a major power. Wilson and his colleagues reckoned that there was no better way for Britain to preserve an international role. The foreign office was pressing for a 'turn to Europe', and, with the Commonwealth divided and the Americans unwilling to treat Britain as an equal, other ways to sustain influence and avoid a drift into isolation seemed to be closed off. Though there was vague talk of long-term economic benefits for Britain, these could only be guessed at, and it was appreciated that the short-term costs of EEC membership were likely to be substantial. Moreover, the fact that Britain's position East of Suez was being reassessed must have reinforced the political arguments for the EEC bid as a compensatory move that would protect status while commitments outside Europe were being given up. The timing of the bid was also largely determined by economic conditions, for the sterling crisis of July 1966 prompted the government to speed up its preparations.[8]

Economic motives cannot be ignored. More and more of Britain's trade was with Europe, the EEC was proving to be a success, and other possible routes to recovery for the British economy—through the Commonwealth, or as part of a wished-for North Atlantic free trade area—were unavailable. Nevertheless, Wilson and his colleagues were also thinking about the political and security benefits offered by a more united Western Europe of which Britain was a part. The intention was for Britain to assume a leadership role in the EEC, which would make up for the loss of influence outside Europe. In addition, there was a wish to gain control over the EEC's development, especially with regard to agriculture, technological progress, and supranationalism. Wilson's policy was also shaped by his need to gratify the Americans, conciliate pro-Europeans in his Cabinet, and score a victory over Heath and the Conservatives, who were in favour of EEC membership.[9]

Despite all these pressing political and economic concerns, Wilson remained cautious. His commitment to the EEC bid was temporary rather than permanent. He was aware of de Gaulle's opinions but hoped that the French president would engage in a fair debate. Wilson miscalculated. Confident that he could get what he wanted from de Gaulle in personal and bilateral discussions, he gave less attention to other tactics, such as persuading the rest of the EEC to put pressure on France. He later admitted that Britain's economic weakness handicapped the application, though he thought it had worried de Gaulle less than it had the French prime minister, Georges Pompidou. Wilson was sure that in the circumstances of the time he had been right to go ahead with the EEC bid. Britain's application was not withdrawn. It remained active, which gave Wilson the flexibility he wanted: if circumstances changed and it no longer seemed appropriate for Britain to join the EEC, he could withdraw it. Wilson was pleased that the bid had been politically useful. Labour's pro-European section was grateful that the attempt had been made; groups opposed to the application considered themselves vindicated; and the Conservatives could no longer claim that they alone had the desire and ability to forge a closer relationship with Europe. There was a significant change in Europe, for those who wished to expand the EEC now knew that both of the major parties in Britain wanted to join. De Gaulle resigned in 1969 and the question of British membership came up again. Opinion within the government, the Labour Party, and the trade unions had become less favourable towards the EEC. In 1970, with a general election approaching, Wilson decided to do nothing until he knew which way the wind was blowing.[10]

De Gaulle's aversion to British membership of the EEC reflected his wider agenda and his taste for active diplomacy. He wanted to change the international order, and in doing so help France economically and gain for France a mediating role between East and West. From 1960 he started to withdraw French units from NATO exercises, and in March 1966 he took France out of the integrated military command. De Gaulle hoped to end what he regarded as Europe's dependency on the United States. He was convinced that the Soviets were ready to bargain, because they were worried about a hostile China and faced dissension within the eastern bloc. De Gaulle officially recognised China in 1964. Soviet foreign minister Andrei Gromyko visited Paris in 1965, and in 1966 the French president went on a state visit to Moscow. In 1967 Soviet premier Aleksei Kosygin visited Paris. In June 1967, during the Six-Day War in the Middle East, France sided with the Arabs and Soviets whereas America and the West supported Israel. Paris was also arranging trade agreements with the eastern bloc, though did not risk offending Bonn by recognising the GDR. By this time, de Gaulle had vetoed Britain's entry into the EEC, rejected an American offer of Polaris missiles, denounced U.S. involvement in Vietnam, and demanded gold for dollars under the Bretton Woods agreement of 1944. Washington was angered by de Gaulle's behaviour, and he caused a wider stir by stepping up France's nuclear weapons programme and disregarding the 1963 Test Ban Treaty. He repeatedly offended Britain with his position on matters connected with the EEC, NATO, and nuclear testing. That he was eager to display his indifference to British interests was also shown by such remarks as those he made in Montreal in July 1967 concerning a 'free Quebec'. This speech was an insult to Queen Elizabeth II, Canada's head of state, and a political interference in another country that de Gaulle would have vilified had it been attempted in France.[11]

The damage he was doing to NATO was particularly irresponsible, claimed the British, for it jeopardised the safety of all. This was a difficult period in NATO's history—not only because of de Gaulle but also because of arguments over nuclear sharing, the cost of keeping U.S. and British forces in Germany, the war in Vietnam, and the likelihood that American involvement in Southeast Asia would have a deleterious effect on the defences of Western Europe. To de Gaulle, meanwhile, his diplomatic, political, and military decisions formed a logical whole. Pushing for détente as well as the reorganisation of NATO, for instance, was part of his scheme to change the western alliance and move international affairs away from their bipolar basis. The withdrawal from NATO's integrated command was also in line with established French strategy, according to which French forces should only engage with an enemy that was directly threatening France. NATO had distinguished between 'major' aggression (extensive penetration) and 'minor' aggression (border incidents). The American and NATO standpoint was that there should be a response to any 'major' aggression, but the French would not class an attack on the FRG as 'major' aggression unless enemy forces headed for France's borders. This was also related to French nuclear policy. In contrast to the 'interdependence' pursued by Britain, France wanted independence in nuclear matters. Beneath the rhetoric, however, there were unresolved problems. France desired freedom of action but also needed to be part of the western alliance, to benefit from its protection. Yet it was also clear that the nation would be devastated unless nuclear weapons were only used away from French territory. Another difficulty existed in relations between Paris and Bonn, for de Gaulle wished to detach the FRG from America but did not offer a firm nuclear pledge to replace the U.S. guarantee that Bonn regarded as indispensable. De Gaulle frequently appeared to care more about domestic political circumstances than about France's military requirements or collective security. This was unwise because France had good reason to make sure that NATO was strong.[12]

Responding to the French withdrawal from NATO's military command, Britain's foreign secretary Michael Stewart told Parliament that all the necessary adjustments were being made, that NATO would remain 'an effective and credible military organisation', and that its members were determined to move ahead with security arrangements, a German settlement, and a thaw in East-West relations. These matters would not simply be left for Paris and Moscow to discuss. *The Times* suggested that even if de Gaulle was right about American domination of NATO and its drawbacks, his tactics were wrong. Quite apart from the military and administrative problems he had caused by taking France out of the command structure, he was damaging the alliance psychologically and discouraging individual members of NATO. It was possible that the alliance might crumble. What had prompted de Gaulle to take such a drastic step? Perhaps he wished to demonstrate his independence as part of his thaw with Moscow, or to protest more openly about U.S. policy in Vietnam. Whatever his motive, he had forced the members of NATO to reconsider the links between the United States and Western Europe and face up to the political and military problems of the day. NATO could certainly survive without France, unlike the EEC. In the EEC, concessions always had to be made to the French, and even now they were blocking reforms. De Gaulle thought he could bully the EEC. He could not bully NATO, but NATO could not risk losing France entirely. *The Times* stood for the strengthening of both Western Europe's unity and its security relationship with the United States. De Gaulle thought he could end the Cold War by separating Europe from America. This was a delusion. Cooperation, not separation, was required, and only on the solid bedrock of unity could NATO be refashioned in a way that enabled its members to deal with internal problems and external challenges.[13]

Britain helped to keep NATO together and limit the damage done by de Gaulle, working closely with the United States and FRG in pursuit of these common objectives. The British bid to join the EEC had an impact, by improving Britain's standing in Europe and disrupting de Gaulle's attack on NATO. Wilson's government was keen to act boldly: this was the way to prove to the Americans that Britain was still important (despite the refusal to send troops to Vietnam and the abandonment of commitments East of Suez). De Gaulle's criticism of the Anglo-American 'special relationship' probably helped to keep it going. Certainly, his withdrawal from NATO's military command created an opportunity for the British to show their worth as allies. One result was an increase in tension between London and Moscow. While de Gaulle had been wooing the Soviets, Wilson's government had also been making overtures, but as Britain assumed a more active role in NATO the Soviet attitude hardened. Wilson did not think that he was getting enough encouragement from Moscow, and the Czech crisis in 1968 reinforced this impression. Annoyed that Moscow preferred Paris to London and unwilling to give up close cooperation with America in order to earn Moscow's trust, the British opted to strengthen NATO rather than improve Anglo-Soviet relations. Wilson accepted the foreign office view that if there was to be a thaw, it had to be pursued by NATO as a whole, not just by Britain.[14]

There was continuing discussion of nuclear issues, especially the MLF, the multilateral force. Wilson's government was no more sympathetic to the MLF than its Conservative predecessors had been, but the Americans persisted because they wanted to lower the status of the British deterrent and merge Britain's nuclear forces with others in a body that would effectively be under U.S. control. London sought to wreck the MLF plan by proposing an alternative, the ANF, or Atlantic Nuclear Force, which would consist of Britain's nuclear submarines, an equivalent number of U.S. submarines, and a small mix-manned element, loosely assigned to NATO. Washington was unenthusiastic and the ANF proposal was not developed, but the Americans accepted that the MLF could not work without Britain's participation and the MLF talks did not progress very far either. When Moscow complained that Britain was not helping to prevent the spread of nuclear weapons, Wilson insisted that his government was committed to nonproliferation. He also stood up to Conservative spokesmen who claimed that he had betrayed the principle of independent deterrence and to members of his own party who were angry about the decision to retain the deterrent. In this he had the support of the defence secretary, Denis Healey, who dismissed the MLF as 'a military monstrosity'. The ANF and MLF plans were both abandoned. Instead, NATO established a nuclear defence committee and a nuclear planning group, to enable nonnuclear members of the alliance to have more of a say in strategic matters.[15]

In general, Wilson and Healey agreed with the line taken by the Macmillan and Home governments that Britain must work with the Americans on strategic matters in pursuit of maximum influence over the United States. Unlike Paris, London had been determined to restore good relations with Washington after the Suez crisis. The exchange of nuclear information and technology was one of the most significant benefits. It quickly led to a reliance on the Americans for the latest weaponry. Before taking office in 1964, Labour leaders had expressed an intention to renegotiate the Nassau Agreement. In the event they chose to drop this idea, recognising that British influence in Washington would quickly decline if they dramatically scaled down the nation's defences or gave up Polaris. Nevertheless, the desire to remain close to the Americans did not mean that the Labour government was prepared to embrace the MLF plan. For years Britain had argued for better consultation on the use of weapons, not joint control of weapons in a multinational force. This remained the position after 1964. In Europe and in Britain there was still some interest in joint projects, procurement, and military arrangements, but the British opposed the MLF and remained sceptical about proposals for a European nuclear force. Nuclear matters and East-West relations were ceaselessly debated in the FRG. To some extent, de Gaulle's independent line and anti-Americanism suited Bonn. West German leaders opposed the Vietnam War and resented the way in which U.S. policy seemed to be based on an acceptance of the division of Germany. They also wanted more input into NATO's nuclear strategy. The U.S. government offered to consult and there was more talk about a nuclear force that would be led by the Americans but with other participants sharing in the decision making. The FRG was in favour. As before, the British and French were not.[16]

During the entire life of the MLF plan, nobody in Britain or Western Europe—of whatever national or political affinity—had anything like the same commitment to it as certain interests in Washington. To these interests, multilateralism offered the way forward in U.S.-European relations and, in particular, in the complicated discussions about NATO's strategy and future. Some of Kennedy's advisers had repeatedly stressed that the MLF would solve several problems. It would deflect pressure from the West Germans, who craved the prestige and influence that they thought would come from acquiring nuclear weapons. It would help to improve America's relationship with France. It would show the British, the French and everyone else that the United States intended to treat all its allies in the same way. It would promote political cohesion in NATO. It would offer all members of NATO a share in nuclear planning and discourage the nonnuclear powers from becoming nuclear, thus serving the cause of nonproliferation. Not all of Kennedy's advisers liked the MLF plan, however, and the president himself thought that the Europeans should be fully consulted. This enabled them to make demands and express misgivings. Then Kennedy decided that a test ban treaty should be the priority and that if he had to sacrifice the MLF to get the treaty, he would do so. Kennedy informed the British that he would not mind if the MLF discussions stalled. London took advantage, and in delaying progress on the MLF the British were also helped by the vague wording in the Nassau Agreement, which had not specifically obliged them to participate in the multilateral nuclear force. When pressed by the Americans, they argued that the MLF plan would be expensive to implement, that it would not greatly improve the West's defences, and that the mixed manning required by the Americans (to ensure that no element of the MLF would be under the FRG's control) was impractical. Britain wished to devote resources to its Polaris fleet, not the MLF. The British could not openly admit that they did not support the MLF, though, for they did not want to endanger the Polaris deal or drive the United States and the FRG more closely together. They hoped that as NATO members made plain their own objections to the MLF, the Americans would abandon it and Britain would not have to carry all of the blame. This is what happened. When President Johnson later pushed for a breakthrough, he found that the project had not advanced as far as some of his advisers were claiming.[17]

Nuclear cooperation between France and the FRG did not gather momentum. De Gaulle's real purpose was to detach the West Germans from the Americans and he did not want the FRG to obtain nuclear weapons, whether American or French. Konrad Adenauer was succeeded as chancellor of the FRG in October 1963 by Ludwig Erhard. While denying that the FRG was dependent upon the United States, Erhard insisted that the U.S. nuclear guarantee was vital and that, because the French were unwilling to offer something of equal worth, the FRG could not fall in with de Gaulle's machinations. Yet American leaders were often as frustrated with the FRG as they were with France in the 1960s. If they disliked de Gaulle's efforts to deal with the Soviets, for example, they were similarly alarmed by West Germany's self-assertion. In May 1967 the FRG agreed to pay more towards the cost of maintaining U.S. and British troops on NATO's frontier, which nullified the threat to withdraw them on financial grounds. The FRG also improved relations with the eastern bloc in May 1969 by abandoning the 'Hallstein Doctrine', by which Bonn severed relations with any state, apart from the Soviet Union, that recognised the GDR. Willy Brandt became chancellor of the FRG in October 1969 and energetically pursued a thaw with his 'Ostpolitik'. The White House national security adviser and future U.S. secretary of state, Henry Kissinger, feared that America was losing influence in Bonn and warned that closer ties between the FRG and the eastern bloc would only strengthen the Soviets and their allies. Kissinger complained that the Europeans, and also the British to some extent, were seeking to redefine their alliance with the United States for their own convenience. They wanted the freedom to negotiate with the USSR while expecting continued U.S. nuclear protection. They refused to increase their contribution to collective defence but required the Americans to provide the

same assistance as before. Kissinger did not want Bonn to place its eastern policy before everything else, including moves for further integration in Western Europe. America, he thought, should aim at strengthening
Bonn's bargaining position with Moscow while setting limits beyond
which Bonn could not go without a general consensus in the West.[18]

The situation in Europe continued to be complicated by events in
Vietnam. In France and the FRG, opposition to U.S. policy in Vietnam
reinforced the desire to deal separately with the USSR, and Moscow
came to realise that this could be exploited. The war in Vietnam made it
more difficult for the Soviets to negotiate agreements with the Americans.
The USSR's support for North Vietnam also represented a response to
China's accusation that Moscow was too eager to appease Washington. It
provided a means to reinforce the Soviet Union's claim to be the leader of
international communism.[19]

De Gaulle's goal for Europe was independence from the United States
and leadership from Paris. British membership of the EEC had no place
in this scenario, and an anti-British front had been solidified by the Franco-German Treaty of Friendship of 1963. The FRG chose France over
Britain, but could de Gaulle persuade Bonn to choose France over the
United States? This proved to be a step too far. De Gaulle had suspected
as much when the West German legislature added a preamble to the 1963
treaty that stressed the FRG's commitment to NATO. Erhard, who was
chancellor from 1963 to 1966, cultivated U.S. friendship. Bonn wanted
to avoid quarrels with Paris but continued to side with Washington on
NATO matters, nuclear policy, international trade and tariff arrangements,
and many other issues. De Gaulle did not share Bonn's sense of reliance
on the United States for security, economic assistance, and the protection
of West Berlin, and underestimated its importance. He offered to push
for German reunification if the Germans accepted the existing border
with Poland and promised not to develop nuclear weapons. In effect, de
Gaulle was telling the politicians in Bonn that if they did not support him
he might recognise the GDR, which would wreck the prospects for reunification and damage Bonn's claim to speak for the whole of Germany.
De Gaulle was trying to control the FRG's eastern policy. He declared

in February 1965 that security issues and disputed frontiers would have to be settled primarily by Germany's neighbours—those most affected by the division of Europe—which really meant France and the USSR, the only nuclear powers on the continent. De Gaulle wanted Bonn to accept that the future of Germany depended more upon decisions made in Paris than upon decisions made in Washington. He sought for France an advantage over the FRG: the idea was to counter the FRG's economic strength through a superior position in security arrangements and thaw diplomacy. This in turn would weaken America's position in Europe. The success of 'Ostpolitik' frustrated de Gaulle's plans. Bonn had its own reasons for taking the initiative, but 'Ostpolitik' soon began to have a much wider effect. In trying to eliminate the tension that was peculiar to relations between the FRG and the USSR, Bonn helped others to take up détente. Without 'Ostpolitik' a wider thaw would not have been possible, and through 'Ostpolitik' Bonn gained for itself more influence and freedom to manoeuvre.[20]

The Adenauer government had attached itself to a 'policy of strength' and Adenauer stuck to this line after he left office. At the Christian Democrat Party Congress of 1966, he spoke out against the 'change by rapprochement' advocated by the Social Democrats. Yet Adenauer had helped to set the ball rolling with his state visit to Moscow in 1955 and his establishment of diplomatic relations with the USSR, and Gerhard Schröder, foreign minister under both Adenauer and Erhard, concluded trade agreements with several of the USSR's satellites in Eastern Europe. The FRG's chancellor between 1966 and 1969 was Kurt Georg Kiesinger, who led a 'grand coalition' of Christian Democrats, the Christian Social Union, and Social Democrats. Kiesinger's constructive approach to relations with the Soviet Union and eastern bloc anticipated the moves made subsequently by Willy Brandt. 'Ostpolitik' developed around the idea that German reunification was not an end in itself, but had to be part of a general thaw that would overcome the Cold War division of Europe. This was the environment within which Brandt (a Social Democrat) operated when he succeeded Kiesinger in 1969. Brandt had no wish to weaken the FRG's security relationship with the United States and NATO, and thought he could use these links to facilitate a lasting East-West thaw, but 'Ostpolitik' became his priority and he put the FRG's goals before European ones. This shaped his attitude towards European unity. He favoured British membership of the EEC, for instance, because he preferred economic union to political integration. The latter, he feared, would get in the way of 'Ostpolitik'. Bonn's willingness to recognise the GDR and renounce territorial claims in Eastern Europe made the FRG much stronger in international affairs, and the Soviet Union approved of 'Ostpolitik' primarily in order to obtain economic benefits. In later life, Brandt claimed that 'Ostpolitik' made an enormous contribution to the undermining of the communist order in Eastern Europe, fostering an interest in reform and a demand for freedom there, yet Kissinger had predicted in 1965 that any effort by the FRG to befriend the GDR would, instead of liberalising the latter, make it even more resistant to change. Until the late 1980s, the leaders of the GDR remained closer to Moscow and more repressive in domestic policy than other governments in the eastern bloc. Timothy Garton Ash has suggested that policymakers in Bonn, and elsewhere in the West, gave in too easily to their own illusions. Ash thinks that if 'Ostpolitik' brought changes, this was more by accident than design.[21]

Bonn did not have everything its own way but had to work with Soviet and eastern bloc leaders and to pay attention to what the Americans, French, British, and others in the West were doing, which meant that compromises were unavoidable. In seeking to promote reforms in the GDR, Bonn could only encourage and could not direct. East German leaders tolerated the talk of reform because they wanted the existence of the GDR to be formally recognised and they wanted trade and hard currency. Bonn treated the East German regime as favourably as it could, in order to liberalise it, which meant that Bonn could do nothing that might hint at support for that regime's opponents. Other states in Eastern Europe pushed for closer ties with the FRG. As they became dependent upon West German trade, Bonn thought, this would provide a lever. In fact, the political impact was limited because trade, credits, and technology were channelled through state organs in Eastern Europe and served not to facilitate reform but as a substitute for reform, hence the argument of historians such as Ash, who deny that 'Ostpolitik' quickened the economic and political modernisation of the eastern bloc. The question of what 'Ostpolitik' could really achieve needs also to be related to a more general point about détente: everything depended on the balance between what might be termed the 'soft' and the 'hard' elements of détente. There was necessarily some ambiguity in what the FRG and indeed other western powers tried to do. In dealing with the USSR and the communist bloc they had to be both supportive and subversive. A framework was provided by NATO's 'Harmel Doctrine' of 1967 (named after the Belgian foreign minister Pierre Harmel), which defined defence and détente as complementary. The West was also keen to bring human rights into the equation, to put more pressure on leaders in Eastern Europe. There was great controversy on these issues and the invasion of Czechoslovakia in 1968 indicated that reform would be quashed if it was carried too far. So the priority could not be promoting reform. Rather than an end in itself, reform was a means. The main goal was to weaken the communist order by exposing it to outside influences.[22]

Brandt's 'Ostpolitik' might not have energetically promoted human rights, but this is hardly surprising. The FRG needed to earn Eastern Europe's trust and could not do so by encouraging protest, although this does not mean that Bonn always opted for stability over change in the bloc. The FRG had to pursue a policy that was both broadly in line with that of the West and distinctive. Washington, London, and Paris were all interested in détente, and the superpower relationship between the United States and the USSR had also to be borne in mind by Brandt and his colleagues. Circumstances facilitated thaw in Europe. The superpowers were willing. The Soviets were looking to alleviate tension in Europe in part because they were worried about the power and hostility of China, and the Americans hoped to gain Soviet help in ending the war in Vietnam. The Americans also wanted more influence over Bonn. Kissinger thought that four-power negotiations on Berlin could be used to this end. 'Ostpolitik' did not exist independently of these other developments within and between the East and the West. Bilateral contact between the FRG and GDR was linked with the Berlin talks and with U.S.-Soviet discussions

232 AN INTERNATIONAL HISTORY OF BRITISH POWER

on arms control and Moscow's concerns about China were to some extent shared in Washington.[23]

The role of the leaders of the FRG and GDR in European détente was important, and clearly there was more to the easing of tension at this time than the relationship between the United States and USSR (hence Wilfried Loth's emphasis on 'a depolarisation of our understanding of the Cold War' and Jussi Hanhimaki's point that European détente began before and continued after the most significant U.S.-Soviet agreements). German reunification and the revision of Germany's eastern frontiers had been among the chief aspirations of the FRG from the time of its establishment as an independent state, but Bonn realised during the 1960s that these goals were incompatible and unattainable in prevalent conditions. In order to make other gains, Bonn had to change tack. The Czech crisis of 1968 imposed limits on what could be attempted and underlined the fact that nothing would be achieved unless Moscow agreed to cooperate. In this context, the FRG's allies in the West, notably France, became relatively less influential in Bonn. There was an increasing gap between the détente activities of Bonn and those of Paris, and Moscow's determination not to lose control over Eastern Europe suited the FRG more than it suited France. De Gaulle had expected the Soviets to relax their control in order to facilitate a thaw, whereas 'Ostpolitik' offered Moscow territorial and political stability involving Bonn's recognition of the GDR and acceptance of the border between Germany and Poland. The Soviets preferred to bargain with Bonn rather than Paris, which helped the FRG to gain the upper hand in its dealings with France. The key point for Moscow was that de Gaulle threatened the established order in the bloc and Bonn's policy did not.[24]

The idea that détente ought to be given a try had been gaining ground in the Kremlin, which hoped to take advantage of the Vietnam War and internal tensions within NATO, trade with Western Europe, and weaken the latter's dependence upon the United States. The Soviets responded favourably to de Gaulle's overtures, but French friendship never mattered more to them than their wish to improve relations with the United States and the FRG. French diplomacy collapsed when the Soviet intervention in

Czechoslovakia in August 1968 confirmed that Moscow would not allow eastern bloc regimes to go their own way. De Gaulle had to backtrack. He suggested that French forces might again feature in NATO plans and manoeuvres. He said that talks on Britain's entry into the EEC could be reopened. The Czech crisis also highlighted the tension that was building up between Paris and Bonn. De Gaulle claimed that the crisis was partly attributable to the FRG's assertive use of its economic strength, which seemed to be drawing the Czechs away from the USSR, whereas Bonn claimed that de Gaulle was to blame because he had been encouraging centrifugal impulses within the eastern bloc.[25]

Continuing quarrels among the western powers brought into question the role and future of NATO. There had been another review of NATO strategy, as advocated by the United States and Britain, and this was completed in January 1967. It endorsed 'flexible response', extending the principle of 'differentiated responses' not only between nuclear and conventional but also between different forms of nuclear action. Strategists in America, Britain, and the FRG no longer assumed that the Soviet Union would automatically use nuclear weapons if war broke out, but they did insist, because war could begin by miscalculation or accident, that the USSR should be left in no doubt of NATO's readiness to fight. Circumstances might arise in which NATO would have to use nuclear weapons first, which meant accepting escalation as a possibility. The wish to keep options open, however, made for ambiguity. More specific guidelines were issued in November 1969. These covered the first and follow-on use of nuclear weapons, but not the ultimate full strategic assault.[26]

To sections of the British press, NATO strategy was flawed and the balance between conventional and nuclear forces unsatisfactory. In February 1969 *The Times* stated that Soviet aggression in Western Europe might not lead to all-out war, in which case a resort to nuclear weapons would be inappropriate and excessive. The defence secretary, Healey, had pointed out that a weakening of Soviet control in Eastern Europe could lead to small and limited clashes. His argument was that NATO should have sufficient conventional forces to police its frontiers. *The Times* agreed that the conventional alternative to nuclear weapons had to be properly maintained and condemned NATO for allowing its conventional forces to run down. By focusing too much on nuclear deterrence, NATO had narrowed its own options. The nuclear fixation was understandable. Nuclear forces were reckoned to be cheaper than conventional forces, and the European members of NATO wished to spend less on defence in order to raise living standards and fund social reforms and services, but overreliance on nuclear weapons reduced flexibility and hastened the moment at which a terrible decision would have to be made regarding their use. Was the deterrent policy even sensible? Could the Soviets not limit their aggression so as not to go beyond the point at which NATO would engage in nuclear retaliation? *The Times* urged NATO leaders to work out a more effective position. Similar remarks were made in the *Observer*, which complained about the 'present non-tough NATO strategy' and called for a new approach, with different options to be pursued simultaneously. To be inflexible would be to 'pre-empt the possibility of any evolution in Russian policy'.[27]

Richard Nixon succeeded Johnson as president of the United States early in 1969. He visited Europe and arrived in London on February 24, 1969. Kissinger advised Nixon to reaffirm America's commitment to NATO, promote further integration in Western Europe, and accept the Anglo-American 'special relationship' as a fact. Although he knew that European leaders and some members of the Nixon administration would object, Kissinger argued against any cutting of ties between the United States and Britain: America did not have such an 'excess of friends' that it could afford to discourage those who feel 'a special friendship for us'. The answer, he thought, was not to demote Britain to a lower level but to raise other countries up. As for the 'special relationship', it was still worthwhile, useful, and important to America, and it was a testament to 'the superb self-discipline by which Britain had succeeded in maintaining political influence after its physical power had waned'. As Kissinger noted of Nixon's visit to Britain in February 1969, the president was received by Harold Wilson 'with the avuncular goodwill of the head of an ancient family that has seen better times but is still able to evoke memories of the wisdom, dignity and power that had established the family name in the first place'.[28]

Wishing to strengthen NATO, Nixon enlisted the help of Britain and the FRG. The Americans also tried to placate de Gaulle, and not only for NATO purposes. Like his predecessors, as president, Nixon was keen for Britain to join the EEC, and if de Gaulle became more flexible, it was thought, he might also help in other ways (in talks with China and North Vietnam, for example). *The Times* did not think that de Gaulle would cooperate and hoped that Nixon would not subject other matters to his desire for reconciliation between the United States and France. De Gaulle soon gave way to a new French president, Georges Pompidou, though the idea of a thaw with the Soviets, in which France would be a key player, did not die away. Pompidou held summits with the Soviet leader, Leonid Brezhnev, and Valéry Giscard d'Estaing, president of France from 1974 to 1981, received Brezhnev on a state visit in December 1974. By this time, however, de Gaulle's earlier realisation that France lacked influence in Moscow and could not restrain Bonn was confirmed. Pompidou even tried briefly to befriend Britain and construct a Franco-British understanding as a counterweight to the strong FRG.[29]

If the Americans were annoyed by West Germany's more assertive approach to international affairs, the British were notably less worried. In fact, when Brandt visited London for talks in March 1970, Wilson recorded that these discussions 'showed a total identity of views', especially on the EEC, European security, and Brandt's eastern policy, 'which we warmly encouraged'. The prime minister subsequently expressed support for Brandt's diplomacy in a speech to the Commons. Wilson also denied that EEC regulations would hinder Britain's trade with Eastern Europe, if and when Britain joined the common market. *The Times* hailed Brandt for 'breaking out of the rigidities of the past twenty years' and creating opportunities for a general thaw. The *Economist* complimented Brandt for his perseverance and noted that the Soviets seemed to be showing 'a more friendly face', probably because they were eager to minimise the ill effects of the invasion of Czechoslovakia.[30]

Wilson had always spoken in favour of an East-West thaw, though as prime minister he did little to promote it and he had an exaggerated idea of his standing in Moscow. Britain's contribution to détente was limited. There were trade deals with the Soviets and various discussions and conferences, and a 'hotline' between London and Moscow was established in October 1967 (after de Gaulle had one), but the Czech crisis damaged Anglo-Soviet relations and underlying animosities (British concerns about Soviet spies operating in Britain, for example, and Soviet opposition to Anglo-American cooperation) did not go away. As for countries in the eastern bloc, Britain had not done much to establish closer links with them, a main consideration here being that London could not officially recognise the GDR, which complicated relations with allies of the GDR in Eastern Europe. Contact with Eastern Europe assumed greater importance at the end of the 1960s when Bonn tried to improve its own relationship with the GDR. Britain hoped for more trade with the eastern bloc, to benefit the British economy, and expected trade to foster political change in the bloc (the Czech crisis was taken to indicate that many people in Eastern Europe were dissatisfied with communism). To some members of Wilson's government, the time was right for Britain to embrace détente more fully. The foreign secretary, Michael Stewart, was not so sure, and argued that Anglo-Soviet relations had in the past been difficult for one main reason: the conduct of Moscow. Even so, the end of the 1960s did see Britain making constructive suggestions for a thaw and helping to arrange talks on various problems, including Berlin. A beginning was made, though little of note was achieved before the general election of 1970, which Labour lost.[31]

The international order was changing more rapidly than it had for some time. Nixon and Kissinger sought to increase America's influence over its allies, try out new ways of containing the Soviets, and end the war in Vietnam without admitting defeat. They were pressed by allies in Europe to make friendly gestures to Moscow and carry forward the thaw in East-West relations. Initially reluctant, Nixon and Kissinger soon decided to commit themselves to détente. In due course, their successes began to alarm Western Europe, which was divided on certain aspects of détente: one of the reasons why Pompidou wanted to deal with the USSR was because he did not want the FRG to set the agenda. Although leaders in Western Europe welcomed the new dialogue between Washington and Moscow, not least because it legitimised their own efforts, they feared that America would act without consulting them and make bargains that directly affected their countries' economic, political, and strategic interests.[32]

London shared these concerns, the 'special relationship' notwithstanding. This was one of the main points of agreement between the British and the continental members of NATO. There were not many others. In fact, on Britain's reassessment of its global commitments, its attitude towards the EEC, its wish to remain close to America, its proposals for the future of NATO, its defence policy and conventional and nuclear capabilities, and its role in and opinion of superpower détente and the thaw in Europe, there was constant controversy abroad as well as in Britain. Challenges and obstacles seemed to be increasing even as international relations shifted and greater flexibility was generated. Through it all, the British were able to retain influence and status, but their position relative to other great powers was less favourable than it had formerly been.

CHAPTER 9

INTERNATIONAL EMERGENCIES

THE SIX-DAY WAR
AND THE CZECH CRISIS

The proactive, assertive diplomacy of Paris and Bonn added a new twist to international relations from the mid-1960s. These years also saw a dramatic increase in tension as a result of the war in the Middle East and the crisis in Czechoslovakia, and it is worth examining these events in greater detail in order to understand their wider impact. British goals and interests were directly affected. It was not easy to decide how to respond, however, and Britain's influence over the course of events in the Middle East and Eastern Europe was not great, which clarified and confirmed the need for Britain to act with others. The Middle East and Eastern Europe were both strategically important. Britain also had economic concerns in these regions, as well as some disquiet about the political ramifications of what was happening. In view of Britain's traditional involvement there, the residual British military presence, and the region's oil, British leaders still regarded the Middle East as a part of the world in which they could and should have a say. Britain's links with Eastern Europe were more tenuous, but attention had to be paid to the region because of the Cold

War. Opportunities seemed to be available in the eastern bloc for trade and détente.

The Arab-Israeli War of 1967 reflected continuing problems in the Middle East. After the Suez affair of 1956, Gamal Abdel Nasser built up Egypt's military capacity with Soviet aid and sought an opportunity to gain revenge over Israel, as did other Arab governments. The United Nations tried unsuccessfully to remove grievances. In addition to the hostility between Arab states and Israel, the situation was further complicated by division among Arab leaders. Although pan-Arab and socialist regimes in Egypt, Syria, and Iraq did not always see eye to eye, they were united in their suspicion of the conservative monarchies in Jordan, Saudi Arabia, and states in the Persian Gulf. The USSR supported the radical governments while the Americans backed Israel and the conservative Arab monarchies. Israel won the Six-Day War of June 1967. American and Soviet leaders used the 'hotline' installed after the Cuban missile crisis to arrange a ceasefire. Washington had imposed an arms embargo and refused to supply weapons when they were requested by Israel. The Soviets did not observe the embargo but the war was so brief that resupplying the Arabs was not possible until the fighting stopped.[1]

Friction had increased quickly in the region in the weeks leading up to the war. On the surface, Britain's response was restrained, but in reality there was fear about the economic consequences of an Arab-Israeli war and talk in the Wilson government of pressurising Israel and drawing the United States into a joint Anglo-American peace initiative. London and Washington had both been warning the Israelis not to take unilateral action. George Brown protested when the UN peacekeeping force that had been stationed on the Egyptian-Israeli border in 1957 was withdrawn on May 19, 1967, at Nasser's request. Brown was unimpressed by the explanation from UN secretary-general U Thant, to the effect that there had been no choice but to comply with the wishes of a sovereign state. Nevertheless, the British government still had some faith in the UN and hoped that various efforts could be made through the UN to prevent war. Wilson's sympathies were with Israel, as were those of other members of the Cabinet and many Labour backbenchers. Brown was more favourable to the Arabs, but like his colleagues he did not want a war. He thought that an international agreement to guarantee free passage for Israeli shipping would defuse the situation and make it easier for Britain and the United States to talk Israel out of steps that could only increase regional instability. As the crisis intensified, intervention had considerable support in the Cabinet, but Richard Crossman and Denis Healey advised against hasty decisions and suggested that Anglo-American action would alienate African and Asian representatives in the UN. Healey also said that the Americans might prove to be unhelpful and that Britain did not have the military might to intervene alone. On May 30 Wilson gave up his idea of a bold move, declaring that Britain should only act with allies. Israel launched its offensive on June 5. As the days passed it became clearer that President Johnson did not intend to help Israel. Arab leaders used their oil as a political tool and the Israelis blocked the Suez Canal, all of which raised alarm in the West, but the British government opted for nonintervention. Crossman did not think that it could do anything else: 'if we had not been neutral our oil would have been stopped and a large part of our sterling balances would have been withdrawn'. The chiefs of staff also opposed intervention, while Brown lamented the unfavourable international circumstances that restricted Britain's freedom of manoeuvre. He knew that the Soviets were pro-Arab and deemed the West to be pro-Israel, but he had hoped for Moscow's help in arranging talks. When the French called for an international conference, however, the USSR refused to participate. The Americans were lukewarm at best. Brown's earlier wish for intervention had diminished by the time the Israelis, frustrated by the failure of international initiatives to prevent war, decided to look after their own security through a preemptive strike.[2]

During a debate on the Middle East in the Commons on July 6, 1967, minister of state for foreign affairs, George Thomson, insisted that Britain's relations with most countries in the region were good. He did not deny that the Arab-Israeli war had caused problems, but he thought that these were often exaggerated by the press. Thomson explained that 'our efforts to avert the war before it broke out, and to contain and limit it after it broke out, were misunderstood and misinterpreted in the Arab world'.

Though some Arab governments had severed relations with Britain, 'we would like to have good relations with these countries...We are not opposed to Arab nationalism and in so far as we have clashed with it our quarrel has been only with certain manifestations of it which seem to us to have worked in a negative and destructive way'. Britain had not been able to support the proposal made by nonaligned states, and backed at the UN by the Arabs and the communist bloc, because this provided for an unconditional Israeli withdrawal from occupied areas and left other key points virtually untouched. It was one-sided and Israel would not have complied. Britain preferred the resolution sponsored by Latin American leaders. This involved the withdrawal from occupied territory, freedom of passage through international waters, and an agreement on the refugee question. Thomson paid tribute to the efforts of the foreign secretary, Brown, who had worked hard at the UN. Thomson also expressed the hope that Israel would do nothing to jeopardise a final settlement and announced that Britain had made extra funds available to relieve refugees, unlike the Soviets, who sent only weapons into the region. Thomson told MPs that Britain would continue to meet its obligations there, helping to keep the peace and protect trade routes. He rejected the claim that Britain's oil interests did not require a continued presence in the region, and argued that the Arabs had only stopped the oil supply because they misinterpreted Britain's efforts to prevent the Six-Day War. Soon the oil would flow again, not least because the Arabs knew that Britain and the West would buy elsewhere if necessary. In the meantime, the government would have to ration oil, which was unavoidable because of the closure of the Suez Canal and the political situation in Nigeria. In this same debate, Brown rounded on those Conservative MPs who accused the government of weakness. He taunted them with references to the Suez crisis. Nasser was Egypt's president, he said, and there could be no settlement unless he participated. Navigation through the Suez Canal, the regional arms race, and the refugee problem had all to be addressed in an international framework, Brown concluded, and it was most important for Israel and the Arab states to accept each other's existence and end belligerency status.[3]

The controversy over Britain's policy before, during, and after the Six-Day War prompted statements from many public figures, including the historian Max Beloff, of All Souls' College, Oxford, who insisted that Britain should side with Israel. Britain should not stand aside and let the Arabs 'extirpate' the Jews, wrote Beloff in a letter to *The Times*, and the tendency to compromise in such matters was 'symptomatic of our disbelief in the values we still proclaim'. What was at stake was the survival of 'a country that is part of our western world, which almost alone among the so-called new states accepts our ideas of political freedom, the rule of law and social justice'. Britain's duty was to assist Israel, not to 'allow ourselves to get caught up in side issues and to deny our right to protect our own without the consent of the United Nations', which meant accepting the veto not only of the USSR, which had 'a legitimate say in world affairs', but also of many new states in Africa and Asia. These states applauded Nasser and condoned Arab aggression but had nothing to commend them: no credit and no political order or rule of law. They 'brandish their swords with one hand and the begging bowl with the other'. Beloff called upon the West to stand firm. Arab ascendancy and Israeli weakness would be disastrous, for the result would be Soviet control of the Middle East. The world would only take Britain and other western powers seriously again if they acted decisively. Above all, they should not try to buy the friendship of developing countries by abandoning Israel.[4]

The Americans had tried to prevent the war of June 1967, but they were torn between the established policy of supporting Israel and the need to restrain Israel, and there were ongoing concerns about oil, regional instability, and the ambitions of the USSR. Though President Johnson wished to deter the would-be belligerents, he avoided drastic gestures in case they backfired. He also knew that U.S. forces were already stretched owing to the struggle in Vietnam. He was annoyed as Israel prepared to fight without consulting Washington. In 1950 the American, British, and French governments had signed a declaration guaranteeing frontiers in the Middle East. They had also agreed that when selling weapons to the Arabs or Israelis, a principle of parity between the two sides would be respected. Here, perhaps, was the basis for collective action in 1967, but the French were reluctant to cooperate. As Johnson attempted to hold Israel back and secure international support for a diplomatic solution, he was obliged to reaffirm the U.S. commitment to Israeli security when asked to do so by Israel. No country in the world received more American aid per capita than Israel, and in April 1967 a subcommittee of Congress reported that the main threat to peace in the Middle East was posed by Egypt and Syria. All this served to legitimise the Israeli offensive of June 1967. Some of the results were advantageous both to the Americans and to Israel: the defeat of Egypt and Syria, the undermining of Nasser's regional influence, and the increased importance of conservative Arab states, especially Saudi Arabia. A less welcome development, as far as the Americans were concerned, was that their role in the politics of the Middle East became much larger than they had wanted or expected. Greater involvement did not mean more influence. In fact, Johnson was repeatedly frustrated by his inability to impose America's will. The president and his advisers had paid more attention to Vietnam than to the Middle East in the spring of 1967, and Johnson was disappointed when the UN peacekeeping force was removed and angered by Egypt's interference with Israeli shipping, which breached an agreement of 1957 relating to free passage through the region's waterways. The Americans were not on good terms with Egypt or with Syria. Relations with Jordan were better, but King Hussein could not break with his Arab allies. Israel was not amenable to U.S. pressure at this juncture. The fact that Israel's main weapons supplier was France, not the United States, put a limit on American influence. Israel was sure that the Arabs were going to attack and accused Washington of doing nothing about it. Once the war broke out, Johnson's main worry was that the Soviets would intervene. Then, after the war, he had to decide how far to press Israel to withdraw from occupied areas. He hoped that military defeat would prompt the Arabs to seek a comprehensive peace treaty and that rapid progress could be made so as to forestall a Soviet move at the UN for Israeli concessions. Israel, however, wanted to take advantage of victory in the war and denied that a quick settlement was needed.[5]

Johnson's handling of the crisis was not very assured. Preoccupied with Vietnam, he appears to have permitted Israeli leaders to believe that he would acquiesce if they decided to go to war against the Arabs. Defence chiefs in Washington and senior figures in the CIA did not discourage an Israeli resort to arms, and many of the president's friends and advisers were pro-Israel in sentiment. At the same time, U.S. ambassadors in the Middle East were urging the White House not to antagonise Egypt. This made for some confusion at the centre of policy making. Official and unofficial signals reaching Israel suggested that the United States would not stand in the way if Israel chose to fight, yet the White House cannot have been unconcerned about the likely results of a war in terms of oil supplies and Soviet influence. Johnson was pulled in different directions. He hoped to avert war, to restrain Israel, and to have British and French help in defusing the situation. There could be no question of unilateral U.S. intervention. Equally, Johnson could not stand aside and let Israel start a war, in case the Israelis suffered reverses and called for help. Nor could he take a hard line with Nasser, in case this made matters worse and reduced America's influence in the region for the foreseeable future. The British plan for international naval patrols had some merit and was favoured by U.S. secretary of state Dean Rusk, but the secretary of defence, Robert McNamara, considered it impracticable and Johnson did not know if there would be enough time for it to work or if it would satisfy Israel. The Israelis, meanwhile, were annoyed that Johnson offered no firm guarantee of support, something he could not do because of its likely impact in the Middle East, in Western Europe, and in the U.S. Congress. Informally, however, he accepted that the Israelis had the right to act alone. He said he would not stop them but warned that they could not expect direct American assistance if the Arabs got the upper hand.[6]

Israel was confident of success and wanted to fight in 1967. The reasons were not unlike those that had prompted the military action of 1956: self-defence and the need to respond to Arab threats, combat terrorism, and ensure free passage for Israeli shipping. Conversely, it would be going too far to argue that Israel actually caused the war, because it was probably not intended or planned by any of the participants, although none of them tried to promote calm through negotiation and compromise. As the crisis mounted in May 1967, the sense of danger in Israel intensified.

The withdrawal of the UN peacekeeping force, the Egyptian advance into Sinai, the overflight of Israel's nuclear research centre at Dimona, and Nasser's closure of the Straits of Tiran put Israeli security at risk.[7]

British newspapers asserted that the Wilson government should have responded more effectively. According to *The Times*, the war and its aftermath demonstrated Britain's lack of influence. Although the government had made sound proposals for a settlement (involving arms limitation, free passage through international waterways, no territorial aggrandisement and provision for refugees), it was not clear how 'past assurances that Britain's presence in the Middle East would safeguard our oil supplies and other interests' could be reconciled with 'the fact that oil supplies are now curtailed, petrol prices threatened, and trade with Arab countries damaged'. World leaders were exchanging ideas about peace and stability in the Middle East but there was no sign of Britain 'at the top table', whereas French prestige was rising. Britain 'seems to have got the worst of all possible worlds—blame from the Arab side with very little credit or compensation from anywhere else'. Meanwhile, de Gaulle 'supplies the weapons for Israel's victory and then manages to win credit almost everywhere with a series of lofty utterances that any parliament which was able to call him to account would justly shred into fairly small bits'. Despite this French posturing, however, the future of the region depended mainly on the Americans and the Soviets. Britain and France would both have to accept what the superpowers decided. This meant that Britain would have to 're-examine some of the assumptions and the style of her diplomacy. It does not mean that Britain is powerless or irrelevant, merely that her power and her relevance can no longer be expressed in old ways if they are to be credible'. The *Guardian* was struck by allegations about pro-Arab bias in the foreign office. Yet George Brown had not been incorrect when he pointed out that the UN Charter explicitly condemned territorial aggrandisement, and that it was not the Arabs who were occupying Israeli land but vice versa.[8]

After the Six-Day War, Brown laid the basis for a settlement. He was largely responsible for the UN Security Council resolution of November 1967, which was designed to facilitate Arab recognition of the state of

Israel. Brown wanted each side to give something up but thought that
this should be expressed in nonspecific terms. According to the resolution, Israel was to withdraw from occupied territories and the Arabs and
Israelis were to terminate 'all claims or states of belligerency'. One of
the problems was that the word 'all' was not used in connection with the
areas from which Israel was going to withdraw, the implication being that
the withdrawal would be less than complete.[9]

Nasser had decided to confront Israel because he considered it a barrier to Egyptian dominance in the region and part of the imperialist West's
design against Arab independence and power. He was also willing to fight
in 1967 because he assumed that the Soviets would assist him and offset
U.S. backing for Israel. Defeat in the Six-Day War was a serious blow, but
Nasser then pursued a 'no war, no peace' policy, keeping up the pressure
on Israel and talking about a settlement while preparing for another conflict. Soviet president Nikolai Podgorny visited Cairo, demonstrating the
USSR's continuing support for Nasser's regime. As for the UN resolution
of November 1967, the Israelis accepted it because they expected also
to have security guarantees from the western powers. Nasser expressed
a willingness to discuss the resolution, but first he wanted to rearm and
to unite the Arabs in order to negotiate from a position of strength, so
he stalled. Border clashes went on. Still there was no peace settlement,
and the Americans were increasingly active in the absence of a decisive
breakthrough at the UN.[10]

If events in the Middle East damaged the reputation of the UN and
brought its peacekeeping role into disrepute, the period after the Six-Day
War was also uncomfortable for Britain. British arms sales in the region,
for instance, became highly contentious. The Labour government tried
to adhere to its stated policy: sales would be limited so that neither the
Arab states nor Israel gained special treatment, particularly with respect
to offensive weaponry. When Israel placed an order for tanks in 1968, the
government approved the deal in order to safeguard jobs and boost the
relevant British companies, but the tanks were subsequently held back
on foreign office advice. Fears had grown about offending the Arabs. The
Arab world was a bigger market than Israel. In addition, the government

did not want to upset the policy of balance or hinder peace efforts in the region. British involvement in these efforts caused trouble. The 'land for peace' principle, which Brown had endorsed at the UN, displeased Israel and provoked quarrels within Wilson's Cabinet. Anglo-Israeli relations did not improve. Indeed, Britain was slow to forget Israel's refusal quickly to reopen the Suez Canal after the Six-Day War (Britain wanted it open for economic reasons but Israel had delayed in order to put pressure on Egypt). The British participated in peace negotiations in the late 1960s, in part as a demonstration of their status and influence, but the talks achieved nothing. Although the foreign secretary from 1968 to 1970, Michael Stewart, suggested that Britain must take the initiative, he could not win over his more cautious colleagues. Wilson argued that there was no point in making proposals unless there was a chance that Israel would accept them, and as time passed and a general election approached, the prime minister was reluctant to do anything that might cause a stir.[11]

The Soviets also became cautious. Peking condemned Moscow for encouraging the Arabs to fight and then abandoning them. Despite these jibes, the Soviets decided not to increase their commitments in the region beyond the point at which they became too expensive and dangerous. The plan all along had been to undermine U.S. influence in the Middle East. The war of 1967 was not in itself alarming, but the possibility that it might spread prompted Moscow to work for a ceasefire. Thereafter, the Soviet position was that Israel and its 'accomplices and protectors' were responsible for the instability in the region and that Israel should not be allowed to use conquered territory as a bargaining tool. The Soviet foreign minister, Gromyko, insisted that the USSR wanted all the peoples of the Middle East to enjoy peace and independence. He called for the satisfaction of legitimate Arab demands, the creation of a Palestinian state, and Israel's withdrawal from all occupied areas. The Soviets respected Nasser for his firm line and his leadership of the Arab states. They were less impressed by Nasser's successor, Anwar Sadat, who became president of Egypt in 1970. Sadat distanced himself from Moscow. As Gromyko saw it, he tried to appease the Americans and weakened Egypt's security by pursuing a thaw with Israel.[12]

But before this there was another war, in October 1973. The 1967 war had settled nothing. One of Nixon's goals when he visited Europe in February 1969 was to arrange four-power talks on the Middle East, to involve the United States, Britain, France, and the USSR. Nixon wanted peace. He also wanted to restrict Soviet involvement in the region. He and Kissinger sought to avoid a return to the pre-1967 situation, for that had been unstable, and yet the Americans had constant difficulty in reconciling their talk of peace with their ongoing support for Israel. Indeed, the need for a strong Israel was reinforced by the so-called 'Nixon-Kissinger Doctrine', according to which the United States, instead of intervening itself in trouble spots around the world, would rely on local friends to keep order. The supply of weapons to Israel continued alongside discussions about giving back occupied Arab territory as part of a peace agreement. Assisted by Britain, the Americans tried to prevent another Arab-Israeli war. Washington and London worked together in September 1970 when Syria intervened in Jordan, and America's reliance on Israel, Jordan, and Iran as regional allies increased as Britain withdrew from East of Suez. With the outbreak of the 1973 war, Kissinger guided a ceasefire resolution through the UN, but the manner in which this had to be done again demonstrated the complicated political complexion of the Middle East. Kissinger had originally wanted Britain to propose a ceasefire, on the grounds that Egypt would not accept it if it came from America or the Soviet Union. Finding that Egypt wanted more than a simple ceasefire the British decided not to make any proposal, and the Soviets refused to act as well, not wishing to annoy the Arabs. The proposal, therefore, had to come from the Americans, and Kissinger only proceeded after gaining Israel's approval. It could be argued that the Americans did not try hard enough to foster agreement in the Middle East. Neither Johnson nor Nixon wished to alienate voters in the United States by increasing their demands of Israel. They admitted that the occupation of Arab land was an obstacle to peace, but did little to prevent the Israelis from establishing settlements there. From 1967, U.S. policy had several basic features that would remain in place for many years. Israel's military capability was to be maintained with American assistance, so that the Israelis would be able to defend themselves against any combination of Arab states. Washington wanted Palestinian rights to be respected but did not envisage the Palestinians' unconditional return to their pre-1967 homes or the creation of an independent Palestinian state. As for the Israeli settlements on occupied land, the Americans sometimes called these illegal and unacceptable but argued also that Israel should not have to give up territory taken in 1967 unless the Arabs made concessions on the 'land for peace' principle embodied in the UN resolution of November 1967. Whenever plans were made for an international conference, the Americans and Israelis were obstructive. The Arabs and Soviets tended to favour the conference route. This distinction is easily explained. The weaker, more numerous parties believed that negotiation gave them a chance to improve their position, while the stronger side suspected that it would lose more than could be gained by negotiating.[13]

The situation in the Middle East continued to disturb international affairs during and after the late 1960s. Instability and tension were also raised by the Czech crisis of 1968. A reform movement had developed in Prague. Its aims included more representative government and economic freedom. Alexander Dubcek rose to become leader of the Czech Communist Party, and, although declaring that Czechoslovakia would remain loyal to Moscow and the Warsaw Pact, he maintained that internal reforms were necessary. His was a more thorough programme than the one the Hungarians had proposed twelve years earlier, and although the Czechs did not wish to pursue a neutral foreign policy as the Hungarians had, they did seek greater independence within the Soviet bloc. Czech reformers wanted more contact and trade with the West and suggested that political liberalisation and economic progress went hand in hand. Moscow decided that its control over the bloc would be undermined if Dubcek and his supporters were given the latitude they desired. Therefore, there could be no relaxation of social discipline or one-party rule, no free speech, and no government posts for noncommunists. Czechoslovakia was invaded on August 20, 1968, and a pro-Soviet regime was eventually restored in Prague. If they expected the West's direct help, the Czech reformers misunderstood the international order and the impact of détente (some historians have stressed the complacency and collusion produced by the thaw of the 1960s). In addition, the West was impressed most by signs of disunity in the bloc, not by reform. Hence the continuing attempts to woo Nicolae Ceausescu of Rumania. Though he was corrupt and authoritarian, he was trying to pursue his own line within the bloc, and Rumania was the only member of the Warsaw Pact not to participate in the invasion of Czechoslovakia.[14]

Czechoslovakia descended into crisis in 1968 largely because of an internal struggle within its communist party. Different factions had their own ideas about political and economic change, and Dubcek's policies unleashed popular forces in Czech society, so much so that pluralism, dissent, and the market gained appeal. The domestic quarrel over reform became an ideological split in Czech communism. Inevitably, hardliners in Moscow and throughout the eastern bloc worried that the process of reform could not be controlled. They did not want change to be challenging. During the spring and summer of 1968, senior figures in the Kremlin grew alarmed. No satellite could be permitted to depart from an approved course in domestic or foreign affairs, they believed, and they were further alienated when the independently minded Tito and Ceausescu both visited Prague in August and were warmly received. Yet Soviet leaders thought long and hard about intervening militarily in Czechoslovakia. They tried to be patient, as did the conservatives in the Czech Communist Party. Much depended on the Kremlin's opinion of Dubcek: Would he be willing and able to limit reform? Perhaps Dubcek was wrong to think that the communist system could be changed by the means he was using; perhaps the Czech reformers became overconfident because there were no Soviet troops on their borders. Dubcek knew that pressure was building for quicker and greater change, but he also knew that Moscow would not accept it. The crisis came at a difficult time for the West, as had the invasion of Hungary in 1956. Then, the western powers had been distracted by the Suez affair. Now, in 1968, the U.S. involvement in Vietnam and the international clamour that this was creating, as well as the antiwar protests within America itself and problems in the Middle East and Europe, made the Soviets think that they could act in Czechoslovakia without fear of a vigorous western response. Moscow did not want to damage East-West relations any more than necessary, however, and sent conciliatory notes to the governments of the United States, Britain, and the FRG on the eve of the invasion of Czechoslovakia.[15]

Concern had been growing in the West since the spring, when Soviet leaders condemned Dubcek's reforms. In July the British government decided not to get involved. Prague had not requested help and it was thought that interference might do more harm than good. Some members of Wilson's Cabinet argued that inactivity would be morally wrong, but the prevalent view was that Britain alone could not influence the course of events in Czechoslovakia. It seemed that the situation there was becoming calmer, only for Britain and other western powers to be surprised by the Warsaw Pact invasion of August 20. NATO lacked information and reliable intelligence was in short supply. In fact, for some time there had been limited awareness of what was going on in the eastern bloc. When news of the invasion reached London, the government issued a protest and some links with the bloc were abandoned. At the same time, there was no wish to destabilise central Europe or disrupt British trade with the region, and Wilson and his colleagues were reluctant to go further than the other western powers in their reaction. In the West, the main results of the invasion were that NATO unity was enhanced, that de Gaulle's independent overtures to the Soviet Union were shown to be unproductive, and that Washington shelved plans to cut the number of U.S. troops in Europe. But it was not automatically assumed that the Soviets would give up on détente. In London, for example, it was still thought that a thaw was worth pursuing (this opinion was particularly strong in the foreign office). Although some critics of the Wilson government attacked its response to events in Czechoslovakia as feeble and foolish, it was in line with the response of NATO as a whole. What else could be done? NATO had no preparations in place to deal with such a crisis and any idea of intervening in the Soviet sphere had been given up after the invasion of Hungary in 1956.[16]

What did the Soviets expect to achieve by invading Czechoslovakia? *The Times* assumed that Moscow aimed to enforce conformity in the eastern bloc, prevent reforms there, and make an example of the Czechs.

Military intervention could not succeed every time, however, and in the future the USSR would find it harder to control its satellites. Moscow had shown itself not to be a reasonable negotiating partner. Governments in Eastern Europe would place less trust in Soviet promises, and loss of trust would also affect East-West relations. Attitudes would harden. The Cold War would be prolonged and the arms race would revive as military spending increased. All of this would disappoint the Soviets, but they had only themselves to blame. As for the United States, recent events made it more likely that Nixon and the Republicans would win the November elections. American foreign policy might become less flexible; perhaps the war in Vietnam would be prosecuted more energetically. Whatever happened, *The Times* argued, the Czech crisis gave grounds for pessimism rather than optimism with regard to the international scene. *The Times* wanted a forceful British condemnation of the USSR. A military operation was out of the question, but Britain could put pressure on the Soviets in other ways, especially through diplomatic channels. There was also a need to reassess some of the assumptions that had been shaping British policy—that superpower détente had acquired 'an automatically continuing momentum', that the military threat to Western Europe had 'permanently receded', that the presence of British forces outside Europe was 'an expensive irrelevance', and that 'the spread of education and material prosperity establishes, whatever the nature of the regime, the liberal virtues of freedom of thought and expression, respect for public opinion, and the abandonment of naked force and terror as political means'. All of this had to be reconsidered, the more so because the Labour government wanted détente to carry on. Now that the Soviets had shown their true colours it was important to be robust. NATO's effectiveness would have to be enhanced and Britain's military role in key areas outside Europe maintained. The government seemed intent on reducing Britain's commitments to the common level, when the prudent course would be for other states to bring their military obligations up to the British level. The Czech crisis suggested that the extra effort was necessary.[17]

Overseeing a military takeover in Czechoslovakia would be easy for the Soviets, commented the *Economist*, but running the country afterwards was another matter and it was possible that Soviet intransigence would make reformers in Czechoslovakia and other satellite states even more determined to promote change. They wanted a form of communism that suited modern, educated, industrial societies, as did the communist parties of France and Italy, which had strongly condemned the invasion of Czechoslovakia. The *Observer* argued that Moscow's problems would only increase. Despite the efficient military operation, the Czech people were refusing to submit.[18]

George Brown was not surprised by the Soviet invasion, bearing in mind what Khrushchev had said in 1956 to the effect that no satellite could be allowed to remove itself from Moscow's control, while Richard Crossman focused more on the unwillingness of America and France to act and on Wilson's unimpressive performance. The prime minister had Parliament recalled for an emergency sitting on August 26 and his remarks, though 'decent', were rather 'superficial'. Crossman found the whole episode 'depressing…because everyone knows that Britain can do nothing to help the Czechs'. Wilson denounced the USSR but also expressed the hope that détente would continue. The invasion, he said, was motivated by 'a grim and cynical determination that no communist country in Eastern Europe should be allowed to decide for itself that it wished to turn away from the deadening uniformity of internal control towards new conceptions of freedom'. Even so, the prime minister added, the West should not ignore opportunities to promote thaw and heal divisions. For the Conservatives, Edward Heath demanded a more vigorous policy from the government. He spoke of the need for a review of NATO strategy, called for more spending on defence, and urged the government to stop abandoning Britain's overseas responsibilities. He argued that only strong forces, and a willingness to use them, would deter the Soviets. What would happen if a similar crisis arose in the Middle East or the Far East, or affected a member of the Commonwealth? Would Britain do nothing except protest? Heath also wondered about détente. The assumption had been made that it was indispensable and irreversible, but the Czech crisis showed how quickly circumstances could change.[19]

The crisis prompted the NATO council to call upon members of the alliance to expand the size of their armed forces. There was a limit to what certain NATO countries could do when domestic political and economic concerns ruled out significant increases in defence spending. The British government set an example and announced an increase in funds for the BAOR with a focus on reequipping. The Czech crisis also saw closer diplomatic collaboration between London and Washington than had been seen for some time.[20]

The invasion of Czechoslovakia confirmed that Brezhnev, who had risen to power in the Soviet Union after the fall of Khrushchev in 1964, was a more conservative figure than his predecessor had been. Brezhnev was determined to keep the Warsaw Pact and Eastern Europe's post-1945 frontiers intact. He assumed that the expansion of nuclear arsenals during the 1960s and a new generation of intercontinental ballistic missiles had enabled the USSR to catch up with America. This meant that a nuclear attack by one side would mean the destruction of both, which seemed to make a conventional war between the two superpowers in Europe more likely. Brezhnev reversed Khrushchev's plans to reduce the Soviet Union's conventional forces and Eastern Europe became even more important strategically. According to the 'Brezhnev Doctrine' of 1968, governments within the bloc were required to maintain an acceptable socialist outlook internally and externally. They had to respect Soviet interests (this was also called the 'doctrine of limited sovereignty'). The Czech crisis proved that the USSR could and would use military force to keep order in its sphere of influence. Invasion became inevitable once the Kremlin decided that other options were unworkable. Cooperation with Dubcek depended on his willingness and ability to keep reform within the limits set by Moscow, and it was thought that he could not be relied upon in this way. After the invasion, however, there was no smooth transfer of power to a compliant Czech leadership. An alternative government was not formed quickly. Even hardliners in the Czech Communist Party opposed the invasion and occupation. A campaign of nonviolent civil resistance began. Eventually, a compromise was worked out. Moscow agreed not to reverse some of the reforms that had been introduced in return for a promise that Czechoslovakia would remain in the Warsaw Pact, the calling off of the civil resistance, and resignations from the Czech government. The West protested about Soviet aggression at the UN, but Moscow pressed Czech leaders to ask for the matter to be taken off the Security Council's agenda, and the Czechs agreed to do this on the understanding that it would speed up the departure of occupying forces.[21]

The short-term consequences of the invasion were unhelpful to the Soviet Union. NATO was reinvigorated. All talk of reducing troop numbers in Western Europe was ended. Some NATO members increased their defence spending. The proposed European security conference was put in jeopardy, as were Soviet thaw policies, especially those involving the FRG. De Gaulle's idea of an independent community of states in Western Europe, led by France and able to stand between the two superpowers, was undermined. In Japan, the opponents of the security pact with America, which was due for renewal in 1970, were weakened. Across the developing world the invasion of Czechoslovakia was condemned. Ratification of a nuclear nonproliferation agreement was postponed as opposition to it increased in the United States, the FRG, and Japan. The opening of the strategic arms limitation talks was delayed. In Britain and Western Europe, unrepentant Cold Warriors and the advocates of closer ties with America gained a fillip.[22]

The 'Brezhnev Doctrine' was disparaged in the West but it did not signify a marked change in Moscow's attitude towards the eastern bloc or in Soviet concepts of sovereignty. Ideas about how socialist countries should relate to each other, and the legal and philosophical framework for this relationship, had long been organised around Moscow's desire to consolidate and control the bloc. The 'Brezhnev Doctrine' rested primarily on a wish to prevent challenges to the Soviet model of socialism and to Soviet world power. The sovereignty of bloc countries was not sovereignty as the West understood it, but Moscow was untroubled by this. Nevertheless, after 1968, Moscow found it increasingly difficult to maintain bloc cohesion as this task was complicated by foreign policy needs, internal bloc relations, and greater global interdependence.

Before and after the Czech crisis, Soviet leaders reminded satellites in Eastern Europe about the limits of acceptable behaviour. Czech reformers did not interpret the signals correctly in 1968, perhaps, although it could also be argued that they did understand Moscow's concerns and did try to show respect for the USSR's interests and avoid a final breach. Even had the Czechs read the signals correctly it is possible that the Soviets would still have invaded, because the Kremlin wanted to be sure that the government in Prague would be led by communists it could trust. Ideologically, the 'Brezhnev Doctrine' was a belief in a uniform state-socialist model for the bloc, and its main purpose was to justify intervention against divergence. Broader security issues were also important, especially those associated with the strength of the Warsaw Pact, the communist order in Czechoslovakia, and even the system of political authority in the USSR itself. Clearly, the relationship between Moscow and the satellites was far from straightforward, before as well as after 1968.[23]

Years later, the official version of what happened in Czechoslovakia was still being maintained by Andrei Gromyko. The Czechs had been enjoying peace, stability, and social and economic progress, he claimed, only to be disturbed by 'forces' that 'cared nothing for the people's welfare or the country's true national interests'. The leaders of this coup gained outside help and intended to impose a counter-revolution, but pleas for help reached Moscow and 'the fraternal countries gave immediate and effective support'. The Czech people wanted to remain in the Soviet bloc and welcomed the increase in internal discipline after the crisis, while the unrealistic Dubcek lacked a mandate and had to be removed.[24]

Despite the contradictions between the West's view of what happened and the Soviet version, détente recovered after the Czech crisis. East-West trade increased, visits and exchanges resumed, Brandt's 'Ostpolitik' took root, other governments in the West promoted thaw, and Nixon's administration decided to go ahead with SALT. The British were not directly involved in SALT, but they favoured arms limitation because they did not wish to fall further behind the two superpowers in military capability. As the tension died down, most leaders in the West accepted that the invasion of Czechoslovakia had been a defensive move to promote stability within the eastern bloc. Détente continued, though in a different form: 'instead of change through rapprochement', writes Jiri Valenta, 'détente became rapprochement without change'. Therefore, the Czech crisis did not end what John Gaddis has called 'the long peace', a period of predictability during which both sides in the Cold War tried to exercise restraint and respected each other's spheres of influence. Nuclear deterrence no doubt contributed to this. Neither side wanted a war over Czechoslovakia. As was typical of the period, both sides preferred to get what they wanted by means other than a direct military clash. If the Cold War brought out the diversity in the western camp, meanwhile, it also made more difficult the expression of diversity in the communist camp.[25]

Yet diversity existed in Eastern Europe even if it could not readily be expressed. The eastern bloc was not monolithic. Bloc governments tried to keep order by giving the people material benefits without weakening state direction of the economy or one-party rule, but economic problems and misgivings about state control began to frustrate this policy. In time, governments became less concerned about the private opinions of the people, provided they conformed in public. There was no demand that everyone should believe in the system. Communist leaders could not avoid making compromises of this kind in the period that followed the Czech crisis, and even before the crisis, during the Khrushchev era, there had been some relaxation of social and economic regulations. At the same time, one can question Khrushchev's assumption that communist systems could be reformed and remain communist (this is not what happened in the USSR and Eastern Europe in the 1980s and 1990s). The Kremlin ordered the invasion of Czechoslovakia in August 1968 not so much because of what was already going on but because of what *might* happen if the Soviet Union did not act. After the crisis, the Kremlin had to learn some give and take in its dealings with the bloc. It was understood that to rely principally on military force would be to risk losing the benefits of détente. It was also understood that stability in the bloc was not compatible with an expectation that the satellites should adhere strictly to norms imposed by Moscow.[26]

In the long run, economic change in the eastern bloc tended to push forward political change. For many years, the pricing policy in Comecon favoured the satellites rather than the USSR. As détente opened up trading relationships outside the bloc, East-West commerce became a feature in bloc planning and integration. In addition, the USSR's oil deposits became a significant asset. The price of oil was rising (not least because of conditions in the Middle East). The Soviets used their oil to pay for western goods and technology, and the growing oil revenue also enabled the USSR to subsidise its satellites. Moscow paid an economic price in order to maintain bloc cohesion. The subsidising was targeted and the main beneficiaries were Czechoslovakia, the GDR, and Poland. In Czechoslovakia, the idea was to satisfy the people as consumers and compensate them for the repression of 1968. Czechoslovakia was also important to the bloc as a supplier and exporter. The GDR was important because it was on the Cold War front line. The most militarily exposed member of the bloc, it was a loyal ally of the USSR and its leaders were staunch opponents of Dubcek in 1968. The GDR was also a source of high technology goods. Poland was important because it was prey to political division and, as such, a threat to bloc stability. It remained a strategic asset, but its economic problems hardly endeared the communist order to the Polish people. During the 1970s, Poland became massively reliant on western credit.[27]

The growth of economic and financial links between East and West meant that problems in the West began to affect the bloc, and this was seen most clearly in relation to the collapse of the Bretton Woods system, which fixed the value of the U.S. dollar to gold and other currencies to the dollar. The U.S. dollar was the main world currency. While the United States had a strong economy and a positive balance of payments there was no reason why its national interest would conflict with its role as currency regulator, but the American economy began to experience difficulties in the 1960s, at a time when trade between Western Europe and Eastern Europe grew rapidly. In 1969 the United States removed some of its prohibitions on trade with communist countries in order to promote economic and political agreements. Unsuccessful economic policies, inflation, slow economic growth, and a monetary crisis then led Washington unilaterally to suspend gold convertibility in 1971. Great confusion ensued in international trade. Oil exporters, including the USSR, took advantage of the West's need for oil while banks in the West, desperate for borrowers, encouraged bloc governments to take on debt. Economic competition within the West and within the bloc intensified. Individual countries on one side thought they could ease their own problems by increasing their trade with the other side. The United States and the USSR both experienced relative economic decline and sought to boost their exports, even at the risk of annoying their allies. This undermined the unity of the West and the unity of the eastern bloc.[28]

Détente weakened established regimes in the bloc, though historians disagree about the extent to which this contributed to the ending of the Cold War. To Moscow, détente was about competing as well as cooperating with the West, and Soviet leaders were loath to prioritise the cooperative aspects. Even so, these aspects gave the West opportunities. In America, Britain, and Western Europe, conservatives often likened détente to retreat and appeasement, but this was to misrepresent the goals of its advocates and authors, who intended to use détente to modify the enemy. Some historians argue that Soviet political ascendancy in Eastern Europe reduced the reformist impact of economic changes. This relates to the question of whether communism collapsed or was dismantled.[29] If Moscow and its satellites wanted more openness to the West, they also knew that this would cause problems. Then again, there was pressure to catch up with those parts of the world that seemed to be making better use of their resources. External contacts were necessary and useful: they could help communist states to improve their economic performance and give them legitimacy and prestige, which would be beneficial both domestically and internationally. Whatever the motives behind the gradual lowering of barriers between East and West, it is clear that the communist bloc was greatly affected over time. Much depended on the economic strength of the Soviet Union, and the slowing of growth rates in the 1960s and 1970s was largely a consequence of the Cold War arms race. Despite détente, the Americans and Soviets continued to compete militarily throughout these decades. The Soviets could not keep up.[30]

By itself, détente did not bring about the disintegration of the bloc or the end of communism in the USSR and Eastern Europe. Neither did trade and credit arrangements, containment, the arms race, western opposition to the USSR's policy and values, or Soviet interventionism and overstretch. These and other phenomena all played their part. Détente did not halt confrontation, most of the bargains made in this period were limited, and negotiation was institutionalised as a form of Cold War competition. Yet it is possible to see ways in which this brought closer the end of the Cold War. More contact between East and West certainly released new ideas and impulses. The invasion of Czechoslovakia in 1968 and the enunciation of the 'Brezhnev Doctrine' confirmed that the Warsaw Pact was a means of maintaining Soviet control over Eastern Europe, but détente frustrated Moscow because it brought to the fore the different national interests of Warsaw Pact members.[31]

The Wilson government did not expect the Cold War to end in the near future but did look forward to a time when Britain could reap more of the political and economic benefits of thaw in Europe. In this sense, London had similar ambitions to those of Paris and Bonn, though the approach was more modest and less idealistic. Britain's response to the Czech crisis of 1968 was restrained. There was little that Britain could do alone to influence developments in Czechoslovakia or in the eastern bloc as a whole, and actions had to be coordinated with allies. Necessity and choice coincided on this point. London wished to put pressure on Moscow and to promote peaceful change in the bloc, but even while arguing that the Soviets should pay a price for the invasion of Czechoslovakia the British hoped that trade with Eastern Europe and the flexibility that was creeping into East-West relations would not be curtailed. Joint action with others was also at the centre of Britain's policy in the Middle East. The Arab-Israeli war of 1967, the rise in tension preceding it, and the peacemaking efforts that followed it led the British to push more clearly and energetically for a regional settlement that would involve 'land for peace' and major concessions from both sides. As in Europe, so in the Middle East, progress towards comprehensive agreements and related breakthroughs that would increase mutual trust was very slow. This was less the fault of Britain or a sign of British weakness than a result of adverse international circumstances and the manner in which interstate relations had become strained during the 1950s and 1960s. The emergencies in the Middle East and Czechoslovakia altered the international environment within which Britain had to operate. Though Britain's influence, prestige, role, and status were not greatly impaired, the need to work with allies (especially the Americans) became clearer, as did the need to adapt quickly to developments abroad rather than make assumptions about the stability and rationality of the international order. Traditional British pragmatism served the nation well in the difficult times of the late 1960s and early 1970s.

CONCLUSION

How did Britain's international role at the beginning of the 1970s compare to its role in the late 1950s? Influence and prestige diminished in this period, but they were not entirely lost and for the most part change was gradual and managed rather than quick and catastrophic. The Suez crisis always looms large in accounts of British foreign policy since the Second World War, and it cannot be denied that Suez was a serious reversal. The crisis did not destroy or even permanently damage Anglo-American relations, however, and it did not end British influence and involvement in the Middle East. The importance of Suez as a turning point needs to be judged carefully, therefore, because it was not taken by each and every observer—at the time and afterwards—as decisive proof that Britain was no longer a world power, and Suez was not the last occasion on which Britain was willing and able to take the initiative. This serves as a reminder that Britain's 'decline' should not be exaggerated. After Suez, there was still a perception at home and abroad of Britain as a great power, with the ability to shape events and act independently in the world, which explains why Macmillan could attempt to broker a deal between the West and the

USSR in the late 1950s and early 1960s, especially on Berlin and the German question, and why Wilson could presume to act as peacemaker during the Vietnam War.

Nevertheless, it can reasonably be argued that the withdrawal from East of Suez in the late 1960s marked a definite retreat, signified the final acceptance of a smaller and less ambitious international role, and made claims about Britain's power and range rather empty. Indeed, Britain's limited role in the Six-Day War and in the Czech crisis underlines the fact that, by the late 1960s, Britain's importance, influence, and relevance had been substantially eroded.

Some historians have been less than charitable in their assessments. With regard to the situation East of Suez, for example, Phillip Darby contends that the loss of India after the Second World War should have been followed by a gradual, intentional scaling down of the imperial defence system, in line with political and economic necessities. Darby thinks that this would have been much better for Britain in the long run, with policymakers in London able to control the process and maintain influence, instead of waiting too long and being obliged by events to make rapid and detrimental compromises.[1] Malcolm Chalmers also argues that British withdrawal should have come sooner: he blames poor leadership and flawed decision making. Chalmers sees the years immediately after 1945 as a time of lost opportunity, when success in securing U.S. assistance pushed British governments down the wrong path. Instead of making 'drastic adjustments' in policy, the British used American help and money to continue the global role. Britain could still consider itself, and appeared to be, a world power. But this was a false position, according to Chalmers, and withdrawal from East of Suez could have been completed 'two decades before it was eventually forced upon the government by later economic crises'. Resources could have been used for 'domestic economic development rather than the doomed attempt to maintain a world role for which only the United States had the industrial muscle'. In addition, the effort to remain a world power distorted Britain's view of Europe. The British opposed supranationalism and kept out of integrationist schemes. They did not think that they needed Europe when they had the empire-Commonwealth and the 'special relationship' with the United States. They forfeited the chance to shape European institutions and protect British interests in that sphere, and when they did turn more towards Europe it was too late, for the rules of membership had been set. These rules did not marry well with Britain's interests. All this might have been avoided, Chalmers insists, had Britain's influence been used differently.[2]

It is easy to be wise after the event, and it should be remembered that British policy was not made in a vacuum: it was shaped in part by the actions of others, including the leaders of America and Western Europe. Even if there was a genuine opportunity to participate fully in discussions about European integration, this was a cooperative exercise and the British would not have had everything their own way. Britain alone could not determine the nature and remit of Europe's new institutions. There were good reasons for Britain's reluctance to commit itself beyond the point of no return, and for most of the period under review Britain's extra-European interests *were* more important than its interests in Europe. Nor were many of Western Europe's leaders sympathetic: they did not go out of their way to help Britain reconsider its approach to integration. They were *un*helpful, even though they benefited from some of Britain's other activities, especially those to do with collective security. Despite the cuts introduced in the 1960s, the British were still spending a greater proportion of their national wealth on defence than their European allies were, which in hindsight might look like a mistake, but it should be recognised that both necessity and choice prompted the British to take their military obligations seriously, in Europe and outside Europe. Britain had to meet its NATO commitments and continued to play a leading part in the defence of Western Europe. For Britain to do less in this respect, its European allies would have had to do more. They were not willing. This hampered a fundamental rearrangement of British defence policy. It was one of the factors that prevented Britain from making the savings that would probably have alleviated the country's wider economic problems. If British governments were at fault, the attitude of the Europeans was hardly irreproachable either.

Much was beyond Britain's control. Perhaps different decisions on the part of the Macmillan, Home, and Wilson governments would have had a significant effect. Then again, it is difficult to see what else they could have done, bearing in mind the goals they had in view and the means that were available. If they made mistakes, at least some of these might be excused, especially if Britain's relative decline as a great power is to be understood primarily in terms of structural economic weaknesses and other long-term trends. In weighing up the evidence—social, cultural, imperial, political, economic, and financial—and the interpretations that have been offered to explain decline, Paul Warwick has suggested that the real answers lie in the late nineteenth century.[3] What governments did or did not do in the years between 1957 and 1970 assumes less importance in this analytical framework.

Britain's withdrawal from East of Suez seems inevitable given the available resources, but as Jeffrey Pickering has pointed out, it would be wrong to focus solely on Britain's economic shortcomings. To Pickering, the decision to withdraw was mainly a political one. Economic pressures were constant after the Second World War, while withdrawal represents a shift in perspective, with British leaders admitting to themselves and to others that Britain's long-existing global military network had to be dismantled. Pickering shows that this shift cannot be explained by referring only to a constant. Indeed, Britain's role East of Suez might have ended long before it did if not for noneconomic considerations. After 1945, commitments in the Middle East and Far East continued because it was generally thought that Britain was and should remain a world power. Then, despite the humiliation and difficulty associated with the Suez crisis, Britain chose not to withdraw from East of Suez. The intention was for the British to remain in those areas where they had traditionally been strong. Although economic problems mounted during the Macmillan years, which prompted increased debate about the affordability of the world role, Pickering stresses that 'overstretch' is natural for great powers and that Britain had managed to cope with it for over a century. The Wilson government came into office in 1964 committed to the preservation of Britain's international status, but within a few years the weakness of sterling created the political context for the East of Suez decision.[4]

Though Pickering's insights are useful, attention must also be paid to other influences on British policy, especially Anglo-American relations and the difficulties surrounding the multifarious give and take arrangements between the two allies on sterling as well as on Malaysia, Vietnam, nuclear matters, Europe, and other issues of the day. Another important factor was the anti-imperial tradition of the Labour Party. This shaped the attitude of many Labour MPs and supporters in the 1960s. Looking back in later years, Denis Healey and Michael Stewart both described the East of Suez presence as anachronistic. Wilson also opined that it had been a mistake to try to sustain the global role.[5]

Healey came to think that it would have been impossible to remain East of Suez because of the growth of nationalism there and the economic situation at home. Washington went on arguing that Britain should have stayed, to help maintain stability. Edward Heath and the Conservative Party had a similar view, at least before they took office in 1970 and realised that Labour's policy could not be reversed, but Healey had seen in the 1960s that the peoples of the Middle East and Southeast Asia wanted the British to leave. It would have been politically unwise to remain, even had the funds been available, which they were not. As for the notion that the Wilson government had been too slow to withdraw, that it should have faced facts and made the necessary arrangements soon after taking office in 1964, Healey disagreed. He believed that while British troops were fighting in Aden and Borneo, assisted by forces from the Commonwealth, it would have been irresponsible to leave abruptly, especially without consulting Britain's partners. Moreover, in the mid-1960s there was still an attachment to the global role. Healey subsequently maintained that the Labour government was to be commended for the way in which it managed withdrawal from East of Suez. Twenty years earlier, Britain's departure from India had been accompanied by serious disorder. Millions of people became refugees and tens of thousands lost their lives. The government of 1964–1970 did better than this, and its measures East of Suez were also more impressive than the American performance in Vietnam.

In addition, Healey thought that the withdrawal did not produce instability. The military operation in Borneo ensured lasting stability there, and although the Aden campaign was problematic the lower part of the Persian Gulf remained at least as stable as it had been when British forces were present. Healey admitted that the upper Gulf area became volatile, but he doubted that British forces could have prevented this. The causes went back to British and American policies of the early 1950s, especially the coup against Iranian prime minister Mohammed Mosaddeq in 1953 and the inclusion of Iran in defence arrangements directed against the USSR, and to Eden's collusion with Israel in 1956, which made Arab leaders reluctant to seek British friendship or protection.[6]

Healey's claims are of course self-serving, but they are not unreasonable and they are not unlike the comments made by some historians. For instance, John Young has suggested that in spite of its failings in other areas, the Wilson government made the tough decisions that were needed to ensure that Britain's role in the world would rest on a more realistic relationship between ends and means. The withdrawal from East of Suez and greater reliance on 'non-military sources to maintain influence in the world' as 'a primarily European power' meant that in the 1970s, in contrast to earlier years, Britain had 'international ambitions that did match resources to aims'.[7]

Even after the withdrawal, Britain still had nuclear weapons and bases all over the world, and Anglo-American cooperation remained close on all the key international issues. However, by 1970 the focus was clearly on NATO and Europe, a departure from the intentions the Labour government had formulated on taking office in 1964. Wilson's government had prioritised the world role, not Europe, and its repeated attempts to reduce the cost of the British Army of the Rhine further demonstrates that this government originally had no idea of making Europe its main responsibility. Young and Pickering are broadly in agreement about the combination of economic and political circumstances that brought about the withdrawal from East of Suez. Young stresses the need to balance commitments and resources; the realisation that Britain's defence expenditure was much higher, as a share of national wealth, than that of its main economic competitors; the assumption that this high spending was holding Britain back; the spread of anti-imperialist opinion; diplomatic requirements linked with the EEC bid; and ministerial changes, with more influence in Cabinet for George Brown and particularly Roy Jenkins. It is true that these circumstances made withdrawal from East of Suez more likely. Yet even at this late stage, was it inevitable? The government wished to avoid alienating Britain's allies, British forces were still involved in the confrontation between Malaysia and Indonesia, and Washington was offering aid in order to encourage the British to rule out withdrawal and put off the devaluation of sterling. In fact, U.S. pressure probably ensured that Britain's resources were depleted more quickly as withdrawal from East of Suez was postponed. Until 1966–1967 Wilson's government believed that Britain could remain a world power. On this point, British thinking and American wishes coalesced. Young considers the economic crises of July 1966 and November 1967 as the events that revealed Britain's financial weakness both to the government and to everyone else. Even more decisive might have been an earlier event, the decision of November 1964 to hold defence spending at £2 billion, for this set a target that could not be met without abandoning overseas responsibilities.[8]

Brian Lapping is also complimentary about the Labour government's handling of the withdrawal from East of Suez. Notwithstanding the intention to remain a world power, writes Lapping, it was clear when Wilson became prime minister in 1964 that commitments would have to be cut. The Americans urged Britain to preserve its global reach, and the emergency in Malaysia meant that any plan to leave the Far East had to be shelved, but once this confrontation was over the government had more flexibility. The government's economic worries were also mounting. Even so, withdrawal could not be rushed. Some account had to be taken of the views of the United States, Australia, New Zealand, Malaysia, Singapore, India, and other countries; of morale in the armed forces, the advice of the service chiefs, and the opinion of strategists and defence experts; and of the need to adjust policies in a way that would not endanger Britain's own security. All this was well done: an unsustainable and outdated role was given up in favour of a more attainable role and the government adapted itself to prevalent conditions instead of 'persisting, like the Americans in Vietnam, until the reason for withdrawal was obvious failure'.[9]

From the version of events offered by Healey and the remarks of Young and Lapping, one gets the impression that the government made a virtue of necessity. Its options were limited because of the lack of resources, but it could not admit defeat and endeavoured to present withdrawal from East of Suez as a sensible, deliberate, and chosen course. This is quite understandable, and it was not as if withdrawal was not in Britain's best interests. For decades the British had successfully accommodated new needs, reassessed commitments, reallocated resources, and stopped doing some things in the world in order to keep on doing other things. Therefore, the adjustments made at the end of the 1960s were not unusual, even if they did redirect British energy and attention for the long term. Britain was still able to intervene in the Middle East and the Far East in an emergency. The large and permanent military presence was no more, but this did not mean that Britain's involvement in distant regions ended completely and for all time.

A number of historians link Britain's economic weaknesses with non-membership of the EEC. Although the British economy enjoyed unprecedented growth in the second half of the twentieth century, the rate of growth was lower than that of Britain's competitors. Peter Clarke has suggested that the most serious mistake on the part of British leaders was the failure to join the EEC much sooner. Britain missed out on the benefits of membership.[10] This is to assume that it was in Britain's best interests to sign the Treaty of Rome and accept the kind of integration that the continentals wanted, which, as indicated previously, is by no means clear. 'The Six' had their own agenda. They refused to make the compromises that would have enabled Britain to be a founder-member of the EEC. They were ready to go ahead without Britain. Labour and Conservative politicians in Britain did not think that participation in supranational European ventures was a good idea. Britain was still a world power with a range of interests and responsibilities that could not be subordinated to what was essentially a Franco-German project designed to suit Paris and Bonn. The decision not to join the EEC when it was established was a sound one. It was not irrational. Later, when Britain did apply to join, there was a willingness to compromise in order to facilitate negotiations. French leader Charles de Gaulle used his veto for his own reasons, refusing properly to consider the merits of Britain's applications, which was hardly Britain's fault.

Britain's position on European integration in the 1950s reflected the realities of the time. If there was an error, it was that British attitudes were slow to change. In time, discussion began to focus more on the terms rather than the principle of entry, but integration remained controversial and political leaders were concerned to keep their parties united and to use European policy for electoral advantage. John Young notes some continuity in this respect, for all governments after 1945 preferred to pursue goals abroad that seemed to have the most support at home. Eventually, important British interests were seen to lie in Europe and it was hoped that membership of the EEC would help Britain to maintain its international status. Another element of continuity was the enduring belief that Europe needed Britain more than Britain needed Europe. The Europeans saw things differently. Indeed, Young does not think that Britain would have emerged as the leader of Europe had there been an earlier British commitment to integration. 'The Six' did not want to accept British leadership. Nevertheless, according to Young there *were* missed opportunities, especially in the 1950s. He explains these in relation to the weakness of Britain's 'European vision'. More enthusiasm about integration would have made a big difference. Instead, the British emphasised their distinctiveness, their island heritage, and their long record of unbroken political development. Even for 'The Six', though, the 'European vision' was a self-serving device. They all put their own national interests first when they could.[11] Britain's history did have a bearing on European policy. As Zara Steiner concludes, the British view of the continent has always been ambivalent. Knowing that they had to be involved in some way, but not always able to decide how to proceed, the British were bound to be 'reluctant Europeans'.[12] During the nineteenth century and into the twentieth, a principal goal was to promote stability on the continent. By the time of the Second World War, this had seriously drained Britain's resources. Economic problems increased and the empire began to break up. After 1945, concerns grew about how to preserve Britain's integrity and independence, which made integration seem hazardous. But did decolonisation make Europe the only option? Was it worth getting closer to Europe, despite the costs? On these questions there was bitter disagreement, and the debate went on long after the withdrawal from East of Suez and Britain's entry into the EEC.

The course of the Cold War also affected British policy. For Britain, peace in Europe was eminently desirable after 1945 and security mattered more than integration. Yet security and integration were soon merged. Taking a longer view of European history, George-Henri Soutou has identified a survival of goals associated with the nineteenth-century concern for the balance of power, to which were added the democratic elements of the twentieth century. After 1945, he thinks, there was a belief that there could still be a new European order despite two world wars and ongoing discord between nations. To achieve this there had to be the necessary minimum of European solidarity, and between the 1950s and 1970s solidarity depended largely on security. Gradually, through arms control, summitry, and attempts at thaw, the West moved to reduce tension by showing the Soviet regime that it was not in danger. The West and the USSR continued to seek gains at each other's expense—the West wanted to undermine communism in Eastern Europe, for instance, while the Soviets wanted to obtain a general acceptance of postwar borders and to limit U.S. influence in Europe—but even though the motives of the two sides were selfish, stability developed, and, according to Soutou, a new European order emerged.[13]

The British helped to bring this about. The aversion to supranational integration did not diminish, and Britain did not welcome the Treaty of Rome and formation of the EEC, but none of the continental states played a more important role than Britain in the evolution of Western Europe's security arrangements after 1945. Eventually, Britain also accepted the necessity and usefulness of economic integration and joined the EEC. European policy remained contentious partly because the benefits of all this to Britain were not self-evident, except perhaps to avid Europhiles.

Membership of international organisations entailed negotiation and compromise, and British leaders often found this difficult and regretted having to abide by decisions with which they disagreed. This was true of NATO, of European bodies, and especially of the Commonwealth and the United Nations. One of the remarkable features of international history between the late 1950s and early 1970s was the decreasing importance of the UN, which was marginalised as the two superpowers and their main allies used other means to sort out problems and disputes. The Security Council met only five times in 1959 compared to 132 meetings per year, on average, between 1946 and 1948.[14] The main reason for the UN's loss of authority was probably the attitude of the United States. Decolonisation and associated changes in the international order led to arrangements at the UN in the mid-1950s whereby the organisation quickly grew in size. New independent states were admitted to the UN almost automatically, which transformed it into a forum for the developing world. Western dominance of the UN was lessened and the Americans, in particular, became disillusioned. They failed to pay all of their dues to the UN and eventually became the most frequent user of the veto in the Security Council, having not used it at all before 1970. What the UN could and could not do increasing depended on U.S. policy, and Washington's approach was unsupportive and unilateral. London also began seriously to doubt the wisdom of referring matters to the UN, in part a legacy of the Suez crisis, and complained that the UN was biased against the interests of the West.

The 'special relationship' with the United States remained by far the most important of Britain's external connections and the question of how to protect and strengthen it was a constant consideration for British policymakers. Anglo-American cooperation persisted through the 1950s and 1960s because of the Cold War and because, for Britain, it offered the best and most convenient way to go on acting and being treated as a world power. It was essential. It helped the British to slow down and hide their relative decline. The 'special relationship' was also useful to America, although the British and Americans saw it differently. In London, there was a hankering to make it more formal and binding and for it to be equally the priority of U.S. as well as British leaders. The Americans preferred to keep it largely informal and from the mid-1960s regarded it as one of several important relationships for the United States, not as the fixed and absolute priority. There were many arguments between London and Washington, which has led some observers to claim that the relationship was not 'special' at all. Conversely, there are those who argue that the common bonds were stronger than the disagreements and that the relationship was never less than unique.[15] Among elites and at the popular level, the Americans cared less about the 'special relationship' than the British did. It could be argued that the concept of 'special relationship' only makes sense as part of the rhetoric and mindset of policy-making groups that used it to rationalise and promote their own decisions. Clearly, the divisions between Britain and America should not be minimised, just as the role and importance of the 'special relationship' should not be exaggerated. Cooperation was conditional. It rested on shared goals and on separate interests that could be served by the same course of action. When there was no mutual gain, it was maintained because schism would have been detrimental. For Britain, the weaker of the two partners, attention always had to be paid to the danger that a hostile America might frustrate British aspirations.

Dependence upon the United States did not prevent Britain's decline relative to the world's other great powers, but it did slow the process. At the same time, this dependence also contributed to Britain's decline. Asserting the 'special relationship' could have been a self-inflicted wound: this is the view of those contemporary and subsequent commentators who think that Britain should have decided much sooner to join Europe. One does not have to be a pro-European to agree that by relying so much on the partnership with America, the British isolated themselves from other partnerships that were necessary in the changing world of the 1950s and 1960s. Yet it cannot be denied that the 'special relationship' did bring significant benefits to Britain. American political support was vital, as were American loans and investment. The British also invested heavily in America (more foreign investment in the United States came from Britain than anywhere else, which underlines the importance of the financial links between the two). The sharing of nuclear technology and information was indispensable to Britain and the Polaris deal confirmed Britain's need for American advanced weaponry. Was this a handicap? The Polaris deal was highly advantageous to Britain, and not just finan-cially. It ensured that the British would have a credible deterrent while guaranteeing them considerable influence in their dealings with the Americans and the other members of NATO.[16]

It was largely owing to American pressure that London kept putting off a major reorganisation of commitments East of Suez. Washington wanted the British to remain East of Suez and was pleased in 1964 when the new Wilson government indicated that there would be no substantial with-drawal of British forces from the Middle East or Far East. This was one of the issues discussed on December 11, 1964, when Wilson and Healey reported to the Cabinet on the recent meetings they had had with President Johnson and his advisers. The prime minister said that there would con-tinue to be thorough consultation with the Americans. 'They want us with them', he explained. When Richard Crossman asked about the American view of Britain's world role, 'Healey replied that what they wanted us to do was not to maintain huge bases but to keep a foothold in Hong Kong, Malaya and the Persian Gulf, to enable us to do things for the alliance which they cannot do. They think our forces are much more useful to the alliance outside Europe than in Germany'. Five days later, Wilson told Parliament that Britain would remain East of Suez. Whatever cutbacks had to be made, Britain would not be giving up its most important over-seas responsibilities.[17] Within five years, many of these responsibilities were abandoned. There was now a timetable for the substantial downsiz-ing of Britain's world role, yet the 'special relationship' did not collapse. For all its reservations and drawbacks, Anglo-American cooperation was still close. It was 'special' because neither Britain nor the United States had anything like the same relationship with any other power.

Withdrawal from East of Suez and the growing concentration of politi-cal, economic, and military activity in Western Europe were the biggest changes in Britain's international role and position between 1957 and the early 1970s. Britain remained a great power, not least as one of the permanent members of the UN Security Council, as one of only a handful of states possessing a formidable nuclear capability, and as a leading member of NATO and other alliances around the world. There were still hopes that the Commonwealth could be made into more of an asset. There was a desire for further engagement with Europe, and Britain joined the EEC in 1973. There was still a 'special relationship' with America, and a residual presence in the Middle East and Far East with the capacity to act in both regions when necessary. British interests still mattered. Britain's favour was still sought and much of the world continued to value Britain's diplomatic and economic assistance and to respect British culture, history, manufactures, and institutions. Some countries still benefited from Britain's political and military protection. In all these ways Britain remained great even while its relative decline became more noticeable.

NOTES

INTRODUCTION

1. Cited in M. Dockrill, *British Defence Since 1945* (Oxford: Basil Blackwell, 1988), 150.
2. *Hansard*, 5th series, 751 (1967), cols 1107–1108.
3. D. Healey, *The Time of My Life* (London: Michael Joseph, 1989), 271, 277.

CHAPTER 1

1. A. Sked and C. Cook, *Post-War Britain: A Political History* (London: Penguin, 1993), 138–139; T. G. Fraser and D. Murray, *America and the World Since 1945* (Basingstoke: Palgrave Macmillan, 2002), 74; A. P. Dobson, *Anglo-American Relations in the Twentieth Century* (London: Routledge, 1995), 117–120; C. J. Bartlett, *The Special Relationship: A Political History of Anglo-American Relations Since 1945* (London: Longman, 1992), 88–90; D. Sanders, *Losing an Empire, Finding a Role: British Foreign Policy Since 1945* (Basingstoke: Macmillan, 1990), 171–173; H. Macmillan, *Riding the Storm, 1956–59* (London: Macmillan, 1971), 240, 242; A. Horne, *Macmillan, 1957–86* (London: Macmillan, 1989), 45–51.
2. D. Reynolds, *Britannia Overruled: British Policy and World Power in the Twentieth Century* (Harlow: Longman, 2000), 199–200; Sked and Cook, *Post-War Britain*, 140; J. W. Young, *Britain and the World in the Twentieth Century* (London: Arnold, 1997), 181; F. S. Northedge, *Descent from Power: British Foreign Policy, 1945–73* (London: Allen and Unwin, 1974), 290; Dobson, *Anglo-American Relations*, 119; Bartlett, *The Special Relationship*, 89–91; Fraser and Murray, *America and the World*, 75, 79–81; Dockrill, *British Defence Since 1945*, 78–79; D. Eisenhower, *Waging Peace, 1956–61* (Garden City, NY: Doubleday, 1965), 178–183; S. Ambrose, *Eisenhower: The President* (London: Allen and Unwin, 1984), 381–388; T. G. Fraser, *The USA and the Middle East Since World War Two* (Basingstoke: Macmillan, 1989), 73–76; N. Ashton, 'Macmillan and the Middle East', in *Harold Macmillan and Britain's World Role*, ed. R. Aldous and S. Lee (Basingstoke: Macmillan, 1996), 51–53.

3. G. Balfour-Paul, *The End of Empire in the Middle East: Britain's Relinquishment of Power in her Last Three Arab Dependencies* (Cambridge: Cambridge University Press, 1991), 118, 144–145; Ashton, 'Macmillan and the Middle East', 61; P. Darby, *British Defence Policy East of Suez, 1947–68* (London: Oxford University Press, 1973), 145–156.
4. *Hansard*, 5th series, 591 (1958): 1438–1439, 1506–1560. Britain's relationship with Jordan remained close and was no mere throwback to the imperial past, for the initiative often came from the Jordanian side. N. Ashton, '"A Special Relationship Sometimes in Spite of Ourselves": Britain and Jordan, 1957–73', *Journal of Imperial and Commonwealth History* 33 (2005): 221–244.
5. *The Times*, July 17, 18, 1958; *Economist*, July 26, 1958.
6. Horne, *Macmillan*, 94–98; Macmillan, *Riding the Storm*, 243, 516–526; J. Turner, *Macmillan* (London: Longman, 1994), 205–207; J. Baylis, *Anglo-American Defence Relations, 1939–80: The Special Relationship* (London: Macmillan, 1981), 63–64; R. Ovendale, *British Defence Policy Since 1945* (Manchester: Manchester University Press, 1994), 119–121; D. C. Watt, *Succeeding John Bull: America in Britain's Place, 1900–75* (Cambridge: Cambridge University Press, 1984), 134–135. Watt considers U.S. intervention in the region under the Eisenhower Doctrine 'an unmitigated disaster'. On Lebanon and Jordan, see also Ambrose, *Eisenhower: The President*, 462–467, 469–475. Ambrose admits that the American action in Lebanon was unhelpful.
7. Sked and Cook, *Post-War Britain*, 137, 139–140; Baylis, *Anglo-American Defence Relations*, 57–63; Dobson, *Anglo-American Relations*, 118–119; Bartlett, *The Special Relationship*, 88–90; Ovendale, *British Defence Policy*, 10–11, 113–116; Eisenhower, *Waging Peace*, 121–125.
8. C. Coker, 'Foreign and Defence Policy', in *Britain Since 1945*, ed. J. Hollowell (Oxford: Blackwell, 2003), 13; C. Gordon, 'Duncan Sandys and the Independent Nuclear Deterrent', in *Politicians and Defence: Studies in the Formulation of British Defence Policy, 1845–1970*, ed. I. Beckett and J. Gooch (Manchester: Manchester University Press, 1981), 132–153; Dockrill, *British Defence Since 1945*, 51, 65–71; Young, *Britain and the World*, 171; Reynolds, *Britannia Overruled*, 198–199, and idem, 'Britain and the World Since 1945: Narratives of Decline or Transformation?' in *The British Isles Since 1945*, ed. K. Burk (Oxford: Oxford University Press, 2003), 168; Northedge, *Descent from Power*, 289–291; Ovendale, *British Defence Policy*, 8, 10, 13, 16, 113–115; Sked and Cook, *Post-War Britain*, 141–142; C. J. Bartlett, *The Long Retreat: A Short History of British Defence Policy, 1945–70* (London: Macmillan, 1972), 132–144; Turner, *Macmillan*, 128–129,

133, 137–139, 154; Horne, *Macmillan*, 45–51; A. J. Pierre, *Nuclear Politics: The British Experience with an Independent Strategic Force, 1939–70* (London: Oxford University Press, 1972), 161–162, 194–195.

9. *The Times*, April 17, 1957; *Observer*, April 21, 1957.

10. *Hansard*, 5th series, 568 (1957): 1758–1759, 1786, 1795. For the whole debate see 1758–1878, 1929–2059.

11. M. S. Navias, 'Terminating Conscription? The British National Service Controversy, 1955–56', *Journal of Contemporary History* 24 (1989): 195–208; W. Rees, 'The 1957 Sandys White Paper: New Priorities in British Defence Policy?' *Journal of Strategic Studies* 12 (1989): 215–229; J. Pickering, *Britain's Withdrawal from East of Suez: The Politics of Retrenchment* (Basingstoke: Macmillan, 1998), 103; M. Chalmers, *Paying for Defence: Military Spending and British Decline* (London: Pluto Press, 1985), 66–72.

12. Dobson, *Anglo-American Relations*, 119–120; Bartlett, *Long Retreat*, 137, and idem, *The Special Relationship*, 92–94; Sked and Cook, *Post-War Britain*, 142; Reynolds, *Britannia Overruled*, 198; Navias, 'Terminating Conscription?' 202–205; Northedge, *Descent from Power*, 291; Dockrill, *British Defence Since 1945*, 68, 71–72; E. R. May and G. F. Treverton, 'Defence Relationships: American Perspectives', in *The 'Special Relationship': Anglo-American Relations Since 1945*, ed. W. R. Louis and H. Bull (Oxford: Clarendon Press, 1989), 168; E. J. Grove, *Vanguard to Trident: British Naval Policy Since World War Two* (London: Bodley Head, 1987), 200, 203, 213–215.

13. Baylis, *Anglo-American Defence Relations*, 60–61; A. L. Friedberg, 'The United States and the Cold War Arms Race', in *Reviewing the Cold War: Approaches, Interpretations, Theory*, ed. O. A. Westad (London: Frank Cass, 2000), 209–210; R. Dietl, 'Une deception amoureuse? Great Britain, the Continent and European Nuclear Cooperation, 1953–57', *Cold War History* 3 (2002): 29–66; D. Murray, *Kennedy, Macmillan and Nuclear Weapons* (Basingstoke: Macmillan, 2000), 18–19.

14. T. J. Botti, *The Long Wait: The Forging of the Anglo-American Nuclear Alliance, 1945–58* (Westport, CT: Greenwood Press, 1987), 175, 182–183, 185–187, 196, 199–200, 210, 226–227, 229, 234, 238–239.

15. J. Simpson, *The Independent Nuclear State: The United States, Britain and the Military Atom* (London: Macmillan, 1983), 124–125.

16. Bartlett, *Long Retreat*, 147–148; Pierre, *Nuclear Politics*, 142–144; Simpson, *Independent Nuclear State*, 226–227, 238–239; Botti, *The Long Wait*, 240–241; Ovendale, *British Defence Policy*, 117–119.

17. B. Heuser, 'The Development of NATO's Nuclear Strategy', *Contemporary European History* 4 (1994): 44–45.
18. K. Pyne, 'Art or Article? The Need for and Nature of the British Hydrogen Bomb, 1954–58', *Contemporary Record* 9 (1995): 562–585; Sked and Cook, *Post-War Britain*, 143; Ovendale, *British Defence Policy*, 113–116; Young, *Britain and the World*, 171; Reynolds, *Britannia Overruled*, 200; Horne, *Macmillan*, 275–277, 428–443; H. Macmillan, *Pointing the Way, 1959–61* (London: Macmillan, 1972), 249–256; P. Kennedy, *The Realities Behind Diplomacy: Background Influences on British External Policy, 1865–1980* (London: Allen and Unwin, 1981), 374–375; J. Dumbrell, *A Special Relationship: Anglo-American Relations in the Cold War and After* (Basingstoke: Macmillan, 2001), 48; Dobson, *Anglo-American Relations*, 120; Bartlett, *The Special Relationship*, 93, 98, and idem, *Long Retreat*, 154–156; Murray, *Kennedy, Macmillan and Nuclear Weapons*, chapter 2.
19. Watt, *Succeeding John Bull*, 135–136; A. P. Dobson, 'Informally Special? The Churchill-Truman Talks of January 1952 and the State of Anglo-American Relations', *Review of International Studies* 23 (1997): 27–47. In his *Anglo-American Relations*, Dobson insists that the 'special relationship' was a reality, but, accepting that there is evidence to suggest the contrary, he also points out that the United States developed many 'special' relationships.
20. S. J. Ball, 'Military Nuclear Relations Between the United States and Great Britain Under the Terms of the McMahon Act, 1946–58', *Historical Journal* 38 (1995): 439–454; Pierre, *Nuclear Politics*, 196–199, 321.
21. Navias, 'Terminating Conscription?' 195–208; Rees, 'Sandys White Paper', 225–226; Pickering, *Britain's Withdrawal from East of Suez*, 103–106.
22. Pickering, *Britain's Withdrawal from East of Suez*, 106–107; *Hansard*, 5th series, 625 (1960): 394–406; *Guardian*, September 21, 1960; *The Times*, September 26, 1960.
23. S. J. Ball, 'Macmillan and British Defence Policy', in Aldous and Lee, *Macmillan and Britain's World Role*, 74–75, 91–92.
24. Coker, 'Foreign and Defence Policy', 6; Dockrill, *British Defence Since 1945*, 71–77; Young, *Britain and the World*, 171; Reynolds, *Britannia Overruled*, 198–199, 202–203; M. Gowing, 'Nuclear Weapons and the Special Relationship', in Louis and Bull, *Special Relationship*, 123–124; Pierre, *Nuclear Politics*, 217–243, 320; Baylis, *Anglo-American Defence Relations*, 77; Simpson, *Independent Nuclear State*, 137–138; M. M. Harrison, *The Reluctant Ally: France and Atlantic Security* (London: Johns Hopkins University Press, 1981), 96–97.

25. J. Darwin, *The End of the British Empire: The Historical Debate* (Oxford: Basil Blackwell, 1991), 7, 114–122; B. Lapping, *End of Empire* (London: Granada, 1985), 317–349, 405–444; M. Kahler, *Decolonization in Britain and France: The Domestic Consequences of International Relations* (Princeton, NJ: Princeton University Press, 1984), 142–160; R. Holland, *The Pursuit of Greatness: Britain and the World Role, 1900–70* (London: Routledge, 1991), 295–302; M. Kitchen, *The British Empire and Commonwealth* (Basingstoke: Macmillan, 1996), 103–104, 111, 123–124, 128, 147; Young, *Britain and the World*, 180–183; E. R. Kantowicz, *Coming Apart, Coming Together* (Grand Rapids, MI: Eerdmans Publishing, 2000), 255–257; Sked and Cook, *Post-War Britain*, 143–147; Reynolds, *Britannia Overruled*, 209–210; J. Hollowell, 'From Commonwealth to European Integration', in Hollowell, ed., *Britain Since 1945*, 68–69; J. D. Hargreaves, *Decolonization in Africa* (London: Longman, 1996), 170–181, 200–207; P. E. Hemming, 'Macmillan and the End of the British Empire in Africa', in Aldous and Lee, *Macmillan and Britain's World Role*, 118.
26. C. K. Mark, 'Defence or Decolonization? Britain, the United States and the Hong Kong Question in 1957', *Journal of Imperial and Commonwealth History* 33 (2005): 51–72.
27. D. Goldsworthy, 'Keeping Change Within Bounds: Aspects of Colonial Policy During the Churchill and Eden Governments, 1951–57', *Journal of Imperial and Commonwealth History* 18 (1990): 81–108; D. J. Morgan, *The Official History of Colonial Development* (London: Macmillan, 1980), 5: 100–102, and see chapter 5 for the period from 1957 to 1961 as a whole.
28. H. S. Wilson, *African Decolonization* (London: Arnold, 1994), 171–172; D. K. Fieldhouse, *Black Africa, 1945–80: Economic Decolonization and Arrested Development* (London: Allen and Unwin, 1986), 7–9; R. F. Holland, *European Decolonization, 1918–81* (Basingstoke: Macmillan, 1985), chapters 7–9; P. Kennedy, *Strategy and Diplomacy: Eight Studies* (London: Fontana, 1989), 217–218.
29. W. D. McIntyre, *The Commonwealth of Nations: Origins and Impact, 1869–1971* (Minneapolis: University of Minnesota Press, 1977), 389, 450; R. Ovendale, 'Macmillan and the Wind of Change in Africa, 1957–60', *Historical Journal* 38 (1995): 455–477; Holland, *Pursuit of Greatness*, 301.
30. J. Kent, 'United States Reactions to Empire, Colonialism and Cold War in Black Africa, 1949–57', *Journal of Imperial and Commonwealth History*

33 (2005): 195–220; Macmillan, *Pointing the Way*, 155–160, 163–164; Hargreaves, *Decolonization in Africa*, 204.

31. A. Mohiddin, *African Socialism in Two Countries* (London: Croom Helm, 1981), 54, 56, 73, 83; A. Low, 'The End of the British Empire in Africa', in *Decolonization and African Independence: The Transfers of Power, 1960–80*, ed. P. Gifford and W. R. Louis (London: Yale University Press, 1988), 70–72; D. Austin, 'The British Point of No Return?' in *The Transfer of Power in Africa: Decolonization, 1940–60*, ed. P. Gifford and W. R. Louis (London: Yale University Press, 1982), 231, 238, 246–247.

32. J. Darwin, *Britain and Decolonization: The Retreat from Empire in the Post-War World* (Basingstoke: Macmillan, 1988), chapter 6, and idem, *End of the British Empire*, 75, 118; S. Strange, *Sterling and British Policy: A Political Study of an International Currency in Decline* (London: Oxford University Press, 1971); A. Hinds, *Britain's Sterling Colonial Policy and Decolonization, 1939–58* (Westport, CT: Greenwood Press, 2001); G. Krozewski, *Money and the End of Empire: British International Economic Policy and the Colonies, 1947–58* (Basingstoke: Palgrave, 2001).

33. Hollowell, 'Commonwealth to European Integration', 59–60; Sked and Cook, *Post-War Britain*, 147–150; G. de Carmoy, 'Defence and Unity of Western Europe Since 1958', in *Troubled Neighbours: Franco-British Relations in the Twentieth Century*, ed. N. Waites (London: Weidenfeld, 1971), 346–348; S. Greenwood, *Britain and European Cooperation Since 1945* (Oxford: Blackwell, 1992), 62–78; D. Gowland and A. Turner, eds., *Britain and European Integration, 1945–98: A Documentary History* (London: Routledge, 2000), 49, 51–60, 88–90; P. Messmer, 'De Gaulle's Defence Policy and the United States', in *De Gaulle and the United States: A Centennial Reappraisal*, ed. R. O. Paxton and N. Wahl (Oxford: Berg, 1994), 351–357; W. C. Cromwell, *The United States and the European Pillar: The Strained Alliance* (Basingstoke: Palgrave Macmillan, 1992), 26–37; M. Camps, *Britain and the European Community, 1955–63* (London: Oxford University Press, 1965), chapters 4–5; H. Simonian, *The Privileged Partnership: Franco-German Relations in the European Community, 1969–84* (Oxford: Clarendon Press, 1985), 34; J. Lacouture, *De Gaulle: The Ruler, 1945–70*, translated by A. Sheridan (London: Harvill, 1991), 333–334.

34. F. Lynch, 'De Gaulle's First Veto: France, the Rueff Plan and the Free Trade Area', *Contemporary European History* 9 (2000): 111–135; Simonian, *Privileged Partnership*, 24, 33–34; M. P .C. Schaad, *Bullying Bonn: Anglo-German Diplomacy on European Integration, 1955–61* (New York: St. Martin's Press, 2000).

35. J. W. Young, *Britain and European Unity, 1945–92* (Basingstoke: Macmillan, 1993), 44–56, and idem, 'The Parting of the Ways? Britain, the Messina Conference and the Spaak Committee, June–December 1955', in *British Foreign Policy, 1945–56*, ed. M. Dockrill and J. W. Young (Basingstoke: Macmillan, 1989), 197–224; W. Kaiser, *Using Europe, Abusing the Europeans: Britain and European Integration, 1945–63* (Basingstoke: Macmillan, 1996), chapter 3; R. Lamb, *The Failure of the Eden Government* (London: Sidgwick and Jackson, 1987), 96–101.

36. Gowland and Turner, *Britain and European Integration*, 88–89.

37. S. Greenwood, 'Not the "General Will" but the "Will of the General": The Input of the Paris Embassy to the British "Great Debate" on Europe, Summer 1960', *Contemporary British History* 18 (2004): 177–188; A. McKinlay, H. Mercer, and N. Rollings, 'Reluctant Europeans? The Federation of British Industries and European Integration, 1945–63', *Business History* 42 (2000): 91–116.

38. Young, *Britain and the World*, 188, and idem, *Britain and European Unity*, 57–71; B. Eichengreen, 'Economy', in *Europe Since 1945*, ed. M. Fulbrook (Oxford: Oxford University Press, 2001), 119, 121; Sked and Cook, *Post-War Britain*, 150–151; P. M. R. Stirk, *A History of European Integration Since 1914* (London: Pinter, 1996), 146–149; Camps, *Britain and the European Community*, chapters 6–7; Kaiser, *Using Europe*, chapter 4; Greenwood, *Britain and European Cooperation Since 1945*, 71–73; Gowland and Turner, *Britain and European Integration*, 51–53, 89–90; D. W. Urwin, *A Political History of Western Europe Since 1945* (London: Longman, 1998), chapter 9.

39. M. Charlton, *The Price of Victory* (London: British Broadcasting Corporation, 1983), 215–217; Camps, *Britain and the European Community*, 506, 510–512.

40. *Hansard*, 5th series, 624 (1960): 677–679; Macmillan, *Pointing the Way*, 57–59.

41. S. George, *Britain and European Integration Since 1945* (Oxford: Blackwell, 1991), 42–43; Kaiser, *Using Europe*, 105–106; Gowland and Turner, *Britain and European Integration*, 49, 51–53.

42. J. G. Giauque, 'The United States and the Political Union of Western Europe, 1958–63', *Contemporary European History* 9 (2000): 93–110; G. Lundestad, *'Empire' by Integration: The United States and European Integration, 1945–97* (Oxford: Oxford University Press, 1998), 51–52; Gowland and Turner, *Britain and European Integration*, 49, 51–60, 88–90.

43. N. Crafts, 'Forging Ahead and Falling Behind: The Rise and Relative Decline of the First Industrial Nation', *Journal of Economic Perspectives* 12 (1998): 193–210; C. Bean and N. Crafts, 'British Economic Growth Since 1945: Relative Economic Decline...and Renaissance?' in *Economic Growth in Europe Since 1945*, ed. N. Crafts and G. Toniolo (Cambridge: Cambridge University Press, 1996), 142–143.
44. Crafts and Toniolo, *Economic Growth in Europe*; G. Toniolo, 'Europe's Golden Age, 1950–73: Speculations from a Long-Run Perspective', *Economic History Review* 51 (1998): 252–267; U. Kitzinger, *The European Common Market and Community* (London: Routledge and Kegan Paul, 1967), 24–25.
45. *The Times*, September 27, 1960.

CHAPTER 2

1. K. Larres, 'International and Security Relations Within Europe', in Fulbrook, *Europe Since 1945*, 211–212; Sked and Cook, *Post-War Britain*, 151; Young, *Britain and the World*, 175; J. G. Richter, *Khrushchev's Double Bind: International Pressures and Domestic Coalition Politics* (Baltimore: Johns Hopkins University Press, 1994), 118.
2. *The Times*, February 6, 20, 27, 1959; *Observer*, March 8, 1959.
3. J. M. Schick, *The Berlin Crisis, 1958–62* (Philadelphia: University of Pennsylvania Press, 1971), 60; J. P. S. Gearson, *Harold Macmillan and the Berlin Wall Crisis, 1958–62: The Limits of Interest and Force* (Basingstoke: Macmillan, 1998), 75–78.
4. R.W. Stevenson, *The Rise and Fall of Détente: Relaxations of Tension in U.S.-Soviet Relations, 1953–84* (Basingstoke: Macmillan, 1985), 81–82.
5. *Hansard*, 5th series, 596 (1958): 1022–1023; 601 (1959): 448–453; 610 (1959): 11–12.
6. P. Johnson, *A History of the Modern World* (London: Weidenfeld and Nicolson, 1984), 586–587, 599; T. Prittie, *Konrad Adenauer* (London: Tom Stacey, 1972), 173, 236, 262–270; R. J. Granieri, *The Ambivalent Alliance: Konrad Adenauer, the CDU/CSU and the West, 1949–66* (Oxford: Berghahn, 2003), 111–127; P. Alter, *The German Question and Europe: A History* (London: Hodder and Stoughton, 2000), 121–123, 127–128; R. Irving, *Adenauer* (London: Longman, 2002), 130–139; M. Roseman, 'Division and Stability: The FRG, 1949–89', in *German History Since 1800*, ed. M. Fulbrook (London: Arnold, 1997), 371–376; Lacouture, *De Gaulle*, 333–339; E. A. Kolodziej, *French International Policy Under De Gaulle*

and Pompidou: The Politics of Grandeur (Ithaca, NY: Cornell University Press, 1974), 264–265, 268; Simonian, *Privileged Partnership*, chapter 2; Harrison, *Reluctant Ally*, 105–106; G. Ambrosius and W. H. Hubbard, *A Social and Economic History of Twentieth-Century Europe* (Cambridge, MA: Harvard University Press, 1989), 298–301; W. F. Hanrieder, *Germany, America, Europe: Forty Years of German Foreign Policy* (New Haven, CT: Yale University Press, 1989), 13–14.

7. A. Sampson, *Macmillan: A Study in Ambiguity* (London: Allen Lane, 1967), 146; Hanrieder, *Germany, America, Europe*, 163–169; Lacouture, *De Gaulle*, 336, 338; R. Challener, 'Dulles and De Gaulle', in Paxton and Wahl, *De Gaulle and the United States*, 161–165; Kolodziej, *French International Policy*, 264–268.

8. H. Adomeit, *Imperial Overstretch: Germany in Soviet Policy from Stalin to Gorbachev* (Baden-Baden: Nomos Verlagsgesellschaft, 1998), 51–57, 159. In his *Détente in Europe: The Soviet Union and the West Since 1953* (Durham, NC: Duke University Press, 1991), John van Oudenaren probably overestimates the Kremlin's commitment to détente. His interpretation can be questioned because he focuses on the Soviet Union's relations with Western Europe, paying insufficient attention to Soviet-U.S. relations. He also neglects the East European aspects of détente, which involved the USSR's security and directly influenced Soviet diplomacy.

9. V. Zubok and C. Pleshakov, *Inside the Kremlin's Cold War: From Stalin to Khrushchev* (Cambridge, MA: Harvard University Press, 1996), 194–195, 198; Adomeit, *Imperial Overstretch*, 100–103; Richter, *Khrushchev's Double Bind*, 101–103, 106–118; S. Talbott, ed., *Khrushchev Remembers*, with notes by E. Crankshaw (London: Deutsch, 1971), 452–454.

10. Zubok and Pleshakov, *Inside the Kremlin's Cold War*, 195–200.

11. J. G. Hershberg, 'The Crisis Years, 1958–63', in Westad, *Reviewing the Cold War*, 305–307; A. B. Ulam, *Expansion and Coexistence: Soviet Foreign Policy, 1917–73* (New York: Praeger, 1974), 618–621.

12. Ulam, *Expansion and Coexistence*, 622; J. L. Gaddis, *The Long Peace: Inquiries into the History of the Cold War* (New York: Oxford University Press, 1987), 230–231; W. Taubman, *Khrushchev: The Man and His Era* (New York: Norton, 2003), 396–419.

13. Richter, *Khrushchev's Double Bind*, chapter 5; Kantowicz, *Coming Apart, Coming Together*, 285–289; Larres, 'International and Security Relations Within Europe', 211; W. LaFeber, *America, Russia and the Cold War, 1945–2002* (Boston: McGraw-Hill, 2002), 212–214; Urwin, *Political History of Western Europe*, 96–98; Hershberg, 'The Crisis Years', 308–311.

14. Kantowicz, *Coming Apart, Coming Together*, 289; Larres, 'International and Security Relations Within Europe', 212; Turner, *Macmillan*, 142–146; Horne, *Macmillan*, 128; Macmillan, *Riding the Storm*, 656; W. J. Tompson, *Khrushchev: A Political Life* (Basingstoke: Macmillan, 1995), 195–196, 203–204.

15. Gearson, *Macmillan and the Berlin Wall Crisis*, 79–87; Turner, *Macmillan*, 146–147; Kolodziej, *French International Policy*, 267–268.

16. S. Ambrose, *Eisenhower: Soldier and President* (New York: Simon and Schuster, 1990), 482–483; O. Troyanovsky, 'The Making of Soviet Foreign Policy', in *Nikita Khrushchev*, ed. W. Taubman, S. Khrushchev, and A. Gleason (New Haven, CT: Yale University Press, 2000), 217–218, 220–221; Tompson, *Khrushchev*, 195–196, 203–204; Kantowicz, *Coming Apart, Coming Together*, 289–290; Young, *Britain and the World*, 175; Fraser and Murray, *America and the World*, 84–86.

17. Richter, *Khrushchev's Double Bind*, 119–122; Taubman, *Khrushchev: The Man and His Era*, 435–439, 443–449, 456–464; Tompson, *Khrushchev*, 210–212, 219–229.

18. Fraser and Murray, *America and the World*, 77–80, 84–86; Bartlett, *The Special Relationship*, 94; K. Burk, 'Introduction', in Burk, *British Isles Since 1945*, 2–3; Ambrose, *Eisenhower: Soldier and President*, 492–494, 507–514; Stevenson, *Rise and Fall of Détente*, 84–94.

19. Eisenhower, *Waging Peace*, 558–559; Ambrose, *Eisenhower: Soldier and President*, 515.

20. Gearson, *Macmillan and the Berlin Wall Crisis*, 118–127, 131–137, 142–156.

21. *The Times*, May 18, 1960.

22. *Hansard*, 5th series, 624 (1960): 999–1010.

23. Gearson, *Macmillan and the Berlin Wall Crisis*, 156–159.

24. Ibid., 2, 4, 32, 97.

25. Fraser and Murray, *America and the World*, 94–96; Johnson, *Modern World*, 614–615; Kantowicz, *Coming Apart, Coming Together*, 290–291; R. Reeves, *President Kennedy: Profile of Power* (London: Papermac, 1993), 36–42, chapters 13–14; Talbott, *Khrushchev Remembers*, 458–459; Troyanovsky, 'Soviet Foreign Policy', 229–231; Bartlett, *The Special Relationship*, 95–96; L. Freedman, *Kennedy's Wars: Berlin, Cuba, Laos and Vietnam* (Oxford: Oxford University Press, 2002), 51–65; J. C. Ausland, *Kennedy, Khrushchev and the Berlin-Cuba Crisis, 1961–64* (Oslo: Aschehoug AS, 1996), 1–12; Tompson, *Khrushchev*, 232–235; F. Costigliola, 'The Pursuit of Atlantic Community: Nuclear Arms, Dollars and Berlin', in

Kennedy's Quest for Victory: American Foreign Policy, 1961–63, ed. T. G. Paterson (New York: Oxford University Press, 1989), 38.

26. R. J. Walton, *Cold War and Counterrevolution: The Foreign Policy of John F. Kennedy* (New York: Viking Press, 1972), 77–84; J. N. Giglio, *The Presidency of John F. Kennedy* (Lawrence: University Press of Kansas, 1991), 45, 72–79; T. G. Paterson, 'John F. Kennedy's Quest for Victory and Global Crisis', in Paterson, *Kennedy's Quest for Victory*, 15–16, 22–23; Freedman, *Kennedy's Wars*, 9, 417.

27. *Hansard*, 5th series, 642 (1961): 928–931.

28. *The Times*, June 5, 1961; *Economist*, June 30, 1961.

29. Fraser and Murray, *America and the World*, 98–99; Ausland, *Kennedy, Khrushchev and the Berlin-Cuba Crisis*, 13–21; Reeves, *President Kennedy*, chapters 17–18; Kantowicz, *Coming Apart, Coming Together*, 291–292; H. Harrison, 'The GDR, the Soviet Union and the Berlin Wall Crisis', in *The Berlin Wall Crisis: Perspectives on Cold War Alliances*, ed. J. P. S. Gearson and K. Schake (Basingstoke: Palgrave Macmillan, 2002), 116; Troyanovsky, 'Soviet Foreign Policy', 232–233; Tompson, *Khrushchev*, 236–237; Taubman, *Khrushchev: The Man and His Era*, 506; Talbott, *Khrushchev Remembers*, 455–458, 460.

30. Adomeit, *Imperial Overstretch*, 103–109; Richter, *Khrushchev's Double Bind*, 140–144.

31. *The Times*, August 19, 1961.

32. *Hansard*, 5th series, 464 (1961): 26–30, 36, 314–318.

33. R. M. Slusser, *The Berlin Crisis of 1961* (Baltimore: Johns Hopkins University Press, 1973), 129–132; Walton, *Cold War and Counterrevolution*, 90–92; Freedman, *Kennedy's Wars*, 75.

34. Gearson, *Macmillan and the Berlin Wall Crisis*, 191–198.

35. D. Nunnerley, *President Kennedy and Britain* (London: Bodley Head, 1972), 68–69.

36. K. P. O'Donnell and D. F. Powers, *Johnny We Hardly Knew Ye: Memories of John Fitzgerald Kennedy* (Boston: Little, Brown, 1972), 304–306; Fraser and Murray, *America and the World*, 99–101; Kantowicz, *Coming Apart, Coming Together*, 292; Reeves, *President Kennedy*, 533–537; Ausland, *Kennedy, Khrushchev and the Berlin-Cuba Crisis*, 73–76, 89; Walton, *Cold War and Counterrevolution*, 149–153; Giglio, *Presidency of Kennedy*, 80–88, 216–219.

37. *The Times*, June 28, 1963.

38. *Guardian*, June 27, 1963.

39. *Hansard*, 5th series, 680 (1963): 198–200.

40. Freedman, *Kennedy's Wars*, 72–91, 268–269; Troyanovsky, 'Soviet Foreign Policy', 233–234; Tompson, *Khrushchev*, 236–237; Slusser, *Berlin Crisis*, chapter 9; G. Schild, 'The Berlin Crisis', in *Kennedy: The New Frontier Revisited*, ed. M. J. White (Basingstoke: Macmillan, 1998), 91–123.

CHAPTER 3

1. L. F. Kaplan, 'The MLF Debate', in *John F. Kennedy and Europe*, ed. D. Brinkley and R. T. Griffiths (Baton Rouge: Louisiana State University Press, 1999), 51–65; Pierre, *Nuclear Politics*, 243–251; Ovendale, *British Defence Policy*, 123–125, 127; Dumbrell, *A Special Relationship*, 49–51, 125, 137–141; Harrison, *Reluctant Ally*, 83–85; A. Horne, 'Kennedy and Macmillan', R. Morgan, 'Kennedy and Adenauer', J. Newhouse, 'De Gaulle and the Anglo-Saxons', and D. Brinkley, 'Dean Acheson and John Kennedy: Combating Strains in the Atlantic Alliance, 1962–63', all in Brinkley and Griffiths, *Kennedy and Europe*, 3–48, 288–316; J. Brain, 'Dealing with De Gaulle', in White, *Kennedy: The New Frontier Revisited*, 160–192; Bartlett, *The Special Relationship*, 93, 95, 98–99; Heuser, 'NATO's Nuclear Strategy', 45–46.
2. Eichengreen, 'Economy', 122; Sked and Cook, *Post-War Britain*, 164–165; Coker, 'Foreign and Defence Policy', 7; Reynolds, *Britannia Overruled*, 200; Young, *Britain and the World*, 171; Baylis, *Anglo-American Defence Relations*, 66–75; Dobson, *Anglo-American Relations*, 120, 127–131; Bartlett, *The Special Relationship*, 98–100, and idem, *Long Retreat*, 154–156, 175–179; Pierre, *Nuclear Politics*, 217–243; Dockrill, *British Defence*, 71–76.
3. Grove, *Vanguard to Trident*, 242–244, 270, 273; B. Heuser, *NATO, Britain, France and the FRG: Nuclear Strategies and Forces for Europe, 1949–2000* (Basingstoke: Macmillan, 1997), 70–71.
4. P. Howlett, 'The Golden Age, 1955–73', in *Twentieth Century Britain: Economic, Social and Cultural Change*, ed. P. Johnson (London: Longman, 1996), 320–324; P. Oppenheimer, 'Muddling Through: The Economy, 1951–64', in *The Age of Affluence, 1951–64*, ed. V. Bogdanor and R. Skidelsky (London: Macmillan, 1970), 117–167; Bean and Crafts, 'British Economic Growth', 142–147; J. C. R. Dow, *The Management of the British Economy, 1945–60* (Cambridge: Cambridge University Press, 1970), 111. Dow is not complimentary about the Conservative economic policies of the 1950s. According to some of the contributors to *The Labour Government's Economic Record, 1964–70*, ed. W. Beckerman (London: Duckworth, 1972), the more interventionist Labour approach was better.

5. V. Keegan, 'Industry and Technology', and L. Stone, 'Britain and the World', both in *The Decade of Disillusion: British Politics in the Sixties*, ed. D. McKie and C. Cook (London: Macmillan, 1972), 125–126, 140.

6. Macmillan, *Pointing the Way*, 251–253; Ovendale, *British Defence Policy*, 121–123; H. Nehring, 'The British and West German Protests Against Nuclear Weapons and the Cultures of the Cold War, 1957–64', *Contemporary British History* 19 (2005): 223–241.

7. B. J. Firestone, 'Defence Policy as a Form of Arms Control: Nuclear Force Posture and Strategy Under John F. Kennedy', in *John F. Kennedy: The Promise Revisited*, ed. P. Harper and J.P. Krieg (Westport, CT: Greenwood Press, 1988), 57–69; Reynolds, *Britannia Overruled*, 202–203; Coker, 'Foreign and Defence Policy', 11–12; Sked and Cook, *Post-War Britain*, 165–166; Baylis, *Anglo-American Defence Relations*, 75–76; Bartlett, *Long Retreat*, 158–160, 176–179; Pierre, *Nuclear Politics*, 224–225; Dumbrell, *A Special Relationship*, 58; R. E. Neustadt, *Report to JFK: The Skybolt Crisis in Perspective* (Ithaca, NY: Cornell University Press, 1999); Murray, *Kennedy, Macmillan and Nuclear Weapons*, 66–69.

8. Murray, *Kennedy, Macmillan and Nuclear Weapons*, 70–71, 74–80.

9. This is the line taken in I. Clark, *Nuclear Diplomacy and the Special Relationship: Britain's Deterrent and America, 1957–62* (Oxford: Clarendon Press, 1994).

10. Neustadt, *Report to JFK*, 88.

11. Pierre, *Nuclear Politics*, 231–272; Simpson, *Independent Nuclear State*, 162–164, 167; Dobson, *Anglo-American Relations*, 128–131; Baylis, *Anglo-American Defence Relations*, 72–85; Dockrill, *British Defence*, 74–88; Bartlett, *Long Retreat*, 179–180; Reynolds, *Britannia Overruled*, 202; Sked and Cook, *Post-War Britain*, 166–167; Horne, *Macmillan*, 437–443; Ovendale, *British Defence Policy*, 125–127.

12. *The Times*, December 22, 1962; *Observer*, December 23, 1962.

13. Murray, *Kennedy, Macmillan and Nuclear Weapons*, 93–98.

14. Nunnerley, *Kennedy and Britain*, 144–145, 149, 160–161; Murray, *Kennedy, Macmillan and Nuclear Weapons*, 98–103.

15. *Hansard*, 5th series, 670 (1963): 955–1074, 1139–1270; A. Thorpe, *A History of the British Labour Party* (Basingstoke: Macmillan, 1997), 155; P. Ziegler, *Wilson: The Authorized Life of Lord Wilson of Rievaulx* (London: Weidenfeld and Nicolson, 1993), 148–149, 208.

16. Greenwood, *Britain and European Cooperation Since 1945*, 79–90; Sked and Cook, *Post-War Britain*, 167–168, 173; Reynolds, *Britannia Overruled*, 203; Young, *Britain and the World*, 175; Bartlett, *The Special Relationship*,

99–101; Gowland and Turner, *Britain and European Integration*, 54–60, 88; Harrison, *Reluctant Ally*, 69, 79–80, 102.

17. Kaiser, *Using Europe*, 173; Baylis, *Anglo-American Defence Relations*, 73; Pierre, *Nuclear Politics*, 161, 208, 214–215, 222–224, 234–235, 239–240, 245.

18. *Hansard*, 5th series, 646 (1961): 928–939, 1493–1494, 1785–1786.

19. Charlton, *Price of Victory*, 293, 307.

20. C. A. Pagedas, 'Harold Macmillan and the 1962 Champs Meeting', *Diplomacy and Statecraft* 9 (1998): 224–242; R. Aldous, 'A Family Affair: Macmillan and the Art of Personal Diplomacy', in Aldous and Lee, *Macmillan and Britain's World Role*, 9–35.

21. S. Lee, 'Staying in the Game? Coming into the Game? Macmillan and European Integration', in Aldous and Lee, *Macmillan and Britain's World Role*, 140–145.

22. Horne, *Macmillan*, 444–451; Macmillan, *Riding the Storm*, 435; Kaiser, *Using Europe*, 197–199.

23. F. Costigliola, 'The Failed Design: Kennedy, De Gaulle and the Struggle for Europe', *Diplomatic History* 8 (1984): 227–251; Cromwell, *The United States and the European Pillar*, 16–26.

24. L. Bell, *The Throw that Failed: Britain's 1961 Application to Join the Common Market* (London: New European Publications, 1995), 25; W. S. Lucas, 'The Cost of Myth: Macmillan and the Illusion of the Special Relationship', and N. Ashton, 'Managing Transition: Macmillan and the Utility of Anglo-American Relations', both in *Harold Macmillan: Aspects of a Political Life*, ed. R. Aldous and S. Lee (Basingstoke: Macmillan, 1999), 16–31, 242–254.

25. N. P. Ludlow, *Dealing with Britain: The Six and the First UK Application to the EEC* (Cambridge: Cambridge University Press, 1997), 242, 244, and idem, '"Ne pleurez pas, Milord": Macmillan and France from Algiers to Rambouillet', in Aldous and Lee, *Macmillan: Aspects of a Political Life*, 108–109.

26. P. Gerbet, 'The Fouchet Negotiations for Political Union and the British Application', M. Vaisse, 'De Gaulle and the British "Application" to join the Common Market', O. Bange, 'Grand Designs and the Diplomatic Breakdown', N. P. Ludlow, 'British Agriculture and the Brussels Negotiations: A Problem of Trust', and G. Schmidt, 'Masterminding a New Western Europe: The Key Actors at Brussels in the Superpower Conflict', all in *Britain's Failure to Enter the European Community, 1961–63: The Enlargement Negotiations and Crisis in European, Atlantic and Commonwealth*

Relations, ed. G. Wilkes (London: Frank Cass, 1987), 51–90, 108–118, 135–143, 191–212.

27. S. Ward, 'Anglo-Commonwealth Relations and EEC Membership: The Problem of the Old Dominions', and K. Newman, 'Legal Problems for British Accession', both in Wilkes, *Britain's Failure*, 93–107, 120–132.

28. Nunnerley, *Kennedy and Britain*, 175.

29. Cromwell, *The United States and the European Pillar*, 26–44.

30. M. Trachtenberg, *A Constructed Peace: The Making of the European Settlement, 1945–63* (Princeton, NJ: Princeton University Press, 1999), ix, 281.

31. *Hansard*, 5th series, 671 (1963): 239–240, 954–955, 962.

32. *The Times*, January 16, 1963; *Economist*, January 19, 1963.

33. Kaiser, *Using Europe*, 199–201.

34. Ibid., 201–202. American leaders continued to hope that Britain would join the EEC: S. Ward, 'Kennedy, Britain and the European Community', in Brinkley and Griffiths, *Kennedy and Europe*, 317–332.

35. Sked and Cook, *Post-War Britain*, 174; Young, *Britain and the World*, 175; Ovendale, *British Defence Policy*, 129–130; C. Leyser, 'The Limited Test Ban Treaty of 1963', in Brinkley and Griffiths, *Kennedy and Europe*, 95–115.

36. K. Oliver, *Kennedy, Macmillan and the Nuclear Test Ban Debate, 1961–63* (Basingstoke: Macmillan, 1998), 14–18, 21, 134–137, 157–161, 163–183.

37. Horne, *Macmillan*, 503–511, 518, 522, 524–526, 528, 549; P. J. Briggs, 'Kennedy and Congress: The Nuclear Test Ban Treaty, 1963', in Harper and Krieg, *John F. Kennedy: The Promise Revisited*, 35–55.

38. Bartlett, *The Special Relationship*, 97–98; Oliver, *Kennedy, Macmillan and the Nuclear Test Ban Debate*, 3, 42, 87, 94, 103, 117, 130, 180, 206; Dobson, *Anglo-American Relations*, 130; Nunnerley, *Kennedy and Britain*, 110.

39. Johnson, *Modern World*, 599; Turner, *Macmillan*, 166–173; Sampson, *Macmillan: A Study in Ambiguity*, chapter 15.

CHAPTER 4

1. Hemming, 'Macmillan and the End of the British Empire', 118.

2. Sked and Cook, *Post-War Britain*, 175–179; M. Hannagan, 'Changing Margins in Post-War European Politics', in *Themes in Modern European History Since 1945*, ed. R. Wakeman (London: Routledge, 2003), 129; Young, *Britain and the World*, 182; Hollowell, 'Commonwealth to European Integration', 68–69; I. R. G. Spencer, *British Immigration Policy*

292 AN INTERNATIONAL HISTORY OF BRITISH POWER

Since 1939: The Making of Multiracial Britain (London: Routledge, 1997), 129–134; R. Hattersley, 'Immigration', in McKie and Cook, *Decade of Disillusion*, 184–186; Z. Layton-Henry, *The Politics of Immigration* (Oxford: Blackwell, 1992), 75–77; Sampson, *Macmillan: A Study in Ambiguity*, 191–192, 216–217; Dockrill, *British Defence*, 87; Kitchen, *British Empire and Commonwealth*, 143–147.

3. These themes are discussed in Gifford and Louis, *Decolonization and African Independence*.

4. D. Welsh, 'The Principle of the Thing: The Conservative Government and the Control of Commonwealth Immigration, 1957–59', *Contemporary British History* 12 (1998): 51–79; Kahler, *Decolonization in Britain and France*, 156–157, 252, 255.

5. W. D. McIntyre, 'Britain and the Creation of the Commonwealth Secretariat', *Journal of Imperial and Commonwealth History* 28 (2000): 135–158.

6. Darwin, *Britain and Decolonization*, 304–305.

7. R. F. Holland, 'The Imperial Factor in British Strategies from Attlee to Macmillan, 1945–63', *Journal of Imperial and Commonwealth History* 12 (1984): 183–184.

8. Reynolds, *Britannia Overruled*, 209–210; Young, *Britain and the World*, 146, 181–182; Hemming, 'Macmillan and the End of the British Empire', 111–112; Macmillan, *Pointing the Way*, 264–266; Darwin, *Britain and Decolonization*, 253; Baylis, *Anglo-American Defence Relations*, 66.

9. C. Young, *Politics in the Congo: Decolonization and Independence* (Princeton, NJ: Princeton University Press, 1965), chapters 3, 12; I. Kabongo, 'The Catastrophe of Belgian Decolonization', in Gifford and Louis, *Decolonization and African Independence*, 381–400; Kantowicz, *Coming Apart, Coming Together*, 276; D. Armstrong and E. Goldstein, 'Interaction with the Non-European World', in Fulbrook, *Europe Since 1945*, 254; S. Meisler, *United Nations: The First Fifty Years* (New York: Atlantic Monthly Press, 1995), 116–118.

10. Young, *Politics in the Congo*, 307–321; Kantowicz, *Coming Apart, Coming Together*, 276–277, 279–280; Hargreaves, *Decolonization in Africa*, 190–197; Armstrong and Goldstein, 'Interaction with the Non-European World', 254; Darwin, *Britain and Decolonization*, 252; Meisler, *United Nations*, chapter 7.

11. L. K. Johnson, *America's Secret Power* (New York: Oxford University Press, 1989), 27–28; V. Marchetti and J. D. Marks, *The CIA and the Cult of Intelligence* (London: Cape, 1974), 31, 117–118, 125–126; R. Jeffreys-Jones,

The CIA and American Democracy (New Haven, CT: Yale University Press, 1989), 97, 126–127, 138.

12. M. G. Kalb, *The Congo Cables: The Cold War in Africa, from Eisenhower to Kennedy* (New York: Macmillan, 1982), 289–290.

13. Kahler, *Decolonization in Britain and France*, 145–148, 156, 281, 305.

14. Darwin, *Britain and Decolonization*, 253–254.

15. Dumbrell, *A Special Relationship*, 51; Baylis, *Anglo-American Defence Relations*, 72; Turner, *Macmillan*, 197–198; Kalb, *Congo Cables*, 370–371.

16. Nunnerley, *Kennedy and Britain*, 201–204.

17. *Hansard*, 5th series, 636 (1961): 1486, 1517–1519, 1523, 1525; 671 (1963): 677–746.

18. *The Times*, January 17, 1963; *Guardian*, December 5, 1962.

19. Darwin, *Britain and Decolonization*, 255; Low, 'End of the British Empire in Africa', 42–43, 50, 56–57; Lapping, *End of Empire*, 392, 437–438.

20. Eichengreen, 'Economy', 117–118. For the wider context, see also I. T. Berend, *Central and Eastern Europe, 1944–93* (Cambridge: Cambridge University Press, 1996), chapter 5; D. H. Aldcroft, *The European Economy, 1914–90* (London: Routledge, 1993), chapter 6; A. Nove, *An Economic History of the USSR, 1917–91* (Harmondsworth: Penguin, 1992), chapter 12; R. J. Crampton, *Eastern Europe in the Twentieth Century and After* (London: Routledge, 2003), chapter 17.

21. Nove, *Economic History of the USSR*, 322, 358–359; R. L. Tokes, *Hungary's Negotiated Revolution: Economic Reform, Social Change and Political Succession, 1957–90* (Cambridge: Cambridge University Press, 1996), 91–92.

22. D. Sassoon, 'Politics', and A. Korner, 'Culture', in Fulbrook, *Europe Since 1945*, 15, 29, 158–159; Larres, 'International and Security Relations Within Europe', 196, 210; S. Morewood, 'Divided Europe: The Long Post-War, 1945–89', in Wakeman, *Modern European History*, 17. For a discussion of social change, education, demography, nationalism and ethnicity, industrialization, and the growth of towns, see Z. A. B. Zeman, *The Making and Breaking of Communist Europe* (Oxford: Basil Blackwell, 1991), chapter 21.

23. D. Bathrick, *The Powers of Speech: The Politics of Culture in the GDR* (Lincoln: University of Nebraska Press, 1995), 1–10; Sassoon, 'Politics', 17; Berend, *Central and Eastern Europe*, chapter 5, and idem, 'The Central and Eastern European Revolution', in Wakeman, *Modern European History*, 190–192; Fraser and Murray, *America and the World*, 41; Aldcroft, *European Economy*, chapters 6, 9; G. Swain and N. Swain, *Eastern Europe*

Since 1945 (Basingstoke: Macmillan, 1998), 121–130; J. Adam, *Economic Reforms in the Soviet Union and Eastern Europe Since the 1960s* (Basingstoke: Macmillan, 1989), part 2; G. Schopflin, *Politics in Eastern Europe, 1945–92* (Oxford: Blackwell, 1993), chapter 6; M. Tepavac, 'Tito: 1945–80', in *Burn This House: The Making and Unmaking of Yugoslavia*, ed. J. Udovicki and J. Ridgeway (London: Duke University Press, 1997), 66–72; M. Vickers, *The Albanians: A Modern History* (London: I. B. Tauris, 1997), chapter 9; T. Gilberg, *Nationalism and Communism in Rumania: The Rise and Fall of Ceausescu's Personal Dictatorship* (Oxford: Westview, 1990), chapter 10; S. Fischer-Galati, *Twentieth Century Rumania* (New York: Columbia University Press, 1970), 185–200; R. Shen, *Economic Reform in Poland and Czechoslovakia* (Westport, CT: Praeger, 1993), chapters 3–4; N. Davies, *Heart of Europe: A Short History of Poland* (Oxford: Clarendon Press, 1991), 12–13; Tokes, *Hungary's Negotiated Revolution*, chapter 2; C. Gati, *Hungary and the Soviet Bloc* (Durham, NC: Duke University Press, 1986), chapter 7; I. T. Berend and G. Ranki, *Hungary: A Century of Economic Development* (Newton Abbot: David and Charles, 1974), 210–246.

24. Kantowicz, *Coming Apart, Coming Together*, 33–35; Crampton, *Eastern Europe*, 255–260; Swain and Swain, *Eastern Europe Since 1945*, 56–60; Tepavac, 'Tito: 1945–80', 66–72; Gaddis, *Long Peace*, 152–164, 187–191.

25. R. L. Russell, *George F. Kennan's Strategic Thought* (Westport, CT: Praeger, 1999), 56; R. West, *Tito and the Rise and Fall of Yugoslavia* (London: Sinclair-Stevenson, 1994), 271; D. Wilson, *Tito's Yugoslavia* (Cambridge: Cambridge University Press, 1979), 68, 74, 98, 114–115, 123, 134–135, 156, 194–195, 213; J. Ridley, *Tito* (London: Constable, 1994), 362–363; W. Zimmerman, 'Yugoslav Strategies for Survival, 1948–80', in *At the Brink of War and Peace: The Tito-Stalin Split in a Historic Perspective*, ed. W. S. Vucinich (New York: Brooklyn College Press, 1982), 11–28.

26. B. Heuser, *Western 'Containment' Policies in the Cold War: The Yugoslav Case, 1948–53* (London: Routledge, 1988), 39–42, 47–49, 66–67, 81–82, 88, 149, 154–155, 161–162, 171–172, 204–207.

27. Sassoon, 'Politics', 29; Larres, 'International and Security Relations Within Europe', 188; D. F. Good and T. Ma, 'The Economic Growth of Central and Eastern Europe in Comparative Perspective, 1870–1989', *European Review of Economic History* 2 (1999): 103–137.

28. Eichengreen, 'Economy', 99–100, 120; Crampton, *Eastern Europe*, chapter 19; Nove, *Economic History of the USSR*, chapter 13; Aldcroft, *European Economy*, chapter 9; Adam, *Economic Reforms*, chapters 6–9;

Berend, *Central and Eastern Europe*, chapter 6; Friedberg, 'The United States and the Cold War Arms Race', 207, 220–222.

29. Johnson, *Modern World*, 549–550; Armstrong and Goldstein, 'Interaction with the Non-European World', 244–246; R. Terrill, *Mao: A Biography* (New York: Harper and Row, 1980), 278–288, 337–341; Talbott, *Khrushchev Remembers*, chapter 18; S. G. Zhang, 'China's Strategic Culture and the Cold War Confrontations', in Westad, *Reviewing the Cold War*, 258–277; C. Pleshakov, 'Nikita Khrushchev and Sino-Soviet Relations', and C. Jian and Y. Kuisong, 'Chinese Politics and the Collapse of the Sino-Soviet Alliance', both in *Brothers in Arms: The Rise and Fall of the Sino-Soviet Alliance, 1945–63*, ed. O. A. Westad (Washington, DC: Woodrow Wilson Centre Press, 1998), 226–294; J. Keep, *The Last of the Empires: A History of the Soviet Union, 1945–91* (Oxford: Oxford University Press, 1996), 147, 227, 415.

CHAPTER 5

1. K. W. Thompson, 'Kennedy's Foreign Policy: Activism versus Pragmatism', in Harper and Krieg, *John F. Kennedy: The Promise Revisited*, 25–34; Johnson, *Modern World*, 614–615; Burk, 'Introduction', 2–3; Walton, *Cold War and Counterrevolution*, chapter 1; Dobson, *Anglo-American Relations*, 124–125.

2. Giglio, *Presidency of Kennedy*, 44–47; Johnson, *Modern World*, 615; Fraser and Murray, *America and the World*, chapter 4; H. Thomas, *Cuba or The Pursuit of Freedom* (London: Eyre and Spottiswoode, 1971), 1226, 1231–1233; T. G. Paterson, *Contesting Castro: The United States and the Triumph of the Cuban Revolution* (New York: Oxford University Press, 1994), 10, 12, 241–254. According to Susan Eckstein, Castro's policies were as much practically motivated as ideologically driven, and Cuba's revolution was characterized by a process of negotiation between the state and the people. S. E. Eckstein, *Back from the Future: Cuba Under Castro* (Princeton, NJ: Princeton University Press, 1994).

3. Johnson, *Modern World*, 622–625; Fraser and Murray, *America and the World*, 82–83, 91–94; Kantowicz, *Coming Apart, Coming Together*, 298–299; LaFeber, *America, Russia and the Cold War*, 223–224; Gaddis, *Long Peace*, 191; S. G. Rabe, *The Most Dangerous Area in the World: John F. Kennedy Confronts Communist Revolution in Latin America* (Chapel Hill: University of North Carolina Press, 1999), 71–73; R. M. Bissell, *Reflections of a Cold Warrior: From Yalta to the Bay of Pigs* (New Haven, CT: Yale

University Press, 1996), 201, 203; Walton, *Cold War and Counterrevolution*, 58–59; P. Wyden, *Bay of Pigs* (London: Cape, 1979), 324–325; T. Higgins, *The Perfect Failure: Kennedy, Eisenhower and the CIA at the Bay of Pigs* (New York: Norton, 1987), 172–173; H. S. Dinerstein, *The Making of a Missile Crisis: October 1962* (Baltimore: Johns Hopkins University Press, 1976), 131; C. Andrew, *For the President's Eyes Only: Secret Intelligence and the American Presidency from Washington to Bush* (London: HarperCollins, 1995), 253–255; T. G. Paterson, 'Fixation with Cuba: The Bay of Pigs, Missile Crisis and Covert War Against Castro', in Paterson, *Kennedy's Quest for Victory*, 135–136.

4. *The Times*, April 17, 18, 21, 1961; *Observer*, April 23, 1961.

5. Higgins, *Perfect Failure*, 99; *Hansard*, 5th series, 638 (1961): 971–974, 1384–1387.

6. J. W. Hilty, *Robert Kennedy: Brother Protector* (Philadelphia: Temple University Press, 1997), 412–431; Giglio, *Presidency of Kennedy*, 48–63; A. M. Schlesinger, *A Thousand Days: John F. Kennedy in the White House* (London: Deutsch, 1965), 211–270; Talbott, *Khrushchev Remembers*, 491–493; Tompson, *Khrushchev*, 232–235, 247–248.

7. Rabe, *The Most Dangerous Area in the World*, 196, 199; R. E. Quirk, *Fidel Castro* (New York: Norton, 1993), 385–387; Kantowicz, *Coming Apart, Coming Together*, 297–300; Zubok and Pleshakov, *Inside the Kremlin's Cold War*, 206–207, 245; Dinerstein, *Making of a Missile Crisis*, chapter 4; Paterson, 'Fixation with Cuba', 136–142; M. J. White, *The Cuban Missile Crisis* (Basingstoke: Macmillan, 1996), 47–59; LaFeber, *America, Russia and the Cold War*, 214–216.

8. Richter, *Khrushchev's Double Bind*, 151–152; Johnson, *Modern World*, 625; Kantowicz, *Coming Apart, Coming Together*, 300; Dinerstein, *Making of a Missile Crisis*, 153–158; White, *Cuban Missile Crisis*, 82.

9. Talbott, *Khrushchev Remembers*, 492–499; Quirk, *Fidel Castro*, 415; Zubok and Pleshakov, *Inside the Kremlin's Cold War*, 259–261; Ausland, *Kennedy, Khrushchev and the Berlin-Cuba Crisis*, 66–73, 76, 99, 102; Hershberg, 'The Crisis Years', 315.

10. M. P. Riccards, 'The Dangerous Legacy: John F. Kennedy and the Cuban Missile Crisis', in Harper and Krieg, *John F. Kennedy: The Promise Revisited*, 83–85.

11. Quirk, *Fidel Castro*, 414–415; Johnson, *Modern World*, 625; Tompson, *Khrushchev*, 248–249; Thomas, *Cuba*, 1393. One of the themes in R. L. Garthoff, *Reflections on the Cuban Missile Crisis* (Washington, DC: Brookings Institution, 1989) is that Castro's role was essentially

passive. The development of Cuban-Soviet relations is also discussed in A. Fursenko and T. Naftali, *One Hell of a Gamble: Khrushchev, Castro, Kennedy and the Cuban Missile Crisis, 1958–64* (London: Norton, 1997).

12. Johnson, *Modern World*, 625–626; Kantowicz, *Coming Apart, Coming Together*, 300–301; Hilty, *Robert Kennedy*, chapter 15; Giglio, *Presidency of Kennedy*, 194; Paterson, 'Fixation with Cuba', 142–145; Dinerstein, *Making of a Missile Crisis*, 223–225; White, *Cuban Missile Crisis*, 112–113, 238.

13. *The Times*, October 23, 24, 1962.

14. *Hansard*, 5th series, 664 (1962): 1053–1064.

15. *The Times*, October 26, 1962; *Economist*, October 27, 1962.

16. *The Times*, October 27, 1962.

17. Fraser and Murray, *America and the World*, 107–112; Giglio, *Presidency of Kennedy*, 209–214; Johnson, *Modern World*, 626; Kantowicz, *Coming Apart, Coming Together*, 301; Talbott, *Khrushchev Remembers*, 504; A. M. Schlesinger, *Robert Kennedy and His Times* (Boston: Houghton Mifflin, 1978), 531; Paterson, 'Fixation with Cuba', 145–148; White, *Cuban Missile Crisis*, 218–231; Thomas, *Cuba*, 1414.

18. Johnson, *Modern World*, 627–628; Giglio, *Presidency of Kennedy*, 213–216; Thomas, *Cuba*, 1418–1419; P. Nash, *The Other Missiles of October: Eisenhower, Kennedy and the Jupiters, 1957–63* (Chapel Hill: University of North Carolina Press, 1997), 34, 170; G. T. Allison, *Essence of a Decision: Explaining the Cuban Missile Crisis* (New York: HarperCollins, 1971), 226; Schlesinger, *Robert Kennedy*, 523.

19. Talbott, *Khrushchev Remembers*, 500, 504; Zubok and Pleshakov, *Inside the Kremlin's Cold War*, 267–270. On Khrushchev's loss of influence within the Soviet government, see parts 3 and 4 of M. Tatu, *Power in the Kremlin* (London: Collins, 1969).

20. Tatu, *Power in the Kremlin*, 260–273; J. L. Gaddis, *We Now Know: Rethinking Cold War History* (Oxford: Clarendon Press, 1998), 278–279; Richter, *Khrushchev's Double Bind*, 153–156.

21. These are among the revelations detailed in Fursenko and Naftali, *One Hell of a Gamble*.

22. R. L. Garthoff, 'U.S. Intelligence and the Cuban Missile Crisis', *Intelligence and National Security* 13 (1998): 18–63, and idem, *Reflections on the Cuban Missile Crisis*, 134, 145, 182–183, 191; G. T. Allison and P. D. Zelikow, *Essence of a Decision: Explaining the Cuban Missile Crisis* (New York: Longman, 1999), 159–160; Fursenko and Naftali, *One Hell of a Gamble*; Hershberg, 'The Crisis Years', 311–314, 316–317; Gaddis,

Long Peace, 225; Dinerstein, *Making of a Missile Crisis*, 230–238; Paterson, 'Fixation with Cuba', 148–149, 151–152; Riccards, 'Dangerous Legacy', 100; White, *Cuban Missile Crisis*, 238–239; Walton, *Cold War and Counterrevolution*, 141–142; Andrew, *For the President's Eyes Only*, 302–305; Tompson, *Khrushchev*, 253.

23. Dobson, *Anglo-American Relations*, 127–128.

24. Reynolds, *Britannia Overruled*, 201; Bartlett, *The Special Relationship*, 97; Dumbrell, *A Special Relationship*, 54–58; Baylis, *Anglo-American Defence Relationship*, 75–76; Pierre, *Nuclear Politics*, 224–225; Nunnerley, *Kennedy and Britain*, 75–77, 83–84, 87.

25. Aldous, 'A Family Affair', 28–29; Horne, *Macmillan*, 380–384.

26. Andrew, *For the President's Eyes Only*, 292, 296; Horne, 'Kennedy and Macmillan', 8–12; L. Scott, 'Close to the Brink? Britain and the Cuban Missile Crisis', *Contemporary Record* 5 (1991): 511.

27. L. Scott, *Macmillan, Kennedy and the Cuban Missile Crisis: Political, Military and Intelligence Aspects* (Basingstoke: Macmillan, 1999), 9, 95.

28. G. D. Rawnsley, 'How Special Is Special? The Anglo-American Alliance During the Cuban Missile Crisis', *Contemporary Record* 9 (1995): 592–597. On the UN's involvement, see Meisler, *United Nations*, chapter 8.

29. Rawnsley, 'How Special Is Special?' 597–598; Horne, 'Kennedy and Macmillan', 4, 8–9.

30. Rawnsley, 'How Special Is Special?' 597–599; Scott, 'Close to the Brink?' 515; Garthoff, *Reflections on the Cuban Missile Crisis*, 79.

31. Horne, 'Kennedy and Macmillan', 11; Scott, 'Close to the Brink?' 509–510, 514; Garthoff, *Reflections on the Cuban Missile Crisis*, 61.

32. The Soviet leader later insisted that his decision to place missiles on Cuba was made in direct response to NATO's deployment of Jupiter IRBMs in Turkey. Talbott, *Khrushchev Remembers*, 493–494.

33. Horne, 'Kennedy and Macmillan', 12; Scott, 'Close to the Brink?' 512–513; Schlesinger, *Robert Kennedy*, 519.

34. Horne, 'Kennedy and Macmillan', 13–14; Fursenko and Naftali, *One Hell of a Gamble*, 236; Garthoff, *Reflections on the Cuban Missile Crisis*, 73.

35. E. R. May and P. D. Zelikow, eds., *The Kennedy Tapes: Inside the White House During the Cuban Missile Crisis* (Cambridge, MA: Belknap Press, 1997), 268–269, 283–287, 384–389, 393–394, 427–430, 480–485.

36. *Hansard*, 5th series, 666 (1962): 18–19.

37. Holland, *Pursuit of Greatness*, 309; Sanders, *Losing an Empire*, 173–174; Watt, *Succeeding John Bull*, 142–143.

38. Larres, 'International and Security Relations Within Europe', 211; Kantowicz, *Coming Apart, Coming Together*, 303; Horne, 'Kennedy and Macmillan', 13–14; Zubok and Pleshakov, *Inside the Kremlin's Cold War*, 270–271; Gaddis, *Long Peace*, 204–205; Stevenson, *Rise and Fall of Détente*, 118–119; K. Dyson, 'European Détente in Historical Perspective: Ambiguities and Paradoxes', and A. Carter, 'Détente and East-West Relations: American, Soviet and European Perspectives', both in *European Détente: Case Studies of the Politics of East-West Relations*, ed. K. Dyson (London: Pinter, 1986), 38, 57; H. Sidey, *John F. Kennedy: Portrait of a President* (London: Deutsch, 1964), chapter 8; Johnson, *Modern World*, 629–630; Riccards, 'Dangerous Legacy', 100. Van Oudenaren, in *Détente in Europe*, claims that the USSR was constantly seeking a thaw in these years. If this is true, Soviet intentions were repeatedly misunderstood in the West.

CHAPTER 6

1. Johnson, *Modern World*, 630–634; Kantowicz, *Coming Apart, Coming Together*, 307; Fraser and Murray, *America and the World*, 114–117; Sidey, *John F. Kennedy*, 57, 286, 386, 411–413; Reeves, *President Kennedy*, 236–237, 255–257, 259–261, 311, 442–450, 519, 528–529, 541–542, 556–577, 586–601, 610, 617–618, 635–652. For a detailed narrative, see M. B. Young, *The Vietnam Wars, 1945–90* (New York: HarperCollins, 1991), 60–106.
2. D. Acheson, *Present at the Creation* (New York: Norton, 1969), 863–864; G. M. Kahin, *Intervention: How America Became Involved in Vietnam* (Garden City, NY: Knopf, 1987), ix; Young, *Vietnam Wars*, ix; D. Halberstam, *The Best and the Brightest* (New York: Random House, 1972), 135, 225–226; Giglio, *Presidency of Kennedy*, 239–254; Freedman, *Kennedy's Wars*, 299–300; L. H. Gelb and R. K. Betts, *The Irony of Vietnam: The System Worked* (Washington, DC: Brookings Institution, 1979), 70–71. Gelb and Betts stress that despite the long-term U.S. commitment to containment in Vietnam, and all the problems that resulted, America's political and bureaucratic system remained intact.
3. Freedman, *Kennedy's Wars*, 347, 363, 397, 419; R. S. McNamara, *In Retrospect: The Tragedy and Lessons of Vietnam* (New York: Times Books, 1995), chapters 2–3. McNamara thinks that had he lived, Kennedy would have pulled out of Vietnam. Richard E. Neustadt, an adviser to several presidents, including Kennedy, also considered that he would have withdrawn.

See R. E. Neustadt, 'Had Kennedy Lived', *Survival* 43 (2001): 177–178, 181–183. See also Schlesinger, *A Thousand Days*, 848. The notion that Kennedy saw Vietnam as the place to make U.S. power credible needs some qualification, for he did not regard Vietnam as a vital sphere of influence for the United States and was reluctant to intervene there without the approval of America's main allies.

4. L. J. Bassett and E. E. Pelz, 'The Failed Search for Victory: Vietnam and the Politics of War', in Paterson, *Kennedy's Quest for Victory*, 223–252.

5. Sked and Cook, *Post-War Britain*, 194; R. Taylor, 'The Campaign for Nuclear Disarmament', in Bogdanor and Skidelsky, *Age of Affluence*, 248; J. W. Young, *The Labour Governments, 1964–70: International Policy* (Manchester: Manchester University Press, 2003), 3.

6. Sked and Cook, *Post-War Britain*, 210–211; B. Lapping, *The Labour Government, 1964–70* (Harmondsworth: Penguin, 1970), 86; Young, *Vietnam Wars*, 117–171.

7. Gelb and Betts, *Irony of Vietnam*, 100–112, 116–118; R. Mann, *A Grand Delusion: America's Descent into Vietnam* (New York: Basic Books, 2001); Neustadt, 'Had Kennedy Lived', 178–181. On the escalation in Vietnam see also K. Bird, *The Colour of Truth: McGeorge Bundy and William Bundy, Brothers in Arms* (New York: Simon and Schuster, 1998), chapters 11–14. The Bundys were senior figures in the U.S. national security establishment and helped to shape the Vietnam policy of both Kennedy and Johnson. On the UN's peace efforts of 1965–67, see Meisler, *United Nations*, chapter 9.

8. Dumbrell, *A Special Relationship*, 148–149; N. Tarling, *The Fall of Imperial Britain in South East Asia* (Kuala Lumpur: Oxford University Press, 1993), 187, 195.

9. P. Busch, *All the Way with JFK? Britain, the United States and the Vietnam War* (Oxford: Oxford University Press, 2003), chapters 3–5; S. Ellis, *Britain, America and the Vietnam War* (Westport, CT: Praeger, 2004), 267–268.

10. D. L. DiLeo, *George Ball, Vietnam and the Rethinking of Containment* (Chapel Hill: University of North Carolina Press, 1991); P. L. Hatcher, *The Suicide of an Elite: American Internationalists and Vietnam* (Stanford, CA: Stanford University Press, 1990), 286; F. Logevall, *Choosing War: The Lost Chance for Peace and the Escalation of War in Vietnam* (Berkeley: University of California Press, 1999).

11. Dockrill, *British Defence*, 79; Young, *Britain and the World*, 178; Sked and Cook, *Post-War Britain*, 211; Armstrong and Goldstein, 'Interaction with the Non-European World', 242.

12. Ellis, *Britain, America and the Vietnam War*, 268–269.

13. D. Watt, 'Introduction: The Anglo-American Relationship', and A. Horne, 'The Macmillan Years and Afterwards', both in Louis and Bull, *Special Relationship*, 6, 9, 101; Young, *Labour Governments*, 20–22; Dobson, *Anglo-American Relations*, 133–135, 138; Bartlett, *The Special Relationship*, 112–115.

14. R. H. Ullman, 'America, Britain and the Soviet Threat in Historical and Present Perspective', in Louis and Bull, *Special Relationship*, 105–106; Baylis, *Anglo-American Defence Relations*, 93–95; Young, *Labour Governments*, 69. For Wilson's version of events, see his *The Labour Government, 1964–70: A Personal Record* (London: Weidenfeld and Nicolson, 1971), 79–80, 95–96.

15. Young, *Labour Governments*, 69; Ellis, *Britain, America and the Vietnam War*, 80–82, 91, 101, 103, 109, 133–134.

16. A. Howard, ed., *The Crossman Diaries: Selections from the Diary of a Cabinet Minister, 1964–70* (London: Methuen, 1979), 104–106.

17. *Hansard*, 5th series, 714 (1965): 1046–1058.

18. *Hansard*, 5th series, 715 (1965): 167; *Guardian*, July 2, 1965; *The Times*, July 2, 3, 29, 1965.

19. Dumbrell, *A Special Relationship*, 150–151.

20. Young, *Labour Governments*, 70–71, 78; Dumbrell, *A Special Relationship*, 150–153; C. Wrigley, 'Now You See It, Now You Don't: Harold Wilson and Labour's Foreign Policy', in *The Wilson Governments, 1964–70*, ed. R. Coopey, S. Fielding, and N. Tiratsoo (London: Pinter, 1993), 125–126.

21. J. Barnes, 'The Record', and H. Young, 'Politics Outside the System', both in McKie and Cook, *Decade of Disillusion*, 38, 40, 45, 48, 64, 218–219, 221–222, 226; Stone, 'Britain and the World', 127–128, 132; Young, *Labour Governments*, 72, 75, 79.

22. Ellis, *Britain, America and the Vietnam War*, 270–271, 273.

23. G. Brown, *In My Way: The Political Memoirs of Lord George-Brown* (Harmondsworth: Penguin, 1971), 141–147; Young, *Labour Governments*, 75–76.

24. Young, *Vietnam Wars*, 181–183; Ellis, *Britain, America and the Vietnam War*, 217, 228–229; Young, *Labour Governments*, 76; J. Dumbrell and S. Ellis, 'British Involvement in Vietnam Peace Initiatives, 1966–67: Marigolds, Sunflowers and Kosygin Week', *Diplomatic History* 27 (2003): 113–149.

25. Dumbrell, *A Special Relationship*, 154–155; Ellis, *Britain, America and the Vietnam War*, 248–251.

26. B. Pimlott, *Harold Wilson* (London: HarperCollins, 1992), 387–388; Ziegler, *Wilson*, 228–229; Young, *Labour Governments*, 55–56; J. Fielding, 'Coping with Decline: U.S. Policy Towards the British Defence Reviews of 1966', *Diplomatic History* 23 (1999): 633–656; Ellis, *Britain, America and the Vietnam War*, 274.
27. Young, *Labour Governments*, 77.
28. Dumbrell, *A Special Relationship*, 155–159; Young, *Labour Governments*, 78.
29. Baylis, *Anglo-American Defence Relations*, 95–96.
30. On these wider changes, see A. W. Daum, L. C. Gardner, and W. Mausbach, eds., *America, the Vietnam War and the World: Comparative and International Perspectives* (Cambridge: Cambridge University Press, 2003).
31. Young, *Labour Governments*, 80–82.

CHAPTER 7

1. Dockrill, *British Defence*, 88, 96–97, 102; Baylis, *Anglo-American Defence Relations*, 97.
2. A. P. Thornton, 'The Transformation of the Commonwealth and the Special Relationship', and J. D. B. Miller, 'The Special Relationship in the Pacific', both in Louis and Bull, *Special Relationship*, 368, 383–384; J. Subritzky, *Confronting Sukarno: British, American, Australian and New Zealand Diplomacy in the Malaysian-Indonesian Confrontation, 1961–65* (Basingstoke: Macmillan, 2000).
3. Lapping, *End of Empire*, 100–101, 488–505; Young, *Labour Governments*, 101–102; Reynolds, *Britannia Overruled*, 208–212; Sked and Cook, *Post-War Britain*, 211–213, 237–238; Darwin, *Britain and Decolonization*, 303, 308–310, 314–318; Hargreaves, *Decolonization in Africa*, 110, 140, 220, 222, 235–239; Stone, 'Britain and the World', 129–133; Kitchen, *British Empire and Commonwealth*, chapters 7–8; McIntyre, *Commonwealth of Nations*, 427–430; B. Porter, *The Lion's Share: A Short History of British Imperialism, 1850–1995* (Harlow: Longman, 1996), 341, 349; Holland, *European Decolonization*, 233–235, 249, 279–283; D. Judd and P. Slinn, *The Evolution of the Modern Commonwealth, 1902–80* (London: Macmillan, 1982), 109–110, 113–115; E. Heath, *The Course of My Life* (London: Hodder and Stoughton, 1998), 276–278, 476–479.
4. Lapping, *Labour Government*, 60–69, 74–78; Nunnerley, *Kennedy and Britain*, 204, 207; P. Murphy, 'By Invitation Only: Lord Mountbatten, Prince Philip and the Attempt to Create a Commonwealth "Bilderberg

Group", 1964–66', *Journal of Imperial and Commonwealth History* 33 (2005): 245–265; McIntyre, *Commonwealth of Nations*, 450–451.

5. *Hansard*, 5th series, 744 (1967): 237–238; 756 (1968): 467–468; 760 (1968): 133; Judd and Slinn, *Evolution of the Commonwealth*, 115.

6. *Hansard*, 5th series, 735 (1966): 34–41.

7. *Hansard*, 5th series, 722 (1965): 2140–2143; 723 (1966): 15.

8. *Hansard*, 5th series, 784 (1969): 443–449.

9. *Hansard*, 5th series, 783 (1969): 3; 787 (1969): 1446–1458.

10. *Hansard*, 5th series, 770 (1968): 576–578, 1587–1589.

11. Howard, ed., *Crossman Diaries*, 128, 141; Young, *Labour Governments*, 65–66; Pimlott, *Harold Wilson*, 366–381, 450–458; Ziegler, *Wilson*, 229–240; Low, 'End of the British Empire', 62–65.

12. Young, *Labour Governments*, 186–187.

13. Brown, *In My Way*, 170–174; Grove, *Vanguard to Trident*, 304.

14. Young, *Labour Governments*, 166–168, 186–187.

15. Young, *Labour Governments*, 196–211; Howard, ed., *Crossman Diaries*, 487–488, 622; McIntyre, *Commonwealth of Nations*, 403.

16. Wilson, *The Labour Government*, 133–134, 138, 169–171, 179–180, 195, 198, 279, 282, 285, 301–302, 317, 391–392, 424, 470–476, 480, 517, 554–561, 564–570, 575–577, 589–590, 592, 597, 600–602, 623–640, 681–682, 690, 729–732, 744–751.

17. Ziegler, *Wilson*, 280, 287–290, 318, 338–340, 361.

18. Kahler, *Decolonization in Britain and France*, 148, 313–314; Lapping, *Labour Government*, 60–68; S. R. Ashton, 'British Government Perspectives on the Commonwealth, 1964–71: An Asset or a Liability?' *Journal of Imperial and Commonwealth History* 35 (2007): 73–94.

19. Bartlett, *The Special Relationship*, chapter 5; Ashton, 'Britain and Jordan, 1957–73'; D. Reynolds, 'A Special Relationship? America, Britain and the International Order Since the Second World War', *International Affairs* 62 (1985): 13, and idem, *Britannia Overruled*, 225; Burk, 'Introduction', 9–10; A. Cairncross, *The British Economy Since 1945: Economic Policy and Performance, 1945–1990* (Oxford: Blackwell, 1992), 174–177; Kennedy, *Realities Behind Diplomacy*, 341–342; W. M. Scammell, *The International Economy Since 1945* (Basingstoke: Macmillan, 1983), 105–106, 110–111; Bean and Crafts, 'British Economic Growth', 142–147; R. Eatwell, 'The Currents of Political Thought', in Hollowell, *Britain Since 1945*, 173. On the economic situation generally, see part 3 of Hollowell, *Britain Since 1945*, and the statistical tables in Eichengreen, 'Economy'. On the respective economic performances of Britain and the FRG during the 1960s, see M. Surrey,

'United Kingdom', and K. H. Hennings, 'West Germany', in *The European Economy: Growth and Crisis*, ed. A. Boltho (Oxford: Oxford University Press, 1982), 485–492, 539–547. On America's links with the FRG, see R. Wakeman, 'Introduction', in Wakeman, *Modern European History*, 4, and idem, 'European Mass Culture in the Media Age', in the same volume, 146–148; Morewood, 'Divided Europe', 18; Armstrong and Goldstein, 'Interaction with the Non-European World', 242–243. See also H. Glaser, 'Daily Life and Social Patterns', and P. K. Breit, 'Culture as Authority: American and German Transactions', in *The American Impact on Post-War Germany*, ed. R. Pommerin (Oxford: Berghahn, 1995), 83–92, 125–148.

20. W. Beckerman, 'Objectives and Performance: An Overall View', in Beckerman, *The Labour Government's Economic Record*, 67–68.

21. Howlett, 'Golden Age', 334–335; A. Cairncross, *The Wilson Years: A Treasury Dairy, 1964–69* (London: Historians' Press, 1997).

22. J. Foreman-Peck, 'Trade and the Balance of Payments', in *The British Economy Since 1945*, ed. N. Crafts and N. Woodward (Oxford: Clarendon Press, 1991), 177–178. For useful summaries of British economic performance in this period, see F. T. Blackaby, 'General Appraisal', in *British Economic Policy, 1960–74*, ed. F. T. Blackaby (Cambridge: Cambridge University Press, 1978), 619–655; L. J. Williams, *Britain and the World Economy, 1919–70* (London: Fontana, 1974), 139–154; B. Supple, 'British Economic Decline Since 1945', in *The Economic History of Britain Since 1700*, ed. R. Floud and D. McCloskey (Cambridge: Cambridge University Press, 1995), 3: 318–346.

23. On all of these problems, see Crafts and Woodward, *The British Economy Since 1945*. For Pollard's ideas see his *The Development of the British Economy, 1914–90* (London: Arnold, 1992) and *The Wasting of the British Economy: British Economic Policy, 1945 to the Present* (London: Croom Helm, 1984).

24. See Cairncross, *British Economy Since 1945*, chapter 3 on the 1950s, chapter 4 on the 1960s, and 302–307 specifically on external factors.

25. A. Cairncross, *Years of Recovery: British Economic Policy, 1945–51* (London: Methuen, 1985), 503, and idem, *British Economy Since 1945*, 275; Scammell, *International Economy Since 1945*, 120; Williams, *Britain and the World Economy*, 147–148, 177–180.

26. Reynolds, 'Britain and the World Since 1945', 168, and idem, *Britannia Overruled*, 197, 211–212, 305; Sked and Cook, *Post-War Britain*, 233–234; Coker, 'Foreign and Defence Policy', 7; Young, *Britain and the World*,

172; Dockrill, *British Defence*, 91–96; Dobson, *Anglo-American Relations*, 129–139; Baylis, *Anglo-American Defence Relations*, 91–98; Bartlett, *The Special Relationship*, 118–119; Kennedy, *Realities Behind Diplomacy*, 327–328, 375–376.

27. Wilson, *The Labour Government*, 40; Young, 'Politics Outside the System', 217–218; Healey, *Time of My Life*, 302–304.

28. Stone, 'Britain and the World', 126–127; Holland, *Pursuit of Greatness*, 318–321; Sanders, *Losing an Empire*, 112–120; Darwin, *Britain and Decolonization*, 329, 333.

29. Holland, *European Decolonization*, 269–272; A. Clayton, 'Deceptive Might: Imperial Defence and Security, 1900–68', in *The Oxford History of the British Empire*, ed. J. M. Brown and W. R. Louis (Oxford: Oxford University Press, 1999), 4: 293, 304.

30. M. Chalmers, 'British Economic Decline: The Contribution of Military Spending', *Royal Bank of Scotland Review* 173 (1992): 35–36, 38–43, and idem, *Paying for Defence*, 112–113.

31. The July 1963 white paper on 'central organization for defence' is summarized in Ovendale, *British Defence Policy*, 128.

32. P. Nailor, 'Denis Healey and Rational Decision-Making in Defence', in Beckett and Gooch, *Politicians and Defence*, 161–163; Pimlott, *Harold Wilson*, 382, 385–386, 388; C. Mayhew, *Time to Explain* (London: Hutchinson, 1987), 170–172.

33. Ovendale, *British Defence Policy*, 8, 11, 13–14, 131–136; Lapping, *Labour Government*, 87.

34. Chalmers, *Paying for Defence*, 84–86; Healey, *Time of My Life*, 270–271, 277–280.

35. Darby, *British Defence Policy East of Suez*, 290–298, 304; Pickering, *Britain's Withdrawal from East of Suez*, 162–163.

36. J. Callaghan, *Time and Chance* (London: Collins, 1987), 211–212; E. Pearce, *Denis Healey: A Life in Our Times* (London: Little, Brown, 2002), 324, 341.

37. *Hansard*, 5th series, 751 (1967): 985, 1108, 1110–1111.

38. *The Times*, July 19, 1967; *Economist*, July 22, 1967.

39. Ovendale, *British Defence Policy*, 142–144; Chalmers, *Paying for Defence*, 86–88.

40. Pickering, *Britain's Withdrawal from East of Suez*, 163–168, and idem, 'Politics and "Black Tuesday": Shifting Power in the Cabinet and the Decision to Withdraw from East of Suez, November 1967–January 1968', *Twentieth Century British History* 13 (2002): 144–170.

41. Pickering, *Britain's Withdrawal from East of Suez*, 169–172; Brown, *In My Way*, 141; Pearce, *Denis Healey*, 353–356; Grove, *Vanguard to Trident*, 304–305; Darby, *British Defence Policy East of Suez*, 316–326.
42. Chalmers, *Paying for Defence*, 88–91; Young, *Labour Governments*, 56.
43. Ovendale, *British Defence Policy*, 144–146; Bartlett, *Long Retreat*, 260–261, 263; Lapping, *Labour Government*, 89–90.
44. Pickering, *Britain's Withdrawal from East of Suez*, 177–184.
45. C. Ponting, *Breach of Promise: Labour in Power, 1964–70* (London: Hamish Hamilton, 1989), 105–106, 397–398.
46. Darby, *British Defence Policy East of Suez*; K. Hack, *Defence and Decolonization in South East Asia: Britain, Malaya and Singapore, 1941–68* (Richmond: Curzon, 2001), chapters 1, 8; W. R. Louis, 'The British Withdrawal from the Gulf, 1967–71', *Journal of Imperial and Commonwealth History* 31 (2003): 83–108; J. B. Kelly, *Arabia, the Gulf and the West* (London: Weidenfeld and Nicolson, 1980), 31–32, 101.
47. Pickering, *Britain's Withdrawal from East of Suez*, 172–173; Ziegler, *Wilson*, 329–332.

Chapter 8

1. M. Camps, *European Unification in the Sixties* (London: Oxford University Press, 1967), 191–195.
2. U. Kitzinger, *The Second Try: Labour and the EEC* (Oxford: Pergamon, 1968), 108–112, 179–188; Sked and Cook, *Post-War Britain*, 235; Urwin, *Political History of Western Europe*, chapter 14; de Carmoy, 'Defence and Unity of Western Europe', 363–368; Gowland and Turner, *Britain and European Integration*, 112–113, 117–125.
3. *The Times*, May 17, 1967; *Guardian*, May 17, 1967.
4. Gowland and Turner, *Britain and European Integration*, 123–125.
5. Young, *Britain and the World*, 191.
6. Brown, *In My Way*, 141, 207, 216–222; Howard, ed., *Crossman Diaries*, 311–312. Fear of federalism was excessive in the 1960s (as it had been in the 1950s). In his *History of European Integration*, Peter Stirk points out that the federalists were never able to impose their vision. The survival of the 'third force' idea that a stronger and more united Western Europe could act on the world stage as the equal of the two superpowers is discussed in G. Aybet, *The Dynamics of European Security Cooperation, 1945–91* (London: Macmillan, 1998).
7. Greenwood, *Britain and European Cooperation Since 1945*, 91–92.

8. A. Daltrop, *Politics and the European Community* (London: Longman, 1986), 32–33; Lapping, *Labour Government*, chapter 6; Young, *Labour Governments*, 159.

9. A. D. Morgan, 'Commercial Policy', in Blackaby, *British Economic Policy*, 538–544; Young, *Britain and European Unity*, 93–101.

10. Wilson, *The Labour Government*, 327–344, 386–391; Ziegler, *Wilson*, 331–338; Pimlott, *Harold Wilson*, 432–442; Young, *Britain and European Unity*, 100–101, and idem, *Labour Governments*, 160.

11. Morewood, 'Divided Europe', 19–20; Wakeman, 'Introduction', 4; Larres, 'International and Security Relations Within Europe', 214–216; Young, *Britain and the World*, 178; Heuser, 'NATO's Nuclear Strategy', 46; D. Johnson, 'De Gaulle and France's Role in the World', in *De Gaulle and Twentieth-Century France*, ed. H. Gough and J. Horne (London: Edward Arnold, 1994), 83–94; de Carmoy, 'Defence and Unity of Western Europe', 352–354; Kolodziej, *French International Policy*, 345–375; Lacouture, *De Gaulle*, 363–398; Ulam, *Expansion and Coexistence*, 723–724; W. Laqueur, *Europe in Our Time: A History, 1945–92* (London: Penguin, 1993), 323–327; Urwin, *Political History of Western Europe*, 150, 156, 160–163; F. Costigliola, 'Kennedy, De Gaulle and the Challenge of Consultation', and L. Gardner, 'Lyndon Johnson and De Gaulle', in Paxton and Wahl, *De Gaulle and the United States*, 169–194, 257–278; P. M. H. Bell, *France and Britain, 1940–94: The Long Separation* (London: Longman, 1997), 164–166, 205–206.

12. Harrison, *Reluctant Ally*, 62–71, 129–131; Heuser, *NATO, Britain, France and the FRG*, 120–123.

13. *Hansard*, 5th series, 729 (1966): 1248–1249; *The Times*, March 9, 14, 1966.

14. Young, *Labour Governments*, 135–136.

15. Ziegler, *Wilson*, 209–210; Young, *Labour Governments*, 116–120, 134–135; Pearce, *Denis Healey*, 232, 264–266; Lapping, *Labour Government*, 92–93; Healey, *Time of My Life*, 304–305.

16. Heuser, *NATO, Britain, France and the FRG*, 84–85, 157–158; Larres, 'International and Security Relations Within Europe', 214; Baylis, *Anglo-American Defence Relations*, 72–74, 77–91; Dumbrell, *A Special Relationship*, 125, 137–141, 223; Dobson, *Anglo–American Relations*, 127–130; Bartlett, *The Special Relationship*, 99, 119; Ovendale, *British Defence Policy*, 127; Urwin, *Political History of Western Europe*, 163–164, 169; Hanrieder, *Germany, America, Europe*, 45–50; Costigliola, 'Kennedy, De Gaulle and the Challenge of Consultation', 176, 185–186, 190–192;

Gardner, 'Lyndon Johnson and De Gaulle', 259–265; Lacouture, *De Gaulle*, 341–344, 354, 359, 374, 376, 413–433; Harrison, *Reluctant Ally*, 83–85.

17. Murray, *Kennedy, Macmillan and Nuclear Weapons*, 151, 155–158.

18. Heuser, *NATO, Britain, France and the FRG*, 151–157; Morewood, 'Divided Europe', 20–21; A. Stent, *From Embargo to Ostpolitik: The Political Economy of West German-Soviet Relations, 1955–80* (Cambridge: Cambridge University Press, 1981), 154–163; T. G. Ash, *In Europe's Name: Germany and the Divided Continent* (London: Jonathan Cape, 1993), 53–67; Swain and Swain, *Eastern Europe Since 1945*, 159–161; W. E. Griffith, *The Ostpolitik of the Federal Republic of Germany* (Cambridge, MA: MIT Press, 1978), 181; Stevenson, *Rise and Fall of Détente*, 148–150; Bartlett, *The Special Relationship*, 128; H. Kissinger, *The White House Years* (London: Weidenfeld and Nicolson, 1979), 408–412.

19. A. B. Ulam, *Dangerous Relations: The Soviet Union in World Politics, 1970–82* (New York: Oxford University Press, 1984), 35.

20. Kolodziej, *French International Policy*, chapter 7; Larres, 'International and Security Relations Within Europe', 215–218; Simonian, *Privileged Partnership*, 13, 34–35; Morewood, 'Divided Europe', 20; L. P. de Menil, *Who Speaks for Europe? The Vision of Charles de Gaulle* (London: Weidenfeld and Nicolson, 1977), chapters 7–9; Harrison, *Reluctant Ally*, 112–114; M. Kreile, 'Ostpolitik Reconsidered', in *The Foreign Policy of West Germany: Formation and Contents*, ed. E. Krippendorf and V. Rittberger (London: Sage, 1980), 123–146.

21. G. A. Craig, 'Did Ostpolitik Work?' *Foreign Affairs* 73 (1994): 162–164; M. Sturmer, 'Deutschlandpolitik, Ostpolitik and the Western Alliance: German Perspectives on Détente', in Dyson, *European Détente*, 134–154; Griffith, *Ostpolitik*, chapters 4–5; R. Morgan, 'The Ostpolitik and West Germany's External Relations', in *The Ostpolitik and Political Change in Germany*, ed. R. Tilford (Farnborough: Saxon House, 1975), 95–108; H. Kissinger, 'The Price of German Unity', *The Reporter* 32 (1965): 14; Ash, *In Europe's Name*.

22. Craig, 'Did Ostpolitk Work?' 164–165, 167.

23. Some of the links between 'Ostpolitik' and the wider context are explored in M. E. Sarotte, *Dealing with the Devil: East Germany, Détente and Ostpolitik, 1969–73* (Chapel Hill: University of North Carolina Press, 2001). Sarotte suggests (175) that Bonn was out to challenge the established order, which goes against the views of those historians who think that 'Ostpolitik' was really about stabilization.

24. W. Loth, 'Germany in the Cold War: Strategies and Decisions', and J. M. Hanhimaki, 'Ironies and Turning Points: Détente in Perspective', both in

Westad, *Reviewing the Cold War*, 254–255, 333; Hanrieder, *Germany, America, Europe*, 186–202.

25. Ulam, *Expansion and Coexistence*, 749–755; Sassoon, 'Politics', 37; Larres, 'International and Security Relations Within Europe', 217; Lapping, *Labour Government*, 94; Simonian, *Privileged Partnership*, 181–182; Lacouture, *De Gaulle*, 467–482; Johnson, 'De Gaulle and France's Role in the World', 94; de Carmoy, 'Defence and Unity of Western Europe', 368–370; Kolodziej, *French International Policy*, 375–390; Swain and Swain, *Eastern Europe Since 1945*, 144–145; Schopflin, *Politics in Eastern Europe*, 156–158; Hanrieder, *Germany, America, Europe*, 198–202, 262–268; Adomeit, *Imperial Overstretch*, 112–115.

26. Heuser, 'NATO's Nuclear Strategy', 46–47.

27. *The Times*, February 3, 1969; *Observer*, February 9, 1969.

28. Kissinger, *White House Years*, 88–91.

29. *The Times*, February 3, 1969; Fraser and Murray, *America and the World*, 148–151; Larres, 'International and Security Relations Within Europe', 217; R. Nixon, *RN: The Memoirs of Richard Nixon* (New York: Grosset and Dunlap, 1978), 370–375; Kissinger, *White House Years*, 80–111; Greenwood, *Britain and European Cooperation Since 1945*, 95; A. Gromyko, *Memories* (London: Hutchinson, 1989), 191–193; Stevenson, *Rise and Fall of Détente*, 149; Bell, *France and Britain*, 222, 243; Kolodziej, *French International Policy*, 391–425; S. Berstein and J. P. Rioux, *The Pompidou Years, 1969–74* (Cambridge: Cambridge University Press, 2000), 25–26; H. Young, *This Blessed Plot: Britain and Europe from Churchill to Blair* (Woodstock, NY: Overlook Press, 1999), 234–238; J. Campbell, *Edward Heath: A Biography* (London: Cape, 1993), 352–360; S. George, *An Awkward Partner: Britain in the European Community* (Oxford: Oxford University Press, 1998), 55, 74.

30. Wilson, *The Labour Government*, 765; *Hansard*, 5th series, 797 (1970): 159, 613, 614; *The Times*, March 20, 1970; *Economist*, March 7, 1970.

31. Young, *Labour Governments*, 129–130, 134. Griffith, *Ostpolitik*, 180 suggests that the Wilson government's support for 'Ostpolitik' and détente made little difference, primarily because of Britain's economic weakness.

32. LaFeber, *America, Russia and the Cold War*, 272–273; Cromwell, *The United States and the European Pillar*, 76–77.

CHAPTER 9

1. T. G. Fraser, *The Arab-Israeli Conflict* (Basingstoke: Macmillan, 1995), 81–85; Johnson, *Modern World*, 666; Kantowicz, *Coming Apart, Coming*

Together, 361, 363, 367; M. Brecher, *Decisions in Israel's Foreign Policy* (London: Oxford University Press, 1974), chapter 7; Fraser and Murray, *America and the World*, 137; Ulam, *Expansion and Coexistence*, 731–737; F. J. Khouri, 'United Nations Peace Efforts', in *The Elusive Peace in the Middle East*, ed. M. H. Kerr (Albany: State University of New York Press, 1975), 58–63.

2. Howard, ed., *Crossman Diaries*, 314–316; Young, *Labour Governments*, 103–105.

3. *Hansard*, 5th series, 749 (1967): 2010–2020, 2115–2118, 2121–2123.

4. *The Times*, June 6, 1967.

5. W. B. Quandt, *Decade of Decisions: American Policy Toward the Arab-Israeli Conflict, 1967–76* (Berkeley: University of California Press, 1977), 39–40; N. Aruri, 'U.S. Policy Toward the Arab-Israeli Conflict', in *The United States and the Middle East: A Search for New Perspectives*, ed. H. Amirahmadi (Albany: State University of New York Press, 1993), 98–99; Fraser, *The USA and the Middle East*, 78–83.

6. W. B. Quandt, *Peace Process: American Diplomacy and the Arab-Israeli Conflict Since 1967* (Washington, DC: Brookings Institution, 1993), 23–26, 29, 33–35, 37, 40–41, 43–48, 60.

7. E. Hammel, *Six Days in June: How Israel Won the 1967 Arab-Israeli War* (New York: Ibooks, 2003), 92, 139, 397; C. W. Yost, 'The Arab-Israeli War: How It Began', *Foreign Affairs* 46 (1967–68): 304–320; M. Brecher and B. Geist, *Decisions in Crisis: Israel, 1967 and 1973* (Berkeley: University of California Press, 1980), 104, 117, 151.

8. *The Times*, June 27, 1967; *Guardian*, June 27, 1967.

9. Brown, *In My Way*, 233–234, 279–280.

10. P. J. Vatikiotis, *Nasser and His Generation* (London: Croom Helm, 1978), 253–260; P. Woodward, *Nasser* (London: Longman, 1992), 103–127; Kantowicz, *Coming Apart, Coming Together*, 368–369; Aruri, 'U.S. Policy', 99–101; Quandt, *Decade of Decisions*, chapters 2–5, and idem, *Peace Process*, chapter 3; Nixon, *Memoirs*, 477–483; Fraser and Murray, *America and the World*, 137–139; Ulam, *Dangerous Relations*, 40; Brecher, *Decisions in Israel's Foreign Policy*, chapter 8; Khouri, 'United Nations Peace Efforts', 63–82, 87–89; J. C. Campbell, 'American Efforts for Peace', in Kerr, *Elusive Peace*, 283–305; Fraser, *Arab-Israeli Conflict*, 85–99, and idem, *The USA and the Middle East*, 83–97; Meisler, *United Nations*, chapter 10.

11. Young, *Labour Governments*, 106–108.

12. Ulam, *Expansion and Coexistence*, 728, 737; Gromyko, *Memories*, 267–272.

13. Quandt, *Decade of Decisions*, 68, 83, 85, 90, 112, 116, 122–123, 182–183, and idem, *Peace Process*, 5–6; R. Cohen, *Culture and Conflict in Egyptian-Israeli Relations: A Dialogue of the Deaf* (Bloomington: Indiana University Press, 1990).

14. Sassoon, 'Politics', 38; Kantowicz, *Coming Apart, Coming Together*, 349–351; Schopflin, *Politics in Eastern Europe*, 152–156; Zeman, *Making and Breaking of Communist Europe*, 278–282; L. R. Johnson, *Central Europe: Enemies, Neighbours, Friends* (New York: Oxford University Press, 1996), 252–254, 257–258; Ulam, *Expansion and Coexistence*, 738–746; Swain and Swain, *Eastern Europe Since 1945*, 140–145; G. Stokes, *The Walls Came Tumbling Down: The Collapse of Communism in Eastern Europe* (New York: Oxford University Press, 1993), 13–14, 65–67; Berend, *Central and Eastern Europe*, 136–146.

15. K. Williams, *The Prague Spring and Its Aftermath: Czechoslovak Politics, 1968–70* (Cambridge: Cambridge University Press, 1997), 5, 110–111; J. Valenta, *Soviet Invasion of Czechoslovakia, 1968: Anatomy of a Decision* (Baltimore: Johns Hopkins University Press, 1979), 130, 147.

16. Young, *Labour Governments*, 132–133.

17. *The Times*, August 24, 1968.

18. *Economist*, August 24, 1968; *Observer*, August 25, 1968.

19. Brown, *In My Way*, 75; Howard, ed., *Crossman Diaries*, 467–468; *Hansard*, 5th series, 769 (1968): 1274–1275, 1277–1278, 1281–1282, 1284–1292.

20. Dockrill, *British Defence*, 97; Baylis, *Anglo-American Defence Relations*, 96.

21. Morewood, 'Divided Europe', 19; Ulam, *Expansion and Coexistence*, 745–746; Larres, 'International and Security Relations Within Europe', 196; J. Dornberg, *Brezhnev: The Masks of Power* (London: Deutsch, 1974), 219–229; Kantowicz, *Coming Apart, Coming Together*, 353, 355; Berend, 'Central and Eastern European Revolution', 190–193; Johnson, *Central Europe*, 258; Laqueur, *Europe in Our Time*, 354–361; Schopflin, *Politics in Eastern Europe*, 157; B. Fowkes, *The Rise and Fall of Communism in Eastern Europe* (Basingstoke: Macmillan, 1993), 132–144; A. Hyde-Price, *The International Politics of East Central Europe* (Manchester: Manchester University Press, 1996), 16, 23, 27, 31, 34–35; K. Dawisha, *The Kremlin and the Prague Spring* (Berkeley: University of California Press, 1984), 315–316; P. Windsor and A. Roberts, *Czechoslovakia 1968: Reform, Repression and Resistance* (London: Chatto and Windus, 1969), 105, 114, 118–127, 132–136; A. Dubcek, *Hope Dies Last: The Autobiography of Alexander Dubcek* (London: HarperCollins, 1993), 203, 205, 213, 219; Williams, *Prague Spring*, 132, 251.

22. Valenta, *Soviet Invasion of Czechoslovakia*, 160–161.
23. R. A. Jones, *The Soviet Concept of Limited Sovereignty from Lenin to Gorbachev: The Brezhnev Doctrine* (Basingstoke: Macmillan, 1990), 17, 27, 237, 257; M. J. Ouimet, *The Rise and Fall of the Brezhnev Doctrine in Soviet Foreign Policy* (Chapel Hill: University of North Carolina Press, 2003), 3, 26–27, 36–37.
24. Gromyko, *Memories*, 232–233.
25. Stevenson, *Rise and Fall of Détente*, 135–136; Young, *Labour Governments*, 133–134; Valenta, *Soviet Invasion of Czechoslovakia*, 161; Gaddis, *Long Peace*, 230, 239, and idem, *We Now Know*, 51; Dawisha, *Kremlin and the Prague Spring*, 380.
26. Stokes, *Walls Came Tumbling Down*, 67–68; C. Gati, *The Bloc that Failed: Soviet-East European Relations in Transition* (Bloomington: Indiana University Press, 1990), 43–48, 57.
27. H. Friedmann, 'Warsaw Pact Socialism: Détente and the Disintegration of the Soviet Bloc', in *Rethinking the Cold War*, ed. A. Hunter (Philadelphia: Temple University Press, 1998), 218–219.
28. Friedmann, 'Warsaw Pact Socialism', 226–228; Berend, *Central and Eastern Europe*, 153, 222–232.
29. See *Dismantling Communism: Common Causes and Regional Variations*, ed. G. Rozman, S. Sato and G. Segal (Baltimore: Johns Hopkins University Press, 1993).
30. Fowkes, *Rise and Fall of Communism*, 194; Friedberg, 'The United States and the Cold War Arms Race', 207, 220–222.
31. Hanhimaki, 'Ironies and Turning Points', 333, 337–338; W. Loth, 'Moscow, Prague and Warsaw: Overcoming the Brezhnev Doctrine', *Cold War History* 1 (2001): 103–118.

CONCLUSION

1. This thesis is advanced in Darby, *British Defence Policy East of Suez*.
2. Chalmers, *Paying for Defence*, 40.
3. P. Warwick, 'Did Britain Change? An Inquiry into the Causes of National Decline', *Journal of Contemporary History* 20 (1985): 99–133.
4. Pickering, *Britain's Withdrawal from East of Suez*, 87, 107, 123, 166.
5. Healey, *Time of My Life*, 277; M. Stewart, *Life and Labour* (London: Sidgwick and Jackson, 1980), 233; Ziegler, *Wilson*, 211.
6. Healey, *Time of My Life*, 299–300.
7. Young, *Labour Governments*, 225.

8. Ibid., 54–56.

9. Lapping, *Labour Government*, 91–92.

10. P. Clarke, *Hope and Glory: Britain, 1900–2000* (London: Penguin, 2004), 441–443.

11. These are among the central themes in Young's *Britain and European Unity*.

12. Z. Steiner, 'British Power and Stability: The Historical Record', *Diplomacy and Statecraft* 14 (2003): 23–44.

13. G. H. Soutou, 'Was There a European Order in the Twentieth Century? From the Concert of Europe to the End of the Cold War', *Contemporary European History* 9 (2000): 329–353.

14. S. Ryan, *The United Nations and International Politics* (London: Macmillan, 2000), 49.

15. Alan Dobson takes this position in his *Anglo-American Relations*.

16. A. Priest, 'In American Hands: Britain, the United States and the Polaris Nuclear Project, 1962–68', *Contemporary British History* 19 (2005): 353–376.

17. Cited in Ovendale, *British Defence Policy*, 131–134.

SELECT BIBLIOGRAPHY

Adam, J. *Economic Reforms in the Soviet Union and Eastern Europe Since the 1960s*. Basingstoke: Macmillan, 1989.

Adomeit, H. *Imperial Overstretch: Germany in Soviet Policy from Stalin to Gorbachev*. Baden-Baden: Nomos Verlagsgesellschaft, 1998.

Aldcroft, D. H. *The European Economy, 1914–90*. London: Routledge, 1993.

Aldous, R., and S. Lee, eds. *Harold Macmillan and Britain's World Role*. Basingstoke: Macmillan, 1996.

———, eds. *Harold Macmillan: Aspects of a Political Life*. Basingstoke: Macmillan, 1999.

Allison, G. T., and P. D. Zelikow. *Essence of a Decision: Explaining the Cuban Missile Crisis*. rev. ed. New York: Longman, 1999.

Alter, P. *The German Question and Europe: A History*. London: Hodder and Stoughton, 2000.

Ambrose, S. *Eisenhower: Soldier and President*. New York: Simon and Schuster, 1990.

———. *Eisenhower: The President*. London: Allen and Unwin, 1984.

Ambrosius, G., and W. H. Hubbard. *A Social and Economic History of Twentieth-Century Europe*. Cambridge, MA: Harvard University Press, 1989.

Amirahmadi, H., ed. *The United States and the Middle East: A Search for New Perspectives*. Albany: State University of New York Press, 1993.

Andrew, C. *For the President's Eyes Only: Secret Intelligence and the American Presidency from Washington to Bush*. London: Harper-Collins, 1995.

Ash, T. G. *In Europe's Name: Germany and the Divided Continent*. London: Jonathan Cape, 1993.

Ausland, J. C. *Kennedy, Khrushchev and the Berlin-Cuba Crisis, 1961–64*. Oslo: Aschehoug AS, 1996.

Aybet, G. *The Dynamics of European Security Cooperation, 1945–91*. London: Macmillan, 1998.

Balfour-Paul, G. *The End of Empire in the Middle East: Britain's Relinquishment of Power in her Last Three Arab Dependencies*. Cambridge: Cambridge University Press, 1991.

Bartlett, C. J. *The Long Retreat: A Short History of British Defence Policy, 1945–70*. London: Macmillan, 1972.

———. *The Special Relationship: A Political History of Anglo-American Relations Since 1945*. London: Longman, 1992.

Bathrick, D. *The Powers of Speech: The Politics of Culture in the GDR*. Lincoln: University of Nebraska Press, 1995.

Baylis, J. *Anglo-American Defence Relations, 1939–80: The Special Relationship*. London: Macmillan, 1981.

Beckerman, W., ed. *The Labour Government's Economic Record, 1964–70*. London: Duckworth, 1972.

Beckett, I., and J. Gooch, eds. *Politicians and Defence: Studies in the Formulation of British Defence Policy, 1845–1970*. Manchester: Manchester University Press, 1981.

Bell, L. *The Throw that Failed: Britain's 1961 Application to Join the Common Market*. London: New European Publications, 1995.

Bell, P. M. H. *France and Britain, 1940–94: The Long Separation*. London: Longman, 1997.

Berend, I. T. *Central and Eastern Europe, 1944–93*. Cambridge: Cambridge University Press, 1996.

Berend, I. T., and G. Ranki. *Hungary: A Century of Economic Development*. Newton Abbot: David and Charles, 1974.

Berstein, S., and J. P. Rioux. *The Pompidou Years, 1969–74*. Cambridge: Cambridge University Press, 2000.

Bird, K. *The Colour of Truth: McGeorge Bundy and William Bundy, Brothers in Arms*. New York: Simon and Schuster, 1998.

Blackaby, F. T., ed. *British Economic Policy, 1960–74*. Cambridge: Cambridge University Press, 1978.

Bogdanor, V., and R. Skidelsky, eds. *The Age of Affluence, 1951–64*. London: Macmillan, 1970.

Boltho, A., ed. *The European Economy: Growth and Crisis*. Oxford: Oxford University Press, 1982.

Botti, T. J. *The Long Wait: The Forging of the Anglo-American Nuclear Alliance, 1945–58*. Westport, CT: Greenwood Press, 1987.

Brecher, M. *Decisions in Israel's Foreign Policy*. London: Oxford University Press, 1974.

Brecher, M., and B. Geist. *Decisions in Crisis: Israel, 1967 and 1973*. Berkeley: University of California Press, 1980.

Brinkley, D., and R. T. Griffiths, eds. *John F. Kennedy and Europe*. Baton Rouge: Louisiana State University Press, 1999.

Brown, J. M., and W. R. Louis, eds. *The Oxford History of the British Empire*. 5 vols. Oxford: Oxford University Press, 1999.

Burk, K., ed. *The British Isles Since 1945*. Oxford: Oxford University Press, 2003.

Busch, P. *All the Way with JFK? Britain, the United States and the Vietnam War*. Oxford: Oxford University Press, 2003.

Cairncross, A. *The British Economy Since 1945: Economic Policy and Performance, 1945–1990*. Oxford: Blackwell, 1992.

———. *Years of Recovery: British Economic Policy, 1945–51*. London: Methuen, 1985.

Campbell, J. *Edward Heath: A Biography*. London: Cape, 1993.

Camps, M. *Britain and the European Community, 1955–63*. London: Oxford University Press, 1965.

———. *European Unification in the Sixties*. London: Oxford University Press, 1967.

Chalmers, M. *Paying for Defence: Military Spending and British Decline*. London: Pluto Press, 1985.

Charlton, M. *The Price of Victory*. London: British Broadcasting Corporation, 1983.

Clark, I. *Nuclear Diplomacy and the Special Relationship: Britain's Deterrent and America, 1957–62*. Oxford: Clarendon Press, 1994.

Clarke, P. *Hope and Glory: Britain, 1900–2000*. London: Penguin, 2004.

Cohen, R. *Culture and Conflict in Egyptian-Israeli Relations: A Dialogue of the Deaf*. Bloomington: Indiana University Press, 1990.

Coopey, R., S. Fielding, and N. Tiratsoo, eds. *The Wilson Governments, 1964–70*. London: Pinter, 1993.

Crafts, N., and G. Toniolo, eds. *Economic Growth in Europe Since 1945*. Cambridge: Cambridge University Press, 1996.

Crafts, N., and N. Woodward, eds. *The British Economy Since 1945*. Oxford: Clarendon Press, 1991.

Crampton, R. J. *Eastern Europe in the Twentieth Century and After*. London: Routledge, 2003.

Cromwell, W. C. *The United States and the European Pillar: The Strained Alliance*. Basingstoke: Palgrave Macmillan, 1992.

Daltrop, A. *Politics and the European Community*. London: Longman, 1986.

Darby, P. *British Defence Policy East of Suez, 1947–68*. London: Oxford University Press, 1973.

Darwin, J. *Britain and Decolonization: The Retreat from Empire in the Post-War World*. Basingstoke: Macmillan, 1988.

————. *The End of the British Empire: The Historical Debate*. Oxford: Basil Blackwell, 1991.

Daum, A. W., L. C. Gardner, and W. Mausbach, eds. *America, the Vietnam War and the World: Comparative and International Perspectives*. Cambridge: Cambridge University Press, 2003.

Davies, N. *Heart of Europe: A Short History of Poland*. Oxford: Clarendon Press, 1991.

Dawisha, K. *The Kremlin and the Prague Spring*. London: University of California Press, 1984.

DiLeo, D. L. *George Ball, Vietnam and the Rethinking of Containment*. Chapel Hill: University of North Carolina Press, 1991.

Dinerstein, H. S. *The Making of a Missile Crisis: October 1962*. Baltimore: Johns Hopkins University Press, 1976.

Dobson, A. P. *Anglo-American Relations in the Twentieth Century*. London: Routledge, 1995.

Dockrill, M. *British Defence Since 1945*. Oxford: Basil Blackwell, 1988.

Dockrill, M., and J. W. Young, eds. *British Foreign Policy, 1945–56*. Basingstoke: Macmillan, 1989.

Dornberg, J. *Brezhnev: The Masks of Power*. London: Deutsch, 1974.

Dow, J. C. R. *The Management of the British Economy, 1945–60*. Cambridge: Cambridge University Press, 1970.

Dumbrell, J. *A Special Relationship: Anglo-American Relations in the Cold War and After*. Basingstoke: Macmillan, 2001.

Dyson, K., ed. *European Détente: Case Studies of the Politics of East-West Relations*. London: Pinter, 1986.

Eckstein, S. E. *Back from the Future: Cuba Under Castro*. Princeton, NJ: Princeton University Press, 1994.

Ellis, S. *Britain, America and the Vietnam War*. Westport, CT: Praeger, 2004.

Fieldhouse, D. K. *Black Africa, 1945–80: Economic Decolonization and Arrested Development*. London: Allen and Unwin, 1986.

Fischer-Galati, S. *Twentieth Century Rumania*. New York: Columbia University Press, 1970.

Floud, R., and D. McCloskey, eds. *The Economic History of Britain Since 1700*. 3 vols. Cambridge: Cambridge University Press, 1995.

Fowkes, B. *The Rise and Fall of Communism in Eastern Europe*. Basingstoke: Macmillan, 1993.

Fraser, T. G. *The Arab-Israeli Conflict*. Basingstoke: Macmillan, 1995.

———. *The USA and the Middle East Since World War Two*. Basingstoke: Macmillan, 1989.

Fraser, T. G., and D. Murray. *America and the World Since 1945*. Basingstoke: Palgrave Macmillan, 2002.

Freedman, L. *Kennedy's Wars: Berlin, Cuba, Laos and Vietnam*. Oxford: Oxford University Press, 2002.

Fulbrook, M., ed. *Europe Since 1945*. Oxford: Oxford University Press, 2001.

———, ed. *German History Since 1800*. London: Arnold, 1997.

Fursenko, A., and T. Naftali. *One Hell of a Gamble: Khrushchev, Castro, Kennedy and the Cuban Missile Crisis, 1958–64*. London: Norton, 1997.

Gaddis, J. L. *The Long Peace: Inquiries into the History of the Cold War*. New York: Oxford University Press, 1987.

———. *We Now Know: Rethinking Cold War History*. Oxford: Clarendon Press, 1998.

Garthoff, R. L. *Reflections on the Cuban Missile Crisis*. Washington, DC: Brookings Institution, 1989.

Gati, C. *The Bloc that Failed: Soviet-East European Relations in Transition*. Bloomington: Indiana University Press, 1990.

————. *Hungary and the Soviet Bloc*. Durham, NC: Duke University Press, 1986.

Gearson, J. P. S. *Harold Macmillan and the Berlin Wall Crisis, 1958–62: The Limits of Interest and Force*. Basingstoke: Macmillan, 1998.

Gearson, J. P. S., and K. Schake, eds. *The Berlin Wall Crisis: Perspectives on Cold War Alliances*. Basingstoke: Palgrave Macmillan, 2002.

Gelb, L. H., and R. K. Betts. *The Irony of Vietnam: The System Worked*. Washington, DC: Brookings Institution, 1979.

George, S. *An Awkward Partner: Britain in the European Community*. Oxford: Oxford University Press, 1998.

————. *Britain and European Integration Since 1945*. Oxford: Blackwell, 1991.

Gifford, P., and W. R. Louis, eds. *Decolonization and African Independence: The Transfers of Power, 1960–80*. London: Yale University Press, 1988.

————, eds. *The Transfer of Power in Africa: Decolonization, 1940–60*. London: Yale University Press, 1982.

Giglio, J. N. *The Presidency of John F. Kennedy*. Lawrence: University Press of Kansas, 1991.

Gilberg, T. *Nationalism and Communism in Rumania: The Rise and Fall of Ceausescu's Personal Dictatorship*. Oxford: Westview, 1990.

Gough, H., and J. Horne, eds. *De Gaulle and Twentieth-Century France*. London: Edward Arnold, 1994.

Gowland, D., and A. Turner, eds. *Britain and European Integration, 1945–98: A Documentary History*. London: Routledge, 2000.

Granieri, R. J. *The Ambivalent Alliance: Konrad Adenauer, the CDU/ CSU and the West, 1949–66*. Oxford: Berghahn, 2003.

Greenwood, S. *Britain and European Cooperation Since 1945*. Oxford: Blackwell, 1992.

Griffith, W. E. *The Ostpolitik of the Federal Republic of Germany*. Cambridge, MA: MIT Press, 1978.

Grove, E. J. *Vanguard to Trident: British Naval Policy Since World War Two*. London: Bodley Head, 1987.

Hack, K. *Defence and Decolonization in South East Asia: Britain, Malaya and Singapore, 1941–68*. Richmond: Curzon, 2001.

Halberstam, D. *The Best and the Brightest*. New York: Random House, 1972.

Hammel, E. *Six Days in June: How Israel Won the 1967 Arab-Israeli War*. New York: Ibooks, 2003.

Hanrieder, W. F. *Germany, America, Europe: Forty Years of German Foreign Policy*. New Haven, CT: Yale University Press, 1989.

Hargreaves, J. D. *Decolonization in Africa*. London: Longman, 1996.

Harper, P., and J. P. Krieg, eds. *John F. Kennedy: The Promise Revisited*. Westport, CT: Greenwood Press, 1988.

Harrison, M. M. *The Reluctant Ally: France and Atlantic Security*. London: Johns Hopkins University Press, 1981.

Hatcher, P. L. *The Suicide of an Elite: American Internationalists and Vietnam*. Stanford, CA: Stanford University Press, 1990.

Heuser, B. *NATO, Britain, France and the FRG: Nuclear Strategies and Forces for Europe, 1949–2000*. Basingstoke: Macmillan, 1997.

———. *Western 'Containment' Policies in the Cold War: The Yugoslav Case, 1948–53*. London: Routledge, 1988.

Higgins, T. *The Perfect Failure: Kennedy, Eisenhower and the CIA at the Bay of Pigs*. New York: Norton, 1987.

Hilty, J. W. *Robert Kennedy: Brother Protector*. Philadelphia: Temple University Press, 1997.

Hinds, A. *Britain's Sterling Colonial Policy and Decolonization, 1939–58*. Westport, CT: Greenwood Press, 2001.

Holland, R. *European Decolonization, 1918–81*. Basingstoke: Macmillan, 1985.

———. *The Pursuit of Greatness: Britain and the World Role, 1900–70*. London: Routledge, 1991.

Hollowell, J., ed. *Britain Since 1945*. Oxford: Blackwell, 2003.

Horne, A. *Macmillan, 1957–86*. London: Macmillan, 1989.

Hunter, A., ed. *Rethinking the Cold War*. Philadelphia: Temple University Press, 1998.

Hyde-Price, A. *The International Politics of East Central Europe*. Manchester: Manchester University Press, 1996.

Irving, R. *Adenauer*. London: Longman, 2002.

Jeffreys-Jones, R. *The CIA and American Democracy*. New Haven, CT: Yale University Press, 1989.

Johnson, L. K. *America's Secret Power*. New York: Oxford University Press, 1989.

Johnson, L. R. *Central Europe: Enemies, Neighbours, Friends*. New York: Oxford University Press, 1996.

Johnson, P. *A History of the Modern World*. London: Weidenfeld and Nicolson, 1984.

———, ed. *Twentieth Century Britain: Economic, Social and Cultural Change*. London: Longman, 1996.

Jones, R. A. *The Soviet Concept of Limited Sovereignty from Lenin to Gorbachev: The Brezhnev Doctrine*. Basingstoke: Macmillan, 1990.

Judd, D., and P. Slinn. *The Evolution of the Modern Commonwealth, 1902–80*. London: Macmillan, 1982.

Kahin, G. M. *Intervention: How America Became Involved in Vietnam*. Garden City, NY: Knopf, 1987.

Kahler, M. *Decolonization in Britain and France: The Domestic Consequences of International Relations*. Princeton, NJ: Princeton University Press, 1984.

Kaiser, W. *Using Europe, Abusing the Europeans: Britain and European Integration, 1945–63*. Basingstoke: Macmillan, 1996.

Kalb, M. G. *The Congo Cables: The Cold War in Africa, from Eisenhower to Kennedy*. New York: Macmillan, 1982.

Kantowicz, E. R. *Coming Apart, Coming Together*. Grand Rapids, MI: Eerdmans Publishing, 2000.

Keep, J. *The Last of the Empires: A History of the Soviet Union, 1945–91*. Oxford: Oxford University Press, 1996.

Kelly, J. B. *Arabia, the Gulf and the West*. London: Weidenfeld and Nicolson, 1980.

Kennedy, P. *The Realities Behind Diplomacy: Background Influences on British External Policy, 1865–1980*. London: Allen and Unwin, 1981.

———. *Strategy and Diplomacy: Eight Studies*. London: Fontana, 1989.

Kerr, M. H., ed. *The Elusive Peace in the Middle East*. Albany: State University of New York Press, 1975.

Kitchen, M. *The British Empire and Commonwealth*. Basingstoke: Macmillan, 1996.

Kitzinger, U. *The European Common Market and Community*. London: Routledge and Kegan Paul, 1967.

———. *The Second Try: Labour and the EEC*. Oxford: Pergamon, 1968.

Kolodziej, E. A. *French International Policy Under De Gaulle and Pompidou: The Politics of Grandeur*. Ithaca, NY: Cornell University Press, 1974.

Krippendorf, E., and V. Rittberger, eds. *The Foreign Policy of West Germany: Formation and Contents*. London: Sage, 1980.

Krozewski, G. *Money and the End of Empire: British International Economic Policy and the Colonies, 1947–58*. Basingstoke: Palgrave, 2001.

Lacouture, J. *De Gaulle: The Ruler, 1945–70*. Translated by A. Sheridan. London: Harvill, 1991.

LaFeber, W. *America, Russia and the Cold War, 1945–2002*. Boston: McGraw-Hill, 2002.

Lamb, R. *The Failure of the Eden Government*. London: Sidgwick and Jackson, 1987.

Lapping, B. *End of Empire*. London: Granada, 1985.

———. *The Labour Government, 1964–70*. Harmondsworth: Penguin, 1970.

Laqueur, W. *Europe in Our Time: A History, 1945–92*. London: Penguin, 1993.

Layton-Henry, Z. *The Politics of Immigration*. Oxford: Blackwell, 1992.

Logevall, F. *Choosing War: The Lost Chance for Peace and the Escalation of War in Vietnam*. Berkeley: University of California Press, 1999.

Louis, W. R., and H. Bull, eds. *The 'Special Relationship': Anglo-American Relations Since 1945*. Oxford: Clarendon Press, 1989.

Ludlow, N. P. *Dealing with Britain: The Six and the First UK Application to the EEC*. Cambridge: Cambridge University Press, 1997.

Lundestad, G. *'Empire' by Integration: The United States and European Integration, 1945–97*. Oxford: Oxford University Press, 1998.

Mann, R. *A Grand Delusion: America's Descent into Vietnam*. New York: Basic Books, 2001.

Marchetti, V., and J. D. Marks. *The CIA and the Cult of Intelligence.* London: Cape, 1974.

May, E. R., and P. D. Zelikow, eds. *The Kennedy Tapes: Inside the White House During the Cuban Missile Crisis.* Cambridge, MA: Belknap Press, 1997.

McIntyre, W. D. *The Commonwealth of Nations: Origins and Impact, 1869–1971.* Minneapolis: University of Minnesota Press, 1977.

McKie, D., and C. Cook, eds. *The Decade of Disillusion: British Politics in the Sixties.* London: Macmillan, 1972.

Meisler, S. *United Nations: The First Fifty Years.* New York: Atlantic Monthly Press, 1995.

Menil, L. P. de. *Who Speaks for Europe? The Vision of Charles de Gaulle.* London: Weidenfeld and Nicolson, 1977.

Mohiddin, A. *African Socialism in Two Countries.* London: Croom Helm, 1981.

Morgan, D. J. *The Official History of Colonial Development.* 5 vols. London: Macmillan, 1980.

Murray, D. *Kennedy, Macmillan and Nuclear Weapons.* Basingstoke: Macmillan, 2000.

Nash, P. *The Other Missiles of October: Eisenhower, Kennedy and the Jupiters, 1957–63.* Chapel Hill: University of North Carolina Press, 1997.

Neustadt, R. E. *Report to JFK: The Skybolt Crisis in Perspective.* Ithaca, NY: Cornell University Press, 1999.

Northedge, F. S. *Descent from Power: British Foreign Policy, 1945–73.* London: Allen and Unwin, 1974.

Nove, A. *An Economic History of the USSR, 1917–91.* Harmondsworth: Penguin, 1992.

Nunnerley, A. *President Kennedy and Britain.* London: Bodley Head, 1972.

Oliver, K. *Kennedy, Macmillan and the Nuclear Test Ban Debate, 1961–63*. Basingstoke: Macmillan, 1998.

Oudenaren, J. van. *Détente in Europe: The Soviet Union and the West Since 1953*. Durham, NC: Duke University Press, 1991.

Ouimet, M. J. *The Rise and Fall of the Brezhnev Doctrine in Soviet Foreign Policy*. Chapel Hill: University of North Carolina Press, 2003.

Ovendale, R. *British Defence Policy Since 1945*. Manchester: Manchester University Press, 1994.

Paterson, T. G. *Contesting Castro: The United States and the Triumph of the Cuban Revolution*. New York: Oxford University Press, 1994.

——, ed. *Kennedy's Quest for Victory: American Foreign Policy, 1961–63*. New York: Oxford University Press, 1989.

Paxton, R. O., and N. Wahl, eds. *De Gaulle and the United States: A Centennial Reappraisal*. Oxford: Berg, 1994.

Pearce, E. *Denis Healey: A Life in Our Times*. London: Little, Brown, 2002.

Pickering, J. *Britain's Withdrawal from East of Suez: The Politics of Retrenchment*. Basingstoke: Macmillan, 1998.

Pierre, A. J. *Nuclear Politics: The British Experience with an Independent Strategic Force, 1939–70*. London: Oxford University Press, 1972.

Pimlott, B. *Harold Wilson*. London: HarperCollins, 1992.

Pollard, S. *The Development of the British Economy, 1914–90*. London: Arnold, 1992.

——. *The Wasting of the British Economy: British Economic Policy, 1945 to the Present*. London: Croom Helm, 1984.

Pommerin, R., ed. *The American Impact on Post-War Germany*. Oxford: Berghahn, 1995.

Ponting, C. *Breach of Promise: Labour in Power, 1964–70*. London: Hamish Hamilton, 1989.

Porter, B. *The Lion's Share: A Short History of British Imperialism, 1850–1995*. Harlow: Longman, 1996.

Prittie, T. *Konrad Adenauer*. London: Tom Stacey, 1972.

Quandt, W. B. *Decade of Decisions: American Policy Toward the Arab-Israeli Conflict, 1967–76*. Berkeley: University of California Press, 1977.

———. *Peace Process: American Diplomacy and the Arab-Israeli Conflict Since 1967*. Washington, DC: Brookings Institution, 1993.

Quirk, R. E. *Fidel Castro*. New York: Norton, 1993.

Rabe, S. G. *The Most Dangerous Area in the World: John F. Kennedy Confronts Communist Revolution in Latin America*. Chapel Hill: University of North Carolina Press, 1999.

Reeves, R. *President Kennedy: Profile of Power*. London: Papermac, 1993.

Reynolds, D. *Britannia Overruled: British Policy and World Power in the Twentieth Century*. Harlow: Longman, 2000.

Richter, J. G. *Khrushchev's Double Bind: International Pressures and Domestic Coalition Politics*. Baltimore: Johns Hopkins University Press, 1994.

Ridley, J. *Tito*. London: Constable, 1994.

Rozman, G., S. Sato, and G. Segal, eds. *Dismantling Communism: Common Causes and Regional Variations*. Baltimore: Johns Hopkins University Press, 1993.

Russell, R. L. *George F. Kennan's Strategic Thought*. Westport, CT: Praeger, 1999.

Ryan, S. *The United Nations and International Politics*. London: Macmillan, 2000.

Sampson, A. *Macmillan: A Study in Ambiguity*. London: Allen Lane, 1967.

Sanders, D. *Losing an Empire, Finding a Role: British Foreign Policy Since 1945*. Basingstoke: Macmillan, 1990.

Sarotte, M. E. *Dealing with the Devil: East Germany, Détente and Ost-politik, 1969–73*. Chapel Hill: University of North Carolina Press, 2001.

Scammell, W. M. *The International Economy Since 1945*. Basingstoke: Macmillan, 1983.

Schaad, M. P. C. *Bullying Bonn: Anglo-German Diplomacy on European Integration, 1955–61*. New York: St. Martin's Press, 2000.

Schick, J. M. *The Berlin Crisis, 1958–62*. Philadelphia: University of Pennsylvania Press, 1971.

Schlesinger, A. M. *Robert Kennedy and His Times*. Boston: Houghton Mifflin, 1978.

———. *A Thousand Days: John F. Kennedy in the White House*. London: Deutsch, 1965.

Schopflin, G. *Politics in Eastern Europe, 1945–92*. Oxford: Blackwell, 1993.

Scott, L. *Macmillan, Kennedy and the Cuban Missile Crisis: Political, Military and Intelligence Aspects*. Basingstoke: Macmillan, 1999.

Shen, R. *Economic Reform in Poland and Czechoslovakia*. Westport, CT: Praeger, 1993.

Sidey, H. *John F. Kennedy: Portrait of a President*. London: Deutsch, 1964.

Simonian, H. *The Privileged Partnership: Franco-German Relations in the European Community, 1969–84*. Oxford: Clarendon Press, 1985.

Simpson, J. *The Independent Nuclear State: The United States, Britain and the Military Atom*. London: Macmillan, 1983.

Sked, A., and C. Cook. *Post-War Britain: A Political History*. London: Penguin, 1993.

Slusser, R. M. *The Berlin Crisis of 1961*. Baltimore: Johns Hopkins University Press, 1973.

Spencer, I. R. G. *British Immigration Policy Since 1939: The Making of Multiracial Britain*. London: Routledge, 1997.

Stent, A. *From Embargo to Ostpolitik: The Political Economy of West German–Soviet Relations, 1955–80*. Cambridge: Cambridge University Press, 1981.

Stevenson, R. W. *The Rise and Fall of Détente: Relaxations of Tension in U.S.-Soviet Relations, 1953–84*. Basingstoke: Macmillan, 1985.

Stirk, P. M. R. *A History of European Integration Since 1914*. London: Pinter, 1996.

Stokes, G. *The Walls Came Tumbling Down: The Collapse of Communism in Eastern Europe*. New York: Oxford University Press, 1993.

Strange, S. *Sterling and British Policy: A Political Study of an International Currency in Decline*. London: Oxford University Press, 1971.

Subritzky, J. *Confronting Sukarno: British, American, Australian and New Zealand Diplomacy in the Malaysian-Indonesian Confrontation, 1961–65*. Basingstoke: Macmillan, 2000.

Swain, G., and N. Swain. *Eastern Europe Since 1945*. Basingstoke: Macmillan, 1998.

Tarling, N. *The Fall of Imperial Britain in South East Asia*. Kuala Lumpur: Oxford University Press, 1993.

Tatu, M. *Power in the Kremlin*. London: Collins, 1969.

Taubman, W. *Khrushchev: The Man and His Era*. New York: Norton, 2003.

Taubman, W., S. Khrushchev, and A. Gleason, eds. *Nikita Khrushchev*. New Haven, CT: Yale University Press, 2000.

Terrill, R. *Mao: A Biography*. New York: Harper and Row, 1980.

Thomas, H. *Cuba or The Pursuit of Freedom*. London: Eyre and Spottiswoode, 1971.

Thorpe, A. *A History of the British Labour Party*. Basingstoke: Macmillan, 1997.

Tilford, R., ed. *The Ostpolitik and Political Change in Germany*. Farnborough: Saxon House, 1975.

Tokes, R. L. *Hungary's Negotiated Revolution: Economic Reform, Social Change and Political Succession, 1957–90*. Cambridge: Cambridge University Press, 1996.

Tompson, W. J. *Khrushchev: A Political Life*. Basingstoke: Macmillan, 1995.

Trachtenberg, M. *A Constructed Peace: The Making of the European Settlement, 1945–63*. Princeton, NJ: Princeton University Press, 1999.

Turner, J. *Macmillan*. London: Longman, 1994.

Udovicki, J., and J. Ridgeway, eds. *Burn This House: The Making and Unmaking of Yugoslavia*. London: Duke University Press, 1997.

Ulam, A. B. *Dangerous Relations: The Soviet Union in World Politics, 1970–82*. New York: Oxford University Press, 1984.

———. *Expansion and Coexistence: Soviet Foreign Policy, 1917–73*. New York: Praeger, 1974.

Urwin, D. W. *A Political History of Western Europe Since 1945*. London: Longman, 1998.

Valenta, J. *Soviet Invasion of Czechoslovakia, 1968: Anatomy of a Decision*. Baltimore: Johns Hopkins University Press, 1979.

Vatikiotis, P. J. *Nasser and His Generation*. London: Croom Helm, 1978.

Vickers, M. *The Albanians: A Modern History*. London: I. B. Tauris, 1997.

332 An International History of British Power

Vucinich, W. S., ed. *At the Brink of War and Peace: The Tito-Stalin Split in a Historic Perspective*. New York: Brooklyn College Press, 1982.

Waites, N., ed. *Troubled Neighbours: Franco-British Relations in the Twentieth Century*. London: Weidenfeld, 1971.

Wakeman, R., ed. *Themes in Modern European History Since 1945*. London: Routledge, 2003.

Walton, R. J. *Cold War and Counterrevolution: The Foreign Policy of John F. Kennedy*. New York: Viking Press, 1972.

Watt, D. C. *Succeeding John Bull: America in Britain's Place, 1900–75*. Cambridge: Cambridge University Press, 1984.

West, R. *Tito and the Rise and Fall of Yugoslavia*. London: Sinclair-Stevenson, 1994.

Westad, O. A., ed. *Brothers in Arms: The Rise and Fall of the Sino-Soviet Alliance, 1945–63*. Washington, DC: Woodrow Wilson Centre Press, 1998.

———, ed. *Reviewing the Cold War: Approaches, Interpretations, Theory*. London: Frank Cass, 2000.

White, M. J. *The Cuban Missile Crisis*. Basingstoke: Macmillan, 1996.

———, ed. *Kennedy: The New Frontier Revisited*. Basingstoke: Macmillan, 1998.

Wilkes, G., ed. *Britain's Failure to Enter the European Community, 1961–63: The Enlargement Negotiations and Crisis in European, Atlantic and Commonwealth Relations*. London: Frank Cass, 1987.

Williams, K. *The Prague Spring and Its Aftermath: Czechoslovak Politics, 1968–70*. Cambridge: Cambridge University Press, 1997.

Williams, L. J. *Britain and the World Economy, 1919–70*. London: Fontana, 1974.

Wilson, D. *Tito's Yugoslavia*. Cambridge: Cambridge University Press, 1979.

Wilson, H. S. *African Decolonization*. London: Arnold, 1994.

Windsor, P., and A. Roberts. *Czechoslovakia 1968: Reform, Repression and Resistance*. London: Chatto and Windus, 1969.

Woodward, P. *Nasser*. London: Longman, 1992.

Wyden, P. *Bay of Pigs*. London: Cape, 1979.

Young, C. *Politics in the Congo: Decolonization and Independence*. Princeton, NJ: Princeton University Press, 1965.

Young, H. *This Blessed Plot: Britain and Europe from Churchill to Blair*. Woodstock, NY: Overlook Press, 1999.

Young, J. W. *Britain and European Unity, 1945–92*. Basingstoke: Macmillan, 1993.

———. *Britain and the World in the Twentieth Century*. London: Arnold, 1997.

———. *The Labour Governments, 1964–70: International Policy*. Manchester: Manchester University Press, 2003.

Young, M. B. *The Vietnam Wars, 1945–90*. New York: HarperCollins, 1991.

Zeman, Z. A. B. *The Making and Breaking of Communist Europe*. Oxford: Basil Blackwell, 1991.

Ziegler, P. *Wilson: The Authorized Life of Lord Wilson of Rievaulx*. London: Weidenfeld and Nicolson, 1993.

Zubok, V., and C. Pleshakov. *Inside the Kremlin's Cold War: From Stalin to Khrushchev*. Cambridge, MA: Harvard University Press, 1996.

INDEX

www.ingramcontent.com/pod-product-compliance
Lightning Source LLC
Chambersburg PA
CBHW022347280326
41935CB00007B/106